The Politics of
Southern Europe

The Politics of Southern Europe

Integration into the European Union

José M. Magone

 PRAEGER

Westport, Connecticut
London

Library of Congress Cataloging-in-Publication Data

Magone, José M. (José Maria), 1962-
    The politics of southern Europe : integration into the European Union /
    José M. Magone.
        p. cm.
    Includes bibliographical references and index.
    ISBN 0-275-97787-0 (alk. paper)
        1. European Union—Europe, Southern. 2. Europe, Southern—Politics and
    government. I. Title.
HC240.25.E854 M34 2003
320.94—dc21   2002070955

British Library Cataloguing in Publication Data is available.

Library of Congress Catalog Card Number: 2002070955
ISBN: 0-275-97787-0

First published in 2003

Praeger Publishers, 88 Post Road West, Westport, CT 06881
An imprint of Greenwood Publishing Group, Inc.
www.praeger.com

Printed in the United States of America

The paper used in this book complies with the
Permanent Paper Standard issued by the National
Information Standards Organization (Z39.48-1984).

10 9 8 7 6 5 4 3 2 1

In memory of

Professor Charlotte Teuber
my kind and generous
Comparative Politics teacher
and her unforgettable
doctoral *privatissima*
in wonderful Vienna

La Mediterranée n'est même pas une mer, c'est un 'complexe des mers' comme on l'a dit, et de mers encombrées d'iles, coupées de penínsules, entourées de cotes ramifiées. Sa vie est melée á la terre, sa poésie est plus qu'a moitié rustique, ses marins sont a leurs heures paysans; elle est la mer des oliviers et des vignes autant que celle des étroits bateaux a rames ou des navires ronds des marchands, et son histoire n'est pas plus à separer du monde terrestre qui l'enveloppe que l'argile n'est à retirer des mains de l'ouvrier qui la modéle. Nous ne saurons donc pas sans peine quel personnage historique exact peut etre la Mediterranée: il y faudra de la patience, beaucoup de démarches et sans doute quelques erreurs inévitables.

Fernand Braudel, *La Mediterranée et le Monde méditerranéen a l'époque de Philippe II.* (Paris: Librairie Armand Colin 1949), pp. ix–x.

Contents

Illustrations

Abbreviations

AN/MSI	Alleanza Nazionale-Movimento Sociale Italiano/ National Alliance-Italian Social Movement (I)
AD	Alianca Democrática/Democratic Alliance (P)
AR	Assembleia da Republica/Assembly of the Republic
BE	Bloco de Esquerda/Block of the Left (P)
BNG	Bloque Nacional Gallego/National Galician Block
CAP	Common Agriculture Policy
CCAA	Comunidades Autonomas/Autonomous Communities
CCOO	Comisiones Obreras/Workers' Commissions (E)
CDS	Centro Democrático y Social/Democratic Social Center (E)
CDS/PP	Centro Democrático Social-Partido Popular/ Democratic Social Center/People's Party (P)
CDU	Christlich-Demokratische Partei/Christian Democratic Party (D)
CDU	Coligação Democrática Unitária/Democratic Unitary Coalition (P)
CDU	Centro dei Democratici Uniti/Center of United Democrats (I)
CEOE	Confederación Española de Organizaciones Empresariales/Spanish Confederation of Business Enterprises (E)
CFP	Common Fisheries Policy
CFSP	Common Foreign and Security Policy

CGIL   Confederazione Generale Italiana del Lavoro/General
              Italian Confederation of Labor (I)
CGTP-In   Confederação Geral dos Trabalhadores Portugueses-
              Intersindical/General Confederation of Portuguese
              Workers-Intersindical (P)
CIP   Confederação da Industria Portuguesa/Confederation
              of Portuguese Industry (P)
CISL   Confederazione Italiana Sindicati Lavoratori/Italian
              Confederation of Workers' Unions (I)
CiU   Convergencia i Unió/Convergence and Union (E)
CPLP   Communidade dos Paises de Lingua Portuguesa/
              Community of Portuguese Speaking Countries
DC   Democrazia Cristiana/Christian Democracy (I)
EAGGF   European Agricultural Guidance and Guarantee Fund
EAR/
Synaspismos   Elliniki Aristera/Greek Left
EC   European Community
EEE   Union of Greek Shipowners (EL)
EH/HB   Euskal Herritarrok-Herri Batasuna/Basque Nation-
              Basque Homeland and Freedom Party (E)
EIA   Environmental Impact Assessment
EMU   Economic and Monetary Union
EP   European Parliament
ERDF   European Regional Development Fund
ETA   Euskadi ta Askatasuma/Basque Country and
              Freedom (E)
ETUC   European Trade Union Confederation
EU   European Union
FI   Forza Italia/Go On Italy
GSEE   General Confederation of Greek Workers (EL)
KKE   Kommounistikó Kómma Elládas/Communist Party of
              Greece
KKE-es   Kommounistiko Komma Elladas-esoterikou
              Communist Party of Greece-Interior (EL)
IMF   International Monetary Fund
IMP   Integrated Mediterranean Programs
IU   Izquierda Unida/United Left (E)
LN   Lega Nord/Northern League (I)
MFA   Moviment das Forças Armadas/Movement of Armed
              Forces (P)
NATO   North Atlantic Treaty Organization
ND   Nea Dimokratia/New Democracy (EL)
PASOK   Panneliniko Sosialistiko Kinima/Panhellenic Socialist
              Movement (EL)

PCE	Partido Comunista de España/Spanish Communist Party (E)
PCI	Partido Comunista Italiano/Italian Communist Party (I)
PCP	Partido Comunista Portugues/Portuguese Communist Party
PDS	Partido Democratico della Sinistra/Party of the Democratic Left (I)
PLI	Partido Liberale Italiano/Italian Liberal Party
PNF	Partido Nazionale Fascista/National Fascist Party (I)
PNV	Partido Nacional Vasco/Basque National Party (E)
PP/AP/CD	Partido Popular (E) (People's Party [E])
PP/CDS	Partido Popular (P) (People's Party [P])
PPI	Partito Popolare Italiano/Italian People's Party (I)
PRD	Partido Renovador Democratico/Democratic Renewal Party (P)
PRI	Partito Repubblicano Italiano/Italian Republican Party (I)
PS	Partido Socialista/Socialist Party (P)
PSD/PPD	Partido Social Democrata/Social-Democratic Party (P)
PSDI	Partito Socialista Democratico Italiano/Italian Social Democratic Party (I)
PSI	Partito Socialista Italiano/Italian Socialist Party (I)
PSOE	Partido Socialista Obrero Español/Spanish Socialist Workers' Party (E)
RC	Partito della Rifondazione Comunista/Party of Communist Refoundation (I)
SEA	Single European Act
SEM	Single European Market
SEV	Union of Greek Industries
UCD	Unión del Centro Democratico/Union of Democratic Center (E)
UGT	Union General de los Trabajadores/General Union of Workers (E)
UGT	União Geral dos Trabalhadores/General Union of Workers (P)
UIL	Unione Italiana del Lavoro/Italian Union of Labor (I)
UN	United Nations
UNDP	United Nations Development Program
UNICE	Union of Industrial and Employers' Confederations of Europe

KEY TO ABBREVIATIONS OF EUROPEAN NATIONS (IN TABLES AND FIGURES)

A	Austria
And	Andorra
B	Belgium
CH	Switzerland
D	Germany
DK	Denmark
F	France
FIN/ST	Finland
E	Spain
El	Greece
EU	European Union
I	Italy
Ic	Iceland
Irl.	Ireland
L	Luxembourg
Liec	Liechtenstein
NK	Norway
NL	Netherlands
P	Portugal
S	Sweden
UK	United Kingdom

Preface and Acknowledgments

For many years I have taught a course called "Politics of Southern Europe." Over time, my accumulated comparative research of Portugal, Spain, Italy, and Greece has grown immensely, so I decided to bring to paper what has been a unique success story in terms of development toward a qualitative democracy. The road toward democracy, always difficult, was different in all countries studied in this book, but they all experienced similar problems and challenges. The main challenge they had to face was integration into what is now commonly called European Union politics. It means that the European Union is bringing all the different European regions (from the Nordic countries to southern Europe) together, and creating a new light polity with its own European public space. This is a long-term process that may now be accelerated due to the introduction of the Euro as palpable currency on January 1, 2002.

In this book, I look at the political development of the past two decades, particularly the 1990s, in the four main southern European member-states. I was interested in studying the impact of the European Union on the southern European political systems. This so-called Europeanization of southern European politics also meant integration into European Union politics through the presidencies of the Council of the European Union and several intergovernmental conferences. Moreover, southern Europe was at the forefront in shaping the politics of the Mediterranean by creating new initiatives such as the Euro-Mediterranean partnership.

The book intends to combine both a comparative as well as a cultural approach that tries to be sensitive to the differences of the four countries studied here.

The main purpose of this book is to draw an accurate map of the complexity of southern European politics, which is becoming increasingly interdependent within the European Union and global governance.

I want to take the opportunity to thank many of my students who always challenged me with new questions about southern Europe. In the past decade, I had the privilege to talk to many eminent scholars of southern Europe. I want to thank them all for interesting discussions about southern Europe. Probably, some of the ideas discussed found their way into the book. One of the greatest instruments for such an endeavour is an excellent library. Therefore, I want to thank the staff of the Brynmor Jones Library at Hull University for doing a great job over the years and for helping me out when I was in search of new and exciting sources. Last, but not least, I want to thank Elisabetta Linton and Greenwood Publishing Group for undertaking this publishing venture.

This was a travel of the mind worth pursuing. The Mediterranean in general, and southern Europe in particular, are again shaping global politics as they have done in the past, only now strengthened by lively democracies full of potential. It is this success story that I want to tell in this book.

The Politics of Southern Europe: A Bird's-Eye View

SOUTHERN EUROPE AS A REGION

All attempts to define a region are more or less artificial. One aims to find common features that make it possible to group countries as part of a region. The four southern European countries—Portugal, Spain, Italy, and Greece—are all members of the European Union (EU). Their political, economic, and social structures are more similar to each other than to those of other members of the European Union. This cluster of countries can be set apart from other clusters in the European continent (see Table 1.1).

The southern European countries are different from other similar artificial regional creations such as Nordic Europe, the British Isles, Benelux, Germanic Europe, the Baltic states, or the Balkans. These different Europes followed different trajectories to democracy based on different historical legacies. Moreover, they have different levels of economic development. Gross domestic product (GDP) per capita in southern Europe is lower than in other regions, in spite of the fact that Italy has a GDP per capita above the EU average. All this makes it difficult to find a homogenous European Union (see Figure 1.1). Instead, differences have to be perceived among the different regions. This becomes even more salient when the candidate countries join in the European Union in several waves. In 2000, the 13 candidate countries (which includes Turkey) had only 35 percent of the EU GDP per capita average (see Figure 1.2). Southern Europe has converged toward the level of the most developed regions of the European Union, but common features of underdevelopment and historical legacy still remain that set it apart from other European regions.

TABLE 1.1 Different European Regions

Regional Clusters	Countries
Benelux	Belgium
	Luxembourg
	Netherlands
Germanic Europe	Austria
	Germany
	Lichtenstein
	Switzerland
Southern Europe	Andorra
	France*
	Greece
	Italy
	Portugal
	San Marino
	Spain
Mediterranean Islands	**Cyprus**
	Malta
Nordic Europe	Denmark
	Finland
	Iceland
	Norway
	Sweden
Baltic Europe	Estonia
	Latvia
	Lithuania
Central Europe	Czech Republic
	Hungary
	Poland
	Slovakia
Eastern Europe	**Bulgaria**
	Romania
Balkan Europe	**Albania**
	Bosnia-Herzegovina
	Croatia
	Macedonia
	Slovenia
	Yugoslavia
British Isles	Ireland
	United Kingdom

* France is here classified as Southern Europe, due to the fact that many French scholars (such as Evelyne Ritaine) tend to classify it as such. In this book, France and the microstates are only treated in comparative perspective. Countries listed in boldface type are discussed in this book.

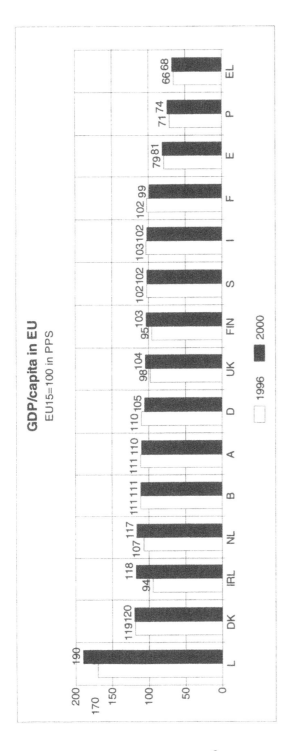

Figure 1.1 GDP per Capita in EU Member-States (EU 15 = 100 in PPS)

Source: Own graph based on data provided by Eurostat in Sijke Stapel, *Statistics in Focus, Economy and Finance, Theme 2,* no. 28 (2001): 5.

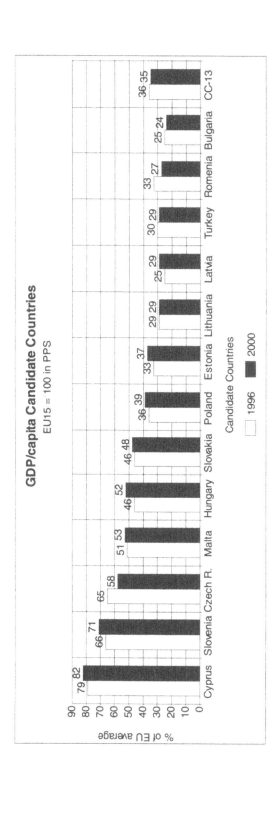

Figure 1.2 Gross Domestic Product per Capita for Candidate Countries (EU 15 = 100)

Source: Own graph based on data provided by Eurostat in Silke Stapel, *Statistics in Focus, Economy and Finance, Theme 2,* no. 28 (2001): 5.

One thing is certain, future enlargement of the European Union will bring even more divergence in economic development, human development, and participation within the European Union. These three aspects are naturally interlinked. According to United Nations figures human development and participation adjusted to gender are still lower in southern Europe and the candidate countries in relation to Nordic Europe and Germany. Southern Europe takes an intermediate position here with differences from country to country between the northern countries and the candidate countries (Figure 1.3 and Figure 1.4). This further reinforces the argument to look at southern Europe as a regional cluster of countries with strong similarities among themselves in terms of political, economic, social, or cultural terms.[1]

One of the most important features is the way democracy is practiced in southern Europe. Although Italy can refer back to a tradition of democracy since its unification in the 1870s, in reality a democratic society based on universal secret suffrage began to emerge only after the collapse of the Fascist regime of Benito Mussolini in 1945. The subsequent Cold War between the United States and the USSR further prevented genuine party competition in Italy. The fear of a Communist takeover led to the establishment of a web of systemic corruption that had at its core the main party of the political system, Christian Democracy (*Democrazia Cristiana* [DC]). Only the investigations of the judiciary under judge Antonio di Pietro on illicit party financing and abuse of power through operation *Mani Pulite* (Clean Hands) led to the final demise of the old system after 1992. The collapse of the old partyocratic structures led to high hopes that Italy may be now moving to a new stage of qualitative democracy, the so-called second Republic. In reality, recent analysts already feel that the opportunity of political transformation was missed by the political elites.[2]

Although the trajectories to democracy of Portugal, Spain, and Greece follow a different political cycle, all three countries had democratic experiences in the nineteenth and twentieth century that were regularly interrupted by authoritarian experiments. In spite of all that, the periods of formal democracy were based on a very reduced electorate that was controlled by political elites. Clientelism and patronage dominated the history of democracy in these countries up to the mid-1970s. It was in the 1970s that Portugal, Spain, and Greece were able to move toward universal and secret suffrage without folding back into authoritarianism. Southern Europe became a region when all authoritarian dictatorships were replaced by modern functioning democracies overnight. Democracy transformed southern Europe into a region. The democratization process was not only limited to the new democracies of Portugal, Spain and Greece—it spilled over to Italy.

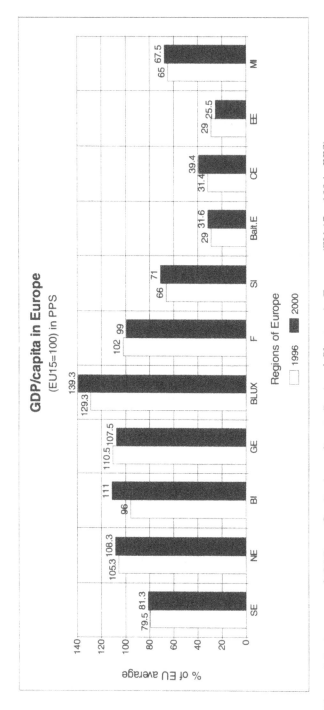

Figure 1.3 Aggregated GDP per Capita According to Regional Clusters in Europe (EU 15 = 100 in PPS)

Source: Own graph based on data provided by Eurostat in Silke Stapel, *Statistics in Focus, Economy and Finance, Theme 2,* no. 2 (2001): 5. **SE:** Southern Europe; **NE:** Northern Europe (w/o Norway); **BI:** British Isles; **GE:** Germanic Europe (w/o Switzerland); **BLUX:** Benelux; **F:** France; **SI:** Slovenia; **Balt.E:** Baltic countries; **CE:** Central Europe; **EE:** Eastern Europe; **MI:** Mediterranean Islands.

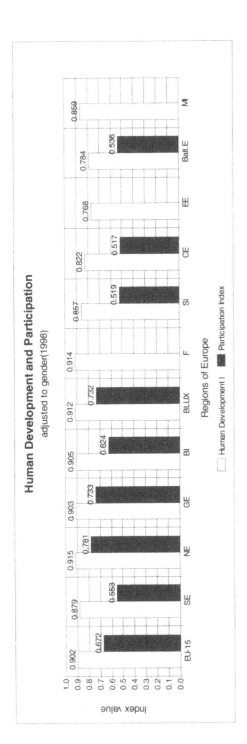

Figure 1.4 Human Development Index and Participation Index, Both Adjusted to Gender (1998) (UN-Database)

Source: Own graph based on data from the Programa das Nações Unidas para o Desenvolvimento, Relatório do Desenvolvimento Humano 2000 (Lisboa: Trinova 2000), pp. 176–177. **SE**: Southern Europe; **NE**: Nordic Europe (w/o Norway); **BI**: British Isles; **GE**: Germanic Europe (w/o Switzerland); **BLUX**: Benelux; **F**: France; **SI**: Slovenia; **Balt.E**: Baltic countries; **EE**: Eastern Europe; **CE**: Central Europe; **MI**: Mediterranean Islands. United Nations Development Programme, *Human Development Report 2000* (New York: United Nations, 2000). The index is calculated according to the mixing of three data: living expectancy at birth between 25 to 85 years; literacy of grown-ups from 0 to 100 percent and the real GDP per head: between $100 and $40,000 PPS.

THE THIRD WAVE OF DEMOCRATIZATION
STARTED IN SOUTHERN EUROPE

The simultaneous democratization of Portugal (1974–1975), Spain (1975–1978) and Greece (1974–1975) started a third wave of democratization across the globe. All three transitions of democracy were uncertain and different from each other. Nevertheless, all led to stable democratic governments. The Portuguese transition of democracy turned into democracy after a coup d'état on April 25, 1974. The uncertain and unstable process almost slid into civil war in the summer of 1975, but the international community in cooperation with the democratic parties was able to redirect the revolutionary process toward democracy. In Spain the process was based on consensualism and negotiations between the authoritarian elites and the opposition. The process was more evolutionary and took four years to reach its final outcome. In Greece, conservative Kostas Karamanlis managed the transition to democracy within a year. He could afford it, because his party—New Democracy—got the absolute majority in the founding elections of November 1974.

The differences in the democratic transition and subsequent consolidation periods in southern Europe became crucial lessons for other regions in Europe and other continents. Countries in Latin America, Asia, Africa, and Central and Eastern Europe changed their totalitarian/authoritarian regimes toward democratic governance systems. "Transitology" became a new stream of political science, which tried to find out the functional and genetic aspects of democratization. The making and sustaining of democracy became a major object of study to which the southern European experiences contributed in the long run (see Table 1.2). The third wave of democratization was regarded as part of the overall change of the global order, which started in the mid-1970s after the first oil shock in 1973.[3]

It was contrasted to the previous democratization processes before and after World War II.[4] The novelty of the democratization processes in southern Europe is that the aim was no longer the establishment of a formal democratic structure, but to make democracy work, to make democracy sustainable. In this respect, the three new democracies became the model for democratization across the globe. The Spanish democratic transition became an important experience for roundtable talks between members of the opposition and of the established authoritarian/totalitarian elites. The role of political actors again gained central stage into the agenda of research.[5]

These democratization efforts of Portugal, Spain, and Greece also highlight one further aspect. The world is becoming more interdependent at the end of the millennium. Democratization has become an

TABLE 1.2   The Sequencing of Democratization in the European Semiperiphery

Phases	Time Frame	Southern Europe	Time Frame	Central and European Countries
Countries Involved		Portugal, Spain, Greece		Poland, Hungary, Czech Republic, Slovakia, Slovenia, Latvia, Estonia, Lithuania, Bulgaria, Romania
Transition	1974–78	The establishment of new democratic constitutions	1989–93	The (re)establishment of democratic constitutions
Consolidation	1978–92	Establishment of rules of game and alternance in power, market economy, independence of justice	1994–	Establishment of rules of game and alternation in power, transformation from planned to the market economy
Negotiations With EU	1976–85	Eight years with Iberian countries, five years with Greece	1995–2004/10	Ten years for the first wave of candidate countries; nine to fifteen years with second wave candidate countries; structured dialogue of collective convergence of negotiations
Europeanization	1981–	Administrative adjustment, absorption of *acquis communautaire* on national legislation, systemic convergence of national and supranational system	1997–	Fulfilment of Copenhagen criteria, annual screening, fulfilment of Maastricht convergence criteria, absorption of *acquis communautaire*, fight against corruption, protection of ethnic minority rights

international endeavor. The international dimension of democratization processes became an important factor to sustain interest in the southern European experiences and those of other new democracies across the globe. International democracy assistance became an essential element to strengthen democratic institutions of new democracies. Such democracy assistance is targeted toward the establishment of new political parties, the monitoring of electoral processes, the strengthening of the judiciary, and the training of different groups such as the police or the army toward democratic values and human rights.[6] At the end of the millennium, democracy assistance institutions contributed to a paradigm change in international relations that replaced the period of the Cold War. The post-national system of international relations envisages the beginning of a new age of pax democratica (democratic peace).[7] This pax democratica is still wishful thinking, but the rhetoric begins to match the reality when we think of the cases of Kosovo, East Timor, or more recently Afghanistan.

The role of the European Union in directing and strengthening southern Europe toward democracy has to be acknowledged. From the very beginning, membership was only possible by complying to a democratic regime and respect for human rights. This was part of the *acquis politique* of the European Union.[8] A so-called technology of democratization, based on the experiences of the southern European and other countries, began to play a major role in sustaining the interest in democratization. Democratization is regarded as the best way to strengthen world peace.

This naturally shows that the knowledge gained from the southern European cases had some impact on the perception of democracy in most democracies around the globe. Particularly, aspects of corruption and democratic transparency became essential topics of study for political scientists in established democracies, creating for the first time comparative indicators on the quality of democracy (e.g., Transparency International). Democracy is not a static phenomenon; on the contrary, democracy has to be regained every day. The best way to do so is to increase accountability and transparency of the political system.

THE UNEASY RELATIONSHIP BETWEEN STATE AND CIVIL SOCIETY

The dominance of the southern European state in relation to civil society created an uneasy relationship between the two. The authoritarian legacy prevented the development of a rational-legal state. The process toward the democratic state based on a universalistic approach toward all citizens was undermined by a culture of neo-patrimonial behavior. Indeed, authoritarian regimes tended to rest on the support of certain military, clerical, and/or economic elites to keep in power. This can be said particularly for the authoritarian dictatorships in Spain and Portugal, but as well as for the Italian fascist state and the Greek colonels' regime. The state was far from being a rational-legal one, even if the formal constitution acknowledged the centrality of a rational-legal order. In all four countries the population was confronted with a repressive state that prevented the development of a civil society. Elections, if allowed, were rigged by the authoritarian regimes.[9]

Such a regime became more and more questionable with industrialization and urbanization in the second half of the twentieth century. The growing erosion of the traditionalist rural society and its replacement by a more urban and industrialized one contributed to the final demise of the authoritarian regimes. The establishment of authoritarian regimes became more difficult in the 1960s. The regime of the Greek colonels can be mentioned as an example of the difficulties that the military or any elites encountered trying to establish an authoritarian regime in the 1960s. The whole authoritarian experiment was a disaster, culminating in the final demise of the dictatorship.

Democracy does not by itself change the rationale of clientelism and patronage that exists in an authoritarian regime. In the end, there must be a will by the political elites to create a rational-legal, universalistic, cultural framework to counteract past forms of behavior. During democratic transition and consolidation, past forms of behavior may coexist for a long period of time with democratic rational-legal universalistic ones. It is a gradual transformation that is achieved by implementing people-oriented policies such as education, judicial reform, and administrative reform that will in the end strengthen the democratic rationale based on transparency and accountability.[10]

This democratic state is still in the making in southern Europe. Even for the Italian case, one must say that the overdominance of DC in the political system between 1948 and 1992 led to the creation of a web of systemic corruption. This means that civil societies in southern Europe had difficulties making their voices heard. Dissatisfaction with domestic democracy in the European Union is highest among southern European populations. Italy ranks as the least satisfied population in democracy in *Eurobarometer* studies.[11] The alienation from the democratic institutions is a widespread phenomenon in present southern European democracies. Most authors tend to call it "democratic cynicism."[12] It is distrust of the political class per se that prevents the southern European populations from being more attached to their democratic institutions. The main problem has been one of legitimacy. Decision-making is not done with sufficient transparency and accountability and the lack of a strong civil society and public opinion prevents this from becoming a reality.[13]

This blurred *mixtum compositum* may create opportunities for criminal organizations such as the Mafia, Camorra, and N'Dranghetta. This was certainly the case in Italy during the DC overdominance.[14]

The Italian *tangentopoli affair* became a warning sign for the political classes of the world to introduce more transparency and accountability in governance processes. For this it is necessary to create an independent civil society. Nongovernmental organizations (NGOs) are still weak in all four countries. In spite of all that, the number of people who join NGOs is growing. They play a crucial role in preventing party-states—such as the one exerted by DC in Italy before 1992 or *Panhellinio Sosialistiko Kinima* (PASOK) in Greece between 1981 and 1989—from becoming a reality in the new millennium. In both cases, the manipulation of the government by political parties to sustain power over a long period included processes of colonization of civil society and the media. Quite important here is education in citizenship, which should make people aware of the dangers of totalitarianism, authoritarianism, and techniques of streamlining (*Gleichschaltung*). One can lose democratic government if civil society is not strong enough to resist possible authoritarian or pseudo-democratic temptations. The southern European democracies have become strong in the past two and a half decades, nevertheless it is important to increasingly include those larger parts of the population that, due to lack of education, unemployment, or other factors, have remained excluded from the political process. The high levels of abstention in Spain and Portugal where voting is not compulsory may indicate that a large part of the population does not express their will regularly. This cannot be completely determined in Greece where high turnout is explained by compulsory voting.[15]

On the whole, the "amoral familism" syndrome, meaning that the center of political life is the family and nothing else, is being eroded by a new individualism that tends to be apolitical or very volatile and looking at political programs in terms of their delivery. This is not particular to the countries analyzed here; it is a trend across the European Union that is transforming European citizens into consumers of an emerging electoral market based on marketing and pragmatic issues. The economization and Americanization of politics may turn out to be an obstacle for emancipatory politics for a part of the populations of southern Europe.

SEMIPERIPHERAL ECONOMIC DEVELOPMENT

The democratic politics of southern Europe are linked to the performance of the southern European economies. This is the crucial pillar for a functioning modern democracy. As Adam Przeworski wrote on the central and eastern European countries, the best regime for new democracies is the creation of a social market economy in long-term perspective.[16] The history of the market economy in these countries is very discontinuous. Indeed, all four countries created modern markets only very late in the twentieth century. Still today the national market integration is weaker and underdeveloped in relation to the other member-states of the European Union. Several factors account for this lack of market integration and development. The most important is certainly the discontinuity of regimes. In Spain and Portugal, the populations experienced a so-called market fascism during the authoritarian dictatorships where certain economic groups were able to dominate the economy through oligopolies.[17] The late unification of Greece and Italy were major obstacles for strengthening market integration as it happened in other European countries. All four countries had fragmented markets in the late nineteenth century. Only slowly were they able to create the necessary conditions for market integration. This process is still going on. The structural funds of the European Union are designed to improve market integration within those countries as well as among the member-states of the European Union. Within one decade, Portugal, Spain, and Greece were able to become more integrated in the European Union, even though their market integration continues to lag behind other west European countries due to underdevelopment of the infra-structures, communications, and distribution networks.[18]

Apart from market integration, one of the factors that prevented the establishment of market economic thinking in these countries was naturally the lack of a contract and market culture throughout the territory. This factor highlighted by Giulio Sapelli was only gradually reversed in the second half of the twentieth century.[19] In spite of all that, pockets of subsistence economy in the rural areas of Portugal, Spain, Italy, and Greece continued to resist against the forces of the market.

Though the Italian economy was able to produce a strong high technological sector in the north of Italy that is based on almost virtual invisible factories, concentrating their efforts on producing new technological products and subcontracting the mass production to other firms,[20] the other three southern European economies are dependent on international foreign direct investment and have a low level of research and development spending.[21] In Portugal, Spain, and Greece the industrial sector is dominated by low-cost labor-intensive industries. This competitive advantage is always at risk of being outstripped by the Asian or central and eastern European economies with a cheaper labor force. Although in the past two decades the occupation structure and GDP distribution in Portugal, Spain, and Greece converged substantially toward the European average, they are still characterized by a higher percentage of people working in the inefficient agricultural sector.

The Portuguese, Spanish, and Greek economies have become extremely dependent on foreign direct investment. Only in Italy can one find more than one transnational corporation that plays successfully in the global market.[22] The tertiary and knowledge-based sector of the economies of southern Europe increased considerably parallel to that of the other EU national economies, but they still lag considerably behind.

In spite of all that, one of the characteristics of southern European economies is the persistence of the dualism in economic development. Although some parts of the country are extremely well developed and can compare to other regions in the European Union in terms of the average GDP per person, other parts are underdeveloped and lagging behind. Regions lagging behind are the Mezzogiorno in Italy, the southwest in Spain, the east in Portugal, and the islands in Greece. The late development of the political economy and the discontinuity of state construction are interlinked, if one wants to understand the underdevelopment in southern Europe.[23] In spite of the structural funds of the European Union, this dualism will continue to persist, because the quality of life is deteriorating in these parts of southern Europe. Young people tend to move to the larger urban centers. The structure of qualifications is still at a low level in Portugal, Spain, and Greece. This can be said about the Mezzogiorno in Italy as well. The improvement has been considerable since the 1970s, but there is a long way to go for these democracies. This is the basis to produce an endogenous research and development technological basis, which may change the structure of the new southern European democracies.

On the whole, the success of the new southern European economies will depend on improving their technological basis and their investment in education.

SOUTHERN EUROPEAN WELFARE STATES

The late development of the modern state and the market political economy are major factors for the development of southern European welfare states. The late development of modern societies in Portugal, Spain, Italy, and Greece strengthened the role of the family in southern Europe. Although in Italy a welfare state began to emerge after World War II in line with all the other more developed European countries, unlike these countries the Italian welfare state became embroiled in the web of systemic corruption institutionalized by DC. At the end of the 1990s, most authors agreed that Italy's welfare state although formally based on universalistic principles degenerated to a clientelistic-particularistic system of distribution, where benefits were targeted toward some groups and to the detriment of others. Another characteristic was the low level of support in financial terms in comparison to other European countries. This inequality inside a system that should actually ensure more equality in society further delegitimized the democratic system. Similarities to this clientelistic-particularistic system can be found in other countries as well.[24]

The development of welfare states in Portugal, Spain, and Greece started only in the 1970s, as emulation of the development in other modern west European democracies. The growing individualization and urbanization of the population in Portugal, Spain, and Greece led to the need by the state to find ways to redistribute some of the produced wealth among the population. The efforts were minimal, and the southern European welfare states were mere imitation of the more developed established ones in west European democracies. With the recession in the 1970s, all welfare states in western Europe entered a crisis. The weak southern European welfare states were even worse off, due to the transition politics and the need to restructure the economy. Clientelistic-particularistic elements continued to shape the southern European welfare states. Due to the weakness, the role of the extended family continued to fulfil the role of a buffer for the lacking support of the state. During crisis these family networks between urban and rural areas acted as an alternative support network.

In the 1990s, individualization of society, diversity of family formations such as the nuclear family, single parenthood, singlehood, and other forms of family life organization contributed to the erosion of the traditional extended family, even if the role of the family continues to be still more important in southern Europe than most other west European countries. The main reason is that, in spite of major reforms of the southern European welfare states, they still lag behind in their delivery of benefits. The social expenditures per inhabitant and family in all four countries is lower than other west European democracies. All are below the EU average, although Italy comes closer to the EU average. The social expenditure of Portugal and Greece are at the bottom of the European Union both in absolute and relative terms. There were some improvements in the second half of the 1990s, but the underdevelopment of these southern European welfare states continues to be the major feature in these countries. The integration into the European Union stabilized and routinized welfare provision in southern Europe. The integration into a community of like-minded states with a higher level of experience with welfare provision contributed to an improvement and modernization of the social services in these countries. The growing integration and coordination in matters of unemployment may have a spillover effect on other social policy areas in long-term perspective.

OVERCOMING CLIENTELISM AND PATRONAGE: THE ROLE OF THE EUROPEAN UNION

The European Union has changed considerably in the past fifteen years. The European Commission under Jacques Delors and Jacques Santer increased the number of policy areas in which the European Union ought to be involved to create a Single European Market (SEM).

From the very start, this external monitoring was directing the new democracies in southern Europe toward a liberal democratic structure based on transparency and accountability. Even if today the European

Union has been attacked for not being sufficiently democratic and lacking accountability and transparency, this was not and is not the view of the southern European member-states. Indeed, the southern European countries felt that the European Union was already more democratic than their political systems, and therefore joining the European Union would have a spillover effect on strengthening democratic governance in those countries. Although the European Union is regarded as a technocratic supranational system,[25] in reality the southern European member-states agree that any technocratic package of modernization coming from the EU toward the southern European member-states contains a rationale of democratic policy-making based on consultation and inclusion of the populations concerned. This could be seen in the negotiation of the Common Support Frameworks since 1988 and in the implementation of larger projects that require the previous consultation of the population as defined in the Environmental Impact Assessment (EIA) directive. The European Union may be regarded as a way to leave the vicious circle of reproduction of the same patrimonial system of politics and change it toward a virtuous circle of rational-legal democratic policy-making. Indeed, Italy, Portugal, Spain, and Greece benefited from the implementation of the Single European Market (SEM) as well as participation in the Economic and Monetary Union (EMU). Their efforts to improve their fiscal, monetary, and budgetary policies changed an old pattern of behavior.

Since January 2001 Greece has been a member of the last stage of the EMU. This naturally puts the government under pressure to undertake major reforms in the public sector as well as in economic policy-making.[26] The same can be said about Italy, which implemented very strict economic policies to achieve this aim. Some authors remain critical about Italy's ability to sustain participation in the EMU without major social and economic costs.[27] This inclusion toward the Eurozone forever changed the ability of southern European states to escape this European regime of low inflation and low interest rates. Although the Eurozone experiment is very young and still needs time to mature, it helped the southern European countries to overcome the long-standing problems of fiscal, monetary, and economic policies. The stabilization of the economies is creating also political and social stability. In the past two and a half decades, southern European economies moved from a growth to a stabilization economy, which clearly contributed to a break from the vicious circle of hyperinflation and high levels of public debt.[28] Instead, the successful participation in the third stage of EMU and subsequently the adoption of the Euro in 2002 reflect the will of southern European political and economic elites to move toward a new democratic, stable era after a long turbulent history of violence and authoritarian experiments.

CONCLUSIONS

The southern European political systems are slowly converging to the political, social, and economic level of the most advanced democracies of the European Union. Their trajectories to democracy were not only discontinuous, but more than that they contributed to the delay in the development toward a modern rational-legal state based on universalistic principles and a market political economy. The southern European democracies are still in the process of catching up in political, economic, social, and cultural terms. Clientelism, patronage, and systemic corruption played a role in delaying this process even in the context of democratic politics. The present democratic political systems have become members of a community of democracies that have been able to change the vicious circle of clientelistic-particularistic politics into a virtuous one based on universalistic principles, accountability, and transparency. This book attempts to make an assessment of the quality of democratic governance in the southern European semi-periphery.

NOTES

1. Jean Barrot, Bernard Elissalde, and Georges Rocques, *Europe-Europes: Espaces en recomposition* (Paris: Vuibert, 1995).

2. Donatella Della Porta, and Alberto Vanucci, *Un Paese Anormale: Come La Classe Politica Ha Perso L'Occasione Di Mani Pulite* (Roma: Editori Laterza, 1999); Donatella Della Porta, "A Judge's Revolution? Political Corruption and the Judiciary in Italy," *European Journal for Political Research* 39, 2001 no. 1: 1–21.

3. Samuel P. Huntington, *The Third Wave: Democratization in the Late Twentieth Century* (Norman: University of Oklahoma Press, 1991); Guillermo O'Donnell, Philippe C. Schmitter, and Laurence Whitehead (eds.), *Transitions from Authoritarian Rule.* 4 volumes (Baltimore: Johns Hopkins University Press, 1986).

4. Klaus V. Beyme, *Systemwechsel in Osteuropa* (Frankfurt a. M.: Suhrkamp, 1993): 10–13.

5. Nikiforos P. Diamandouros, "Southern Europe: A Third Wave Success Story," in *The International Dimension of Democratization: Europe and the Americas,* ed. Lawrence Whitehead (Oxford: Oxford University Press, 1996), 3–25; Arend Lijphardt, Thomas Bruneau, and Richard Gunther, "A Mediterranean Model of Democracy? The Southern European Democracies in Comparative Perspective," *West European Politics,* no. 2 (1985): 8–25; Geoffrey Pridham, "Comparative Perspectives on the New Mediterranean Democracies: A Model of Regime Transition?" *West European Politics,* no. 1 (1984): 1–29.

6. Larry Diamond, *Promoting Democracy in the 1980s: Actors and Instruments, Issues and Imperatives* (New York: Carnegie Corporation of New York, 1995); European Commission, "On the Inclusion of Respect for Democratic Principles and Human Rights in Agreements between the Community and Third Countries." Communication from the Commission and the European Union and the External Dimension of Human Rights Policy: From Rome to Maastricht and Beyond. Communication from the Commission to Council and to the European

Parliament. Document drawn up on the basis of COM (95) 216 final and COM (95) 567 final, in *Bulletin of the European Union, supplement 2/95*; IDEA, *International Election Observation: Seventeen organizations share experiences on electoral observation.* October 10–12, 1995, in Stockholm (Stockholm: IDEA, 1995); IDEA, *Roundtable on National Capacity-Building for Democracy. Report of Proceedings.* February 12–14, 1996 (Stockholm: IDEA, 1996).

7. James Robert Huntley, *Pax Democratica. A Strategy for the 21st Century* (Basingstoke, U.K.: Macmillan, 1998).

8. Geoffrey Pridham, "The Politics of the European Community. Transnational Networks and Democratic Transition in Southern Europe," in *Encouraging Democracy: The International Context of Regime Transition in Southern Europe,* ed. Geoffrey Pridham (London: Leicester University Press, 1991), 211–254, particularly p. 37; Geoffrey Pridham, "The International Context of Democratic Consolidation: Southern Europe in Comparative Perspective," in *The Politics of Democratic Consolidation. Southern Europe in Comparative Perspective* , ed. Richard Gunther, Nikiforos P. Diamandouros, and Hans-Jürgen Puhle (Baltimore: Johns Hopkins University Press, 1995), 166–203; particularly pp. 189–193; Lawrence Whitehead, "Democracy by Convergence and Southern Europe: A Comparative Politics Perspective," in *Encouraging Democracy. The International Context of Regime Transition in Southern Europe,* ed. Geoffrey Pridham (London: Leicester University Press, 1991), 45–61, particularly pp. 50–52; Lawrence Whitehead, ed., *The International Dimension of Democratization* (Oxford: Oxford University Press, 1998).

9. Edward Malefakis, "The Political and Socioeconomic Contours of Southern European History," In *The Politics of Democratic Consolidation. Southern Europe in Comparative Perspective,* ed. Richard Gunther, Nikiforos P. Diamandouros, and Hans-Jürgen Puhle (Baltimore and London: Johns Hopkins University Press, 1995), 33–76, particularly pp.59–76; Salvador Giner, "Political Economy, Legitimation and the State in Southern Europe," in *Transitions from Authoritarian Regime. Vol.II: Southern Europe,* ed. Guillermo O'Donnell, Philippe C. Schmitter, and Laurence Whitehead (Baltimore: Johns Hopkins University Press, 1986), 11–44, particularly pp. 17–29.

10. James Kurth, "A Tale of Four Countries: Parallel Politics in Southern Europe 1815–1990," in *Mediterranean Paradoxes: The Politics and Social Structure of Southern Europe,* ed. James Kurth and James Petras (Providence, Oxford: Berg, 1993), 27–66, particularly pp. 54–66.

11. Leonardo Morlino and Maurizio Tarchi, "The Dissatisfied Society: The Roots of Political Change in Italy," in *European Journal for Political Research* 30 (July 1996); 41–63; *Eurobarometer* 48 (1997): 1–2; *Eurobarometer* 56 (Autumn 2001): 16–17.

12. Leonardo Morlino and José Ramon Montero, "Legitimacy and Democracy in Southern Europe" in *The Politics of Democratic Consolidation. Southern Europe in Comparative Perspective,* ed. Richard Gunther, Nikiforos P. Diamandouros, and Hans-Jürgen Puhle (Baltimore and London: Johns Hopkins University Press, 1995), 231–60, particularly p. 252. Democratic cynicism is widespread in older democracies as well. In the two Anglo-Saxon democracies turnout was down considerably. In the, British general elections of June 7, 2001, turnout was down to 59.2 percent (record lowest); over 40 percent did not bother to vote. In the U.S. presidential elections of November 7, 2000, elections turnout was below 50 percent. Interestingly, the recent Italian elections of May 13, 2001, led to a turnout of over 80 percent . Most polling stations had to be open until the early hours of the morning. Any considerable decline of turnout is naturally a sign of a crisis of legitimacy of the political system. It may lead to decision-making taken by a

minority for a minority. On the relationship between the working poor and voting behavior in the United States, see the excellent contribution by James Petras and Steve Vieux, "Neoliberalismo y vida cotidiana" in *Buen Gobierno y politica social,* ed. Salvador Giner and Sebastián Sarasa (Barcelona: Ariel, 1997), 49–59.

13. Here we come to the central topic of the whole book—the study of the quality of democracy in southern Europe. On this see Nancy Bermeo, *A Teoria da Democracia e as Realidades da Europa do Sul* (Lisboa: Difel, 2000), 171–251; David Campbell, Karin Liebhart, Renate Martinsen, Christian Schaller, and Andreas Schedler (eds.), *Die Qualität der Österreichischen Demokratie* (Wien: Manz, 1996); and David Beetham, *The Democratic Audit of the United Kingdom: Auditing Democracy in Britain* (London: Charter 88 Trust, 1993).

14. Stefano Guzzini: "La Longue Nuit de la Premiére Republique. L'implosion clienteliste en Italie," *Revue Française de Science Politique,* 44, no. 6 (December): 979–1013.

15. In Italy, compulsory voting was abolished in the mid-1990s, but it continues to be valid in Greece.

16. Adam Przeworski, *Democracy and the Market: Political and Economic Reforms in Eastern Europe and Latin America* (Cambridge: Cambridge University Press, 1991); Adam Przeworski and others, *Sustainable Democracy* (London: Manchester University Press, 1995).

17. Giovanni Arrighi, "From Fascism to Democratic Socialism. Logics and Limits of Transition," in *Semiperipheral Development: The Politics of Southern Europe in the Twentieth Century,* ed. Giovanni Arrighi (Beverly Hills, CA: Sage, 1985), 249–79.

18. Gabriele Tondl, "EU Regional Policy in the Southern Periphery: Lessons for the Future," *South European Society and Politics* 3, no. 1 (Summer 1998): 93–129, particularly pp. 96–104.

19. Giulio Sapelli, *Southern Europe since 1945: Tradition and Modernity in Portugal, Spain, Italy, Greece and Turkey* (London and New York: Longman, 1995), 103.

20. Robert Leonardi and Rafaella Y. Nanetti (eds.), *The Regions and European Integration: The Case of Emilia-Romagna* (London: Pinter, 1990); Rafaella Y. Nanetti, *Growth and Territorial Policies: The Italian Model of Social Capitalism* (London: Pinter, 1988).

21. Whereas in the period 1989–1999 countries such as Sweden, Finland, and Denmark spent between 2 and 3 percent of GDP for research and development in the private and public sectors, Portugal, Spain, and Greece spent below 1 percent. Italy spent over 1 percent of GDP. In comparison to the United States and Japan spending yearly 2.8 percent of GDP, the EU spent on average 1.8 percent of GDP. Eurostat, *100 Basic Indicators from Eurostat Yearbook 2001. The Statistical Guide to Europe. Data 1989–99* (Luxembourg: Office of the Official Publications of the European Community) 30.

22. European Commission, *Sixth Periodic Report on the Social and Economic Situation and Development of the Regions of the European Union* (Luxembourg: Office of the Official Publications of the EC, 1999).

23. Evelyne Ritaine, *Hypothéses pour le Sud de l'Europe: Territoires et Médiations,* EUI Working Papers, RSC, 1996 no. 96/33, p. 10.

24. Maurizio Ferrera, "The 'Southern Model' of Welfare in Social Europe." In *Journal of European Social Policy* 6, no. 1 (1996): 17–37. For a general overview of the southern European welfare states see Bruno Pallier (ed.), *Comparing Social Welfare Systems in Southern Europe* (Paris: MIRE, 1997). In terms of statistics and

European Union comparison, see European Commission, *Social Protection in Europe 1998* (Luxembourg: Office of the Official Publications of the European Community, 1997). See also the recent study on the future of the welfare state in Europe by Maurizio Ferrera, "Integrazione Europea e Sovranità Sociale dello Stato-Nazione: Dilemmi e Prospettive," *Rivista Italiana di Scienza Politica*,Anno 30, no 3 (2000): 393–421. On the Italian state, see Maurizio Ferrera and Elisabetta Gualmini, "Reforms Guided by Consensus: The Welfare State in the Italian Transition," *West European Politics* 23, no. 1 (2000): 187–208.

25. Maurizio Bach, *Die Bürokratisierung Europas. Verwaltungseliten, Experten und politische Legitimation in Europa* (New York: Campus, 1999).

26. Kevin Featherstone, "'Europeanization'and the Centre Periphery: The Case of Greece in the 1990s," *South European Society and Politics* 3, no. 1 (1998): 23–39, particularly pp. 28–29; and Kevin Featherstone and George Kazamias, "Introduction: Southern Europe and the Process of 'Europeanization,'" in *Europeanization and the Southern Periphery*, ed. Kevin Featherstone and George Kazamias (London: Frank Cass, 2001), 1–22.

27. Kenneth Dyson and Kevin Featherstone, "Italy and EMU as a 'Vincolo Esterno': Empowering the Technocrats, Transforming the State," *South European Society and Politics* 1, no. 2 (Autumn 1996): 272–99.

28. George Pagoulatos, "Economic Adjustment and Financial Reform: Greece's Europeanization and the Emergence of a Stabilization Pact," in *Europeanization and the Southern Periphery*, ed. Kevin Featherstone and George Kazamias (London: Frank Cass, 2001), 191-214, particularly pp. 204–210.

2

Trajectories to Democracy in Southern Europe

In comparison to most countries in northern Europe, southern Europe has been characterized by a discontinuous process toward democratization. (See Table 2.1.)

After the French Revolution of 1789 all west European countries moved gradually from a system of absolutist monarchical rule to democratic rule. Some countries emphasized the aspect of gradual and peaceful evolution, whereas in others democratization had to be forced upon the dominant oligarchical groups closely linked to the monarchy. The United Kingdom and Scandinavia are representatives of the first group; all four southern European countries have to be counted as part of the second group. The major contrasting feature between one group and the other is that the first group had a very continuous process toward democracy based on constant electoral reform and enlargement of the universal suffrage toward complete inclusion of the whole adult population, whereas in the other group this process was manipulated and controlled by the oligarchy through clientelism, patronage, and corruption. With the passing of time, this process of manipulation of the electoral system to sustain an oligarchy in power became less and less viable. The most drastic solution was to establish an authoritarian dictatorship. This abuse of power has been called "neopatrimonialism," because although it was informed formally by a democratic constitutional settlement, in reality the oligarchy in power tended to manipulate the system for its own purpose. This became more and more difficult with the growth of adult literacy and the emergence of new social movements such as the labor, the republican, or even the anarchosyndicalist movements to achieve change radically by not shying away

TABLE 2.1 Democratic Discontinuity and Universal Suffrage in Europe

Country	Periods of Authoritarian Rule or Foreign Occupation	Universal Suffrage (Male)	Universal Suffrage (Male and Female)
Continuous Democracies			
Belgium	Nazi Occupation (1939-1945)	1919	1948
Denmark	Nazi Occupation (1939-1945)	1915	1915
France	Nazi Occupation (1939-1945)	1848	1944
Ireland		1921	1928
Luxembourg	Nazi Occupation (1939-1945)	1918	1918
Netherlands	Nazi Occupation (1939-1945)	1917	1919
Finland		1906	1906
Sweden		1909	1921
United Kingdom		1918	1928
More or Less Discontinuous Democracies			
Germany	Nazi Regime (1933-1945)	1867	1918
Austria	Ständestaat (1934-1938) Nazi Occupation (1938-1945)	1907	1918
Italy	Fascist State (1922-1945)	1919	1945
Very Discontinuous Democracies			
Portugal	Dictatorship of Sidonio Pais (1917-1918) Authoritarian Regime of Salazar (1926-1974)	1975	1975
Spain	Dictatorship of Primo de Rivera (1923-1931) Civil War (1936-1939) Authoritarian Regime of Franco (1939-1975)	1931/1977	1931/1977
Greece	Dictatorship of Metaxas (1936-1941) Nazi and Italian Occupation (1941-1945) Civil War (1947-1949) Authoritarian Regime of the Colonels (1967-1974)	1949	1952

from violent means if necessary. Neopatrimonialist arrangements informed a deviation from the modern party system based on genuine political pluralism, political market rationality, equal access to the market following the principle "one man, one vote," clear distinction between state and civil society, and last but not least, the ability of alternation in government. (Figure 2.1)

Moreover, the importation of political democratic institutions and their adaptation to the reality of patrimonial political systems are another factor in understanding external causes of the discontinuous process toward democracy. A historical approach toward democratization trajectories has to take into account the dissemination of a market rationality as well. The creation of a genuine economic market culture makes people aware of the importance of having a choice among a variety of goods. This competitive spirit of the market is transferred gradually to the political field and becomes an essential element of modern competitive party politics.

Such rationality was only partly established in southern Europe shortly before World War II. Nevertheless, this is an essential precondition of modern and postmodern democracies to establish "one man, one vote" universal suffrage electoral systems, which are the very basis of modern democratic politics. Indeed, all four countries of southern Europe deviated from the pattern found in the rest of west European countries, because even in democratic periods patrimonial forms of behavior continued to prevent the establishment of a genuine democratic system based on universal suffrage and controlled by accountability and transparency. The Italian case clearly shows that even if democracy was formally institutionalized, it could be informally hijacked by patrimonial forms of behavior based on clientelism, patronage, and corruption.[1] The trajectory toward democracy in these countries is the best explanation for understanding the present problems of establishing a sustainable democracy based on transparency and accountability.

In this chapter, we delineate the main obstacles and facilitators in the trajectories toward democracy in the southern European countries. In the next section, the main historical stages toward a genuine democratic system are briefly discussed before we turn to actual processes of democratization in Italy, Portugal, Spain, and Greece from World War II to the mid-1970s.

Since the mid-ninteenth century, democratic regimes were characterized by clientelism, patronage, corruption, and manipulation of electoral systems. Here is not the place to make a full account of the process of democratization; it suffices to delineate the main developments (see Table 2.1.)

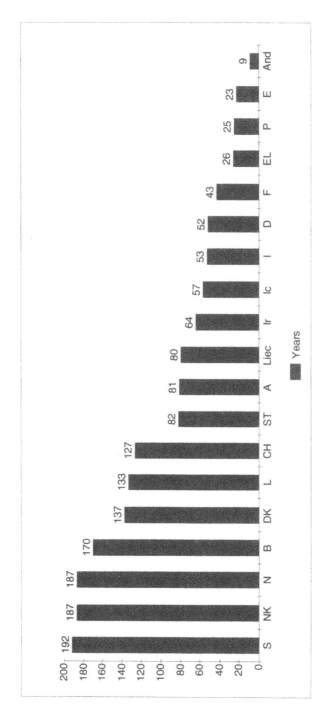

Figure 2.1 Constitutional Longevity in Western Europe (2001)

THE PERSISTENCE OF NEOPATRIMONIALISM IN DEMOCRATIC REGIME BUILDING (NINETEENTH TO TWENTIETH CENTURIES)

In spite of all the differences among the four countries, the trajectories toward democracy show extremely similar features. In the second half of the nineteenth century all four countries developed some kind of two-party systems based on a very restricted electoral college that was manipulated through a clientelistic electoral machinery. This machinery was highly centralized in the corresponding ministries of the interior. A further similarity is that all attempts to move toward genuine democratic political systems were accompanied by political violence. Sooner or later the military or more authoritarian political parties used political violence to prevent processes toward democratization during the interwar period (1918–1939).

Rise and Fall of the Electoral Machines of the Nineteenth and Twentieth Centuries: Between Manipulation and Political Violence

In all four countries the British political system became an important model for the oligarchies. The two-party system was regarded as a device to create stability and control of the emerging mass democracy. Southern European democracies were transformed into oligarchies, which used electoral machines to stay in power.

In Portugal and Spain the two-party system was established in the 1870s. They were called *rotativismo* (rotation of two parties) and *turno pacifico* (peaceful alternation) respectively. Both of them were based on an electoral machine administered by the ministry of the interior in the government. In both cases, a huge nationally organized clientelistic network called *caciquismo* became the main basis for the rigging of elections.

Caciques were influential local bosses (priests, lawyers, land owners) who acted as intermediators between the government and the local community. *Caciques* offered votes of local communities to the parliamentary oligarchies in the capital in exchange for favors from the center, which could include all kinds of exemptions, construction of roads, or other public works.[2] This system prevailed until the turn of the century. The emergence of new social movements influenced by socialism and republicanism made it more difficult to control the extension of suffrage. Political violence and political instability led to the collapse of the constitutional monarchy in the two cases.

In Portugal, the Republican revolution of October 5, 1910, led to the abolishment of the monarchy. In spite of this change, the new Republican elite turned to the same practices of clientelism but now to prevent the return of the monarchists. After sixteen years of political and parliamentary instability, political violence, and authoritarian experiments, the Republic collapsed and an authoritarian dictatorship under Antonio Oliveira Salazar was established.[3] In Spain, a dictatorship under Primo de Rivera was established in 1923 and delayed the necessary reforms to achieve a more democratic system. The dictatorship wanted to restore law and order in Spain. It used mechanisms of corporatism to integrate the working class in the regime.[4]

After the overwhelming victory of the left in the local elections of April 12, 1931, the Second Spanish Republic was proclaimed two days later. In spite of all hopes, the second Republic turned into an ideological fight between left and right. Political instability, political violence, and lack of compromise contributed to the demise of this genuine democratic experiment.[5] The polarization led to civil war between 1936 and 1939, which ended with the establishment of an authoritarian dictatorship by General Francisco Franco.

After the unification of Italy between 1860 and 1870 a new political system emerged. The constitution of the kingdom of Piedmont, the Statuto Albertino, was extended to the rest of the country. The main party became the Liberal Party, which integrated a left-wing and a right-wing faction. Similar to the Iberian countries, the new liberal elite based its power on a system of clientelism called *transformismo*, meaning the reconversion of economic interests of land owners of the south and industrialists of the north into electoral support. In the early twentieth century the new leader Giovanni Giolitti extended *transformismo* to the emerging working classes.[6] With extension of suffrage and the emergence of new mass parties such as the Socialist and the Fascist parties, the liberal constitutional monarchy collapsed in 1922. Benito Mussolini took over power and established a fascist dictatorship until the end of the second world war.[7]

In Greece, the whole process of democratization was even more complicated. Nevertheless one can find similarities to the other countries mentioned previously. Between 1881 and 1897 a two-party system was in operation dominated by Kharislaos Trikoupis who alternated in power with his opponent Theodoros Deliyannis. The party system was based on a quite restricted electorate and an electoral machine. An exchange-of-favors system seemed to keep the political field under control. After 1910, Eleftherios Venizelos, leader of the liberal party, became the dominant political figure. Until 1936, Greek politics was polarized between the Venizelist and anti-Venizelist groups. This period was characterized by a high level of political instability. Since the late 1920s, Greece was formally a Republic, but monarchists wanted a return to the constitutional monarchy. Moreover, democratic periods were interrupted by authoritarian periods such as the dictatorship of General Theodoros Pangalos in 1925–1926. Political instability was the major feature in the 1930s. Coalition governments did not last very long. On November 25, 1935, the constitutional monarchy was restored after an affirmative vote in a rigged referendum. Due to growing social conflict and violence, King George II decided to install a dictatorship under General Ioannis Metaxas. This dictatorship, introduced by the so-called Regime of the Fourth August 1936, lasted between 1936 and 1941. Metaxas tried to emulate other Fascist movements in Europe, but the annexation of the country by the Axis powers led to the demise of his regime. His dictatorship gained some respectability in the resistance of Greece against the Axis powers. His death at the end of January 1941 led to the collapse of this resistance under his successor Alexandros Koryzis.[8]

The national resistance was now undertaken by communist and monarchist partisans. The Greek government had to flee in exile to London. After World War II, Greece continued to be polarized between left and right. After a bloody civil war between communists and monarchists, the constitutional monarchy was again restored.

Between 1951 and 1965, the anticommunist environment of the Cold War prevented a normalization of the relationship between left and right. Right-center governments were able to manipulate elections in order to keep left-wing parties out of power. The conservative Greek Rally (*Ellinikos Synagermos* [ES]) under the leadership of Field Marshal Alexander Papagos between 1952 and 1955 and later on the National Radical Union (*Ethniki Rizopastiti Enosis* [ERE]) under the leadership of Kostas Karamanlis dominated political life in Greece between 1955 and 1963. Opposition became more virulent in the 1960s leading to the resignation of Karamanlis and the rise of George Papandreou as leader of the Center Union (*Enosis Kentrou* [EK]). He intended to introduce a social democratic program promoting education and social welfare. This was regarded by the military and the conservative establishment as a Communist threat. Rumors around his son Andreas Papandreou, who allegedly was involved in a military plot under the codename "Aspida" to overthrow the monarchy, clearly increased the tensions in the 1960s.[9] This perceived imminent danger of a possible left-center government after 1965 contributed to the preventive intervention of a military junta of colonels on April 21, 1967, that stopped abruptly once again the prospects of democratization in Greece.[10]

Rise and Fall of the Authoritarian Regimes

The present southern European democracies emerged from the breakdown of authoritarian regimes. They all clearly show similarities of development. A southern European pattern of authoritarian dictator-ships can be recognized, which, after a short period of mobilization and streamlining, becomes less ideological and more lax in the whole ap-proach toward the original design. In spite of the fact that Mussolini's fascist Italy wanted to be a totalitarian dictatorship and dominate all aspects of life, by the 1930s, Italian fascism had lost its dynamics. The same can be said for the halfhearted emulations in Portugal and Spain. In Greece, the dictatorship was so unpopular that it never was able to present an alternative model.

Elements of the Italian philosophy of action, nationalism, futurism, and proletarian imperialism were brought together to create a new legitimacy for the new political system. Fascism established itself as a new authoritarian political regime in 1925. It would last until 1943. Although the fascistization of state and society was thorough, the constitution of the liberal state, the Statuto Albertino, continued to prevail, and the king kept his place as head of state. Mussolini created the myth of the "duce" (leader) and an artificial civil religion around his personality. In spite of all that, the totalitarian pretention never reached the same degree of thoroughness as in Nazi Germany or Stalin's Soviet Union.

The authoritarian regime tried to implement a new kind of economic and social organization based on corporatism. The National Charter of Labor (*La Carta Nazionale del Lavoro*) in 1927 specified the rights of workers; nevertheless they remained unfulfilled. The "corporate state" established a social organization of labor, in which unions were in-cluded both as representatives of labor as well as capital. These vertical trade unions undermined workers' organizations.

Italy entered war on the side of Nazi Germany, nevertheless its army was not as well equipped and prepared. It suffered several disasters in Greece and Africa. In 1943, the growing protests by workers in Turin made it apparent that domestically the fascist regime was becoming weaker.[11]

Indeed, since the invasion of the Allied armies in Sicily on July 10, 1943, Mussolini lost the support of King Vittorio Emanuelle II.[12] Al-though antifascist resistance was quite dominant before 1943, it was the dismissal of Mussolini that led to a broadening of the resistance move-ment. Resistance spread throughout the country. In the south land labourers occupied the land estates in the countryside. The collapse of the authoritarian regime in Italy is quite different from other countries. Indeed, the war was the catalyst of regime collapse and democratiza-tion. Although the breakdown of the Fascist regime was induced from outside, it was complemented by an upsurge of civil society in north Italy. If Italy had stayed out of the war, the Fascist regime might have developed in the direction of the Iberian countries and survived longer.[13]

After the nomination of António Salazar, Professor for Political Economy at the University of Coimbra, as finance minister in 1928 and later on as Prime Minister in 1932, an authoritarian dictatorship called the *Estado Novo* (New State) was created that imposed a single-party system on the Portuguese population. The regular elections in the *Estado Novo* lacked any competition by other parties.[14] The electorate was restricted. Although the opposition could present party lists to the elections, the actual control of the whole electoral campaign, process, and results just confirmed the victory of the single-party National Union (*União Nacional* [UN]), later renamed People's National Union (*Acção Nacional Popular* [ANP]). Salazar was interested in controlling society and preventing the modernization of the *Estado Novo*.[15]

The colonial wars that started in the 1960s became the catalyst for the demise of the authoritarian regime. From then on until the fall of the regime the colonial wars became unpopular domestically and internationally. On the eve of the coup d'état of April 25, 1974, the "regime was not more than its war."[16] It was already evident in the early 1970s that the wars could not be won militarily. Industrialization and modernization of the economic structure led to a transformation of society. A modern society was emerging that resembled west European ones. In this period, emigration, mass media, tourism, and liberalization were major factors in transforming mentalities. Marcelo Caetano, the successor of Salazar, attempted to liberalize the political system under the slogan "evolution in continuity," but he was not very successful. The experiment started in 1969 and had a disappointing end in 1973, when the conservative faction within the regime—the so-called ultras, among them president Américo Thomaz—prevented a further liberalization. The dissatisfaction within the middle-ranking officers grew in the 1970s. Operation "end of the regime" took place in the early hours of April 25, 1974, after the song *"Grandôla Vila Morena"* was played on the radio as a starting signal. Within hours the movement of armed forces (*Movimento das Forças Armadas* [MFA]) was able to achieve control over the strategically important places of the capital. The authoritarian regime fell like a house of cards.[17]

After the civil war General Franco established an authoritarian dictatorship and a single-party system. The new Spanish *Falange* (Spanish Phalanx), later called National Movement (*Movimiento Nacional* [MN]), became the single party of the regime. The new regime was based on the ideology of corporatism. On the whole, it restored the conservative idea of unitary Spain. It repressed regionalist-nationalist claims. Catholicism and nationalism became two ideological foundations of the new regime. The corporatist architecture was based on three columns—

the family, the municipalities, and the vertical syndical organization. The *Cortes*, the Spanish Parliament, continued to exist throughout the Francoist period, but the representatives were recruited from the Francoist administration. Most of the *procuradores* were elected indirectly; only about 20 percent were elected directly by 9.4 million heads of family and 6.9 million married women (1967–1968).[18]

In the late 1960s, Spain was characterized by an authoritarian dictatorship with "limited pluralism." The level of social discontent increased in the 1970s, particularly in the historical regions of Catalonia and Basque Country. In Catalonia, resistance was restricted to peaceful protest; but in Basque Country, the new separatist organization Basque Country and Freedom (*Euskadi ta Askatasuma* [ETA]) stepped up its actions against the autoritarian dictatorship. The most spectacular one was the assassination of Admiral Carrero Blanco, the number two in the regime, in December 1973.[19]

The main pillar of the authoritarian regime, the Catholic Church, was also undergoing a social change. A younger generation influenced by Marxism, active in illegal trade unions, and socially engaged challenged the Catholic hierarchy and the regime.[20]

The political opposition was divided and weak. The two main parties of the opposition, PSOE and the Communist Party, were not able to come together because of the experiences of the civil war.[21] Divergence of opinions became quite important inside the authoritarian regime. A rejuvenation of the political elite was already taking place in the 1960s.[22] Most of these younger members of the regime wanted to achieve a reform, or even a complete break with it, and make a move toward democracy. This was opposed by the hard-liners of the Francoist regime. The isolation of the government increased in 1973. After Carrero Blanco's assassination, the new prime minister, Arias Navarro, tried to relaunch the strategy of *aperturismo* (opening up) that existed before 1969. In reality, Arias Navarro was too weak to reform the regime. He continued to pursue a ruthless policy of repression, and the promise of liberalization soon vanished from his plans when facing the opposition coming from the conservative protagonists of the regime, the so-called bunker. In this period, Franco's health deteriorated considerably. The future king Juan Carlos took up his place between July 19 and September 1, 1974, indicating that he would be Franco's successor. Indeed, Franco had already nominated Prince Juan Carlos as his successor after his death in the Law of Succession of 1967. On November 20, 1975, Franco died. From now on the process of transition to democracy was initiated.[23]

The collapse of democracy on April 21, 1967, led to the establishment of the dictatorship of the colonels. The right-wing coup d'état wanted to prevent a victory of the party of George Papandreou, the Center

Union, in the elections of May 1967. The new junta led by Giorgios Papadopoulos, Nikolaos Makarezos, and brigadier Stylianos Pattakos called their coup d'état the "Revolution of 21 April."[24] Their intention was to prevent an allegedly imminent communist coup d'état. The opposition was unprepared. Ideologically, the military dictatorship presented itself as defender of traditional values of the "Helleno-Christian civilization." The idea of the "perfect world of the village" was combined with anti-individualistic feelings. At the same time, it advocated economic development and modernization.[25]

Most people of the former political elite were purged from office. New people who adhered to the new ideology were offered the vacant positions. The opposition was ruthlessly persecuted. Many left-wing and other opponents were deported to the islands of Jaros and Leros. The ambivalent position of the United States further contributed to the consolidation of the power of the colonels. During the Nixon administration, Vice President Spiro Agnew, who was half of Greek origin, supported the colonels.[27] A new constitution was proclaimed by the Junta on September 29, 1968, which was accepted unsurprisingly with 92.1 percent of the cast votes through a massive manipulation of the results. Already in December 1967 the King tried to dismiss the colonels without success. Constantine II had to flee abroad. The resistance became more intense in the 1970s. The decline of support of the lower middle classes to the regime became quite evident in 1974. The growing fragmentation of the military junta created major problems for a cohesive leadership. Nevertheless, the single most important factor leading to the fall of the regime was the attempt to carry out a coup attempt against Archbishop Makarios, the president of Cyprus, in July 1974. Indeed the intervention of the junta was intended to achieve *enosis* (unification) and regain some legitimacy of its regime in Greece. In reality, this led to the intervention of the Turkish troops on behalf of the Turkish minority in Cyprus and the subsequent partition of Cyprus. In this situation, President Ghizikis decided to hand over the power to civilians. The solution was proposed by Evangelos Averoff-Tossiza, a right-center politician who held close links with the military leadership and the deposed democratic opposition. He proposed that Kostas Karamanlis should return from the exile in Paris and take over from the military.

In sum, all four countries show similarities in the process toward democracy. The discontinuity in the democratization process can be witnessed in all four countries. The electorate is extremely restricted. Patrimonialist forms of representation dominated the political field through large electoral machines established by the ruling classes. Modernization, industrialization, and, in three countries, the impact of external wars led to the demise of these dictatorships.

DEMOCRATIZATION IN SOUTHERN EUROPE

Democratic Transition and Consolidation

In the mid-1970s, one could witness the collapse of the authoritarian regimes in the Iberian countries and Greece. Such simultaneous breakdown of authoritarian regimes initiated what later was called by Samuel P. Huntington "The Third Wave of Democratization." All three countries were affected by different factors, which clearly leads us to the insight that trajectories to democracy, even in the same region, are always very different (see Table 2.2).

Meanwhile the bulk of literature on democratic transition brought to the fore that there are several factors affecting this process toward democratization. Democratic transition is highly contingent on domestic and international factors.[28] This provisional situation creates its own transitional legality that is highly uncertain. *Uncertainty* is, therefore, the first feature of democratic transition processes.[29] Uncertainty pervades the public and private sphere as well as the future of political organization.[30] In fact, transition is a process of "inconclusive struggles" that at some stage, hopefully, lead to a decision phase.[31] The agreement upon a constitution may be regarded as the final point in a minimalist definition of transition toward democracy. A constitutional settlement does not mean that the transition to democracy was successful. On the contrary, a long-term process of consolidation and democratization is needed to make democracy sustainable.[32]

A second feature of transition is the importance assigned to political actors and their behavior. The elite of transition comprises different types of actors. The different ways in which the authoritarian regime collapsed may produce a different elite configuration. It is their action that will lead, in the end , to democracy. In this regard, political actors do matter in a situation of institutional vacuum.[33]

The third feature shaping the process of democratic transition is the international context. The growing interdependence among states and nongovernmental actors has increased the influence of the international community upon democratic processes.[34]

Italy: From Consensus to Conflict (1945–1948)

Before we start to analyse the southern European democracies that emerged in the 1970s, it is important to look at the chronologically earlier transition of Italy. Indeed, the Italian case shows that the three factors were quite relevant in shaping the transition and consolidation of democracy.

In Italy in June 1945 a new unity government under the premiership of Ferrucio Parri, leader of the Action Party, consolidated the economic

TABLE 2.2   Democratic Transitions in Southern Europe

	Portugal	Spain	Italy	Greece
Time Period	1974–1976	1975–1978	1945–1948	1974–1975
Background Condition	Collapse of authoritarian regime after 48 years	Collapse of authoritarian regime after 36 years	Collapse of authoritarian regime after 21 years and World War II	Collapse of authoritarian regime after 7 years
Nature of Transition	Revolutionary/ conflictual	Evolutionary/ consensual	Evolutionary/ consensual	Dominant/ managerial/ conflictual
Uncertainty	High level	High level	High level	Low level
Political Actors and Behavior	Military (MFA) and civilian/ inconclusive conflictual struggles	Bargaining between old Francoist elites and new democratic civilian elites; military excluded from process	Bargaining among left- and right-center democratic forces/National coalition governments	Imposed managerial style of Kostas Karamanlis based on absolute majority of his party in founding elections; other parties more or less integrated, but too weak to influence
International Dimension	Strong influence by U.S. administration, German political foundations, Socialist International, European Union, Soviet Union	Low level of international influence during transition	Strong American influence in postwar period; some influence of the Soviet Union	Influence by the European Union; strong anti-Americanism of the Greek population

and social situation in Italy. His main task was to purge former fascist activists and Nazi collaborators from local and central administration. This was prevented by the Courts, which felt themselves to be as culpable as the perpetrators accused. A general amnesty was granted to prevent further tensions with the court system and public administration.[35]

On June 2, 1946, the elections to the Constituent Assembly gave to *Democrazia Cristiana* (Christian Democracy [DC]) under the leadership of Alcide de Gasperi a strong majority in relation to Socialists and Communists and other parties. DC got 35.2 percent and 207 seats, followed by Socialists with 20.7 percent and 115 seats and the Communists with 19 percent and 104 seats. On the same day, a referendum was held asking which kind of regime form the population wanted for Italy. About 54.2 percent decided for a Republic form and 45.8 percent for a monarchy form. The main cleavage was between the North of Italy voting predominantly for the Republic and the South casting its vote mainly for the monarchy. This referendum shows how deep the support for the monarchy still was, in spite of the very subordinate role Vittorio Emanuelle III played during the Fascist period. His attempt to regenerate the monarchy by resigning in favor of his son Umberto one month before the referendum did not change the end result.

After the results were known, there was tension for some time, which also involved rumors of an imminent coup d'état by the army. In the end, the results were accepted. The New Republic now needed a new constitution. The Constituent Assembly worked through 1946 and 1947. The constitution came into force on January 1, 1948. It contained many programmatic long-term aims such as "the right to work for all Italians." Indeed, it was regarded as the most progressive constitution in the West during the Cold War.

Although the confrontation between the communists and the Christian-Democrats was quite intense before the elections of April 1948, the communist leader Palmiro Togliatti asked his party to be moderate. Indeed, the elections of April 1948 brought an unexpected success for Alcide de Gasperi. DC won with a comfortable majority of 48.5 percent of the votes and an absolute majority in the Chamber of Deputies—305 out of 574. The Popular Front uniting Communists and Socialists achieved a disappointing 31 percent. Nevertheless the Communists were able to increase their number of seats from 106 to 140. The Socialists declined from 115 to 41 seats and became only the third largest group in the new parliament. With this election, post-War Italian politics was defined by the overdominating Cold War *Zeitgeist*. The DC became a bulwark against communism. The transition to democracy was shaped by the personality of Alcide de Gasperi, while democratic consolidation was assured by the moderation of the communist leader Palmiro Togliatti. On July 14 he was shot by an isolated fanatic named Antonio Pallanti. He was seriously injured. Nevertheless, he asked communist militants to remain moderate and accept the results. This was the beginning of what would later be called imperfect bipartism (*bipartitismo imperfetto*)—the dominance of DC in government and the permanent opposition of the second largest party, the PCI.[36]

The democratic transitions in Portugal, Spain, and Greece show similarities to the Italian experience, particularly in relation to the international factor and uncertainty. The Portuguese experience clearly shows strong similarities due to the role of the Communist Party and the military during the transition process. Even more interesting is that although the Italian transition has to be contextualized in the early period of the Cold War, the transitions to democracy in Portugal, Spain, and Greece are located at the very end of this period. Although the global bipolarism between the United States and the U.S.S.R. was still existent in the 1970s, the strategies were quite different. But let us have a look at the individual cases.

Portugal: The Revolutionary Transition (1974–1976)

In Portugal three groups of political actors were dominant in the democratic process: the military, the political parties and their leaders, and the social movements that emerged during the revolutionary process. The military organized themselves in the Movement of Armed Forces (*Movimento das Forcas Armadas* [MFA]) and became political when they realized that there was a vacuum after the collapse of the authoritarian regime. The MFA started as a moderate movement, but the more institutionalized it became, the more it became indistinct from the provisional governmental structures. Most of the decision-making process was taken by the Council of the Revolution (*Conselho da Revolução*), and this was advised by the so-called Assembly of the MFA (*Assembleia do MFA*). Both institutions became more radical after February 1975. This was partly due to infighting, partly because the conservative general Antonio Spinola staged coup attempts in September 1974 and March 1975 that remained unsuccessful. The main figure of the MFA movement became Prime Minister Vasco Gonçalves, who presided over most of the provisional governments and allowed the Communist party to colonize most of the state structures during this period. Vasco Gonçalves was only removed in September 1975 and replaced by the more moderate General Pinheiro de Azevedo. This led to a radicalization of the extreme wings of the MFA and military creating a very chaotic situation in autumn 1975.

The second group was the political parties and political leaders. Among them, the three most important ones were Mário Soares, leader of the Socialist Party (*Partido Socialista* [PS]), Alvaro Cunhal, leader of the Communist Party (*Partido Comunista Portugues* [PCP]), and Francisco Sá Carneiro, leader of the liberal Social Democratic Party (*Partido Popular Democrático* [PPD]). Both Mário Soares and Alvaro Cunhal were living abroad and were pleasantly surprised by the coup d'état. They returned hastily to Portugal. From the very beginning the politicians had to take a subaltern position to the military. They were only able to gain democratic legitimacy after the founding elections of April 25, 1975. The political parties were asked to sign a pact with the MFA on April 12, 1975, which guaranteed the supervising and leading role of the MFA for the time being and its extension after the elections to the Constituent Assembly. In return, the MFA allowed the conduct of free elections on April 25.[37] The elections of April 25 led to a victory of the moderate Socialist and People's Democratic Parties. The Socialist Party won the elections with 37.87 percent and

115 of the seats, the PPD got over 26.38 percent and 80 seats. The PCP was only able to get 12.53 percent and 30 seats. Surprisingly, the conservative Democratic Social Center (*Centro Democrático Social* [CDS]) was able to become the fourth largest party with 7.65 percent of the vote and 16 seats. Two smaller parties, the left-wing Portuguese Democratic movement (*Movimento Democrático Portugês* [MDP-CDE]) and the albanist Democratic People's Union (*União Democrática Popular* [UDP]) achieved to get Members of Parliament (MPs) elected.[38] From this moment on the parties legitimized by the population were in the position to contest the "revolutionary legality" imposed arbitrarily by the military. Mário Soares, the socialist leader, adopted an anti-Communist line in this phase of the Revolution, because the PCP was penetrating the political institutions and the mass media. From then on, the PS and PPD became main democratic parties opposing the military dominance and the Communist party and pleading for the establishment of liberal democracy in Portugal.[39]

Prime Minister Vasco Gonçalves was very keen to reduce the importance of the parties by endorsing a people's democracy model inspired by the central and eastern European communist regimes. This led to the split of the MFA into three main factions: two of them advocating extremist models, and one supporting a moderate model of democratic socialism. An alliance between the main moderate democratic parties and the latter faction led to a steering of the whole revolutionary process toward liberal democracy.[40]

The whole process was complicated by the fact that social movements became quite radical in 1975. Three kinds of social movements established different models of socialism inspired by extreme left-wing groups. The workers' commissions (*comissões dos trabalhadores* [CTs]) made efforts to unite all CTs into a megastructure so that they could create a people's power Socialist democracy. The residents' commissions (*comissões dos moradores* [CMs]) were promoting a connection to the CTs in the larger towns of Setúbal and Lisbon. The collective production units (*unidades colectivas de produção* [UCPs]) were established in the occupied land estates of the southern province of Alentejo and intended to create collective farms similar to those in the Soviet Union. The Communist party was very keen to control the process.[41] After 1976 all three social movements lost in significance.

A second pact between parties and the MFA was signed on February 26, 1976. It guaranteed the supervisory role of the MFA for the next five years. Nevertheless, the political field was left now to the politicians.[42] The proclamation of the new constitution on April 2, 1976, finalized this transition process. Furthermore, General Antonio Ramalho Eanes was elected first president of the new republic with an overwhelming majority of 61.5 percent on June 27, 1976. He became an important factor for the stabilization of the young political system.

Spain: The Consensual Transition

A more ordered transition to democracy could be found in the other countries. The role and behavior of political actors was crucial in preventing a less conflictive process. At the end of the Portuguese transition, Spain started its own process toward democracy. Indeed, the Spanish transition was heavily conditioned by the events in neighboring Portugal.[43] The transition to democracy in Spain became known as a *ruptura pactada* based on a negotiation between old and new elites. This form of transition to democracy became a model for many countries in Latin America, Asia, and Eastern Europe. This so-called transition through transaction[44] took longer than the democratic transitions in Portugal and Greece, but it was fully negotiated between the main actors. After General Franco's death, Prime Minister Arias Navarro still tried to reform the system. His strategy of *reforma pactada* was not supported by the opposition, which saw that Arias Navarro was not able to impose himself in relation to the conservative *bunker*. Moreover, the successor of General Franco, King Juan Carlos, was regarded by the opposition with reluctance. He was seen as a man of the regime, so in late 1975, opposition groups perceived the chances to achieve a *ruptura pactada* quite considerably diminished. Indeed, on July 1, 1976 Arias Navarro was dismissed by the king. In his period, he did not achieve an institutional reform, although civil society was beginning to feel more freed after the death of the dictator.

Juan Carlos decided to choose Adolfo Suarez, the former minister of the single-party National Movement, as the new prime minister. The opposition regarded Suarez as a man of the regime, so Juan Carlos's choice was met with skepticism.[45]

In reality, it was Adolfo Suarez who steered the transition process from *reforma pactada* to *ruptura pactada*. Adolfo Suarez proved to be the right person to negotiate with the opposition and the bunker. He was able to convince the *Cortes* to accept the "law of political reform" in December, which was then confirmed by the population in a referendum on December 15, 1976. The population accepted the law of political reform with the exception of the historical regions of Catalonia and Basque Country.

Adolfo Suarez could now start a process of negotiation with the political opposition. One of the preconditions was the legalization of the Communist Party. This was the most difficult issue, because the conservative military bunker, which was extremely anticommunist, resisted against it. Adolfo Suarez tried first to get approval from the Supreme Court, but this was denied by the judges. After consultation with some of its ministers, he decided to legalize the Communist Party by a decree-law on April 9, 1977. This led to protest from the military. The minister of the Marine, Admiral Pitta de Veiga, resigned from office. Reluctantly, most generals accepted. This was facilitated by the moderate stand of the Communist Party, which accepted the monarchy and was interested in a strong settlement with the Francoist regime.[46] The elections of June 15, 1977, had a participation rate of 79.24 percent of the population—around 18 million voters—and led to a victory for Adolfo Suarez. The Center Democratic Union (*Unión de Centro Democratico* [UCD]) got 39.9 percent of the vote, the PSOE 28.8 percent, the post-Francoist Popular Alliance (*Alianza Popular* [AP]) led by former Francoist minister Manuel Fraga Iribarne 8.2 percent and the Communist party 9.2 percent. Apart from these parties Catalan and Basque regionalist parties were also represented in the Constituent Assembly as well as the smaller Christian-Democratic parties and the Socialist People's Party. José Maria Maravall explained the results of the PSOE and the PCE in terms of the historical memory of many voters and the enduring traditions of republicanism. The new parties still had no party organization, so that they were merely nominal electoral entities.[47]

Afterwards, Suarez successfully integrated the trade union confederations into a corporatist arrangement to stabilize the difficult economic situation. Although among political elites consensualism prevailed, the number of political and economic strikes increased considerably since 1975.[48] The so-called *Pactos de Moncloa* were signed in October 1977 in the hope of introducing difficult austerity measures and stabilizing the economy.[49]

The government was able to gain the support of the opposition for a plan to cut any wage increases, severe credit restrictions, reduction of public spending, and new taxes. Suarez was able to reconcile with the regional governments in exile. He was able to bring back Josep Tarradellas, the president of *Generalitat*, by restoring the Catalan government. Tarradellas came back on October 23, 1977, to Catalonia.

The case of Basque Country was a bit different. A commission had to be set up consisting of a Socialist, a Basque nationalist, and a Centrist to decide over the creation of a General Basque council designed to fulfill the functions of an autonomous government. Both historical regions had to wait until the constitution was approved.[50] The final constitutional settlement granted autonomy to the historical regions through the formula of a "state of autonomies" (*estado de autonomias*).

Indeed, in this period the main aspect that had to be dealt with was the constitutional issue. The discussion between different parties led to a culture of compromise. The referendum in December 1978 was approved overwhelmingly by the population. High levels of abstention could only be registered in Basque Country and Catalonia.

The elections on March 1, 1979, represented the final moment of transition to democracy. The UCD won the elections with 35 percent of the vote, the PSOE came in second with 30.4 percent, AP declined to 5.8 percent, and the PCE remained stable with 10.7 percent. Several regionalist parties managed to get MPs elected.

Greece: A Hegemonic Transition (1974–1975)

The transition to democracy in Greece was quite different from the Portuguese, Spanish, and Italian ones. Konstantinos Karamanlis's return to Greece was celebrated by the population as the return of *paraklitos* (savior). Karamanlis's long years in exile gave him now the opportunity to establish a more stable and democratic political system. His charismatic personality shaped the trajectory of the transition in Greece. On August 1, he restored the constitution of 1952 so that the legacy of the military dictatorship could be neutralized.[51] He introduced also several laws to liberalize political life. Due to the threat coming from the military, elections were held on November 17, 1974, the anniversary of the uprising in the National Polytechnic in Athens. This was done to establish as quickly as possible democratic legitimacy against the military.

The elections to the Constituent Assembly produced an absolute majority for Karamanlis's Party New Democracy (*Nea Dimokratia* [ND]). He was able to win over the Center Union Party (*Enosis Kentrou* [EK]) under the leadership of Georgios Mavros and the Panhellenic Socialist Movement (*Panhellenio Sosialistiko Kinima* [PASOK]) and both Communist parties (KKE and KKE-es).[52]

ND gathered 54 percent of the vote and 220 seats, EK 20 percent and 60 seats, PASOK 14 percent and 12 seats, and the United Left 10 percent and 8 seats. One month later Karamanlis decided to hold the referendum on the future form of the regime. On December 8, 69.18 percent of the population voted for a republic and 30.82 percent for a parliamentary monarchy.

In 1975, Karamanlis had to struggle against potential threats coming from the military. Indeed, in February 1975 a coup attempt was discovered including about thirty-nine officers and led by one of the prominent military of the Junta, Ioannides. Later in August they went to trial; fourteen out of twenty-one suspects got sentences between four and twelve years.[53]

Meanwhile the new constitution was adopted in Parliament, replacing the constitution of 1952 on June 11, 1975. The new constitution was approved only by the votes of the government party on June 7—the opposition walked away and abstained from the vote. On June 19, Konstantinos Tsatsos was elected by the *Vouli*, the Greek parliament, as first president of Greece.

An important event closed the transition to democracy in Greece. The trial against those mainly responsible for the coup d'état of April 1967 was regarded as crucial to deal with the horrid chapter of the military dictatorship. In the trial G. Papadopoulos, Stelios Pattakos and N. Makarizos were condemned to death. Further, eight charged officers got lifelong prison sentences. Two days later, on August 25, the Greek government suspended the death sentences and changed them to life-long prison. In September the members of the military police ESA went to trial and received jail sentences ranging from five months to twenty-three years. The transition to democracy became complete with elections on November 20, 1977. ND again won a considerable majority of 42 percent of the vote and 171 seats, followed by PASOK with 25 percent and 43 seats, EDIK with 12 percent and 16 seats, the Stalinist Communist Party of Greece (KKE) 9 percent and 11 seats, the National Camp a (splinter group of ND), with 7 percent and 5 seats, and the Alliance of Progressive and Left-wing forces with 3 percent and 2 seats.[54] In this sense, the Greek transition diverges completely from the Iberian ones, because after the constitutional settlement new elections were held only two years later, thus establishing a continuity between democratic transition and consolidation. Karamanlis's success was related to the ability to give a new direction to the country by pursuing a fast membership to the European Community (EC). This was possible because the other parties were electorally too weak to challenge ND and the charismatic personality of Karamanlis.

In sum, transitions to democracy in southern Europe were quite diverse. This shows that a great part of a successful transition to democracy is due to the interplay among the political actors. Nevertheless, a major supporting factor was that transition to democracy in the four countries happened during periods favorable to such a transition.

FROM DEMOCRATIC CONSOLIDATION TO EUROPEANIZATION

The institutionalization of democracy has to be regarded as a long-term multidimensional process. The degree of consolidation and institutionalization of certain dimensions (economic, social, political, and cultural) may be achieved at a faster pace in some than in others. Guillermo O'Donnell and Philippe Schmitter in their pioneering study on transitions from authoritarian rule in Latin America and southern Europe liken consolidation to a multiple chessboard, each following a different rhythm of play.[55]

Since the mid-1980s, all countries of the European Union have been under considerable pressure to introduce legislation and implement

European public policy for the creation of a Single European Market (SEM) and an Economic and Monetary Union (EMU). This process is being called Europeanization. In the case of the southern European countries, this was an important process to overcome many past habits of public policy by introducing the European rationale into public administration and government. This new stage of European democratic trajectories is changing qualitatively the nature of national democracies toward a common space of democracy and peace. In this section we want to outline briefly the main political events leading to democratic consolidation and Europeanization.

Democratic Consolidation

Italy
The "First" Italian Republic was established after the approval of the constitution of 1948 and ended abruptly in 1992 when the majority of the ruling Italian political class was charged with corruption. The so-called *tangentopoli* initiated by the Milanese judge Antonio di Pietro affected mainly the parties of government DC, the Italian Socialist Party (PSI), and three smaller parties: the Italian Liberal Party (PLI), the Italian Republican Party (PRI), and the Italian Social Democratic Party (PSDI). The fall of the Italian political class closed a chapter in Italian history that became known as *partitocrazia* (the rule of parties). For almost fifty years the culture of patronage and clientelism was prevalent in Italian politics, undermining the development of a strong democracy based on accountability and transparency. Connections of politicians to the Mafia, such as allegedly the case of Giulio Andreotti, the longtime prime minister of DC, as well as the role the DC played in Naples and Palermo made people aware of the fact that at least part of the Italian political economy was based on clientelism, patronage, and corruption. Although the constitutional settlement in 1948 was achieved through consensualism and elite bargaining, after the elections of the same year the DC became the dominant actor in the party and political systems. Indeed, the Cold War period that started with the Truman doctrine in 1947 should have been helpful for the consolidation of power of the DC in the 1950s and 1960s. Furthermore, this dominance of the DC was strengthened by the economic boom called bluntly the "Italian miracle." which transformed the country from an agrarian to an industrial nation within two decades. The "blocked democracy" (*la democrazia bloccatta*) was based on the exclusion of the Italian Communist Party (PCI) from governmental responsibility. This imperfect bipartyism (*bipartitismo imperfetto*) remained the most stable feature of the new political system. Another feature was the centrality of the parliament (*centralità dell parlamento*), meaning that the fragmented

party system led to an increasing importance of the parliament in relation to the weak coalition governments.[56] Between 1948 and 1992 Italy experienced fifty governments of short duration.[57]

The governmental instability did not lead to a chaos, mainly because the political elite remained quite stable and was characterized by continuity. The same people tended to be coopted government after government, changing maybe only the portfolios that they were allocated. Another reason was the stability of the party composition in government. The DC formed coalitions only with the three smaller lay parties: the Italian Republican Party (*Partito Repubblicano Italiano* [PRI]), the Italian Liberal Party (*Partito Liberale Italiano* [PLI]), and the Italian Social Democratic Party (*Partito Social Democratico Italiano* [PSDI]). In the 1960s this constellation was replaced by a coalition between the DC and the Italian Socialist Party (*Partito Socialista Italiano* [PSI]). In the 1970s, the DC was increasingly challenged by the second largest party, the PCI. The gap between the two main parties in electoral terms narrowed. The Cold War period is being steadily replaced by an atmosphere of debate and peaceful coexistence. In Italy, a process of rapprochement between PCI and DC changed the culture of the country.

The so-called historical compromise (*compromesso storico*) initiated by the secretary-general of the PCI, Enrico Berlinguer, and the DC leader, Aldo Moro, was a major step in transforming the PCI from an antisystemic force to a supporter of the political system. The two major parties found a formula of cooperation with the historical compromise. This was quite important, because after decades of alienation, many social movements erupted during the 1970s. Some of them even chose the path of terrorism and violence.[58] The historical compromise found its final point when DC Prime Minister Aldo Moro, one of the architects of the historical compromise, was kidnapped by the Red Brigades. On the eve of the assassination of Aldo Moro in May 1978 by the Red Brigades (*Brigate Rosse*), a leftwing terrorist group, the historical compromise collapsed. In the 1980s, a further realignment of the voters took place. The PSI strengthened its position and under the leadership of Bettino Craxi became one of the governing parties. The dominance of the PSI in government formation and stabilization was regarded as positive. The leadership of Bettino Craxi made it possible for the five-party government (*pentapartito governo*) to have the longest duration in the history of the first Italian Republic.[59]

Afterward the decline of both main parties in the elections of 1987 again created a very unstable situation in Italy. The fragmentation of the electorate, the collapse of the Soviet Union, and the crisis of the patronage and clientelistic network embroiling firms of the economic sector such as ENI, the parties, industrial entrepreneurs, and the Mafia led to the breakdown of a whole party system in 1992. The so-called *tangentopoli* affair (kickback city) discovered during the *Mani Pulite* (Clean Hands) operation of Judge Antonio di Pietro led to the imprisonment of hundreds of party leaders across the country charged with accepting commissions in exchange for granting or facilitating contracts with public enterprises. The most extensive networks were found in Naples, which was dominated by DC leader Gava and in Sicily by Salvo Lima. The latter had intimate connections with the most prominent leader of the DC, Giulio Andreotti.[60] Andreotti was put on trial in 1995 for murdering journalist Mino Pecorelli in 1979 who wanted to report on the political figures behind the assassination of Prime Minister Aldo Moro in 1978, and for having links to the Mafia through the DC Sicilian leader Salvo Lima.[61] He was acquitted in both cases by courts in Perugia and Palermo respectively.

Portugal

The Portuguese case of democratic consolidation was extremely conditioned by the nature of democratic transition. The legislative elections and the presidential elections of 1976 strengthened liberal democracy. Although the transition to democracy had been successfully accomplished, the new political system was affected by extreme political and economic instability. The economic disarray after the revolution was regarded as a major obstacle to the consolidation and institutionalization of democracy. This was reinforced by a weak executive who had no governmental experience and lacked a strong stable majority in the new Assembly of the Republic (*Assembleia da República* [AR]), the Portuguese Parliament. Between 1976 and 1985, Portuguese governments had only a very weak support in Parliament. The two socialist governments until 1978 were too unstable to introduce any kind of economic and political reforms. Afterward President Antonio Ramalho Eanes decided to take over the initiative and appoint technocratic governments led by independents that were regarded by the Portuguese parliament as illegitimate. They lacked support in parliament and were not able to improve the political and economic situation. Coalition governments existed between 1979 and 1985 that were extremely unstable.[62] A complete civilianization of the political system was only achieved when the Council of the Revolution, enshrined in the constitution, was abolished in 1982 after a constitutional revision spearheaded by the coalition government of the Social-Democratic Party (PSD), CDS, and PPM. This revolutionary institution was replaced by a Constitutional Court.[63]

This civilianization of the political system was achieved by a weakening of the powers of the presidency in relation to parliament and government. The experience with the semipresidential position of President Ramalho Eanes between 1976 and 1980 created a joint effort of the AD government and the main opposition party PS to change the relation of powers between the three main institutions. In this sense, the potential semipresidentialism was transformed into a presidency that fulfilled merely a representative role. In the new elections of April 25, 1983, the PS won the elections and formed a coalition government with the PSD. The bad economic situation required from this coalition the implementation of a package of austerity measures prescribed by the International Monetary Fund (IMF). This second standby credit of the IMF led to very high social costs leading even to the bankruptcy of several small firms and arrears in salaries of several months.[64] Problems between the coalition partners in 1985, particularly due to leadership change in the PSD, led to the breakdown of the coalition. The year 1985 marked the beginning of a new phase of democratic consolidation in Portugal. The integration of the country into the European Community after the solemn signature of the Treaty of Accession on June 10, 1985, and the victory of PSD leader Anibal Cavaco Silva in the legislative elections of 1985 changed this situation radically. The charismatic leader remained in power for the next decade. Although his first government relied only on a very weak relative majority in parliament, Silva transmitted to the electorate an image of eficiency and competence. In 1987, after a motion of nonconfidence against the government introduced by the new Democratic Renewal Party (*Partito Renovador Democrático* [PRD]), he called for early elections. In the elections of July 17, Cavaco Silva transformed his relative majority into an absolute majority. He was able to repeat this victory in the subsequent elections of 1991. The success of Cavaco Silva led to a further revision of the constitution in 1989 that focused on liberalizing the economic section and removed all the references to the revolutionary period. This completed more or less the period of consolidation and institutionalization. From then on, pressure for further modernization and democratization came from the European integration process.

Spain

Comparing Spain's political system with Portugal, one can say that the former achieved political stability at a very much earlier stage. In October 1982, the Spanish Socialist Workers Party (PSOE) won the elections with 48.2 percent of votes and achieved the absolute majority in both chambers of Parliament (Congress and Senate). The other national parties ([AP/CD/PP], UCD, and the Spanish Communist Party/United Left [PCE/IU]) were too weak to attain such a high number of votes. PSOE remained in power until 1996.

But the consolidation of democracy began before the victory of the Socialist Party. In the elections of 1979, Adolfo Suarez repeated his electoral success of 1977. With its share of 35 percent, the UCD was able to retain his pivotal position in the party system. The period between 1979 and 1982 was also the most difficult one in the processes of transition and consolidation of Spanish democracy. Basque terrorism, left- and right-wing terrorism, and the danger of a military coup d'état dominated political life. Apart from it, the economic situation had to be stabilized by a new social pact.

The retreat of Prime Minister Adolfo Suarez and the desintegration of the UCD during 1981 represented a factor of instability of the new regime. Before Calvo Sotelo could be invested as the new prime minister, Colonel Tejero seized the Cortes and its members and hoped to create a nationwide support, including the king's, for his action. This action of February 23, 1981, was the last action of the conservative bunker in the military hierarchy to reverse the process of democratization in Spain. King Juan Carlos played an important role to solve the situation and save democracy in Spain. The supporters of Colonel Tejero were worried about the position of politicians in relation to the regional question. Their centralistic conception of the state seemed to be eroded by the constitutional granting of autonomy statutes to the regions.[65]

In June 1981, UCD and PSOE signed the Law for the Harmonization and Ordering of the Autonomy Process (*Ley de Ordenación y Armonización del Proceso Autonómico* [LOAPA]) introducing a very restrictive interpretation of the Basque, Catalan, and Galician statutes and sharply reducing the powers of the regional parliaments, obliging them to seek the approval of all legislation in the Cortes in Madrid. This was regarded by the regions as a rollback in the process of regional devolution. This early period of the habituation phase was very unstable, because the state was still in (re-)construction, but the main factor that contributed to the general crisis of disenchantment (*desencanto*) of the population and the end of the politics of consociationalism was the desintegration of the UCD under Adolfo Suarez and later under Calvo Sotelo. Several political families, that made up the UCD began to split from the party.

In October 1982, the social basis of the UCD almost eroded. In the parliamentary elections the UCD received only 6.8 percent of the vote and finished third after the PSOE and AP. The "party of transition" dissolved itself shortly afterward.[66]

The overdominating party became the PSOE. The new president of the government, Felipe Gonzalez, presented a program of economic and social liberalization. A two-phase strategy was developed. The first phase was intended to heighten the competition ability and efficiency of the Spanish market. In the second phase, social policy and the measures to build up a welfare state would be introduced to improve the life of the lower classes.

The economic situation in 1982 was rather bad to implement a more Keynesian style of policy, in which social policy could have a priority over all other policies. A strategy oriented toward the international economic system was designed to restore the competitiveness of the Spanish economy. The concept of a Spanish internal market-oriented economic policy was dropped.[67]

The integration of Spain into NATO and in the EC in 1986 documents also the development of the PSOE from a socialist-left (1974–78) over a social-democratic (1979–82) to a technocratic standpoint. In 1989 the PSOE was able to achieve an absolute majority with 39.55 percent. Its loss in votes did not affect its position in the political system. This is related to the fragmented character of the non-PSOE electorate among different parties of different ideological currents. The PSOE was accused during the 1980s of abusing its power and practicing corruption in some cases. More evident are 25,000 administrative posts that were created between 1984 and 1987.[68] This tendency to allocate administration posts to potential voters for coming elections is very similar to the patronage politics of Andreas Papandreou and the PASOK during the 1980s in Greece. In 1993 the PSOE achieved only a relative majority. Afterward several scandals of PSOE corruption during the absolute majority governments of the Socialists came to the fore. After the SEM came into force on January 1, 1993, an economic recession set in, which would contribute to the downfall of the PSOE in government.[69]

Greece

After approval of the constitution in 1975, Konstantinos Karamanlis was very keen to promote the integration of Greece into the EC. This aspect dominated his politics in the late 1970s. He began the negotiations with the commission in Brussels in July 1976. The commissioners hesitated to recommend the integration of Greece into the EC, but the Council of Ministers decided to open up negotiations. Karamanlis promoted the Europeanization of Greece so that education, the economy, and social policy could be reformed. He was opposed by many vested interests: businessmen, bankers, trade unions, the academic establishment, and the ecclesiastical hierarchy.[70]

In the early elections of 1977, Karamanlis again received the absolute majority. This gave him enough legitimacy to pursue his policy of European integration. On May 28, 1979, the treaty of accession was signed and approved in Parliament. PASOK boycotted the voting.

In 1980, Karamanlis became the new president of the Greek republic and was replaced by Giorgios Rallis as the new leader of *New*

Democracy (ND). The following year, PASOK won the elections. The radical discourse of PASOK was seen by the EC and potential investors as a danger. PASOK tried first to fulfill the promises of the election campaign by introducing a Keynesianist policy to promote the demand in the Greek market. This caused major problems to the economy, due to its higher levels of imports. The Greek economy began to have difficulties in the mid-1980s. PASOK had to introduce austerity measures in 1985-1987 to stabilize the economy under the guidance of the European Community.[71] In spite of those measures between 1987 and 1989 PASOK returned to the politics of expansionism in view of the forthcoming elections in 1989. The high budget deficit, high inflation, and high unemployment were the main worries of the Greek economy.[72]

The PASOK era was also conditioned by a high level of political violence and anti-Americanism, which did not help to stabilize the political system. PASOK with its comfortable majority was not able to present an alternative to the dominant liberal policies of Western Europe. Political violence came predominantly from Greek left-wing and right-wing terrorism, as well as from Arab terrorism, which saw Greece as a very good field to prepare attacks against Western and American institutions based in Greece. In 1989 a coalition government between the Alliance of the Progressive Left and the New Democracy was formed. It was a transitional coalition, due to the fact that both main parties were not able to win a relative majority. The main purpose of this coalition was *katharsis*. This meant the cleaning up of political life from the scandals that emerged after eight years of absolute majority Socialist government. In an analysis of 1986 it was found that of the 70 percent of PASOK members who had joined the party since 1981, 89 percent were employed in the state sector, a figure that increased to 96 percent in the case of Central Committee members.[73]

Parliament was the dominant institution in dealing with this *katharsis*. In 1990 the New Democracy formed a coalition government with PASOK and the Progressive Alliance of the Left to endorse a very austere economic program. This was replaced in the autumn of the same year by a New Democracy government led by the controversial Kostas Mitsotakis. The Mitsotakis government introduced major changes in the Greek political economy by starting important privatization and liberalization processes of the public sector. He relied on the support of a team of the European Union to guide the Greek economy toward macroeconomic stability.[74] This was only partially achieved and under strong resistance from the trade union confederation GSEE, PASOK, and opposition within his own party. Particularly, the intention to privatize the public main telecommunications provider OTE contributed to his downfall when businessmen with vested interests joined in with the opposition. The erosion of his majority in the Vouli led to the resignation of Prime Minister Mitsotakis. Allegations of telephone tapping of the opposition leader Andreas Papandreou contributed further to discrediting his government.[75] In 1993 PASOK returned to power. It learned from past mistakes and was more committed to European integration. It actually followed policies similar to those of New Democracy with the rhetoric of the left.[76] Democratic consolidation and institutionalization in Greece were overshadowed by old political practices such as clientelism and patronage. This is still dominant in Greek politics.

Europeanization of Political and Economic Systems Since the Mid-1990s

The Europeanization of the political systems of southern Europe became an important new qualitative step toward reinforcement of democratization. Indeed, all four countries are now integrated in a process of economic, political, social, and certainly also cultural convergence. One could notice a change of political culture among political elites from a mere ideological conflictual approach toward the adversary to a more rational and technocratic approach to government and governance. Throughout this book, we deal with the Europeanization of political systems. In the following pages, we want only to sketch the changing nature of national politics in the four countries in view of growing convergence and integration.

Portugal
The Cavaco Silva period became a successful phase in Portuguese politics sustained in large part by the large amount of structural funds flowing to Portugal originating from the European Community. For the first time in the history of this young democracy, long-term policies had to be designed so that Portugal could adjust to the policies of the European Community. Cavaco Silva was able to present the image of a technocratic government interested in modernizing the country. Within one decade, Portugal's economy experienced an economic boom. Cavaco Silva introduced more stability in policy making, changed the culture of government vis-à-vis the international community, and enhanced the self-confidence of the Portuguese executive within the European Union. An important test for the new government was the presidency of the European Community in 1992, which had in its agenda the process of ratification of the Maastricht Treaty, the reform of the Common Agricultural Policy (CAP), and the important conference on environment organized by the United Nations in Rio de Janeiro. Domestically, Cavaco Silva was accused by the opposition as being

authoritarian and uncompromising. He used to avoid public debates with the main opposition leaders on television. Its reluctance toward the European integration process was steadily replaced by a more positive attitude. Although the opposition noticed that Cavaco Silva inaugurated new roads shortly before elections and used that to promote the image of the government, the decade of *Cavaquismo* has to be regarded as crucial for the consolidation and institutionalization of democracy in Portugal.[77]

His successor, the socialist Antonio Guterres, was very keen to present a different image than that of Cavaco Silva. He was reelected in 1999. He held regular meetings with the opposition leaders, and he was able to compromise with different political actors. This was a sign that elite culture had become more democratic and more concerned with demands of civil society. Once again, the structural funds of the European Union as well as the entry in the third stage of Economic and Monetary Union (EMU) had spillover effects on the efficiency of the policies of the Portuguese government. In spite of the structural funds, in 2001 the Portuguese government had to make major cuts to avoid an economic crisis. Indeed, in the past twelve years, Portuguese government expenditure has risen considerably, due to massive investment in infrastructures, education, and the welfare system. Moreover, due to unwillingness to reform public administration with 700,000 civil servants, about 8 percent of the population, Guterres had difficulties rallying support from his own party and the opposition for his policies. It was also difficult for Guterres to get approval for his budget 2000–2001 and 2001–2002 in parliament due to the lack of an absolute majority by one vote. He had to rely on the support of MP Fernando Campelo of the opposition party, the Democratic Social Center/People's Party (CDS/PP). Subsequently Campelo was expelled from the party.[78] In the local elections on December 16, 2001, the PS lost control of the major cities Lisbon, Porto, and Coimbra. This led Guterres to resign and allowed President Jorge Sampaio, after consultation with the main political parties and the Council of State, to call for early elections.[79] In the March 17, 2002, legislative elections, Manuel Durão Barroso, the leader of the PSD, was able to defeat the ruiling Socialist party and form a coalition government with the People's Party, which became a junior partner. The new government announced several austerity measures to contain public expenditure. Indeed, false accounting practices by the previous government led to a revision of the original estimation of the budget deficit of the year 2001 from 2.8 percent of GDP, still below the criteria of Maastricht of 3 percent of GDP, to 4.1 percent in July 2002. This naturally will lead to a substantial cut of the annual rate of public expending that Portuguese society was used to since the early 1990s.

Spain

The People's Party of José Maria Aznar was able to increase the share of votes between 1993 and 1996, but the PSOE under the leadership of charismatic Felipe Gonzalez was kept in power due to a parliamentary pact with the main regionalist party of Catalonia, *Convergencia i Unió* (Convergence and Union [CiU]). This changed the way of doing politics in Spain, because for the first time, regionalist parties got more significance as coalition partners at the national level. Throughout 1994 and 1995 several scandals in which the PSOE was involved came to the fore. The crucial scandal was the alleged involvement of Felipe Gonzalez in the establishment of a terrorist organization called Anti-terrorist Liberation Group (*Grupos Anti-terroristas de Liberación* [GAL]), set up by the Spanish Secret Services, CESID, and with the aim to destroy the Basque separatist organization ETA. The GAL consisted of mercenaries from France and Portugal who would target family members of alleged ETA terrorists. This was regarded as "state terrorism" by public opinion and the opposition parties. Minister of the Interior José Barrionuevo was charged later with this crime, but no link to Prime Minister Gonzalez was ever found. Other cases of sleaze and corruption dominated the agenda until 1996.[80] This led to the withdrawal of support of the coalition with the PSOE by the Catalan Convergence and Union (*Convergencia i Unió* [CiU]).

In the elections of March 3, 1996, the electorate gave only a relative majority of 1 percent over the PSOE to the PP. Leader José Maria Aznar had to enter in coalition negotiations with the main regionalist-nationalist party of Catalonia, CiU. It took over two months to agree upon a program, due to the demands of CiU to devolve more rights to Catalonia and the other autonomies. The PP could count on the support of the main party in the Basque Country, the Basque Nationalist Party (*Partito Nacional Vasco* [PNV]), to introduce a different system of interterritorial cooperation in Spain. This inability of both main parties to gain a decisive absolute majority and its dependency on the regionalist-nationalist parties indicate a change of the relationship between the central and the regional political fields. The position of the PP in relation to the autonomies changed substantially since 1989, leading even to a reversal of policy. José Maria Aznar was supported by the most prominent member of the party, Manuel Fraga Iribarne, presently the president of the *Xunta de Galicia* (the Galician regional government).[81] After two decades Spain was democratically institutionalized. Although corruption scandals made people aware of the difficulties in establishing a strong democracy, one has to say that simultaneously the control institutions of the new democracy are being challenged and responding quite well to the problems that accumulated in the past two decades. From a democratic standpoint, decentralization and deconcentration of policy making is changing Spain from a centralized country to a semifederal polity.

This may lead in the long run to more wealth and democracy. In March 2000, José Maria Aznar's PP was reelected with an absolute majority in spite of or probably because of an electoral pact signed between PSOE and IU. Aznar's government was and is very successful in stabilizing the Spanish economy and using the structural funds and the pressure coming from European public policies to introduce major reforms of the political and economic system.[82] The main target has been the reform of the labor market. Some reform was done with the support of the main trade union confederations, UGT and CCOO, and the main employers' organization, CEOE, in 1997. In spite of that, since the elections of March 12, 2000, the conciliatory and compromise policy of PP changed considerably due to the fact that it achieved an absolute majority. Particularly, the will to further reform the labor market has found opposition from the trade union confederations. Aznar has been successful in bringing down unemployment to almost 13 percent of the active population, but after the September 11 (2001) events, this figure may go up again. By the end of 2001, trade union confederations and the main representative of Spanish business were able to restore the social dialogue and sign an Interconfederal Agreement.[83]

Aznar is faced with a renewed campaign of Basque terrorism, which started in December 1999, after a year of cease-fire. The elections of May 13, 2001, in the Basque Country clearly strengthen the moderate nationalism of the Basque Nationalist Party (*Partito Nacionalista Vasco* [PNV]) and the *Eusko Askartasuna*, but Aznar is uncompromising even in relation to these nationalist groups.[84] After the September 11 events, Aznar's strategy of nonnegotiation gained new momentum. A multiple strategy targeting the financial and formal political organizations linked to ETA including Herri Batasuna gained support from the main opposition party, PSOE. ETA and Herri Batasuna are to be included in the list of terrorist organizations against which the European Union will fight in the context of the international war against terrorism.[85] Another major issue is the new law of immigration (*ley de extranjeria*) that led to major protests in Spanish society because of its discriminatory and tough nature. In spite of its implementation, which restricts the ability of illegal immigrants to work in Spain, immigration from the southern Mediterranean continues to be a major concern for the Spanish authorities.[86] Aznar's government also faced strong criticisms from the opposition parties and public opinion in relation to the denial of responsibility for the financial scandal caused by the investment firm *Gescartera* that led to huge losses of investments of several clients, including several Catholic institutions. Allegedly there was a strong collusion between *Gescartera* and the controlling institution of the sector the National Commission for the Bond and Security Markets (*Comisión Nacional del Mercado de Valores* [CNMV]).

Moreover, huge protests were organized by students and teachers of the public higher education sector against the introduction of privatization and a more marketlike reform in Spanish universities. The culmination of the protests was a megademonstration in Madrid of over 350,000 students and teachers against the introduction of the Organic Law for Universities (*Ley Organica de Universidades* [LOU]) on December 1, 2001. The protests were joined by the main trade union confederations and PSOE. This naturally made things difficult for Minister of Education Pilar del Castillo.[87]

Italy

The widespread corruption became normality in Italian politics since the 1940s. In this sense, the continuity of features of a political culture based on clientelism and patronage since the establishment of the Italian nation may be regarded as the most evident aspect of an incomplete democratization, which would foster universal rational-legal values instead of particularistic clientelistic ones, transparency instead of diffuseness, accountability instead of personal favoritism.

Growing regionalism contributed to the collapse of *partitocrazia*. Indeed, the Lombard League (*Lega Lombarda*) under the leadership of Umberto Bossi was a major force exposing the clientelistic nature of the Italian state. The introduction of regional elections in the 1970s, although agreed much earlier in the 1948 constitution, established an intermediary electoral arena between local and national levels. This became the main arena for the Lega Lombarda, which, later on, joined by other smaller leagues, created the *Lega Nord* (Northern League [LN]). Although, these new social movements were regionalist in character, they demanded a more federal structure for Italy, or even the breakup of Italy. This is quite important, because Lega Nord is characterized by a very xenophobic discourse against North African immigrants and southern Italians. One of the main criticisms is what the Lega calls the "southernization of the administration" and the extensive network of patronage of clientelism, perpetuating the inefficiency of the civil service.[88]

Since 1993, Italy has operated under a new mixed electoral system. Seventy-five percent of all seats in both parliamentary chambers are elected by a simple majority system, and twenty-five percent are elected by a proportional representation system. This led to the creation of very loose electoral coalitions on the left and the right. Governmental instability is still quite common, and the polarization between left and right continues to predominate. In 1994, the right-wing center electoral coalition Pole of Freedom/Pole of Government (*Polo della Libertà/Polo del Buon Governo*) led by Silvio Berlusconi's *Forza Italia* (FI) won the elections. The new party was formed within three months and used new marketing techniques to place itself as the new DC in the new party system. Within nine months the coalition fell apart due to corruption allegations of the judiciary against Silvio Berlusconi and his brother. After a technocratic government led by Lamberto Dini in 1995–1996, early elections were called and a left-wing center coalition under the name Olive Tree (*Ulivo*) came to power whose leader Romano Prodi was as well the chairman of the Italian People's Party (*Partito Popolare Italiano* [PPI]).[89] Prodi's main objective was to bring Italy into the third stage of EMU by complying with the criteria set up in the Treaty of the European Union (TEU). He was successful to achieve this objective within two years. He used the route of taxation to finance integration into the first wave of membership. Afterward the coalition lost the support of the Communist Refoundation (*Rifondazione Comunista* [RC]) and Prodi was replaced by Massimo D'Alema, the leader of the Party of Democratic Left (*Partito Democratico della Sinistra* [PDS]), who had difficulties keeping the alliance together. Already in December 1999, the government collapsed and a new government had to be negotiated among the main parties of the Olive tree coalition. This showed that governmental instability continued to be a major problem for Italian politics.[90] The continuing fragmentation of the Ulivo alliance and the defeat in the regional elections of March 2000 led to the resignation of Massimo D'Alema, who was replaced by a technocratic government under Giuliano D'Amato in May 2000. Many members of the government belonged to the Ulivo alliance. This government was quite successful in completing the one year that was left of the normal legislature time of five years. In the elections of May 13, 2001, the House of Freedoms under the leadership of media tycoon Silvio Berlusconi won the elections against the very fragmented left-center alliance Ulivo under the leadership of Francesco Rutelli, the former very popular mayor of Rome. One of the most salient features was the complete demise of the Lega Nord and the transfer of vote to Silvio Berlusconi's Forza Italia. The LN ended officially without seats, but according to the coalition agreement Berlusconi allocated some seats to the Lega. On the whole, Italian politics has become more stable in comparison to the pre-1992 situation, but there is still a strong volatility between the ideological blocks. The electorate is still experimenting with different options.[91] The Berlusconi government inherited many economic problems, particularly related to the budget deficit. According to the new economy minister Giulio Tremonti, the public deficit figures of the D'Amato government had to be revised from 0.8 percent to probably 1.9 to 2.6 percent of GDP.[92] Moreover, Prime Minister Berlusconi's conflict of interests and problematic past in relation to alleged fraud in accounting of his firms continued to haunt him since he was elected. His attempt to use the September 11 events to get the approval of legislation that would lead to his acquittal retrospectively was criticized in the European Council of Laeken in mid-December 2001.[93] Moreover, at the end of 2001, Minister of Foreign Affairs Renato Ruggiero resigned, because Berlusconi's cabinet was moving toward a more Euroskeptic position against the introduction of the Euro, at the beginning of the year. Euroskepticism was expressed by Minister of Economy Giulio Tremonti, Interior Minister Umberto Bossi, and Defense Minister Antonio del Martino. This naturally shows that the coalition government is showing the first signs of instability.[94]

Greece

After the death of Andreas Papandreou in 1995, a new leader emerged who strengthened the commitment of Greece to European integration. Kostas Simitis' technocratic approach toward SEM and EMU is regarded as positive for the improvement of the integration efforts into the European Union by Greece. Most of his policies were monitored by the European Commission, which was very keen to integrate Greece into EMU. The policies of the Greek government have been more rational in recent times. The positive rapprochement between Greece and Turkey is improving the climate within the European Union. According to the European Central Bank and other reports, Greece has made huge progress in the past two years and has fulfilled most of the Maastricht criteria. Still lagging behind is the huge public debt, which is over 100 percent of GDP. Very detailed reform programs are targeting particularly the public sector to reduce the deficit in long-term perspective. At the moment we are still in a transition phase within the third stage of EMU. It will take at least a decade to make a final assessment of how the dynamics of the SEM and EMU will further affect the whole political and economic structures of these political systems. The main task ahead for Kostas Simitis is to reform the social security system. This is opposed by the trade unions. Simitis also faces some left-wing opposition inside PASOK, which halfheartedly is supporting his program of modernization. Another major task is to reform public administration and to create more confidence of the population in the civil service, which has been quite intransparent for decades. Particularly, the taxation system has to be reformed, as well as the privatization process of eleven state-owned entreprises such as the national telecommunications company OTE, Olympic Airways, and the energy sector. Several reforms in the banking and financial sector are contributing to a revitalization of the Greek economy. It is now one of the fastest growing economies of the European Union.[95] One major achievement, though, was the integration into the Eurozone since January 1, 2001. Any further reforms of the public sector will be very relevant to sustain participation in this first wave of members. Simitis is also very keen to use the structural funds available in the third common framework program (2000–2006) to improve infrastructures, business, and education. In the horizon lies one prestigious project that may have a strong impact on the country: the Olympic Games in 2004.[96] Although Simitis has not been very successful in reforming the pension system, which was rejected by the left-wing faction inside the party and the trade unions, nevertheless it still can count on a strong mandate. In the last party conference on October 10–14, 2001, he emerged once more strengthened against his left-wing rival, the aging defense minister Akis Tsochatzopoulos. Instead, Simitis used his success to remodel his cabinet and promote Christos Doulakis, former deputy economy and finance minister, as chief of the most important ministry.[97]

CONCLUSIONS

The transformation of the political systems of southern Europe from authoritarian rule toward democracy was a lengthy and painful process. It was difficult to overcome aspects of neopatrimonialism that prevented the establishment of a democracy based on universalistic principles. Still today, the highest level of democratic cynicism can be found among the populations of southern Europe. In spite of all that, in the 1980s and 1990s the reinforced European integration process has increased the pressure on these southern European countries to overcome their past behavior and move toward more accountability and transparency in government. The political corruption findings of the 1990s in all four countries strengthened the cause for democracy and stronger European integration that is more and more based on reliable comparative data. On the one hand, this makes it possible to compare and expose mismanagement, corruption, or sleaze. On the other hand, it may have spillover effects on becoming a much better democracy by learning from common experiences shared among the member states of the European Union.

NOTES

1. Giuseppe Di Palma, *Political Synkretism in Italy: Historical Coalition Strategies and the Present Crisis* (Policy Papers in International Affairs; Berkeley: Institute of International Studies, 1978).

2. Robert W. Kern, *Liberals, Reformers and Caciques in Restoration Spain, 1875–1909* (Albuquerque: University of New Mexico Press, 1974); and José Manuel Sobral and Pedro Ginestal de Almeida, "Caciquismo e Poder Politico. Reflexoes em Torno das Eleições de 1901," *Analise Social*, 18, no. 72–74 (1982–1983): 649–71; particularly pp. 661–69.

3. Kathleen Schwartzman, *The Social Origins of Democratic Collapse. The First Republic in the Global Economy* (Kansas City: University of Kansas Press, 1989);

Douglas L. Wheeler, *Republican Portugal: A Political History, 1910–1926* (Madison: University of Wisconsin, 1978); Fernando Farelo Lopes, *Clientelismo e Poder Politico na Primeira Republica* (Lisboa: Estampa, 1994).

4. Manuel Tuñon de Lara, *Poder y Sociedad en España 1900–1931* (Madrid: Coleccion Austral, 1992); Shlomo Ben-Ami, *Fascism from Above: The Dictatorship of Primo de Rivera in Spain 1923–1930* (Oxford: Oxford University Press, 1983).

5. Juan Linz, "From Great Hopes to Civil War: The Breakdown of Democracy in Spain," in *The Breakdown of Democratic Regimes. Vol. 2: Europe*, ed. Juan J. Linz and Alfred Stepan (Baltimore, London: Johns Hopkins University, 1978), 142–215; particularly p. 145.

6. Spencer Di Scala, *Italy: From Revolution to Republic, 1700 to the Present* (Boulder, CO: Westview Press, 1995), 130–38; Margot Hentze, *Pre-Fascist Italy: The Rise and Fall of Parliamentary Democracy* (London: Allen and Unwin, 1939), 73–74; William A. Salomone, *Italy in the Giolittian Era: Italian Democracy in the Making 1900–1914* (Philadelphia: University of Pennsylvania Press, 1960), 108.

7. Paolo Farnetti, "Social Conflict, Parliamentary Fragmentation, Institutional Shift, and the Rise of Fascism," in *The Breakdown of Democratic Regimes. Vol. 2: Europe*, ed. Juan J. Linz and Alfred Stepan (Baltimore, London: Johns Hopkins University, 1978), 3–33; Christopher Seton-Watson, *Italy from Liberalism to Fascism,1870–1915* (Madison, Milwaukee: University of Wisconsin Press, 1968).

8. For a thorough assessment of the Metaxas dictatorship see Robin Higham and Thanos Veremis (eds.), *The Metaxas Dictatorship: Aspects of Greece 1936–1940* (Athens: Hellenic Foundation for Defense and Foreign Policy, 1993).

9. Jane and Andrew Carey, *The Web of Modern Greek Politics* (New York: Columbia, 1968), 148–94.

10. Gunnar Hering, Georg Demetriou, and Michael Kelpanides, "Politisches System," in *Südost Europa Handbuch. Bd. III: Griechenland*, ed. Klaus Detler-Grothusen (Gottingen: Vandenhoeck and Ruprecht, 1980), 54–121, particularly pp. 70–72; Richard Clogg, *Parties and Elections in Greece: The Search for Legitimacy* (London: Hurst Company, 1987), 57–73.

11. Roberto Bataglia, *Storia della Resistenza Italiana*. 8 settembre 1943–25 Aprile 1945 (Torino: Giulio Einaudi, 1964), 46–54.

12. Danilo Veneruso, *L'Italia Fascista (1922–1945)* (Bologna: Il Mulino, 1981), 395–99.

13. Paul Ginsbourg, *The History of Society and Politics in Contemporary Italy* (Harmondsworth: Penguin, 1989).

14. Presidencia do Conselho de Ministros/Comissão do livro negro sobre o fascismo, *Eleicões no regime fascista* (Lisboa: PCM, 1979); Philippe C. Schmitter, *Portugal: Do Autoritarismo à Democracia* (Lisboa: Instituto de Ciencias Sociais, 1999), 71–102.

15. Marcelino Passos, *Der Niedergang des Faschismus in Portugal. Zum Verhältnis von Ökonomie, Gesellschaft und Staat. Politik in einem europäischen Schwellenland* (Marburg: Verlag fur Arbeiterbewegung und Gesellschaftswissenschaft, 1987).

16. Kenneth Maxwell, *The Making of Portuguese Democracy* (Manchester: Manchester University Press, 1995), 40–44; Boaventura de Sousa Santos, "A Crise e a Reconstituição do Estado em Portugal (1974–1984)," *Revista Critica de Ciencias Sociais* 14 (1984): 7–29.

17. Otelo Saraiva de Carvalho, *Alvorada em Abril* (Lisboa: Ulmeiro, 1984); José Medeiros Ferreira, *Ensaio Histórico sobre a Revolucao de 25 de Abril* (Lisboa: Casa da Moeda, 1981), 17–36.

18. José Amodia, *Franco's Political Legacy: From Dictatorship to Facade Democracy* (London: A. Lane, 1977).

19. Raymond Carr and Juan Pablo Fusi, *España: De la Ditadura a la Democracia* (Madrid: Planta Siglo XX, 1979), 209–73; Daniele Conversi, *The Basques, The Catalans and Spain. Alternative Routes to Nationalist Mobilisation* (London: Hurst, 1997), 98–107.

20. Audrey Brassloff, *Religion and Politics in Spain. The Spanish Church in Transition, 1962–96* (Basingstoke, U.K.: Macmillan, 1998), 42–60.

21. José Maria Maravall, *La Politica de la Transición* (Madrid: Taurus 1984(2)), 165–66.

22. José M. Cuenca Toribio, "Soledad Miranda Garcia, La Elite Ministerial Franquista," *Revista de Estudios Politicos*, no. 5–7 (July–September 1987): 107–46.

23. Robert Graham, *Spain: Change of a New Nation* (London: Michael Joseph, 1984); Charles T. Powell, *Juan Carlos of Spain: Self-Made Monarch* (Basingstoke, U.K.: Macmillan, 1996), 62–84.

24. Stephen Rousseas, *The Death of a Democracy: Greece and the American Conscience* (New York: Grove Press, 1968).

25. Richard Clogg, "The Ideology of the 'Revolution Of 21 April 1967,'" in *Greece under Military Rule*, ed. Richard Clogg and George Yannopoulos (London: Secker and Warburg), 36–58.

26. Hering, Demetriou, and Kelpanides, *Politisches System*, 76.

27. C.M. Woodhouse, *Karamanlis: The Restorer of Democracy in Greece* (Oxford: Oxford University Press, 1982).

28. For a typology attempt, see Christian Welzel, "Systemwechsel in der globalen Systemkonkurrenz: Ein evolutionstheoretischer Erklärungsversuch," in *Systemwechsel 1: Theorien, Ansätze und Konzepte der Transitionsforschung*, ed. Wolfgang Merkel (Opladen: Leske and Budrich, 1996), 47–79.

29. Adam Przeworski, "Democracy as a Contingent Outcome of Conflicts," in *Constitutionalism and Democracy*, ed. Jon Elster and Rune Slagstad (New Rochelle, NY: Cambridge University Press, 1988), 59–80; Adam Przeworski, *Democracy and the Market: Political and Economic Reforms in Eastern Europe and Latin America* (Cambridge: Cambridge University Press, 1991); Giuseppe Di Palma, *To Craft Democracies: An Essay on Democratic Transitions* (Berkeley: University of California Press, 1990).

30. Guillermo O'Donnell, Philippe C. Schmitter, and Laurence Whitehead (eds.), *Transitions from Authoritarian Rule*. 4 vols. (Baltimore: Johns Hopkins University Press, 1986).

31. Dankwart W. Rustow, "Transitions to Democracy: Towards a Dynamic Model," *Comparative Politics* 3 (1970): 337–63.

32. Adam Przeworski and others, *Sustainable Democracy* (London: Manchester University Press, 1995).

33. Gianfranco Pasquino, "Political Leadership in Southern Europe: Research Problems," *West European Politics* 13, no. 4 (1990), 118–130; John Higley and Richard Gunther (eds.), *Elites and Democratic Consolidation in Latin America and Southern Europe* (Cambridge: Cambridge University Press, 1992).

34. Lawrence Whitehead (ed.), *The International Dimensin of Democratization* (Oxford: Oxford University Press, 1998); Geoffrey Pridham, "The International Context of Democratic Consolidation: Southern Europe in Comparative Perspective," in *The Democratics of Democratic Consolidation. Southern Europe in Comparative Perspective*, ed. Richard Gunther, Nikiforos P. Diamandouros, and Hans-Jürgen Puhle (Baltimore: Johns Hopkins University Press, 1995), 166–203; particularly pp. 189–93.

58   The Politics of Southern Europe

35. Christopher Duggan, *A Concise History of Italy* (Manchester: Manchester University Press, 1994), 246.

36. The international factor played a major role in conditioning the development of Italian politics. The American Truman doctrine, named after its president, envisaged the exclusion of the Communist parties from government in Western Europe. In the first months of 1948, the American government was very explicit in influencing the Italian population to vote for DC and against the communists. The European Recovery Plan, devised by U.S. Secretary of State George Marshall, was used to impose the desired result. The DC used an electoral strategy that denigrated the Left, particularly the PCI. The campaign "Christ against Communism" was supported by the Church. (See Robert Leonardi, "Democratic Transition in Postwar Italy," in *EncouragingDemocracy: The International Context of Regime Transition in Southern Europe*, ed. Geoffrey Pridham [London: Leicester University Press 1991], 62–84, particularly pp. 74–78.) The victory of DC would institutionalize the permanent exclusion of the PCI from power and create the conditions for a web of systemic corruption until 1992.

37. "Plataforma de Acordo Constitucional Com os Partidos Politicos," in *Movimento. Boletim Informativo das Forcas Armadas*, no. 15 (April 16, 1975), supplement without numbering.

38. *Eleições em Abril: Diário de Campanha* (Lisboa: Liber, 1975), 511-12.

39. In Portugal, the Socialist international was a major supporter of democracy. During and after the founding elections of April 25, 1975, the Socialist Party was able to mobilize the international community against an eventual transformation of Portugal into a socialist country. The so-called Committee of Solidarity with Socialism Democracy in Portugal, which consisted of important social democratic leaders like Olaf Palme, Willy Brandt, and Bruno Kreisky, used their influence to support the democratic parties in Portugal. Particularly, the Friedrich Ebert Foundation, closely linked to the German Social Democratic Party (*Sozialdemokratische Partei Deutschland* [SPD]), was instrumental in helping the Socialist Party logistically and financially against the organizational dominance of the Communist Party. Some authors refer to the fact that in the context of the Cold War, the SPD was working closely with the American Central Intelligence Agency (CIA) so that a communist takeover could be prevented. The Communist Party was also supported by the Communist sister party—the East German Party of the Socialist Unity of Germany (*Partei der Sozialistischen Einheit Deutschlands* [SED])—in logistical and financial terms. In this situation, the Portuguese transition to democracy was extremely dominated by the international environment of the Cold War (Rainer Eisfeld, *Sozialistischer Pluralismus in Europa: Ansätze und Scheitern and Beispiel Portugal* [Köln: Wissenschaft und Politik, 1984]; Maxwell, 1995, [FN13]). Quite important is, naturally, the pressure coming from the European Community, which through the whole revolutionary period kept close contacts with the military and civilian elites making people aware that any membership would depend on the development of a liberal democratic regime in Portugal. Any financial support was made dependent on this development toward a genuine liberal democracy. (José M. Magone, "A Integração Europeia e a Construção da Democracia Portuguesa," *Penelope* no. 18 (1998): 123–63, particularly pp. 134–39).

40. Rainer Eisfeld, Revolutionäre und Gegenrevolutionäre Bewegungen in Portugal seit 1974: Rolle und Entwicklung der Streitkräfte," *Politische Vierteljahresschrift* 23, Heft 2 (1982): 163–64; Douglas Porch, *The Portuguese Armed Forces and the Revolutoni* (London: Croom Helm, 1977), 195–215.

41. Nancy Bermeo, *The Revolution within the Revolution: Workers' Control in Rural Portugal* (Princeton: Princeton University Press, 1986); Charles Downs, *Revolution at the Grassroots in the Portuguese Revolution* (New York: State University of New York, 1989).

42. Thomas Bruneau and Alex Macleod, *Politics in Contemporary Portugal. Parties and the Consolidation of Democracy* (Boulder: Lynne Rienner, 1986), 80–81.

43. Josep Sánchez Cervelló, *A Revolucão Portuguesa. E A Sua Influencia na Transicao Espanhola (1961–1976).* (Lisboa: Assirio e Alvim, 1993), 331–412.

44. Donald Share, "Transitions to Democracy and Transition through Transaction," *Comparative Political Studies* 19, no. 4 (January 1987): 525–48.

45. Robert Graham, *Spain*, 138.

46. Carr and Fusi, *España*, 287–89.

47. Maravall, *La Politica*, 203–12; Mario Caciagli, "Spain: Parties and the Party System in the Transition," in *The New Mediterranean Democracies: Regime Transition in Spain, Greece and Portugal*, ed. Geoffrey Pridham (London: Frank Cass, 1984), 84–98, particularly p. 86; Ramon Cotarelo, "El Sistema de Partidos," in *La Transicion Democratica Espanola*, ed. José Felix Tezanos, Ramon Cotarelo, amd Andres De Blas (Madrid: Editorial Sistema 1993), 347–88, particularly p. 355.

48. Maravall, *La Politica*, 26–31.

49. Keith Salmon, *The Modern Spanish Economy: Transformation and Integration into Europe* (London: Pinter, 1995), 10–11.

50. Carr and Fusi, *España; The Basques, the Catalans and Spain*, 141–61.

51. Nikiforos P. Diamandouros, "Transition to, and Consolidation of, Democratic Politics in Greece 1974–1983: A Tentative Assesment," *West European Politics* 7, no. 2 (1984): 50–71, particularly p. 57.

52. Roy C. Macridis, "Elections and Political Modernization in Greece," in *Greece at the Polls: The National Elections of 1974 and 1977*, ed. Howard R. Penniman (Washington, London: American Enterprise Institute for Public Policy Research, 1981), 14–25, particularly pp. 14–15.

53. Harry J. Psomiades, "Greece: From the Colonels' Rule to Democracy," in *From Dictatorship to Democracy: From Authoritarian to Democratic Legacy*, ed. John Herz (London: Greenwood, 1982), 251–73.

54. Macridis, 15–17.

55. Guillermo O'Donnell and Philippe Schmitter, *Transitions from Authoritarian Rule, vol. 4, Conclusions* (Baltimore: Johns Hopkins University Press, 1986), 66.

56. Maurizio Cotta, "The Italian Parliament and Democratic Consolidation," in *Parliament and Democratic Consolidation in Southern Europe: Greece, Italy, Portugal, Spain and Turkey*, ed. Ulrike Liebert and Maurizio Cotta (London and New York: Pinter Publishers, 1990), 51–91.

57. Geoffrey Pridham, *Political Parties and Coalitional Behaviour in Italy* (London, New York: Routledge, 1988).

58. Sidney Tarrow, *Democracy and Disorder in Italy* (Oxford: Oxford University Press, 1989).

59. David Hine, *Governing Italy: The Politics of Bargained Pluralism* (Oxford: Oxford University Press, 1993).

60. Sarah Waters, "'Tangentopoli' and the Emergence of a New Political Order in Italy," *West European Politics* 17 (1994): 169–82; Mark Donovan, "Political Corruption in Italy," in *Distorting Democracy: Political Corruption in Spain, Italy and Malta*, ed. Paul Heywood (Bristol: Centre for Mediterranean Studies, University of Bristol). Occasional paper no. 10 (1994): 15–24; Stefano Guzzini, "La Longue Nuit de la Premiére Republique: L'Implosion Clienteliste en Italie,"

Revue Française de Science Politique 44, no. 6 (December 1994): 979–1013; Mark Gilbert, *The Italian Revolution* (Boulder: Westview Press, 1995).

61. Attilo Bolzoni, Giuseppe D'Avanzo, "I Processi A Giulio Andreotti: Palermo" (72–87); Carlo Bonini, "I Processi A Giulio Andreotti: Perugia" (88–99), in *Mafie E Antimafia: Rapporto' 96*, ed. Luciano Violante (Roma: Laterza, 1996).

62. José M. Magone, "Portugal: The Rationale of Democratic Regime Building," in *Coalition Governments in Western Europe*, ed. Wolfgang C. Müller and Kaare Strom (Oxford: Oxford University Press, 2000), 529–58.

63. Thomas Bruneau, *Politics and Nationhood: Post-Revolutionary Portugal* (New York: Praeger, 1984),138–40.

64. João Cravinho, "The Portuguese Economy: Constraints and Opportunities," in *Portugal in the 1980s: Dilemmas of Democratic Consolidation*, ed. Kenneth Maxwell (New York: Greenwood Press, 1986), 111–65.

65. Powell, *Juan Carlos*, 157–80; Alberto Olliart, "La Noche en que se afianzó la Corona," in *El Pais*, Extra Juan Carlos I (special report on King Juan Carlos 1), November 22, 2000, p.13.

66. Jonathan Hopkin, *La Desintegración de la Union de Centro Democratico: Una Interpretacion Organizativa* (Madrid: Centro de Estudios Constitucionales, 1993).

67. Wolfgang Merkel, "Sozialdemokratische Politik in einer post-keynesianischen Ära? DasBeispiel der sozialistischen Regierung Spaniens (1982–1988)," *Politisches Vierteljahresschrift* 30 (1989): 629–54.

68. Richard Gillespie, "Political Parties and Democratic Consolidation in Spain," in *Securing Democracy: Political Parties and Democratic Consolidation in Southern Europe*, ed. Geoffrey Pridham (London, New York: Routledge, 1990), 126–46.

69. José Magone, "The Logics of Party System Change in Southern Europe," in *Comparing Party System Change*, ed. Paul Pennings and Jan-Erik Lane, (London: Routledge, 1998), 217–40; Jonathan Hopkin, "A 'Southern' Model of Electoral Mobilisation? Clientelism and Electoral Politics in Spain," *West European Politics* 24, no. 1 (January 2001): 115–36.

70. J.C. Loulis, "The New Face of Conservatism," in *Greece at the Polls: The National Elections of 1974 and 1977*, ed. Howard R. Penniman (Washington, DC and London: American Enterprise Institute for Public Policy Research, 1981), 49–83, particularly pp. 67–68.

71. George Pagoulatos, "Economic Adjustment and Financial Reform: Greece's Europeanization and the Emergence of a Stabilization State," in *Europeanization and the Southern Periphery*, ed. Kevin Featherstone and George Kazamias (London: Frank Cass, 2001), 91–214; particularly pp. 194–96.

72. James Petras, "Spanish Socialism: The Politics of Neoliberalism," in *Mediterranean Paradoxes: The Political and Social Structures of Southern Europe*, ed. James Kurth and James Petras (Providence, RI: Berg Publishers, 1993), 95–127.

73. Geoffrey Pridham and Susannah Verney, "The Coalition of 1989–90: Inter-Party Relations and Democratic Consolidation," *West European Politics* 14, no. 4 (1991): 42–69, particularly p. 59.

74. Pagoulatos, "Economic Adjustment," in Featherstone and Kazamias, 198.

75. George Mavrogordatos, "Greece," in Political Data Yearbook 1994, *European Journal for Political Research* 26, no. 3/4 (December 1994): 313–18.

76. Pagoulatos, "Economic Adjustment," in Featherstone and Kazamias, 199.

77. José M. Magone, *European Portugal: The Difficult Road to Sustainable Democracy* (New York: Macmillan, St. Martin's Press, 1997); David Corkill, "Party Factionalism and Democratization in Portugal," *Democratization* 2, no. 2 (1995): 64–76.

78. "A Survey of Portugal," *The Economist*, December 2, 2000, pp. 9–12; *The Economist* December 21, 2001, pp. 36–37.

79. *O Publico*, December 17, 2001; December 18, 2001; *El Pais*, December 18, 2001, p. 8; *El Pais*, December 19, 2001, p. 10

80. Antonio Rubio and Manuel Cerdan, *El Origen Del Gal: "Guerra Sucia" Y Crimen De Estado* (Madrid: Temas De Hoy, 1997).

81. Sebastian Balfour, "'Bitter Victory, Sweet Defeat:' The March 1996 General Elections and the New Government in Spain," *Government and Opposition* 31, no. 3 (Summer 1996): 275–87; José Amodia, "Spain at the Polls: The Elections of March 3, 1996," *West European Politics* 19, no. 4 (October 1996): 813–19.

82. *The Economist*, March 11, 2000, pp. 25–28; Elisa Roller, "The March 2000 General Elections in Spain," *Government and Opposition* (2001): 209–29; Raj S. Chari, "The March 2000 Spanish Election: A Critical Election?" *West European Politics* 23, no. 3 (July 2000): 207–14.

83. *El Pais*, December 19, 2001, p. 48.

84. *The Economist*, May 12, 2001, p. 52; *The Economist*, May 19, 2001, pp. 44 and 47; *El Mundo*, May 15, 2001, pp. 1–8; *El Pais*, May 15, 2001, pp. 13–22; *El Pais*, May, 17, 2001, pp. 13–15.

85. *El Pais*, November 28, 2001, p. 17.

86. *El Pais*, June 1, 2001, p. 26: In 2000, 4,025 were detained; by July 2001 it was already 2,251. This is supported by criminal organizations that specialize in organizing illegal immigration.

87. *El Pais*, October 21, 2001, p. 32; *El Pais*, December 2, 2001, pp. 22–23.

88. Hilary Partridge, "Can the Leopard Change Its Spots? Sleaze in Italy," *Parliamentary Affairs* 48, no. 4 (October 1995): 711–25; Dwayne Woods, "The Rise of Regional Leagues in Italian Politics," *West European Politics* 15, no. 2 (April 1992): 56–76; Dwayne Woods, "The Crisis of Center-Periphery Integration in Italy and the Rise of Regional Populism: The Lombard League," *Comparative Politics* 27 (1995): 2; Carlo Ruzza and Oliver Schmidtke, "Roots of Success of the Lega Lombarda: Mobilisation, Dynamics and Media," *West European Politics* 14, no. 1 (1993): 1–24.

89. Vittorio Buffachi, "The Coming of Age of Italian Democracy," *Government and Opposition* 31, no. 3 (1996): 322–46.

90. Sergio Fabbrini, *Chi Guida L'Esecutivo? Presidenza della Repubblica e Governo in Italia (1996–1998)* (Siena: Centro Interdipartimentale di Ricerca sul Cambiamento Politico. Occasional Papers no. 3, 1998); Sergio Fabbrini, "Dal Governo Prodi al Governo D'Alema: Continuitá o Discontinuitá? In *Politica in Italia. I fatti dell'anno e le interpretazioni*, ed. David Hine and Salvatore Vassalo (Bologna: il Mulino, 1999), 139–59.

91. *The Economist*, April 28, 2001, pp. 23–25; *The Economist*, May 19, 2001, pp. 43–44; *The Economist*, May 26, 2001, p. 46; *L'Espresso*, May 24, 2001, p. 41 and pp. 48–49; *La Stampa*, May, 15, 2001, pp. 1–15.

92. *The Economist*, July 21, 2001, p. 36.

93. *El Pais*, December 18, 2001.

94. *El Pais*, January 6, 2002, p. 8.

95. *The Economist*, July 21, 2001, p. 38.

96. Athens News Agency, June 2, 2001, Greece now: *http://www.greece.gr/POLITICS/InternalAffairs/structuralreform.stm*

97. He was re-elected for the third time president of PASOK with 71.16 percent of over 6,000 delegates present at the conference The Athens News Agency, October 15, 2001 (http://www.ana.gr); *Die Zeit*, November 22, 2001, p. 33.

3

Institution Building in Southern Europe

CONSTITUTIONAL SETTLEMENT AND INSTITUTIONAL DESIGN

The debate over a future constitution is an important exercise. It is mainly an agreement over the rules of the democratic game of the new political system. Therefore actors are required to find a minimal common denominator to agree upon the essential rules of democratic society. The constitutional settlement is not merely an elitist project. More than that, it is influenced by direct experiences during the transition process as well as interaction between the population and the elites. The nature of the transition will influence considerably the constitution-drafting process. The institutions created during the transition to democracy may acquire an important role in the institutional framework enshrined in the constitution. In this regard, we can already differentiate between different constitutional settlements: conflictual, hegemonic, and consensual, which are conditioned by transition and will condition post-transitional political processes.

Another factor that influences the final outcome of the constitutional settlement is the historical past. Former experiences of ideological conflict entailing political violence may lead to a more consensual stand of certain parties. The Spanish example may account for this aspect. Conflict and consensus lead also to different constitutional settlements. A conflictual atmosphere will lead to ideological, programmatic constitutions, whereas consensualism may lead to more pragmatic ones.

Another aspect is the constitutional history of the country. All these countries were characterized by a discontinuous constitutional history, highly influenced by exogenous models. Such failed constitutional projects may shape considerably the drafting of the new constitution.

On the whole, the constitutional design will have to be adjusted in the long-term perspective to new realities. Constitutional behavior may diverge completely from the postulated constitutional norms. In schematic terms we may place the main factors constraining the constitutional settlement in this way (as shown in Table 3.1).

From the start the Portuguese constitution-drafting process was shaped by a left-wing atmosphere. The final draft was very much conditioned by this atmosphere. Although the liberal democratic element prevailed after 1976, the constitution itself is very ambiguous in relation to the predominance of liberal democratic institutions.[1] Article

TABLE 3.1   Factors Affecting the Constitutional Settlement

Factors	Portugal	Spain	Italy	Greece
Constitutional Legacy	Five constitutions between 1822 and 1974	Ten constitutions between 1808 and 1978	One constitution, 1870–1945	Four constitutions 1844–1974
Previous Regime	Authoritarian dictatorship (1926–1974)	Authoritarian dictatorship (1939–1975)	Authoritarian dictatorship (1922–1945)	Authoritarian dictatorship (1967–1974)
Nature of Democratic Transition	Conflictual/ revolutionary (1974–1975)	Consensual/ evolutionary (1974–1978)	Consensual (1945–1948)	Hegemonic/ charismatic (1974–1975)
Actors Involved	Civil politicians, military, social movements	Old authoritarian elites and new democratic elites	Civil politicians from new democratic political elites	Civil politicians, overdominance by Kostas Karamanlis's New Democracy
Outcome	Semi-presidentialist unitary controversial constitution with a military and political realm of decision-making (1976)	Consensual, monarchic constitution based on moderate regional autonomy (1978) after referendum	Consensual, Republican unitary constitution, based on administrative regional autonomy (1948)	Hegemonic imposed constitution by New Democracy on other parliamentary parties by absolute majority (1975)
Post-Constitutional Settlement	Conflictual permanent revision of the constitution toward liberal democratic principles (1982; 1989; 1992; 1997; 2001)	Remained untouched, interpretation of regionalization and autonomy was widened and developed	Several constitutional reforms failed to materialize due to governmental instability and lack of support in Parliament. Administrative regionalization achieved only in the 1970s	Powers were watered down in 1985 under PASOK government

1 of the constitution of 1976 stresses that Portugal is a sovereign Republic, based on the dignity of human beings and popular will. She is
engaged in her transformation into a classless society. Article 2 goes
even further by mentioning that the ultimate objective is to ensure the
transition to socialism through the creation of conditions for the working classes to empower them to exercise their democratic right. The
section on the political organization included the Council of the Revolution (*Conselho da Revolucão* [CR]) as a supervisory body of the democratic process. In the new political system, the president is elected
directly and exercises a strong role.

The Council of the Revolution was given the power to rule upon the
constitutionality of laws. The revision of 1982 ended the dominance of
the military in the political system and finally transferred the powers
of the abolished Council of the Revolution to a newly created Constitutional Court whose main power was to watch over the constitutionality
of laws.

The presidency was also restricted in its powers, so that a semi-
presidentialist situation such as between 1978 and 1979 could be
avoided. Although the Marxist vocabulary continued to be included in
the constitution, the revised constitution had achieved a civilianization
of the political system.[2]

In 1989, the second revision of the constitution removed the last
remainders of the Socialist rhetoric. Moreover, the irreversibility of the
nationalization in the economic sector was changed, opening up the
way to privatization.

In December 1992, the third revision of the constitution was undertaken to adapt it to the new Treaty on the European Union, which came
into force on November 1, 1993. The third revision increased the role of
the Assembly of the Republic in scrutinizing the adoption of European
legislation.[3] In 1997, a fourth minor revision of the constitution slightly
changed the electoral system enshrined in the constitution by introducing more uninominal constituencies. The aim was to strengthen the
linkage between MP and their constituencies, which has been almost
nonexistent in Portugal until today. In the end, neither of the main
parties was able to find a compromise solution to put the revision of the
electoral system into practice.[4]

In the aftermath of the events of September 11 in the USA, a further
revision of the constitution was undertaken on October 4, 2001, which
aimed at strengthening the constitutional provisions in the fight
against terrorism. This included the acknowledgment of the International Crime Court as part of the Portuguese law in the Portuguese
constitution. The Spanish constitutional settlement was less spectacular. The *ruptura pactada* required a growing necessity to compromise
with other parties. After the elections to the *Cortes*, a committee

(*ponencia*) was established to draft the first version of the constitution. The whole process was carried out through consensus. All relevant groups were integrated into the process, and it was fully negotiated before it was submitted to both the plenary of the congress of the deputies and the plenary of the Senate. One of the main reasons for this procedure was the intention of the political elites to avoid a conflictual violent situation as was the case during the Second Spanish Republic and the Civil War in the 1930s. Hence, ideological polarization led to the breakdown of democracy. Particularly, the Communist Party under the leadership of Santiago Carrillo played an important role in moderating the discourse. The PSOE was more radical than the PCE. Nevertheless, the pivotal actor was Adolfo Suarez's UCD, which acted as a broker of the constitution.[5]

Two issues were at stake and a matter of controversy. First, the domestic political order needed to be defined. After many negotiations, it was agreed to establish a parliamentary monarchy. This was even supported by the PCE represented by Solé Tura, because they were more concerned to overcome the gulf that existed between enemies and partisans of the democracy than with the question of the monarchy.

More controversial was the question of the relationship between center and the peripheries. This issue was related to the historical regions Catalonia and Basque Country. Representatives of these two countries were present in the *Cortes*. In the end, the compromise was the State of the Autonomies (*Estado de Autonomias*). It meant that the centralized state would continue to prevail and that some autonomy would be granted to the historical regions. A widening of the competences for the regional governments was agreed to. Nevertheless, the Basques demanded a full restoration of the *fueros*, the special autonomy rights granted to the Basque Country in the Middle Ages. This led to an abstention by the Basque representatives in the voting of the first draft. The constitution was accepted with an overwhelming majority of 325 MPs (4.2 percent) to 6 (1.8 percent) and 14 abstentions in the congress of deputies and 226 (94.5 percent) against 5 (2.3 percent) and 8 abstentions in the Senate.[6]

In the referendum of December 1978 87.87 percent of the votes cast accepted the new constitution. Only a small percentage—7.83 percent—was against it. Nevertheless, about 32.89 percent abstained from voting, mainly in the Basque Country where the constitutional settlement was accompanied with skepsis. Subsequently, central-regional relations became the major element in transforming Spain into a semi-federal state. This has become quite relevant in view of the coalitions between PSOE and the Catalan *Convergencia i Unio* (CiU) between 1993 and 1995 and between PP and CiU until 2000.[7] The Spanish constitution was only recently changed to adjust to the Maastricht criteria, but it remained a widely accepted and uncontested document.

The Italian constitution of December 27, 1947, can be considered as a break with the former constitutional history. Until that date, the so-called *Statuto Albertino* imposed by the kingdom of Piedmont on the rest of Italy after 1860 was the constitutional framework of Italy. The new constitution was Republican. It implemented the decision of the Italian population in the referendum held on June 2, 1946.

This new Constituent Assembly elected on June 2, 1946, nominated a committee to prepare a first draft. This was divided in three subcommittees. Although the left socialist-communist bloc was the strongest ideological group, the *Democrazia Cristiana* was in fact the strongest force in the assembly. At the beginning, the fragmented composition of the assembly led to cooperation between the groups. This cooperation lasted until early 1947. Afterward, the Cold War was a disturbing factor of the parliamentary work. The socialist-communist bloc moderated its position, and the Catholic center tried everything to reconcile its position with the other forces. This led to the construction of a political design that included the best of all ideological traditions. The so-called *Stato sociale* (social state) integrated the values of liberty and equality, individuality and sociability, private interest and respect for minorities, national unity and deconcentration, political decision and long term commitments into a coherent whole.[8]

The constitution stresses predominantly social and political rights. The right to work for all Italian citizens, for example, was quite radical. It led to the declaration by the *Corte di Cassazione* in February 1948 that one had to distinguish between those parts of the constitution that were of immediate actuation (*norme precettizie*) and those that would become reality only at a later stage (*norme programmatiche*).[9]

Although the socialist-communist bloc resisted until the last minute against the introduction into the constitution that Catholicism should be regarded as the official religion of the country, in the end, this was accepted reluctantly by the left-wing MPs. Another question was the indissolubility of the family. After an intervention of the communist Giovanni Grili, this was prevented by a marginal vote in the Assembly.[10] In 1996 a Joint Committee on Constitutional Reform (*Bicamerale Constituzionale*) was set up to make a major revision to the constitution. When the leader of the *Bicamerale*, Massimo D'Alema, replaced Romano Prodi as Prime Minister in 1998, the whole enterprise came to a standstill. The only reform that was undertaken concerned the federalization of Italy. Indeed, in 1999 several articles (articles 121, 122, 123 and 126) in the chapter on regional government were changed. It introduced the direct elections of regional presidents, it enhanced presidential power and provided them with a working majority in the council. The process of devolution is expected to last over a long period of time. On the whole, the Italian constitution has remained quite unchanged until today. Similar to the Spanish case, it adapted to new circumstances. Consensualism, even during the emerging Cold War, determined the outcome of one of the most radical constitutions of the Western world. The constitution was approved with an absolute majority of 453 votes (88 percent) to 62. It came into force on January 1, 1948. Several attempts to introduce major reforms to the constitution, even after 1996, failed because of lack of agreement or the unstable climate of Italian politics.[11]

The Greek constitutional settlement was dominated by the personality of Konstantinos Karamanlis. The new constitution replaced that of 1952. The opposition saw the constitution as tailored to the personality of Karamanlis. Indeed the word *dimokratia* means both democracy as well as republic in Greek. After the referendum of December 1974, the Greeks decided against the monarchy and for the Republic, and this led to the establishment of a Republic strongly influenced by the French Fifth Republic. At that time Karamanlis's constitution was called a *crowned* democracy. The new *presidential* democracy acknowledged the centrality of parliament, but in reality the president, elected by parliament, was an important factor in stabilizing the political system. The new Republic was highly influenced by the negative experiences of the postwar crowned democracy and the military junta, therefore it emphasized substantially the aspect of the state of law (Art. 2, 4–25, 26, 29, 49, 50, 87–100). The new constitution also mentioned the commitment to the welfare state. The special relationship with the Greek Orthodox Church was enshrined in the constitution.[12]

On June 7, the new constitution was adopted by New Democracy with 208 votes, but the opposition did not show up at the voting session in protest. On the whole, the Greek constitutional settlement was imposed by the hegemonic configuration of forces. It was very much a document shaped by the "savior" Konstantinos Karamanlis.[13] In 1985, the Vouli adopted a constitutional revision that reduced the powers of the president. Further changes were undertaken in the 1990s, which diminished the appearance of a crowned monarchy. In 2001, a further revision of the constitution was undertaken to bring the country more in line with the European integration process.

Constitutional settlements have different outcomes, because of the configuration of forces drafting them. All this shows that to understand southern European democracies, one has to take into account their constitutional trajectories. In the postconstitutional period consolidation and institutionalization of democracy will depend on the founding experiences of politics in each of the countries. Conflictual, ideological antagonism throughout the postconstitutional period like in Greece and Portugal may delay development toward a stable democracy. On the other hand, a consensual outcome will lay the foundations for stable government and politics. In certain circumstances, influenced partly by external factors, what was a consensual constitutional outcome may turn into a conflictual antagonistic approach to government and politics after the constitutional settlement, destroying the very foundations of an emerging democracy, as happened in Italy between 1948 and 1992.

CREATING STABLE INSTITUTIONS IN SOUTHERN EUROPE

One of the striking features of the political systems in Portugal, Spain, Italy, and Greece is the high level of centralization of decision-making and concentration of administration. This can be attributed to the fact that all four countries had authoritarian experiences that tended to centralize and concentrate government and administration respectively. Subnational government remained underdeveloped. The process toward decentralization and deconcentration has become one of the major policies of all four countries in the past three decades. In Italy such a process started in the 1970s with the implementation of regions as an intermediate administration unit between the national and local levels. But still today regional government is a mere extension of central government. Reforms in the 1990s were designed to make administration more efficient and closer to the citizen. It will take some time for these reforms to show any tangible effects on a public administration that is regarded as very inefficient and distant from the people.

In Spain, such a process of decentralization and deconcentration was imposed by the seventeen autonomous communities that strived to widen their competences and keep the dynamics of the devolution process alive since the adoption of the Spanish constitution of 1978. In Portugal, regionalization was a central issue for the Socialist government in 1998, in spite of the fact that in a referendum on November 8, 1998 the majority of two thirds of voters (turnout slightly below 50 percent) rejected the division of the country into eight administrative regions. The Socialist government hoped that the introduction of re-gionalization, which is enshrined in the constitution, would lead to a more efficient administration and the enhancement of democracy. In Greece, regionalization was imposed by the European Union so that the Integrated Mediterranean Programs and later the structural funds could be implemented more efficiently. All this shows that southern European democracies are in the process of overcoming long-term deficiencies in the relationship between civil service and citizens and in the delivery of social services.

Governmental Dominance

One major feature of government in southern Europe is that it gained more stability in the 1990s and at the beginning of the new millenium after decades of instability. Particularly, Portugal and Italy had to struggle with governmental instability in the 1970s and 1980s. Spain was able to create a culture of governmental stability, and Greece's governmental stability is related to the overdominance of PASOK in the political system. The reasons for growing stabilization of political government are different in each country.

Portugal

In the first constitutional elections in Portugal, no party was able to achieve a strong majority. The electorate remained ideologically split until 1987. (See Table 3.2.) Between 1976 and 1987, Portugal experienced all kinds of unstable governments. Minority, coalition, and technocratic governments dominated the scene. They were characterized by a short life span of less than one year on average, which prevented a fast political consolidation of the political system. Both main parties, PS and PSD, tended to approach government in highly ideological terms, preventing a routinization of democratic rules. The constitution was blamed for the inability of the inexperienced politicians to develop a more rational approach toward government. The governmental programs were never implemented and tended to be drafted directly by the prime minister. The instability of government also prevented the development of coordination mechanisms between the different ministries. A reform of public administration was delayed to a later date.[14]

After 1985, government became more stable. The emergence of a new generation of leaders who were more pragmatically and technocratically oriented changed the whole approach toward government.

Prime Minister Anibal Cavaco Silva was in office for a decade and introduced major reforms in public administration and the decision-making process. After a short minority government, he was able to gain the absolute majority both in the 1987 and 1991 elections (as shown in Table 3.2). During his period, a secretariat for the modernization of the administration (*Secretariado para a modernização da administração* [SMA]) was established, and the process of deconcentration of public administration was started. His autocratic leadership style gave discipline to the cabinet, which increased in members considerably between 1985 and 1995. The government tended to dominate the parliament due to its abolute majority. Cavaco Silva certainly contributed to stabilization and modernization of government in Portugal. His successor Antonio Guterres, from the Socialist party, was able to receive a strong majority from the electorate in the

TABLE 3.2   Governments in Portugal (1974-2002)

Prime Minister	Date In	Resignation	Party Composition	Kind of Government
		Provisional Governments (1974–76)		
Palma Carlos	5.16.74	7.11.74	Provisional	All-Party
Goncalves I	7.18.74	9.30.74	Provisional	All-Party
Gonvalves II	9.30.74	3.11.75	Provisional	All-Party
Goncalves III	3.26.75	8.8.75	Provisional	All-Party
Goncalves IV	8.8.75	9.8.75	Provisional	MFA-PCP
Pinheiro de Azevedo	9.19.75	7.22.76	Provisional	All Party
		Constitutional Governments (1976–2002)		
Mario Soares I	7.23.77	12.9.77	PS	Minority government
Mario Soares II	1.23.78	7.28.78	PS-CDS	Coalition government
Nobre Costa	6.22.78	9.15.78	Independent	Technocratic
Mota Pinto	11.22.78	6.11.79	Independent	Technocratic
Pintassilgo	7.31.79	12.27.79	Independent	Technocratic
Sá Carneiro	1.3.81	1.9.81	AD (PSD-CDS-PPM)	Coalition government
Balsemão I	1.9.81	8.14.81	AD (PSD-CDS-PPM)	Coalition government
Balsemão II	9.4.81	12.23.82	AD (PSD-CDS-PPM)	Coalition government
Soares III	6.9.83	11.3.85	PS-PSD	Coalition government
Cavaco Silva I	11.4.85	7.17.87	PSD	Minority government
Cavaco Silva II	7.17.87	10.31.91	PSD	Absolute majority
Cavaco Silva III	10.31.91	10.31.95	PSD	Absolute majority
Guterres I	11.3.95	10.10.99	PS	Strong majority
Guterres II	10.10.99	3.17.02	PS	Strong majority
Barroso	6.4.02		PSD-PP	Coalition government

Source: Own computation from Keesing's *Contemporary Archive*, several years.

elections of 1995 and 1999. More or less, he continued the work of reform of Cavaco Silva and adopted as well a technocratic and pragmatic approach to government. The European integration process is one of the factors that reinforced the transformation of democratic government in Portugal. The growing integration into a transnational European culture of government was certainly a modernizing factor for Portuguese government and administration.[15]

Spain

In the Spanish institutional framework the government is the dominant institution in relation to Parliament (*Cortes*) and the Monarch. The constitutional monarchy gives only a very restricted, symbolic role to King Juan Carlos. Even the possibility to influence the process of investiture remains very formal. The executive is dependent on the vote of confidence coming from the parliament. In this sense, the prime minister is central in the Spanish political system. In Spanish he is called the president of government (*El Presidente del Gobierno*). This naturally strengthens his position within the framework.[16] Another factor protects the prime minister from being exonerated from parliament. The Spanish parliament is requested to sucessfully present a constructive motion of censure against the prime minister, which includes the presentation of an alternative name to fill in the position of prime minister with an alternative program. In this regard, the prime minister is quite strong in Spanish politics. The main difficulties arising may be related to the nature of his majority in parliament. A weak majority, which requires the voters of other parties, diminishes the ability of the prime minister to play a more dominant role within the cabinet.[17] This was the case for the government of José Maria Aznar, which was only formed after extensive bargaining between Aznar's PP and Jordi Pujol's CiU and other minor regionalist parties represented in *Cortes*. Such a weakening of the prime minister's role could also be observed between 1993 and October 1995, because the PSOE Minority Government under Gonzalez needed the support of Jordi Pujol's CiU to govern. The withdrawal of support to the PSOE by Catalan leader Jordi Pujol in October 1995, due to the forthcoming Catalan elections and the growing knowledge of political scandals around the PSOE, showed that the prime minister may be vulnerable to parliamentary defeat when he/she loses the majority in the *Cortes*.[18]

This contrasts completely with the period between 1982 and 1993 when the Socialist Party had a comfortable majority and could produce the required majority in the *Cortes*. This period was characterized as majoritarian, where the executive was able to control the legislative. This was due to the fact that the PSOE government could count on a highly disciplined parliamentary group that lacked serious factionalist tendencies within it. Therefore, Prime Minister Felipe Gonzalez was able to shape a more assertive leadership style in the cabinet, in the party, and subsequently in the parliamentary group. Previously, Prime Minister Adolfo Suarez was in a different situation. After the successful implementation of transition to democracy, he had to face a very fragmented party that lacked any cohesion. This lack of cohesion led to his resignation at the end of 1981 and his replacement by Leopoldo Calvo Sotelo. Nevertheless, the party literally disintegrated and made it possible for the PSOE to occupy the center. In this sense, Spanish government can be strong, if it can count on a strong majority in the *Cortes* and just survive as a minority government, and the prime minister is able to make deals with other parties, including the possibility of a coalition, to pass legislation.

The cabinet has remained quite small and stable in comparison with other countries such as Austria and Italy. In the 1980s, Gonzalez tended to recruit ministers with a technical competence; therefore decision-making followed a technical style. Although Prime Minister Gonzalez was an uncontested leader, different departments tended to have conflicts among themselves in the meetings of the Council of Ministers, which took place on Friday morning. Particularly, the Minister of Economy and Finance accounted for about a quarter of all conflicts taking place within government, followed by the Minister of Industry and the Vice President (about a sixth), the Minister of Defense (about one in eight), and the Minister of Foreign Affairs (about one in twelve).[19] The Aznar cabinets are also quite small, comprising less than twenty ministers. The most recent one, formed after the 2000 elections, comprises seventeen ministers.[20] Although the cabinet, which meets once a week, is the formal place of decision-making, the prime minister can create minicabinets in crisis situations. Most recently, this was the case during the Kosovo war, which required a fast response from the Spanish government.[21]

In the 1990s, the decision-making process became more complex. José Maria Aznar's success has been also related to his stronger consultation of other parliamentary parties, particularly the regionalist-nationalist parties, until his victory on March 12, 2000. This indicates that the two decades of democracy have contributed to a routinization and professionalization of Spanish government. Aznar gained in self-confidence after his absolute majority victory. More or less the cabinet was able to survive all possible criticisms of the opposition. Recently, foreign minister Josep Piqué was targeted by the opposition in relation to the Gescartera scandal. The PP used its absolute majority to prevent any further parliamentary inquiry into its dealings (as shown in Table 3.3).

Italy

The recent upheaval of Italian politics has brought to the fore the many problems that the political system faced since the adoption of the constitution in 1948. The dominance of partyocracy in the institutional framework was a major factor preventing a strong professionalization and routinization of interinstitutional relationships. The *Mani Pulite* operation of Judge Antonio di Pietro in 1992, exposing the web of systemic corruption that existed for over forty years, was a sign for renewal of Italian politics. Similar signs were already visible during the 1980s, when judges such as Giovanni Falcone and magistrates such as Paolo Borsellino dared to stand courageously against the linkage between politics and organized crime. The spreading of corruption at national, regional, and local levels embracing politicians, civil servants, and criminals had attained, after almost a half-century, the legitimacy of being the normal way and only way to achieve something within the political system.[22]

TABLE 3.3 Governments in Spain (1975–2000)

Prime Minister	Date In	Resignation	Party Composition	Kind of Government
Provisional Governments (1975–1979)				
Arias Navarro II	12.5.75	7.1.76	Provisional	Elites of authoritarian regime
Adolfo Suarez I	7.3.76	8.5.77	Provisional	Elites of authoritarian regime
Adolfo Suarez II	8.5.77	4.4.79	UCD	Minority government
Constitutional Governments				
Adolfo Suarez III	4.4.79	2.15.81	UCD	Minority government
Leopoldo Calvo Sotelo	2.25.81	12.2.82	UCD	Minority government
Felipe Gonzalez I	12.2.82	6.22.86	PSOE	Absolute majority government
Felipe Gonzalez II	6.22.86	10.29.89	PSOE	Absolute majority government
Felipe Gonzalez III	10.29.89	7.14.93	PSOE	Absolute majority government
Felipe Gonzalez IV	7.14.93	5.3.96	PSOE	Minority government/ agreement with CiU; it collapsed in October 1995
José Maria Aznar I	5.4.96	3.12.00	PP	Minority Government/agreement with regionalist-nationalist parties
José Maria Aznar II	3.12.00		PP	Absolute majority government

Source: Own compilation from Keesing's *Contemporary Archive*, several years.

In this sense, today's political system is a response to this widespread network of complicity around corrupt practices. The most well-known offender was the former secretary-general of the Italian Socialist Party (*Partito Socialista Italiano* [PSI]), Bettino Craxi, who was sentenced to prison in absentia in 1994, because he had fled to Tunis to avoid his arrest. He died in March 2000 in Tunisia.

Government in Italy was extremely unstable since its early beginnings. Cabinet life was extremely short. The cabinet with the longest duration was led by the Socialist Craxi between 1983 and 1986, which lasted for twenty-three months. In contrast, the shortest cabinet lives were experienced by the Alcide de Gasperi government of mid-July 1953 and the Amintore Fanfani government of January-February 1954, both lasting not more than one month. All the other forty-eight governments had a duration between these two extremes. On the average, Italian governments lasted for ten months.[23] This governmental instability was quite stable in terms of its personnel. The main party of the political system was *Democrazia Cristiana*, which was the key actor in the coalition game. As Geoffrey Pridham asserts, a kind of a coalition language (*coalizionese*)[24] developed out of government formation throughout the postwar period of Italian politics. The continuity of the personnel recruited from the DC, the Italian Liberal Party (*Partito Liberale Italiano* [PLI]), Italian Republican Party (*Partito Repubblicano Italiano* [PRI]), the Italian Social Democratic Party (*Partito Social-democratico Italiano* [PSDI]) and later on, the Italian Socialist Party (*Partito Socialista Italiano* [PSI]) counterweighted the short duration of cabinet life in some way.

On the contrary, the largest party, DC, achieved a strong relative majority, but it lacked an absolute majority. Therefore, it tried to forge an absolute majority government with the smaller lay parties, and excluded the second largest party, the Italian Communist Party (*Partito Comunista Italiano* [PCI]), from government. This was regarded as the main objective of the DC until the 1970s, an objective that was influenced by the Cold War. The PCI was regarded as too close to the Soviet Union to be allowed into government. A kind of détente was initiated in the 1970s with the Historical Compromise (*Compromesso Storico*) carried out by both main parties, but it never allowed for a participation of Communists in central government.[25] In the 1980s, the electoral share of the DC declined, which led to coalition formation with the lay parties and the PSI, which was increasing its electoral base. Throughout this period, government became dominated by Bettino Craxi, the secretary-general of PSI, who became a successful prime minister between 1983 and 1987. The period between 1986 and 1992 can be described as the demise of *partitocrazia*, which had its climax in 1993 with the appointment of the independent Azeglio Ciampi for prime minister by president Oscar Scalfaro.

Nevertheless, instability continued to persist after 1994. The breakup of the coalition government led by Prime Minister Silvio Berlusconi forced president Oscar Scalfaro to again nominate an independent for prime minister. Lamberto Dini, a former president of the National Bank of Italy, took over a caretaker government until the next elections. After the elections of 1996, the situation did not change very much. The Olive Tree governments of Romano Prodi (1996–1998) and the Massimo D'Alema (1998–2000) governments clearly made people aware that *coalizionese* will continue to prevail in Italian politics. The fragmentation of parties in the legislative assembly created major difficulties in establishing stable governments.[26] More stable than party governments has been the phenomenon of the caretaker technocratic governments such as that under Giuliano D'Amato in May 2000, which succeeded the very short Massimo D'Alema II government. They are normally more successful in reforming the political system.

The recent victory of the coalition of House of Freedoms under the leadership of media tycoon Silvio Berlusconi gives the impression of being more stable than the 1994 coalition. The main reason is that the *Lega Nord* has been weakened following the May 13, 2001, elections, from which it emerged without a single MP. According to the coalition agreement, it is entitled to ministerial positions and also seats in both chambers, but the mere fact that it did not win single seat forces Umberto Bossi to support the coalition government. Although Berlusconi's coalition government is quite stable in relation to the previous center-left government of Prodi and D'Alema, it is too early to say if internal dissent will lead to a breakup of the coalition. The resignation of foreign minister Renato Ruggiero at the end of 2001 over the new currency, which is regarded with skepticism by most members of the Berlusconi cabinet, may document some signs of disagreement within the new government.

In the pre-1992 period, the position of the prime minister was weak in relation to the other ministers and conflict[27] between the members of the cabinet was quite high.[28] This is one reason coalitions break up so easily. Nevertheless, conditions were replaced by coalitions with the same composition and same parties in charge of the same ministries, giving at least a kind of continuity in personnel.[29]

A salient feature of the decision-making process is that it focused mainly on particularistic decisions for certain categories and groupings. This means that Italian governments did not legislate in universalistic terms but tended to create particularistic welfare regimes for all kinds of population groups. Such a web of particularistic decisions and commitments was a major factor in creating a huge public debt, which continues to be a major constraint for Italian government. This web of particularistic legislative acts was embedded in a general culture of clientelism, patronage, and corruption, which led to the final demise of *partitocrazia* after 1992.[30] Therefore, policy formulation and implementation was quite fragmented. Policy coordination was not very efficient, and this was reinforced by an administrative elite who lacked an administrative culture with a stronge policy coordination capacity.[31]

In the 1990s, Italian governments were trying to make government more efficient and accountable, but a tradition of instability cannot be overcome in a couple of years. The nature of the present governments, which consisted of highly heterogenous coalition partners, further undermines the regeneration of the political system. At least, "political ossification" has given way to more volatile and less compromising coalition governments (as shown in Table 3.4).

Greece

The Greek political system can be regarded as highly stable. Since its emergence in 1975, the Greek institutional framework successfully cre-

TABLE 3.4 Governments in Italy (1945–2001)

Prime Minister	Date In	Resignation	Party Composition	Kind of Government
		Provisional Governments		
Parri		11.24.45	PdÁz.-DC-PCI-PLI-PSIUP-PDL	All-Party Coalition Government
De Gasperi I	12.9.45	7.1.46	DC-PCI-PSI-PÁz-PDL-PLI	All-Party Coalition Government
De Gasperi II	7.13.46	1.20.47	DC-PCI-PSI-PDL-PRI	All-Party Coalition Government
De Gasperi III	5.31.47	5.12.47	DC-PCI-PSI	Coalition Government
De Gasperi IV	5.31.47	5.12.48	DC-PLI-Tech	Coalition Government
		Constitutional Governments (1948–1994)		
		Center Governments (1948–60)		
De Gasperi V	5.23.48	1.12.50	DC-PSDI-PLI-PRI	Coalition Government
De Gasperi VI	1.21.50	7.16.51	DC-PSDI-PRI	Coalition Government
De Gasperi VII	7.26.51	6.29.53	DC-PRI	Coalition Government
De Gasperi VIII	7.16.53	7.28.53	DC	Minority Government
Pella	8.17.53	1.15.54	DC	Minority Government
Fanfani I	1.18.54	1.30.54	DC	Minority Government
Scelba	2.10.54	7.22.55	DC-PSDI-PLI	Coalition Government
Segni	7.6.55	5.16.57	DC-PSDI-PLI	Coalition Government
Zoli	5.19.57	6.19.58	DC	Minority Government
Fanfani II	7.1.58	1.26.59	DC-PSDI	Coalition Government
Segni II	2.15.59	2.24.60	DC	Minority Government
Tambroni	3.25.60	7.19.60	DC	Minority Government
		Center-Left Governments (1960–1975)		
Fanfani III	7.26.60	2.12.960	DC	Minority Government
Fanfani IV	2.21.62	5.16.63	DC-PSDI-PRI	Coalition Government
Leone	6.21.63	11.5.63	DC	Minority Government
Moro I	12.4.63	6.15.68	DC-PSI-PRI-PSDI	Coalition Government
Leone II	6.24.68	11.19.68	DC	Minority Government
Rumor I	12.12.68	7.15.69	DC-PSI-PRI	Coalition Government
Rumor II	8.5.69	2.17.70	DC	Minority Government
Rumor III	3.27.70	7.16.70	DC-PSI-PSDI-PRI	Coalition Government
Colombo	8.6.70	1.15.72	DC-PSI-PSDI-PRI	Coalition Government
Andreotti I	2.17.72	2.26.72	DC	Minority Government
Andreotti II	6.26.72	6.12.72	DC-PSDI-PLI	Coalition Government
Rumor IV	7.7.73	3.2.74	DC-PSI-PSDI-PRI	Coalition Government
Rumor V	3.14.74	10.3.74	DC-PSI-PSDI	Coalition Government
Moro II	11.23.74	1.7.76	DC-PRI	Coalition Government
Moro III	2.12.76	4.30.76	DC	Minority Government
		National Solidarity Governments (1976–1979)		
Andreotti IIIa	7.29.76	1.16.76	DC	Minority Government
Andreotti IIIb	3.11.78	1.31.79	DC	Minority Government
Andreotti IV	3.20.79	3.31.79	DC-PSDI-PRI	Coalition Government

TABLE 3.4 *(continued)*

Prime Minister	Date In	Resignation	Party Composition	Kind of Government
Five-Party Coalition (1980–1992)				
Cossiga I	8.4.79	3.19.80	DC-PSDI-PLI	Coalition Government
Cossiga II	4.4.80	9.28.80	DC-PRI-PSI	Coalition Government
Forlani	10.18.80	5.26.81	DC-PSI-PRI-PSDI	Coalition Government
Spadolini	6.28.81	8.7.82	PRI-DC-PSI-PSDI-PLI	Coalition Government
Fanfani V	12.1.82	4.22.83	DC-PSI-PSDI-PLI	Coalition Government
Craxi I	8.4.83	7.27.86	PSI-DC-PRI-PSDI-	Coalition Government
Craxi II	7.28.86	4.17.87	PLI	
Fanfani VI	4.17.87	4.28.87	DC	Technical Government
Goria	7.28.87	3.11.88	DC-PSI-PRI-PSDI-PLI	Coalition Government
De Mita	4.13.88	5.19.89	DC-PSI-PRI-PSDI-PLI	Coalition Government
Andreotti V	7.23.89	3.29.91	DC-PSI-PRI-PSDI-PLI	Coalition Government
Andreotti VI	4.13.91	4.24.92	DC-PSI-PSDI-PLI	Coalition Government
D'Amato I	6.28.92	4.22.93	PSI-DC-PLI-PSDI	Coalition Government
Ciampi	4.29.93	1.13.94	DC-PSI-PSDI-PLI	Technical Government
Governments under New Electoral Law (1994–)				
Berlusconi I	5.11.94	12.22.94	FI-LN-AN-CCD	Electoral Coalition Government
Dini	1.17.95	1.7.96		Technical Government
Prodi	5.18.96	10.9.98	PDS-Greens-PPI-RIN	Electoral Coalition Government
D'Alema I	10.21.98	12.18.99	DS-Greens-PPI-RI-SDI-UDR-PdCI-Independents	Electoral Alliance Government
D'Alema II	12.21.99	4.28.00	DS-Greens-PPI-RI-SDI-UDR-PdCI-Independents	Electoral Coalition Government
D'Amato II	4.28.00	6.11.01		Technocratic
Berlusconi II	6.11.01		FI-LN-AN-PSI-CCD	Electoral Alliance

Source: Updated from Luca Verzichelli and Maurizio Cotta, "Italy: From 'Constrained' Coalitions to Alternating Governments?," in *Coalition Governments in Western Europe*, ed. Wolfgang C. Müller and Kaare Strom (Oxford: Oxford University Press, 2000), 454-55; Sergio Fabbrini, "Dal Governo Prodi al Governo D'Alema: Continuitá o Discontinuitá?," in *Politica in Italia: I Fatti dell'Anno e le Interpretazioni*, ed. David Hine and Salvatore Vassalo (Bologna: Il Mulino, 1999); Piero Ignazi, "Italy," Political Data Yearbook 2000 (special issue), *European Journal for Political Research* 38, no. 3–4 (2000): 434–35; Piero Ignazi, "Italy," Poltical Data Yearbook 2001 (special issue), European Journal for Political Research 40, no. 3–4 (2001): 341.

ated a web of stable interinstitutional relationships. The government remained majoritarian, leading to a peaceable alternation of the two main parties, the conservative New Democracy and the socialist PASOK, in government. In this regard, the election of the president of the Republic by the parliament and the dependency of government on a stable majority in parliament enhances the role of parliament in the political system. After 1989, executive-legislative relations were dominated for a short while by the latter. The scandals of the PASOK government of the 1980s were scrutinized by the parliament. Several committees of inquiry dealt with several corruption scandals that were related to the abuse of power by Socialist leaders. The so-called *katharsis* period was carried out by the ND and the Communist coalition, called *synaspismos*. This coalition government had only a temporary character. At stake was the Koskotas scandal, which involved former members of the Socialist government. It seems that Papandreou's Justice Minister Menos Koutsogiorgas had received a $2 million bribe from George Koskotas to obstruct an investigation of the Bank of Greece into the activities of the Bank of Crete. Other cases were related to the "Warplanes Kickback," which involved an excessive cost of purchases from French and American suppliers; the Yugoslav Maize Fraud (an attempt to defraud the EC over import levies); and the Telephone Tapping Racket, which involved even Prime Minister Andreas Papandreou.[32] Some of the charges pressed against Papandreou were dropped at a later stage. In terms of colonization of civil society organizations, the PASOK was able to control the mass media and the trade unions.[33] Maybe the most evident cases of abuse of power concerned the over-employment of party adherents in public administration shortly before elections. This contributed to further inefficiency in the administration.

Since 1974 Greek government has been dominated by single parties with an absolute majority. (See Table 3.5.) This is also one of the main characteristics of Greek politics, which count on a party to achieve the absolute majority. This will automatically lead to the nomination of the party leader who achieved the absolute majority as new prime minister by the president according to the stipulations of Article 37 of the Greek Constitution. This characteristic was only interrupted between June 1989 and April 1990 with the two coalition governments. The establishment of the strong absolute majority governments are a product of the proportional representation system, which favors larger parties and is less friendly toward smaller parties. In the Greek political system, one has to speak of a bipolar party system. Government was so far dominated by two parties: ND and PASOK.

In both cases, the governments were led by strong charismatic personalities who dominated cabinet life and the administration. In this respect, although government was overwhelmingly stable, it did not

TABLE 3.5   Governments in Greece (1974–2000)

Prime Minister	Date In	Resignation	Party Composition	Type of Government
Karamanlis I	7.26.74	11.19.77	ND	Absolute Majority Government
Karamanlis II	11.28.77	5.6.80	ND	Absolute Majority Government
Rallis	5.6.80	10.17.81	ND	Absolute Majority Government
Papandreou I	10.21.81	7.26.85	PASOK	Absolute Majority Government
Papandreou II	7.26.85	6.17.89	PASOK	Absolute Majority Government
Tzannetakis	7.2.89	11.4.89	ND-Synaspismos	Coalition Government
Zolotas	11.22.89	4.7.90	ND-Synaspismos-PASOK	Coalition Government
Mitsotakis	4.26.90	10.25.93	ND	Minority Government
Papandreou III	10.25.93	2.1.96	PASOK	Absolute Majority Government
Simitis I	2.1.96	10.13.96	PASOK	Absolute Majority Government
Simitis II	10.13.96	4.25.00	PASOK	Absolute Majority Government
Simitis III	4.25.00		PASOK	Absolute Majority Government

Source: Own compilation from Keesing's Contemporary Archive, several years.

manage to be very efficient. One of the reasons for the lack of efficiency was that alternating governments tended to reverse the reforms undertaken by the previous government, thus reinforcing the problem of a waste of resources.

Such a practice would be observed in the case of administrative reform in the 1990s[34] and in the elaboration of the Common Support Framework in conjunction with the European Union.[35] The bipolarization is sometimes reinforced by the charismatic leadership style of personalities such as Andreas Papandreou and Kostas Mitsotakis. The government is dominated by the prime minister, who tends to accumulate the position of party leader as well. Such concentration of power created what Christos Lyrintzis called *bureaucratic clientelism*.[36] State and party became very close—they tended to create an intransparent symbiosis. The influence of the party over administration led to abuse of power. Government infiltrated all aspects of civil society. Party influence was particularly widespread among the mass media. The manipulation of television for political purposes was common among the two PASOK cabinets of the 1980s. Although PASOK cabinets were cohesive in the 1980s and tended to follow—at least in the early period—the radical program set up in 1981, that implementation lacked the necessary efficiency and financial conditions to make it lasting reforms. More difficulties surfaced in the ND government chaired by Kostas Mitsotakis, who had to face massive resignations in 1991 and 1992. The party was affected by internal squabbles thus creating a very negative atmosphere in public opinion.[37] Party politics had until now been the main factor shaping governmental work. A colonization of state structures by parties made it very difficult to achieve administrative reform. Nevertheless, the impact of the European Union has been considered a major factor limiting the abuse of state structures by parties.

Between 1993 and 1995 under the premiership of Andreas Papandreou one could see the end of a leadership style based on patrimonial behavior. This became quite visible during 1995, when Andreas Papandreou began to promote his new wife Dimitra Liani Papandreou to the powerful job as director of the private office of the prime minister. This led to major criticisms by the opposition and within his own party. He expelled one leader of the so-called "rebels," Kyriakos Spyriounis, during summer of 1995. Criticisms from Costas Simitis and former European Commissioner Vasso Papandreou were the consequence.[38] Such a patrimonial attitude toward party and government became even more clear before his death in January 1996. During November and December 1995 he was bedridden, but nevertheless refused to resign from office.[39]

The emergence of the more pragmatic PASOK prime minister Kostas Simitis in 1996 introduced a more efficient style in government in Greece.[40] He gave more importance to the cabinet and parliament, although naturally the office of prime minister clearly still gave him great power protected by an absolute majority conquered twice in 1996 and 2000. The recent election of Kostas Karamanlis as party leader of ND is allowing for a more consensual cooperative climate between the two parties before and after achieving membership in the EMU by January 2001 (as shown in Table 3.5). In spite of that, populism continues to play a major part in Greek politics, although the clientelistic resources no longer exist due to growing disciplining pressure coming from the EU to sort out budgetary and public debt figures in the framework of the EMU. One characteristic that reinforces the power of the prime minister is the creation within the government of "mini-cabinets" related to specific crucial policy areas. This has been enshrined specifically in law since 1976. The so-called government mini-cabinet deals with the coordination of the program of the government and its implementation. The economy mini-cabinet and the currency mini-cabinet under the leadership of the coordinating minister decide all important economic measures and issues related to currency and interest rate policy. The president of the Bank of Greece was a member of the currency mini-cabinet. Last but not least, the prime minister chairs the

Highest Council for National Defense related to questions of defense and appointment of leading positions in the Armed Forces. The Highest Commander of the Armed Forces is also a member of this council. This naturally strengthens the power of the prime minister and allows for abuse, as happened during the Papandreou years. The collegiality of the cabinet is undermined by too much power concentration in the hands of the prime minister.[41] In spite of all these coordinating mini-cabinets that may be convened or not depending on the personality of the prime minister, coordination has been poor.

Apart from the Italian case, southern European politics has been characterized by strong governments dominating all aspects of political life. The most extreme cases could be found during the Socialist absolute majority governments in Spain and Greece in the 1980s, which due to longevity in government allowed for forms of bureaucratic clientelism.

Parliamentary Weakness

Parliamentarianism in southern Europe is still quite incipient in comparison to other countries. The low level of professionalization and routinization can be found in all four parliaments. The dominance of the executive over the legislative and the lack of scrutiny of governmental work are salient features of southern European parliamentarianism.

Portugal

Until 1987, the Portuguese parliament was fragmented and characterized by a low level of institutionalization and routinization. None of the legislatures completed its full term. This situation presented an obstacle to the strengthening of parliamentarianism in the Portuguese case. Nevertheless, one could notice a growing professionalization of MPs and their specialization in certain fields, in spite of a lack of resources for committee work. Parliamentarianism lacked a democratic tradition, so outbursts of personalism and authoritarianism tended to reappear in Portugal. One of the crucial features of Portuguese parliamentarianism was the dominance of university teachers and lawyers and the underrepresentation of other social classes. This was due to the need for more professional MPs who had an extensive knowledge of legal procedures of policy-making.[42] Today, the Portuguese parliament resembles most other west European parliaments. (See Figure 3.1)

In terms of legislation, the first legislatures were characterized by ideological polarization. Nevertheless, during the AD governments there was limited cooperation between the two main parties, PS and PSD. This was reinforced during the Central Block government between 1983 and 1985. A more conflictual behavior between the parties took place during the minority government under the leadership of Cavaco

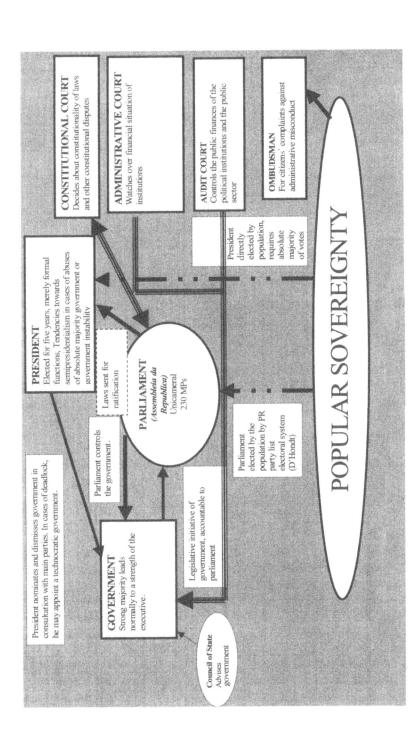

Figure 3.1 Institutional Framework of Portugal

Silva. After the victory of Cavaco Silva in 1987, interparty conflict broke out, nevertheless the absolute majority of the party in the general elections strengthened the executive in relation to the legislative. Although the proportion of private member bills in relation to government bills increased since 1976, the success rate of the latter is much higher and overdominant after 1987.[43]

Indeed during the Cavaco Silva years, president Mário Soares increased its engagement in the process of scrutiny of approved government bills, due to the fact that sometimes it did not tend to include the changes proposed by other parliamentary parties. During Cavaco Silva's government, efforts were made to moralize parliamentary life and make attendance of MPs in plenary sessions compulsory. The government under Antonio Guterres sought good relations with parliament. This led to a strengthening of the image of the Assembly of the Republic as a stabilizing influence. For the time being, one can assert that parliamentarianism in Portugal is becoming more professionalized and routinized. The contact with parliamentarians of other European countries and a modest improvement in human and material resources are important reinforcing elements in the recently regained self-confidence.[44] The New Portuguese government was sworn in on April 6, 2002. It is a coalition government between the PSD and the PP. Prime Minister Manuel Durão Barroso announced a major austerity program to achieve convergence with the rest of Europe in terms of the convergence criteria set up by the Treaty of Maastricht. The first three months of the government were negatively perceived by the population. The government had to revise the figure for the budget deficit of 2001, which was carried throught the former Socialist government, from 2.8 percent of GDP to 4.1 percent. The new government is quite small, comprising only 17 ministers. IT clearly wants to set an example for the need to reduce public spending in Portugal.

Spain

The Spanish *Cortes* originated from regional parliaments in the historical regions and became only naturally represented during the Napoleonic occupation in the early nineteenth century. The *Cortes* of Cadiz between 1808 and 1812 became the cradle of Spanish constitutionalism and democracy. Presently, the *Cortes* consists of two chambers: the lower house, the *Congreso de Deputados* (congress of deputies), and the upper house, *Senado* (senate). There is an asymmetrical relationship between the two chambers. The congress is by far the more important of the two. The congress consists of 350 members elected in 50 multimember constituencies by a D'Hondt representation electoral system and two single member constituencies Ceuta and Melilla, situated in northern Africa. (See Figure 3.2.)

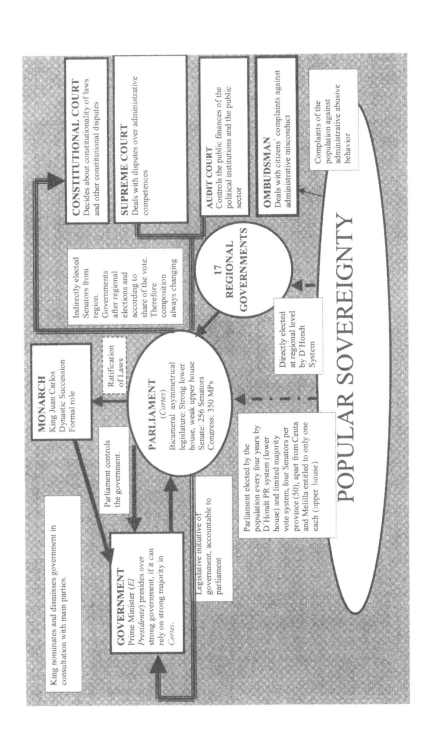

CONSTITUTIONAL COURT
Decides about constitutionality of laws and other constitutional disputes

SUPREME COURT
Deals with disputes over administrative competences

AUDIT COURT
Controls the public finances of the political institutions and the public sector

OMBUDSMAN
Deals with citizens' complaints against administrative misconduct

Complaints of the population against administrative abusive behavior

17 REGIONAL GOVERNMENTS

Indirectly elected Senators from region. Governments after regional elections and according to share of the vote. Therefore composition always changing

Directly elected at regional level by D'Hondt System

MONARCH
King Juan Carlos
Dynastic Succession
Formal role

Ratification of Laws

PARLIAMENT
(*Cortes*)
Bicameral asymmetrical legislature: Strong lower house, weak upper house
Senate: 256 Senators
Congress: 350 MPs

Parliament elected by the population every four years by D'Hondt PR system (lower house) and limited majority vote system, four Senators per province (50), apart from Ceuta and Melilla entitled to only one each (upper house)

POPULAR SOVEREIGNTY

King nominates and dismisses government in consultation with main parties.

Parliament controls the government.

GOVERNMENT
Prime Minister (*El Presidente*) presides over strong government, if it can rely on strong majority in *Cortes*.

Legislative initiative of government, accountable to parliament

Figure 3.2 Institutional Framework of Spain

The upper house, the *Senado* (senate) consists of 256 members elected partly in 52 multimember constituencies (each province is allocated three to four senators, and Ceuta and Melilla elect two senators) by a limited vote system and partly indirectly co-opted within the legislative assemblies of the *Autonomous Communities*, according to their own rules of procedure, on a proportional basis (each of the seventeen Autonomous Communities returns one senator, plus one more for each 1 million inhabitants).

The legislative process is centered in the lower house, with the *Senado* having a mere right to approve and amend the bill. The Spanish parliament is the central source of legitimacy of the regime according to the constitution of 1978 based on the principle of popular sovereignty. In terms of the legislative process, most of the legislation is worked through, discussed, and approved by the permanent committees. Due to the fact that permanent committees have been more subject to media coverage, subcommittees (*ponencias*) were created that discuss the legislative proposals behind closed doors and with a smaller representative number of MPs. This has been inofficially called a first reading, before the matter is resubmitted to the committee and later to the plenary session. These committes are the central place of Spanish parliamentarianism. The composition of each permanent committee is a mere reflection of the strength of the parliamentary groups in the plenary sessions. This opens opportunities for Spanish parties to work together more professionally on legislation. The plenary sessions are used to show differences of opinion that, in general, were integrated into the legislative act discussed in the permanent sessions. One important aspect is that any motion of censure against a government has to be accompanied by an alternative candidate to the present prime minister and an alternative program. This so-called *constructive motion of censure*, influenced by the German Grundgesetz, strengthens the role of the prime minister in the overall decision-making process. A kind of presidentialism of the prime minister may become evident. The overdominance of the Socialist executive between 1982 and 1989 prevented Parliament from being more salient. In fact, a study shows a different image of the relationship between the parliamentary groups in legislative matters. The level of cooperation and consociationalism was quite high throughout the period between 1982 and 1992. In this sense, executive-legislative relations have to be differentiated from the internal system of relationships inside the parliament. It seems that government bills were widely supported by the opposition parties, even if in the plenary sessions the self-presentation of the main parliamentary groups was more conflictual. In the second legislature (1982–1986) the absolute majority of the Socialist party seemed to overdominate the process of legislation, due to the fact that the opposition was weak and very fragmented.

Consociationalism seems to set in after 1986 due to the fact that the opposition parties became stronger. After 1989, the PSOE had to compromise more often with the opposition, because it lacked an absolute majority. According to a report of the Spanish ministry of the presidency, this consociational style of parliamentary relationships continued to exist throughout the past fifth legislature (1993–1996). Although most of the bills were forwarded by the government, they were approved with the votes of the other parliamentary groups and, vice versa, the Socialist parliamentary groups tended to support the private bills of other parliamentary groups. Indeed about 305 legislative acts out of 313 presented by other parliamentary groups were supported by the Socialist party.[45]

Nevertheless, the parliament gained some salience in dealing with abuse of power by Socialist governments between 1982 and 1996. Several political scandals since 1990 caused major problems for the Socialist government. The extent of political corruption strengthened parliament in its controlling function of the government. Several committees of inquiry were set up to investigate these different alleged abuses of power such as the terrorist Anti-Terrorist Groups of Liberation (*Grupos Anti-terroristas de Liberacion* [GAL]), which was targeted family members of alleged Basque terrorists belonging to the terrorist organization ETA (*Euskadi ta Askatasuna* [Basque Country and Freedom]). It was discovered that the Minister of the Interior sponsored these actions against ETA, which led to a cry of indignation in the population.[46] In the 1990s, there was a call from the regionalist-nationalist parties to transform the *Senado* into a genuine territorial chamber, in which the autonomous communities would have more possibilities to influence the decision-making process of national European Union policy coordination. Although a special bicameral committee was set up to look into this question, no political party compromise was achieved to make this happen. On the contrary, the process of reform of the Senate is presently in a standstill and the second chamber may continue to lose power in relation to the *congreso*, because it has been completely neglected by the government after their absolute majority victory on March 12, 2000.[47] Instead, plans for a stronger presence of the central administration in the autonomous communities has been presented in a document of the PP called *The State in the Twenty-First Century: The New Responsibilities*.[48]

Like the Portuguese case, Spanish parliament has still not achieved a high level of routinization and professionalization. Indeed, the rate of renewal of committee members and presidents is quite high. Very few MPs really have an institutional history. This naturally undermines a strengthening of a parliamentary culture in Spain. Similar to Portugal, the relationship to voters and interest groups is a distant one. Normally,

MPs spend a very small amount of time with voters and interest groups (13.06 percent of working time). Most of the time is devoted to plenary sessions (26.46 percent). This is followed by work in subcommittees which consumes 16.44 percent of the working time. Other minor activities that fill the working time of Spanish MPs are formal representations before public administration (9.89 percent), work on private bills (9 percent), tabling of questions and interpellations (8.55 percent), meetings of the parliamentary group (8.19 percent), preparatory committee work (5.38 percent) and other activities (3.03 percent). This obviously confirms a distance between voters or civil society and parliament.[49]

Italy

As regards Italy, the centrality of parliament (*La centralitá dello parliamento*) was one of the major features of the pre-1992 political system. The weak government and the more symbolic role of the president strengthened the position of parliament. This was even more true, because the bicameral parliament has a symmetrical structure. Both the lower house, Chamber of Deputies (*Camera dei Deputati*), as well as the upper house, the Senate (*Senato*) have the same legislative powers. Although parliament continues to have the same structure, its centrality has been weakened by the recent judiciary investigations of politicians who were involved in corruption scandals. The abuse of parliamentary immunity to obstruct the judiciary work was regarded as negative and damaging to Italian parliamentarianism. Another factor negatively affecting the centrality of parliament was the complicity of MPs in supporting a huge web of particularistic interests that were created by clientelistic and patronage practices. The collapse of *partitocrazia* and subsequently of the political class made people aware that democratic representation was subverted by corruption, clientelism, and patronage.[50]

Before 1992, both houses were elected by a system of proportional representation, but since the electoral law reforms of 1992 and 1993, both houses are elected by a mixed system of partially simple majority and partially proportional representation. The Chamber of Deputies consists of 630 members, 75 percent elected in single-member constituencies by a simple majority (475) and 25 percent by proportional representation and party list (155) elected for a period of five years. Each voter casts two ballot papers, one under each of the distinct systems. If a party wins less than 4 percent of the vote nationwide, it is not entitled to proportional representation seats. The Senate consists of 326 members, 75 percent elected in single-member constituencies by a simple majority (232) and 25 percent elected by proportional representation on the basis of regional voting results (83); additionally 9 are appointed by the president and 2 are ex-officio Senators.[51] (See Figure 3.3.)

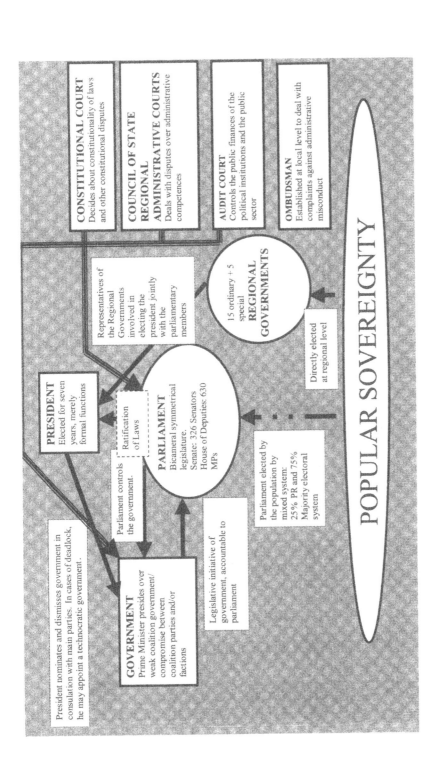

CONSTITUTIONAL COURT
Decides about constitutionality of laws and other constitutional disputes

COUNCIL OF STATE REGIONAL ADMINISTRATIVE COURTS
Deals with disputes over administrative competences

AUDIT COURT
Controls the public finances of the political institutions and the public sector

OMBUDSMAN
Established at local level to deal with complaints against administrative misconduct

Representatives of the Regional Governments involved in electing the president jointly with the parliamentary members

15 ordinary + 5 special **REGIONAL GOVERNMENTS**

Directly elected at regional level

POPULAR SOVEREIGNTY

PRESIDENT
Elected for seven years, merely formal functions

Ratification of Laws

PARLIAMENT
Bicameral symmetrical legislature.
Senate: 326 Senators
House of Deputies: 630 MPs

Parliament controls the government.

Parliament elected by the population by mixed system:
25% PR and 75% Majority electoral system

President nominates and dismisses government in consulation with main parties. In cases of deadlock, he may appoint a technocratic government.

GOVERNMENT
Prime Minister presides over weak coalition government/ compromise between coalition parties and/or factions

Legislative initiative of government, accountable to parliament

Figure 3.3 Institutional Framework of Italy

Presently, the Italian parliament is learning to act according to the new rules of the game. The collapse of the former political class initiated an overall renewal of the two chambers. According to Luca Verzichelli, in the 1994 parliament over 70 percent of members were elected for the first time, whereas only 17.5 percent were elected in 1992 and 11.1 percent before 1992. Still today the parliamentary elite is extremely volatile, changing parties all the time, thus creating major difficulties in consolidating the new party system.[52] The centrality of parliament does not directly relate to its legislative efficiency, due in large part to the features of Italian parliamentarianism after the 1994 elections. The main reason seems to be that pieces of legislation have to be agreed upon by a majority, which neither government nor opposition can be sure of because of the low level of discipline within the parliamentary groups. Like in the pre-1992 DC-dominated political system, there is no clear-cut division between government majority and opposition or even the government and the parliamentary group. To complicate things, even within the opposition parliamentary groups, dissent is very common. Another factor is the high number of absentees in plenary sessions or in the committees. The need to bargain legislation has increased the status of the parliamentary committees.

According to Article 72, some pieces of legislation can be passed in parliamentary committees and avoid the plenary voting of both houses. This is one of the aspects of the *centralitá dello parlamento*, a major target for lobby groups. Legislation had been, until 1992, quite particularistic in nature, satisfying the interests of certain groups and categories. It is still too early to tell if this will continue to be the case. Indeed, several reforms in the 1980s and 1990s reduced the abusive nature of legislation both coming from the government as well as from the MPs in the committees. A dramatic decline of committee-approved legislation was the consequence. Italian government is under considerable strain to cut public spending and the budget deficit to keep in line with the criteria set up by the European central bank.[53]

Until the 1970s lobbies were quite strong in shaping the outcome of legislative bills. The so-called *leggini* (small laws) were the main bulk of legislation produced in parliament and an important element in the whole web of systemic corruption. After the *tangentopoli* affair, this practice is less tolerated.[54]

From 1988, the secret vote was abolished in the plenary sessions. This was an important instrument to block legislation. MPs could avoid the voting discipline of parliamentary groups. In 1978 an open roll-call on government decree-laws was introduced to assure the working of the government, but a second secret vote on the contents of legislation continued to prevail. Finally in 1988 a reform abolished the secret vote. Consequently, many MPs choose to be absent from the plenary sessions, leading very often to a lack of quorum to pass legislation. The Italian parliament is now challenged to improve its efficiency. Nevertheless it will take some time to make an assessment of how parliamentary work is affected by the recent developments in the party and political system. European integration has become a major catalyst in this quest for more efficiency.

Greece

The Greek unicameral *Vouli* (see Figure 3.4) has remained quite insignificant since its establishment. The main reason has been the fact that out of the eleven governments, nine were absolute majority governments. Another feature is that Greek MPs are only semi-professionalized—they are entitled to pursue their normal jobs during their parliamentary time.[55] Most of the parliamentary sessions are held at the end of the day and tend to run throughout the evening and early morning hours. Moreover, the lack of extensive committee work, which may last between five and eight days, leads to the elaboration of bad legislation that clearly is predominantly drafted by the government with a limited impact by the opposition. Following the French model, there are only six committees, each consisting of thirty members. Similar to the British Parliament, there is a strong relationship between government, parliamentary majority, and parliament. Normally one third of the MPs of the governing party are engaged in government. This was quite extreme during the Papandreou years. Similar to the German case, the prime minister cannot be challenged very easily. Although there are mechanisms of control (such as question time, interpellations, request for viewing of documents, and written questions and objections), the quorums for being successful are too high. Whereas the government needs only a simple majority of 120 to get a program or a motion of confidence approved, the opposition has to achieve an absolute majority for a motion of censure.[56] Between 1974 and 1999, out of 2,774 approved bills, only 8 originated from the parliament.[57] In the 1990s, some reforms had been initiated to improve the situation, but in reality a culture of parliamentarianism is in some way undermined by the populist and controversial style of Greek politics between the two main parties. Still today, the Greek parliament has not lost the impression of being solely a talking parliament.[58]

In sum, parliamentarianism in southern Europe has been dominated by partyocratic arrangements. The overdominance of the executive over the Portuguese, Spanish, and Greek political systems was intentional, so that more governmental stability could be achieved (as shown in Table 3.6). Similar weakness can be found in the Italian parliament, which is more related to the growing fragmentation in terms of political parties of the two chambers.

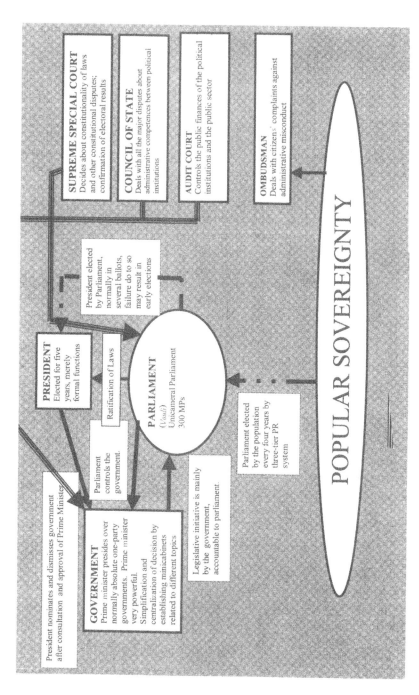

SUPREME SPECIAL COURT
Decides about constitutionality of laws and other constitutional disputes; confirmation of electoral results

COUNCIL OF STATE
Deals with all the major disputes about administrative competences between political institutions

AUDIT COURT
Controls the public finances of the political institutions and the public sector

OMBUDSMAN
Deals with citizens' complaints against administrative misconduct

President elected by Parliament, normally in several ballots, failure do to so may result in early elections

PRESIDENT
Elected for five years, merely formal functions

Ratification of Laws

PARLIAMENT
(*Vouli*)
Unicameral Parliament
300 MPs

Parliament controls the government.

Parliament elected by the population every four years by three-tier PR system

Legislative initiative is mainly by the government, accountable to parliament.

President nominates and dismisses government after consultation and approval of Prime Minister.

GOVERNMENT
Prime minister presides over normally absolute one-party governments. Prime minister very powerful. Simplification and centralization of decision by establishing minicabinets related to different topics.

POPULAR SOVEREIGNTY

Figure 3.4 Institutional Framework of Greece

92

TABLE 3.6 Structure and Functions of Parliaments in Southern Europe

	Portugal	Spain	Italy	Greece
Structure of Parliament	Unicameral (230) *Assembleia da Republica*	Bicameral Lower House: *Congreso de Deputados* (350). Upper House: *Senado* (256). Dominance of Lower House	Bicameral. Lower House: *Camera die Deputati* (630). Upper House: *Senato* (325). Symmetrical importance of both Houses	Unicameral (300) *Vouli*
Governmental Bills	Submission to parliament. Two readings. First reading: general discussion about the bill after elaboration by committee; after redrafting of the bill, second, final reading takes place that approves legislation.	*Proyectos de Ley:* Three stages: 1) Submission to Congreso and discussed by corresponding committee; 2) submission to Senate and discussed in appropriate committee; 3) if amendments or veto, discussed and approved in Congreso.	Presentation to one of the chambers has to be approved by both chambers. Process may take several stages until it is approved. Most of the bills are decided at committee level. Decentralized legislative process. Time limits were set up.	Limited debate and involvement of standing committees. Voting and debate in three stages in principle, by specific article, and as a whole.
Strength of Committees	Strong engagement	Strong engagement	Strong engagement	Weak engagement
Submission of Private Bills	Submission by individual MPs	*Proposiciones de Ley:* Submission by MP + 14 signatures of other MPs or parliamentary group (in Senate by parliamentary group or 25 Senators). Government decides if it wants to accept as part of its legislative program. If yes, same procedure as a *proyecto de ley.*	Can be presented by individual MPs, institutions of civil society or popular initiative with the support of 50,000 votes. It may take several stages until it is approved. Decentralized legislative process. Time limits were set up.	Can only submit private law proposals
Motion of Censure	It has to be submitted by 25% of MPs and approved by absolute majority. The voting and discussion happens only two days after submission.	Overall majority and name of alternative prime minister coming from the opposition has to head the motion of censure.	Overall majority in one of the chambers brought forward by one tenth of MPs and discussed three days later. It leads to resignation of government.	Absolute majority of total membership and only every six months.

TABLE 3.6   *(continued)*

	Portugal	*Spain*	*Italy*	*Greece*
Motion of Confidence	It has to be approved by simple majority.	Simple majority; failing to achieve it leads to dissolution of both Houses and new elections.	Simple majority; failing to achieve it leads to resignation of the government.	Simple majority of the MPs present, but not less than 2/5 of MPs. Failure leads to resignation of government.
Question Time	Perguntas, Interpelacoes Question time is every second week.	Preguntas and Interpelaciones Weekly (Wednesday afternoons for twenty minutes).	Questions, interpellations, and motions. First forty minutes of each parliamentary day reserved for questions to the government.	Petitions delivered to ministers through speaker, requests for official documents, oral questions, question time (Friday) and interpellations (Tuesday).
Control of EU Legislation	Post-facto	Post-facto	Post-facto	Post-facto
Election of the President	NO Directly elected by population	NO Does not apply— Monarchy	YES	YES

The Head of State

The role of the head of state in modern liberal constitutions is very much a legacy of west European republicanism. In comparison with the Americas, parliamentary government is the main form of government in Western Europe in contrast to presidential government. This characteristic of west European government is widespread in the four southern European democracies we are studying here. In all cases, the head of the state is regarded as an important integrative figure who helps to smooth the dominance of party politics in the political culture of the four countries. In the end, all four countries decided for different forms of head of state.

Portugal

In Portugal, the president of the Republic was designed as a counterpart to partisan politics. Therefore, the constitution of 1976 and the subsequent revisions confirmed that the president is directly elected by the population. This was certainly quite important during the phase of governmental and parliamentary instability until 1985. During this early period the presidency was the only stable factor in the institutional framework and certainly contributed to a strengthening of democracy in Portugal. Due to his direct election, the president of the

Republic is essentially an important referee in difficult phases of political life. The conflict with the prime minister is a common feature of
former presidents such as Ramalho Eanes with Francisco Sá Carneiro
or Mário Soares or later on Mário Soares with Prime Minister Anibal
Cavaco Silva.[59]

It seems that the president intervenes more strongly in politics
when there is a phase of political instability, as happened particularly
in 1978–1979 after the resignation of the second Soares government
or in phases when the absolute majority of the government may lead
to the imposition of legislation that has not been accepted by the
opposition. This happened particularly between 1991 and 1995 when
several bills of the government of Cavaco Silva III were vetoed by
president Mário Soares and sent by him to the Constitutional Court
for review. Apart from that, Portuguese semipresidentialism is weaker
than the French one, because the Portuguese presidents are not sharing
the executive with the government.[60] On the contrary, the president
is restricted to a formal representative role and to be a moral political
figure during his mandate. Furthermore, the president can only be
elected for a second consecutive time. Afterwards it has to pause at
least for one mandate. One of the quite popular events of the
five-year-long presidency is the so-called open presidency (*presidência
aberta*), when the president goes for a lengthier period of time to one
of the regions of Portugal and meets the population on several
occasions. The relationship between the president Jorge Sampaio and
the prime minister Antonio Guterres was quite consensual and
friendly, probably because both politicians were from the Socialist
party. The resignation of Prime Minister Guterres after defeat in the
local elections of December 16, 2001, led to a stronger intervention
of President Sampaio. After discussion with all parties and consultation with the state council, it nominated an interim technocratic
government and called for early elections scheduled for March 17,
2002 (as shown in Table 3.7).[61]

Spain
In Spain, during the constitutional settlement, parties agreed con-
sensually to reinstate the monarchy. This means that the present
monarchy breaks with the past one. It represents a new monarchy
under a democratic regime. This naturally makes the monarchy quite
Republican in character. The consensualism of the constitutional
settlement intended to create a monarchy that would have merely
formal representative powers and fulfill the role of an integrative
figure for the whole of Spain. His powers are extremely restricted,
and they always imply consultation with the government and/or
political parties. King Juan Carlos became the new king of Spain after

TABLE 3.7   Presidents of Portugal Since 1976

President	Period	Elections (%)			Type of Relationship with Prime Minister
General Ramalho Eanes	1976–1981	Ramalho Eanes		61.54	Conflictual
		Otelo S. Carvalho		16.52	
		P. de Azevedo		14.36	
		Octavio Pato		7.58	
General Ramalho Eanes	1981–1986	Ramalho Eanes		56.44	Conflictual
		Soares Carneiro		40.23	
		Otelo S. Carvalho		1.49	
		G. de Melo		0.84	
		Pires Veloso		0.78	
		Aires Rodrigues		0.22	
Mário Soares	1986–1991		1st	2nd	Consensual/
		Mário Soares	25.4	51.2	Cohabitation
		F. do Amaral	46.3	47.8	
		Salgado Zenha	20.9		
		Pintassilgo	7.3		
Mário Soares	1991–1996	Mário Soares		70.4	Conflictual/End of
		Basilio Horta		14.1	Cohabitation
		Carlos Carvalhas		12.9	
		C. Marques		2.6	
Jorge Sampaio	1996–2001	Jorge Sampaio		53.91	Consensual/same
		Cavaco Silva		46.09	party
Jorge Sampaio	2001–2006	Jorge Sampaio		55.76	Consensual/same
		Ferreira do Amaral		34.54	party
		Antonio Abreu		5.13	Cohabitation since
		Fernando Rosas		2.98	2002
		Garcia Pereira		1.59	

Source: Commissao Nacional de Eleicões (http://www.cne.pt)

the death of the dictator, who had appointed the king as his successor in the 1968 Succession Act. King Juan Carlos used his powers to move Spain toward democracy. This evolutionary transformation of Spain from authoritarian dictatorship to democracy is certainly one the biggest achievements of King Juan Carlos. Moreover, after the constitution was approved, he was prominent in pushing the cause of democracy among the resilient right-wing circles. This became evident when Colonel Tejero seized the *Cortes* on February 21, 1981, and hoped to make the king reverse the process of democratization. Instead, King Juan Carlos condemned the act and used his loyal forces to arrest the insubordinate officers. This determination to protect democracy in Spain strengthened the Spanish monarchy and democracy as intertwined elements of stability. The monarchy has a very high level of acceptance in Spain (as shown in Figure 3.5).[62]

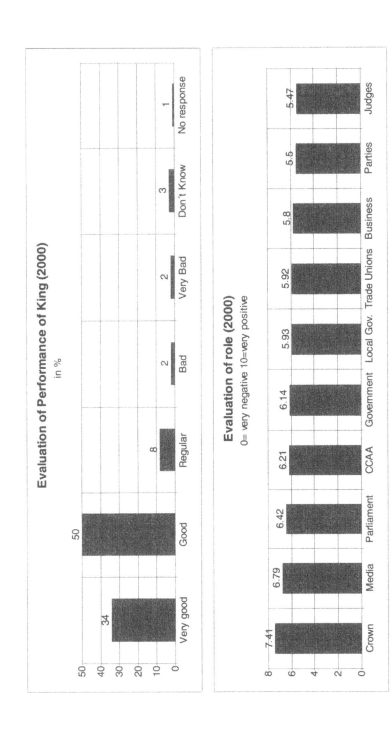

Figure 3.5 Positive Evaluation of the Spanish Monarchy

Source: Own graphs based on data from *El País*, November 22, 2000, p. 4.

Italy

In Italy, the president is indirectly elected by the members of parliament and representatives of the regional governments (three from each region; Val d'Aosta has only one representative). This college elects the president, a process that can take a long period of time. All presidents elected until now have been very experienced politicians. The president is elected for a period of seven years. Although most of the powers of the Italian president are formal and quite restricted, in the end the level of governmental and parliamentary instability assigns the president an exceptional managerial role of re-creating stability. During *tangentopoli*, Oscar Scalfaro had to deal with the collapse of an entire political class. He had to appoint two technocratic governments, in 1993 under Carlo Azeglio Ciampi and in 1995 under Lamberto Dini. This strong involvement in the construction of government has been the rule, not the exception. As already mentioned earlier in this chapter, most governments since 1948 had a brief life span. The Italian presidency is certainly the most stable element of the political system (as shown in Table 3.8).

The president is entitled to appoint one third of all judges of the Constitutional Court and is the official president of the High Council of the Judiciary, the organ supervising the administration of the judiciary sector. Under the presidency of Francesco Cossiga, a big discussion broke out on how independent the judiciary is. Indeed, it seemed that the judiciary tried to gain more autonomy from the dominance of the executive in 1990–1991. This naturally created conflicts with the political class on the eve of *tangentopoli*.[63]

One major issue of dispute with the weak governments is the role that presidents may assign themselves in foreign policy. Although the president represents Italy inside and outside the country, foreign policy is normally a domain of government and the president has to consult the

TABLE 3.8   Presidents of Italy since 1946

President	Period
Enrico de Nicola	1946–1948
Luigi Einaudi	1948–1955
Giovanni Gronchi	1955–1962
Antonio Segni	1962–1964
Giuseppe Saragat	1964–1971
Giovanni Leone	1971–1978
Alessandro Pertini	1978–1985
Francesco Cossiga	1985–1992
Oscar Luigi Scalfaro	1992–1999
Carlo Azeglio Ciampi	2000–

government, before he makes any statements in foreign policy. Such a dispute existed particularly between President Sandro Pertini and the Ministry of Foreign Affairs. Pertini tended to condemn international terrorism and dictatorial regimes without previously consulting with the Ministry of Foreign Affairs.[64] The present president, Carlo Azeglio Ciampi, is well regarded among the political class and the population. This may lead to a different climate in Italian politics.

Greece

Similar to Italy, the Greek president is indirectly elected by the *Vouli*. Although the constitution was designed to allow some form of semi-presidentialism following more or less the French example, in the end the constitutional reality limited and restricted the powers of the president. In 1986, PASOK introduced a major constitutional revision to acknowledge this constitutional reality. The Greek president has merely representative powers inside and outside the country.

In the past twenty-six years the Greek president has been quite a silent, but important moral figure (as shown in Table 3.9). The most charismatic of the presidents was naturally Kostas Karamanlis between 1980 and 1985. In spite of the friendly relationship between Karamanlis and Prime Minister Papandreou, PASOK restricted the powers of the president in the 1985 constitutional revision and did not propose Karamanlis for reelection. Instead PASOK put forward and elected Kostas Sartzetakis to strengthen the position of the government. Due to the reinforced proportional representation system, PASOK has been able to dominate the selection of a government-friendly candidate since 1985. The present president Kostas Stephanopoulos had almost no difficulty getting elected in 1995 and recently in 2000. He is well regarded by the population. He is over 75 and he clearly keeps a low profile in the Greek political system.

In sum, in all four countries the constitutional reality transformed the head of state into a mere ceremonial figure who watches over the constitutionality of legislation, preserves the unity of the country, and represents the country abroad.

TABLE 3.9   Presidents of Greece Since 1975

President	Period
Konstantinos Tsatsos	1975–1980
Konstantinos Karamanlis	1980–1985
Christos Sartzetakis	1985–1990
Konstantinos Karamanlis	1990–1995
Konstantinos Stephanopoulos	1995–2000
Konstantinos Stephanopoulos	2000–

The Judiciary

In the 1990s, the judiciary was able to gain more importance in relation to the other powers of the political system. Accountability and transparency became important issues in dealing with the government. Although the judiciary is in appalling condition in all four countries, the controlling higher courts were able to develop a more independent role in the past two decades.

Portugal

The Portuguese political system provides for three main higher courts related directly to the political system: the Constitutional Court, the Audit Court, and the Supreme Administrative Court. Accountability has become a major factor in moralizing and bringing more transparency into the executive branch. During Cavaco Silva's government these controlling institutions were quite active. They were characterized by Cavaco Silva as the "blocking forces" (forças de bloqueio). Nevertheless, the activity of the Constitutional Court and the Audit Court were backed by President Mário Soares. Prime minister Antonio Guterres was more keen to accept the importance of auditing instances.

The Constitutional Court (Tribunal Constitutional) was established in 1982, and it replaced the Revolutionary Council inherited from the revolutionary constitution. The Constitutional Court's main task is to scrutinize the constitutionality of parliamentary bills and other issues that may violate the constitution. This can be forwarded by the president of the Republic, the president of the Assembly of the Republic, the prime minister, the ombudsman, the attorney general, or one-tenth of the deputies. During the Cavaco Silva governments, President Mário Soares sent several bills approved by the majority party to the Constitutional Court. About twenty out of twenty-seven legislative acts were deemed illegal by the Constitutional Court.[65]

The Auditing Court (Tribunal de Contas), too, gained in importance in the 1990s. It audits the public expenditure of public institutions. The former president Professor Antonio Sousa Franco created major embarassment to the president of the regional government of the island Madeira, Alberto João Jardim, by exposing major irregularities in payments by Madeira's regional administration. The Audit Court made it known in July 2002 that the former Socialist government tended to exclude many accounts from the budget, which belonged in it, so that it could offer to the European institutions a budget deficit that was below the 3 percent GDP. This naturally created problems (now major) for the government of Manuel Durão Barroso, because of the Statistical Office of the European Union dfid not except these false accounting practices.

The Supreme Administrative Court (*Supremo Tribunal Administrativo*) has been less prominent. Since its foundation in 1976, it has not been able to achieve the implementation of some of its decisions by the government. This is partly due to the permanent restructuring of administration since 1976, partly because of a lack in accountability in administration.[66] The Supreme Court of Justice oversees the different courts that deal with civil and criminal matters. The president of the Supreme Court of Justice is elected by the judges.

In the 1990s, due to political stability, interinstitutional relations became more routinized and strengthened. Accountability and transparency became part of the vocabulary of policy makers and administrators. In spite of substantial improvements, the basic problems of the Portuguese judiciary sector continue to be the lack of human and material resources and the slowness of trials, which sometimes creates unsurmountable backlogs. Moreover, the restructuring of the overall judiciary system began only in the late 1980s.[67] The creation of an ombudsman in 1976 was intended to improve the accessibility of the population to the justice system.[68]

Spain

The Spanish judiciary shows similar features to the Portuguese judiciary. Its role grew in prominence in the 1990s due to the amount of corruption scandals of the former PSOE government. This became an opportunity for judges such as Baltazar Garzón to become important charismatic figures in the struggle to improve accountability and transparency in Spain. Super-Garzón became a model for the new self-confident judiciary.[69]

Three courts are quite important in the core institutional framework: the Constitutional Court (*Tribunal Constitucional*), the Supreme Court of Justice (*Tribunal Supremo de la Justicia*), and the Higher Courts of Justice (*Tribunales Generales de la Justicia*).

The Constitutional Court deals with the constitutionality of laws approved by the *Cortes*, decree-laws issued by the government, disputes between central and regional governments over constitutional issues, and citizens' protests against infringement of their rights. The number of cases submitted to the Constitutional Court has increased over the years, which indicates the importance that it has acquired in the political system. Nevertheless it is quite slow in resolving cases.[70]

The Constitutional Court was able to gain in reputation since its first resolution of January 23, 1981. In the past fifteen years, the Spanish style of scrutinizing the constitutionality of laws became established. Most of the resolutions are not concerned about the interpellations and policy options referring to the law. More than that, the concern is with the boundaries of the corresponding law within the constitutional framework.[71] The twelve judges nominated by the *Cortes* are of outstanding reputation (minimum of fifteen years of practice). Moreover, they are elected by a complicated process to ensure impartiality. The Congress and Senate elect four judges each by a three-fifths majority so that they are less a partisan choice of the largest party two are elected by the government; and two are elected by a General Council of the judiciary power (*Consejo General del Poder Judicial* [CGPJ]), which is the body appointing judges and maintaining ethical standards within the legal professions.[72]

The Supreme Court of Justice and the Higher Courts of Justice are the highest bodies of the judiciary hierarchy at the national and regional body respectively. They are the last resort of appeal for sentences issued against criminal acts. Especially during the GAL affair, involving former interior minister José Barrionuevo, the Supreme Court intervened and nominated the experienced judge Eduardo Moner to deal with the case in 1995. Nevertheless Judge Moner had difficulties getting the alleged secret documents of the Spanish secret police, CESID, due to the fact that these were regarded as classified information. This was decided by the Court of Jurisdiction Conflicts (*Tribunal de Conflictos de Jurisdicción*). The PP government also had to distance itself from the promise it made during the elections that it would declassify the documents of CESID and send them to Judge Moner.[73] Later, the documents were leaked to the daily newspaper *El Mundo*, creating a major embarrassment for both the government and the opposition. In comparative terms, the Spanish judiciary is slow and not very efficient. In comparison to Germany with 26,000 judges for 80 million citizens and Portugal with 2,000 for 10 million, Spain has only 4,000 for 40 million citizens. This naturally contributes to delay and inefficiency.[74]

Italy

The recent emergence of the judiciary in Italy in the political system is leading to a thorough reform of the entire political structure. The judiciary was well known for its quiet, conservative role until well into the 1970s. Nevertheless, the politicization of Italy during that decade led to a factionalization of the main institution administering the Italian judiciary system, the so-called Higher Council of the Judiciary, an intermediate agency between the judiciary and the political world. The President of the Higher Council is the President of the Republic. The thirty judges are elected by various branches of the judiciary (two thirds) and by parliament (one third). On the whole, the judiciary system is slow and lacks in enough human and material resources. The waiting time for all kinds of trials is quite long. Nevertheless, the recent *Mani Pulite* operation, initiated by the Milanese judge Antonio di Pietro against several politicians involved in accepting illegal commissions for the speeding up of licences and the granting of orders from public institutions, the so-called *tangentopoli*, enhanced its role as a controlling institution within the political system.

The Court of Accounts (*Corte dei Conti*) is actually an "auxiliary" agency to the government. Its main task is to control public expenditure of the government. Over 500 magistrates are part of this institution.

The Council of State (*Consiglio di Stato*) fulfils the dual function of adviser of the government and highest court of appeal on legal and administrative matters. Over 400 councillors, partly nominated by the government, partly recruited on a competitive basis, are engaged in the Council.

Last but not least, the important Constitutional Court (*Corte Costituzionale*) is the highest body dealing with constitutional issues. The Court is highly regarded and highly respected in Italy. It is even above the highest Court of Appeal of the judiciary system, the so-called Court of Cassation (*Corte di Cassazione*). The fifteen judges are elected by the different high courts (three members from the Court of Cassation, one from the Council of State, one from the Court of Accounts) from parliament (five judges nominated by both Chambers) and the president (five judges). It deals with constitutionality of legislative acts adopted in Parliament and is an important institution in regulating certain controversial areas in the public sector (such as in the broadcasting field).

The recent rise of the judges is related to their form of recruitment based on competitive examinations and the protection guaranteed by law to prevent interference. This led to a transformation of the once conservative authoritarian culture inside the judicial profession. A new generation grew up with a different attitude toward the legal system.

At some stage, politicians of all parties were afraid that after a politicization of the judiciary a judicialization of the political system would follow.[75] Since 1995, politicians try to gain control over the whole process. Only in 2000 were they able to agree on the setting up a bicameral committee on illicit party financing, seven years after the outbreak of *tangentopoli*.[76] In spite of the strong performance of the judiciary in the 1990s, the tangible results of reform are quite disappointing. A general assessment clearly tends to see little change in the way politics is run in Italy.[77]

Greece

The Greek judicial system was not very successful in dealing with the scandals related to the PASOK government of the 1980s.[78] The whole structure of the judicial system is quite complicated. In comparison with the other southern European countries, one can find similar controlling institutions.

The Supreme Special Court fulfills the role of a constitutional court, dealing with the constitutionality of laws and the confirmation of electoral results. The Audit Court audits public expenditure of the government. The high level of public spending and budget deficit are indicators that it has not been very efficient in the past. The Council of State is the highest institution deciding over administrative issues and complaints of citizens against this administration. The Higher Special Court deals with all aspects related to the Courts as well as constitutional matters.

Moreover, among the Courts, there are two more worth mentioning. The Special Court on the Revision of Law decides about issues that lead to the misinterpretation of the law; the Special Court dealing with complaints of ministers and others against the president of the Republic is a further important court sorting out conflicts between the institutions. On the whole, the structure is still building its own legal culture, which has been partly undermined by the dominance of the executive in the political system.[79]

In sum, the judiciary is quite an important controlling instance of the political system. The danger of politicization of judges is always imminent as the cases of Antonio di Pietro in Italy and Baltasar Garzón in Spain show. The strong interference of government in the judicial system in Greece has been quite problematic. In spite of that, these efforts are first signs of an emerging strong legal culture that wants to reform negative aspects of the political system and withstand attempts by the political class to make webs of systemic corruption.

Problems of Public Administration: Overcoming the Patrimonial Legacy

Public administration and the public economic sector are two areas that the different governments of southern Europe were very keen to reform in the 1990s, due to the growing pressures coming from the EU. For decades, reform of public administration has been neglected, making it a playing field for clientelistic and patronage politics. Public employment was used and abused by governments of southern Europe to strengthen their positions in power.

Portugal

In Portugal, governmental instability prevented a reform of public administration inherited from the former authoritarian regime. Most heads of the General-Directorates continued to exist after the collapse of the authoritarian regime. This naturally showed that past forms of patrimonial clientelistic behavior continued to prevail in the 1980s.[80] Although the Portuguese case is perceived as less corrupt than the other southern European countries, one can find similar patterns where clientelistic networking can lead to political corruption in the end. Indeed, during Cavaco Silva's government between 1985 and 1995 the media and opposition tended to call it the Orange state (*estado laranja*), referring to the color of the party emblem. During the *Cavaquismo* period, several political scandals related to abuse of power or traffic of influences became known to the public. This tells a lot about one of the main causes of corruption: longevity in power. The lack of appointment rules led to the establishment of a widespread clientelistic practice in the distribution of top jobs in health, public television and the public telecommunications sector. This was later extended to the deconcentrated administrative structures in the regions, which were, in 70 to 95 percent of the cases, filled with people close to the PSD.[81]

One major problem of public administration in Portugal was the low level of education among civil servants and the lack of resources to implement most of the policies. Even more problematic were the poor results in implementation and control of policy-making. After entry into the EC/EU on January 1, 1986, Cavaco Silva's government introduced major reforms in the administration.[82] A Secretariat for Administrative Modernization (*Secretariado de Modernização Administrativa* [SMA]) was set up to improve the relationship between public administration and citizens. Moreover, the deconcentration process of the public administration was started, which ended the inheritance of an extremely centralized administration. This transformation of public administration was continued by the Guterres government. Guterres wanted to go even further and introduce administrative regions with a devolution of decision-making competences, but he failed to achieve a majority for it in a referendum on November 8, 1998. Two thirds of the voters opposed the governmental intention to establish eight administrative regions in Portugal.[83] In 1996, of the 531,663 civil servants, 81 percent were employed in central administration, but only 19 percent at the local level. Although about one third of all civil servants from central government are deconcentrated, the level of decentralization of public administration decision-makers is still very low.[84] A National Institute of Administration (*Instituto Nacional de Administracao* [INA]) was founded in the mid-1980s to train civil servants in specific subjects. In spite of all these attempts of reform, there is still the need to reduce the current number of civil servants. This is quite important in view of the adjustment to the Economic and Monetary Union. Such difficult decisions were not taken on by the Guterres government.[85] This contributed to the resignation of the prime minister.[86]

Spain

Similarly in Spain, deconcentration and decentralization have been happening since the new constitution was approved in 1978. The creation of autonomous communities (*comunidades autonomas*) led to a devolution program in competences, finances, and human resources that is still going on. Modernization of the Spanish public administration became another priority. Already at end of the Francoist regime, attempts were made to transform public administration as the instrument of a state of law. During transition, no purges of former civil servants was undertaken, so most of the public administrative structures were inherited from the authoritarian regime.[87] The pressure for transformation and modernization came from the regions. As Jeanie Bukowski clearly stated, most west European countries were under pressure to devolve authority to the supra- or the subnational level. Spain's process was a devolution in both directions that clearly transformed the former highly centralized political system into a new modernized system, convergent with other European countries.[88]

According to official figures, the number of civil servants in the autonomous communities surpassed the number of central administration civil servants in the 1990s. The present PP government just consolidated and reinforced the trend (as shown in Table 3.10). Less spectacular has been the rise of the local administration, which in some sense had to deal with a renewed centralization of competences at the autonomous community level in lieu of central level. Indeed, the PP government strengthened the dialogue with the regional governments in terms of renegotiating the Inter-territorial Compensation Fund (*Fondo de Compensación Inter-territorial* [FCI]) and advocating the leveling of similar competences for all the autonomous communities, thus ending the differences that exist between historical regions (Catalonia, Basque Country, Galicia, and Andalucia) and the other autonomous communities. This shows the commitment to make the whole process of devolution more transparent and equal across the territory.[89]

This devolution of human resources has also been followed by a stronger financial devolution. In 1998, 63.49 percent of public expenditure was undertaken by central administration, whereas 24.06 percent was controlled by the governments of seventeen autonomous communities and 12.45 percent by local government. A magic orientation figure

TABLE 3.10   Public Administration in Spain

Level of Administration	1996	1997	1998	1999
Central	602,980	601,039	595,579	570,565
Autonomous	636,559	661,133	677,160	690,370
Local	425,470	442,286	440,972	450,710

Source: *El Pais*, March 1, 2000, p. 28.

has been until now a 50:25:25 share between the central, regional, and local governments. It is local government that has still to be provided with more cash, so that it can better fulfill its competences. In spite of all that, Spain can be considered as one of the most decentralized multilevel governments in the European Union. It fares well against Germany with a public expenditure ratio of 62:65:20 in comparison to the Spanish 67:16:68 ratio in 1998.[90] After the elections of March 12, 2000, the absolute majority government of Aznar put on hold further developments of the state of autonomies. The present discussion in the government is to restore the presence of the central administration through deconcentrated services in the autonomous communities. This is regarded as important because it allows for a better central coordination of policies. This naturally affects the administrative devolution process, in spite of the fact that between 1996 and 2000 the minority government of Aznar clearly contributed to a strengthening of the decentralized Spanish state.

Italy

In comparison with the Iberian cases, the Italian and Greek public administrations did not manage to make major reforms in the past decades. In Italy, public administration is still today quite intransparent and inefficient. The main problem seems to be that both countries had to deal with a legacy of clientelism and patronage that in the end spilled over into cases of systemic corruption. The use and abuse of public administration and the public economic sector by the former DC governments until 1992 makes it difficult to change the cultural pattern of behavior overnight. The culture of *tangenti* (kickback) in Italy is still in place, in spite of the fact that *tangentopoli* was exposed by the judiciary in 1992.[91] One of the factors leading to this situation is the fact that the whole bureaucratic procedure is too complex, giving power in some way to the underpaid civil servants. One source of the complexity of the process is the astronomical number of laws that exist in Italy. The estimation is that Italy has produced over 150,000 laws in the past four decades in comparison to 7,325 in Germany and 5,587 in France.[92] It seems that civil servants are quite unsatisfied with their jobs, which are low paid and with few avenues for personal progress. This is naturally related to the fact that too many people are in the civil administration in the wrong places, thus creating a culture of dissatisfaction.[93] Such a feeling is also expressed across Italy among citizens.[94] An important thesis of Cassese seems to be the fact that the civil service is dominated by graduates coming from the south. In the early 1990s, over 70 percent of civil servants originated from the south, leading to the phenomenon of a "southernization of the public administration." This process has been happening steadily over the past century.[95] Another factor is the fact that many civil servants were hired without any state examination. The figure amounts to 350,000 civil servants who entered into public administration without any entry examination between 1973 and 1990. This contrasts negatively to the 250,000 civil servants who entered with entry examinations.[96] The problem does not seem to be the total number of civil servants in Italy at central, regional, local, and public sector agencies, but their low quality, poor morale, inefficient training, and sometimes over- or understaffing in certain sectors.[97] Italian devolution to the regions took twenty-two years following the approval of the constitution. Only in the 1970s were fifteen administrative regions and five special regions established that are in themselves regional political systems with electoral procedures. Until today, regional governments are regarded as extended arms of central administration, which certainly makes it difficult to distance themselves from this pattern of administrative behavior. In the 1990s, the government started a major reform of public administration in view of making it more transparent, accountable, and simplified. The privatization of the public sector during the Dini and Prodi administrations were major factors in modernizing the public sector. Although there is a long way to go, more competences were devolved to the regions during the D'Alema government under a new Bassanini local government law.[98] Accompanying this is a major reversal of the financial organization of the state. A so-called fiscal federalism is emerging slowly in Italy, which not only gives most of the competences to regions and communes but moreover allows them to raise taxes, something that was prevented until the 1990s.[99] The impact of European public policy and the fulfilment of the Maastricht criteria by the Prodi government were major factors in introducing major reforms in Italian administration.

Greece

In Greece, the legacy of public administration has been one of clientelism and patronage. This did not change after 1974. In reality, the whole process developed toward a web of systemic corruption. Similar to Italy, competitive examinations were almost eliminated or changed to allow sympathizers of the major party PASOK to enter public administration. This process of recruitment was naturally related to temporary positions that eventually were made permanent. This became quite prominent in all areas of public administration, but particularly in the public economic sector such as the Hellenic Telecommunications Organization (OTE), the Public Power Company (DIE), and the National Bank. Interestingly, when New Democracy came to power under Kostas Mitsotakis in 1990, it only emulated the policies of PASOK and started to dismiss all sympathizers of PASOK and replace them with ND people.[100] One particular problem of Greek administration is its lack of autonomy from political parties. Subservience toward political parties makes civil servants vulnerable to clientelistic strategies. Another factor is the fragmentation of the civil service in over 890 corps and a lack of horizontal coordination between ministries. The strong centralization of public administration enhances the power of the ministers in relation to the civil service, who are almost excluded from the central political bodies such as the cabinet.[101] In the end, administrative reform has been delayed until today. Indeed, any attempts at administrative reform did not rely on consensual agreement between the major parties, so one party tended to replace the administrative reform of the other party with its own proposals.[102] Some timid reforms have been undertaken under the Simitis government, but the Greek state continues to be heavily centralized. After joining the EC/EU, administrative regions were created for the sole purpose of managing the structural funds. These regions are naturally dominated by the central government and do not attempt to decentralize decision-making.

Since 1995, a major reform of the administration was introduced to make it more efficient. This is partly financed by the European Union. One of the principles of this reform is to improve the quality of service for the citizens by simplifying access to citizens' documents.

Decentralization through the new regions and the use of new technologies has become central to the modernization of the Greek administration. Success will depend on the ability to overcome the low level of functional efficiency and politicization of the decision-making process, the absence of stability and continuity of top-ranking personnel, and lack of coordinating mechanisms to make policy making more cohesive.[103] The National School of Public Administration and the National Center of Public Administration have been contributing since the mid-1980s to an improvement of the qualifications of civil servants.[104] In spite of all that, Simitis will have to make the difficult decisions in relation to downsizing public sector expenditure, which is a precondition for a sound integration in the Economic and Monetary Union.

National EU-Policy Coordination

Since the mid-1980s, all member states of the EC/EU are experiencing a growing pressure coming from the supranational level to adjust their political institutional setting to the demands of SEM and EMU. The pressure has been a constant one in the past twelve years and may increase in the near future. The main change can be observed in the processes of decision making. The main discussion is around the issue that the sovereignty of nation-states is being eroded by this European integration process. The growing Europeanization is leading to a shifting of decision-making processes from the national to the supranational level. This could be observed during the inclusion of European law into national law and the implications for national parliaments. In reality the context of erosion of national sovereignty is more complex. The recent thrust of European integration was only a response to a globalization thrust that is affecting all countries alike since the early 1970s. Today, one has started to talk and write about the "hollow" state, which has difficulties controlling processes inside its territories related to international criminal gangs and financial transactions.[105] What seems to emerge is what may be identified as a collective or shared sovereignty.[106] The European Union may be considered as such a strategy of nation-states to regain some lost sovereignty by creating a more flexible multilevel structure comprising the supranational, national, regional, and local levels. The present reshaping of the political systems in southern Europe may be seen in this context.

Portugal

The Portuguese political system had to introduce major changes to adjust to the European integration process. The Portuguese parliament was not very active in European affairs until the early 1990s. Although several laws assured the participation of the *Assembleia da Republica* in community affairs, the inertia of parliamentarians prevented a more efficient way of dealing with European legislation. This changed in 1992, when Portugal was incumbent of the presidency in the first half of the year and the general euphoria over membership was replaced by a more down-to-earth position of all political parties. The CDS-PP and the PCP were fierce opponents of further thrusts of European integration. They vehemently opposed the TEU. Nevertheless, on December 10, 1992, the TEU was overwhelmingly ratified in the Portuguese parliament. At the same time, parliament worked on a law to ensure better control of the government in European affairs. Law 20/1994 provided an adequate instrument to enhance the role of the Committee of European Affairs in the Portuguese Parliament.[107] Although several governmental reports were presented before 1994 to the Portuguese Parliament, the quality of work of this committee changed considerably in 1994–1995. For the first time, the committee managed to issue an opinion on the annual report of the government, that included opinions from all the specialized committees. The flow of information between government and parliament has improved considerably. Quite important was the performance of the Secretariat for European Affairs attached to the Ministry of Foreign Affairs during the Cavaco Silva period, which attempted to enhance the role of the Committee of European affairs.[108] The Socialist government managed to establish a reputation in European affairs. The former Secretary of State Francisco Seixas da Costa was quite competent, even if he tended to emphasize formalities in dealing with Portuguese representatives working in Brussels.[109] The climax of EU policy coordination is naturally the presidency of the Council of the European Union for a six-month period. Due to the fact that the Portuguese administration was not ready to organize such an event in 1986, it just delayed to the next possible event. In the first half of 1992 the Portuguese administration finally had the opportunity to organize a presidency. Although it had to deal with the negative referendum on Maastricht in Denmark and the crisis in Yugoslavia, it was regarded by Jacques Delors as a big success.[110] In the first half of 2000, the Socialist government had the opportunity to organize a presidency, which clearly was only a preparation for the Nice treaty at the end of the year. In spite of that, Portuguese administration was able to organize a very successful European Council in Lisbon in March, which led to the establishment of an Open Method of Coordination (OMC) in employment issues.[111] In this sense, Portuguese administration was quite successful in projecting the country in the European Union.

Like other countries the Portuguese government has and had difficulties coping with the amount of European matters coming from Brussels in due time, although the new law 20/94 and other measures have improved considerably the transposition of EC law into national law. Portugal is among the best performing member states regarding this issue. Another question, more difficult to evaluate, is the real transposition in policy making. Nevertheless, in relation to the period previous to 1992, the coordination of EU matters has improved substantially.[112]

Spain

Unlike in Portugal, the process of national EU policy coordination became more complex in Spain in the past fifteen years. Since 1985 a Joint Committee of Congress and Senate for Community Affairs (*Comision Mixta de Congreso y Senado para las Comunidades Europeas*) has been set up to deal with EC/EU legislation. Its competences were enhanced in a law issued in 1988. After Maastricht a new Law 8/1994 was adopted by the *Cortes*, which enhanced the rights of information of the Joint Committee in relation to EU matters. Presently the Joint Committee is entitled to receive regular reports after each European Council Meeting, regular information on the EU activities of the EU institutions, regular information on the guidelines of the European policy, and before each European Council a report on developments during the outgoing presidency. The Joint Committee has a posteriori government control powers. Moreover, the joint committee is more strongly involved in the EC law-making process, because the law stipulates that the joint committee is entitled to receive legislative proposals from the Commission on time, and issue opinions on them. Nevertheless, parliament has lost legislative powers in relation to EC legislation. Most of the European directives are transposed to national law via the administrative route through decree laws. Most of the EU legislation is technical in nature and requires mere changes of existing legislation.[113]

The main coordinator of European Union policy is the Secretariat for European Affairs attached to the Ministry of Foreign Affairs. In the past it proved to be quite efficient in promoting Spanish interests. It comprises two general-directorates: one dealing with technical coordination of community matters and the second coordinating juridical and institutional aspects of European integration. On the whole, the performance of Spain in community matters has been quite competent and well organized, in spite of its novelty for the country.[114]

The European integration process also changed the position of the autonomous communities within the political system. They lost substantial powers to the institutions in Brussels. After the Basque Country and Catalonia set up their own European offices,[115] all other autonomous communities followed suit.[116] Since the late 1990s, the regions are more strongly involved in the national EU policy coordination and—similar to Germany, Belgium, Austria, and the UK—are able to send representatives to the Council of Ministers. This is the reason why in 1993 a major debate was held in the Senate to transform it into a more genuine and efficient territorial representation chamber. The discussions are still going on, but in principle there is general consensus that the balance between supranational, national, and subnational levels has to be redesigned to assure the full participation of regions in the whole process of European integration. A further proposal is the establishment of an autonomous communities observatory that would make people aware of imbalances between central and regional institutions. It is quite important that the number of meetings between the national government and the governments of the autonomous communities has increased considerably to assure that there is some coordination of Spanish representatives in the commissions and in the COREPER committees.[117] A similar system of fusion through cooperative federalism like in the German case is emerging in Spain. Growing consultation and participation of the regions in central decision-making and of the central government in regional decision-making is the likely outcome of a process that is still going on.[118] The two Spanish presidencies of 1989 and 1995 were able to launch new initiatives in the European Union. In 1989, the presidency chaired by Felipe Gonzalez was very keen to promote issues related to Social Europe, particularly the *Charter of Fundamental Workers' Rights*. The second Spanish presidency, in the second half of 1995, pushed forward the Euro-Mediterranean partnership, also called the Barcelona process, and naturally the Euro. The third presidency, under the leadership of José Maria Aznar in the first half of

2002, had to dedicate itself to issues related to EU-Mercosur relations, particularly the crisis of Argentina, which is adversely affecting the Spanish economy, the Euro-Mediterranean partnership, and consolidation of the Euro as a currency.

Italy

The Italian political system was and is regarded as inefficient. The instability of government and the fragmentation of parliament are major factors in perpetuating this situation. The aspect of European integration was not very relevant until the adoption of the Single European Act. The Italian political system entered into dire straits when pressure to implement the SEM-Program by the end of 1992 created a backlog upon the institutional setting. In the period between 1987 and 1992 Italy was the country with the worst rate of transposition of European directives into national law. In 1991, Italy had only achieved transposing 76.1 percent of all laws, and in the same year the European Court of Justice had to deal with 288 cases of directives, which the Italian government failed to transpose. One of the main reasons is that the relationship between parliament and government was not very well coordinated in European affairs, so for a long time Italian governments tended to recur to the institution of governmental decree laws.[120]

Evaluation of European directives by the parliament was almost missing. After 1987, two laws changed this situation and contributed to an enhancement of the position of the Italian Parliament. The Fabbri Law (183/1987) was devised to speed Community legislation through the administration route and ensure consultation with regional assemblies and parliament. It also was meant to contribute to a process of "delegislation" in a highly legally oriented political system. Even more important became the La Pergola Law (86/1989), which established the centrality of parliament in the process of European policy making. The law stipulates that the government has to submit a report to the parliament on the conformity of national law with European law. The specialist committees of both houses of parliament express their opinion about the changes to be undertaken in domestic law. Furthermore, there is a report every six months on Italy's participation in the formation of European public policy. Moreover, a report on the sentences of the European Court of Justice that may entail changes to Italian legislation is a further duty of governments. Within parliament, the specialist committees of European Affairs have recourse to the opinions of different specialist committees, normally with one leading European Community specialist in each one, and elaborate the proposed changes to the legislation presented by the government.[120]

The main problem is not the legal instruments in place, but the overall EU affairs coordination by the Italian government. Until the late 1980s, the dominant body dealing with Community affairs was the Directorate for General and Political Affairs attached to the Ministry of Foreign Affairs. It was an important body to represent Italy in the Community institutions. It is linked to all important ministries of the Italian government and is the main channel to the Delegation of Permanent Representatives (COREPER) in Brussels. Until recently all fifty representatives were attached to the Ministry of Foreign Affairs.[121] Nevertheless, the growing impact of European legislation on Italy requested the establishment of a more specialized department that would deal with the specialized aspect of transposition of Community law into national law. A department for the coordination of European Community Policies had already existed for a long time, but it was endowed with more powers in Law 400/1988. The former Minister without Portfolio was now called the Minister of Community Affairs. The huge task of this minister, who was attached to the prime minister's office without any independent staffing and resources, could be only partially fulfilled until now. The rivalry with the Minister of Foreign Affairs continued to be a major problem for a more salient performance. During the 1990s, three interministerial committees were established in the areas of economic planning, industrial policy, and external trade policy, of which the Minister of European Affairs is a member. Nevertheless, the main problem seems to be the chronic understaffing of a body that not only has to coordinate policies at the central, regional, and local levels, but also is faced with an increasing number of new tasks.[122] Presidencies chaired by the Italian government always had the impression of being improvized at the last moment. This is naturally related to governmental instability and the confusion about the center of EU policy coordination.

Greece

The Greek political system has been always affected by the bipolarization between New Democracy and PASOK. The organisation of EU policy coordination was characterized by discontinuity in the past two decades. Nevertheless, one can witness general improvements since accession to the EC/EU in 1981. The scrutiny role of parliament of EU matters was stipulated in the law adopted by the Greek parliament during the ratification of the accession treaty. It foresaw that the Greek government had to submit a report to the parliament at the end of each parliamentary session. In reality, the first report was only submitted in 1989. It included a report of the first eight years of EU membership. Parliament failed to debate it. In 1990, a joint committee on European Affairs of twelve national MPs and twelve MEPs was set up to monitor the transposition of EU legislation into national legislation.[123] Nevertheless, their success was quite weak. In reality, it retained its role of rubber-stamping parliament. A recent revision of the constitution in March 2001 enshrined in the constitution that the Committee should be informed about European Union affairs—this did not lead to a major improvement.[124] On the contrary, very recently, Kostas Karamanlis, leader of the opposition party ND, expressed his frustration that the prime minister has avoided to give any account to parliament for months.[125]

The main coordinating body is the Secretariat for European Affairs attached to the Ministry of Foreign Affairs. It plays an important role in organizing the permanent representation (COREPER) in Brussels, consisting of officials of both the Ministry of Foreign Affairs and the other technical ministries. The number of representatives is about ninety, which is quite large. About 30 percent are co-opted from the Ministry of Foreign Affairs and 70 percent from the technical ministries. The reason for the large number of representatives has to do with the fact that all technical ministries want to have firsthand information about policy making in Brussels. Another, less official reason is that the Permanent Mission is used for patronage purposes and as a stepping-stone to enter into Community institutions. The process of coordination is further complicated by the lack of institutionalization of representation in the many working groups in the Council and Commission. Most of the ministries have a European unit that deals with aspects of European integration related to the specialized ministries. The main problem is that in the past two decades Greek administration was highly politicized by the two main parties, which created a situation of discontinuity of administrative culture and structure.[126]

Until now the Ministry of National Economy was able to preserve an independent position in relation to the Ministry of Foreign Affairs, monopolizing most issues related to finance and economy. The last decision-making instance is the prime minister's office with its cabinet, governmental council, and governmental committee. The prime minister has the last word in any policy aspect.[127]

Greek presidencies were in place in the 1980s and 1990s. A pattern emerged that is similar to that of the Italian presidencies. In spite of that, one can witness an improvement over time.[128]

In sum, public administrations and the systems of national EU policy-coordination had to be remodeled and improved in the 1990s due to the growing importance of EU legislation. All four countries had to adjust rapidly to the new demands. This adjustment was more successful among the Iberian countries, which saw an opportunity to enhance the prestige of their administrations by improving their coordinating structures in Brussels. Particularly, the Spanish national EU policy-coordination became more democratic due to the inclusion of the regional governments into the overall process. Italy and Greece have been less successful, the former because of excessive fragmentation at the center; the latter because of excessive centralization and overstaffing. All these reforms have to be related to the efforts of the European Union toward a convergence of public administration performance linking the fifteen administrative systems among themselves and the European bureaucratic structures. The so-called Europe of the administrations[129] is a less studied aspect of European integration, but making an extraordinary impact on southern European democracies in terms of creating the conditions for a more open, accountable, better administration. Introductions of elements of new public management and the transition from government to governance patterns are all part of this big transition that are more visible in southern European democracies.

DECENTRALIZATION, REGIONALIZATION, AND DEMOCRACY

In southern Europe, centralization and concentration of power is and has been a salient factor of the political system. Traditionally, all four countries had only two tiers of administration until the late twentieth century: national and local. Regional government began to emerge in the 1970s. Indeed, devolution is still in process. Several reasons account for the necessity to decentralize and deconcentrate the administrative structure of the political system. (See Table 3.11.) First, regionalization is related to the necessity to make national economies more flexible. The region is regarded as a more flexible unit to allocate new plant sites of transnational corporations. This economic dimension of regionalization enhanced the significance of regional and local elites for fostering regional and local development.

Second, regionalization responds to the need to make public policy more accountable to the regional population. Democratization of the decision-making process via decentralization and deconcentration strengthens the legitimacy of the political system and provides the population with a possibility to influence decision-making. A more decentralized democratic structure increases the level of transparency.

Third, regionalization is linked to regionalism/regionalist politics. This dimension enhances the diversity of the nation-state. This can be observed in Spain, where regionalism and regionalist politics are shaping the national political system. Regionalization can be regarded as an important element in creating a strong democracy. The southern European countries are still having to deal with these recent trends. The European Union is a major factor in fostering the reconstruction of national territories. Such reconstruction is accompanied by a territorial rationale that focuses on regional and local development.[130] Therefore, the following pages are dedicated to the growing importance of the local and regional dimension of the political system. This fits in the recent discussion about the "Europe of the Regions," which envisages a multi-level governance in the European Union consisting of several dimensions of decision-making: supranational, national, and subnational.[131]

The Regions

Portugal

In Portugal, the constitution of 1976 provides for the establishment of administrative regions (*regiões administrativas*) with partly directly elected regional assemblies and a regional government. The main task was to coordinate efforts of local authorities and serve as intermediary between local and central government. The Socialist party tried to achieve a compromise with the main opposition party to establish administrative regions, but in a referendum on November 8, 1998, two thirds of the voters decided against the division of the country in eight administrative regions. For the moment, the administration of the territory is coordinated by five deconcentrated Regional Coordinating Commissions (*Comissões Coordenadoras Regionais* [CCRs]) in Algarve, Alentejo, Lisboa, and Vale do Tejo, Centre, North of Portugal; the intermediary decentralized tier is the preconstitutional administrative unit of the district (*distrito*). The provincial assembly is co-opted by the local authorities and president by a civil governor (*governador civil*) appointed by the government. One main topic of discussion aspects is the fear that decentralization will lead to the desintegration of the traditionally unitary Portuguese state. This was used extensively by the right-center opposition parties during the referendum campaign.

Spain

The growing importance of the autonomous communities in Spain deserves special attention in this book. The Spanish regional level consists of three levels: the regional, the provincial, and the local governments. The regional level is regarded as a coordinating tier that shapes policy making at the provincial and local levels. The name for the regional level is autonomous communities (*comunidades autonomas* [CCAA]), which resemble, with minor differences, the institutional framework at the central level. The names adopted for the different institutions of the autonomous communities are related to their historical inheritance. For example, Catalonia's government is called *Generalitat de Catalunya*; in Galicia its equivalent is *Xunta de Galicia*. The dynamics of the autonomous communities have led to a devolution of powers from the central to the regional and local levels. Recently, one witnesses an increase of competences in foreign policy in the Basque Country and Catalonia. This is particularly the case of Catalonia, which is committed to the Europe of the Regions and follows the approach of regional government practiced by the German *Land* of Baden-Württemberg. Catalonia has increased its importance in the national political system since the mid-1990s due to its role as kingmaker. This contributed to a more active role of the other autonomous communities. Quite interesting is the rise of smaller regional governments such as the *Generalitat Valenciana*.[132]

Regionalist parties from these regions were integrated in the negotiations over the constitutional settlement. The formula was ill-defined and open-ended and led to a dynamic that contributed to the transformation of a highly centralized state into a semifederalist one. Between December 1979 and August 1983, seventeen autonomous communities came into existence, with their respective governmental structures. Faced with the regionalist dynamics, the UCD government tried to bring more uniformity and governmental control over a phenomenon that was getting out of hand. The Organic Law for the Harmonization of the Autonomy Process (*Ley Organica para la Armonizacion del Proceso Autonomico* [LOAPA]), enacted by the *Cortes* to rationalize the autonomy process in June 1982, was extremely opposed by the existing regions, particularly the Basque Country and Catalonia. Indeed, the Constitutional Court annulled LOAPA and thus strengthened the position of the Spanish regions—although the Socialist government after 1982 had several conflicts over the transfer of competences with the more historic regions of the Basque Country and Catalonia.[133]

Although the constitution provided two ways to achieve the statute of regional autonomy in Spain, the highest level of autonomy was granted to the historic regions of the Basque Country and Catalonia, which were already recognized during the Second Republic. In the second tier are the Galicians and Andalucians, which remained at same level as the other autonomous communities as soon as their statutes were approved. Later on, Valencia, Navarre, and the Canaries achieved autonomy, although with a lower level of power. Last but not least, all the other ten autonomous communities—Castilla y León, Castilla La Mancha, Extremadura, the Balearic islands, Madrid, Aragón, Asturias, Cantabria, Murcia, and Rioja— remained at the bottom level of granted competences.[134] The four-tier division of autonomous communities is in constant review due to the fact that the boundaries between the central and regional level are shifting continuously toward the latter. During 1995, six regional parliaments decided to reform their statutes— Canarias, Baleares, and Aragon, and later on, on a more modest scale, the regions of Asturias, Cantabria, and Castilla La Mancha. The case of Aragón was the most extreme, asking for a special regime of finance such as it exists for the Basque Country and Navarre. Another aspect is the growing devolution of competences in the fields of education and health to the autonomous communities to bring them to equal footing with the seven other regions, with a high level of competences. Competence disputes between central and regional governments declined substantially in the past two or three years. On the whole, regionalism is a dynamic process that is still ongoing. The growing self-confidence of regions, its recent impact on the national political system, and the development of multiple identities made Spain an interesting example among many other countries. At the moment, almost 40 percent of the national budget is spent at the regional and local levels. Nevertheless, the allocation of resources is still very centralized. Only the Basque Country and Navarre have the right to tax collection (as long as the two communities follow the national guidelines). The special regime is related to the *fueros* (historic charters of rights) acquired in the past. All the other regions are allocated tax-sharing funding from the central government. The seven autonomous communities with a high level of competence are able to take part in the decision-making process related to education and health. In Catalonia and the Basque Country the competences extend to policing. All autonomous communities are subject to the common financing regime with the exception of the Basque Country and Navarre due to the historical *fueros*. Some autonomous communities such as Asturias, Cantabria, Madrid, Murcia, La Rioja, and Navarre are allowed to levy provincial revenues. Moreover, regional taxes can be levied by six regions (Andalucia, Canary Island, Catalonia, Murcia, Valencia, and Basque Country).

TABLE 3.11 Subnational Territorial Organization in Southern Europe

	Regions	Subregional units	Local authorities
Portugal	5 Administrative regions (nonelected) 2 autonomous regions (Azores, Madeira) (elected)	22 Provinces (nonelected)	308 municipalities (elected)
Spain	17 autonomous communities (elected)	52 provinces (nonelected)	8,000 municipalities and communities (elected)
Italy	15 ordinary regions and 5 special regions (Val D'Aosta, Friuli-Venezia; Trentino-Adige; Sardinia; Siciliy)	54 provinces (elected)	8,000 municipalities and communities (elected)
Greece	13 administrative regions (nonelected)	54 counties (elected)	900 municipalities and 133 small communities (elected)

Still today Spanish regions are underfunded. Very few taxes are collected by the regions, nevertheless the Interterritorial Compensation Fund (*Fondo de Compensación Interterritorial* [FCI]) was devised to transfer funds from the richer regions to the less advantaged ones such as Andalucia and Extremadura. The main cleavage of regional disparities is southwest to northeast. Extremadura and Andalucia have a Spanish GDP average below 70 percent, whereas the provinces in Catalonia, Baleares, and Aragon achieve values above 100 percent. Also the rate of unemployment follows the same southwest/northeast cleavages. Unemployment is particularly high in Andalucia—between 31.5 percent and 23.5 percent; in Catalonia and Aragon, it is below 9 percent.[135]

The dynamics of the semi-federal organization of the Spanish state are reinforced by the role that representatives of regional government are playing in the upper house of the Spanish *Cortes*, the Senate. It is hoped that this chamber may be transformed into a stronger territorial chamber that is able to play an influential role in matters concerning regional, provincial, and local issues. A committee was established to discuss the change of the role of the Senate. In the legislature between 1993 and 1996 no agreement was achieved. After years of compromise with regionalist parties, the present PP government put devolution on hold for the time being. In spite of that, the PP electoral manifesto clearly wants to level the powers among the seventeen autonomous communities and give more say to the autonomous communities in the distribution of the structural funds.

Italy

Regional devolution in Italy is very recent. Although it is enshrined in the constitution of 1948, Italians had to wait until the early 1970s for the implementation of regionalization. The outcome was the establishment of fifteen so-called ordinary regions and five special regions. It took several years to draft regional constitutions, transfer administrative responsibilities, and get the agreement on financial arrangements worked out.

The Italian subnational government consists of three tiers: the commune (municipality), the province, and the region. The smallest unit is the commune. There are approximately 8,000 communes throughout Italy, which vary in size. Some towns can be regarded as large communes, but villages may be quite small. Sometimes communes are identical to the provinces. The province is the in-between unit. The region is the only unit with real powers. Although this has been enshrined in the constitution, the region is in reality a mere arm of centrally decided policies.

The regional bureaucracies are still very small in scope—176,000 civil servants in comparison with 3.4 million in the public service in total.

The process of regionalization is sustained by a general feeling of attachment of Italians to their regions against the southern poorer ones. Regionalist political movements such as the *Lega Lombarda* and *Lega Veneta* founded an umbrella organization called *Lega Nord* to achieve the independence of the northern regions from Italy. The main leader, Umberto Bossi, wants to establish the Republic of Padania, which shall comprise all rich regions of the north. The discourse of the *Lega Nord* is quite xenophobic in relation to the Italian south. Moreover, they attacked the Italian state as being dominated by southerners. The so-called southernization of public administration is regarded as the main reason the political system is so inefficient.[136]

A recent study on the performance of regional governments made people aware of the differences in efficiency between north and south. The south is lagging behind because regional governments are not supported by a strong civil society. In contrast, the regional governments in the north could recur to historical traditions of civil association existent since the Middle Ages. Such an explanation is further bolstered by factors such as long-term planning and efficient implementation. The study helped to clarify the importance of historical traditions upon today's performance of regional government, but refuses to take a deterministic stand by leaving the outcome of policies open to the possibility of change in behavior of local authorities.[137] It introduced the concept of social capital for analyzing the economic strength of a particular region. This was the main explanation for the gulf that exists between north and south. Regionalization has contributed substantially to the democratization of the political system, although some regional governments such as Sicily were involved in corruption scandals.[138]

According to Article 117 of the Constitution, the regions have legislative and administrative competences under seventeen headings mostly related to the setting up of infrastructures. Some of the headings such as regional transport networks, regional industrial development, vocational training and assistance, as well as health policy have become more important over time. A turnover of the regional political class after *tangentopoli* similar to the central political class did happen only after the regional and administrative elections of April–May 1995. According to Di Virgilio, 74.5 percent of the regional political class elected in 1995 was new in office.[139]

In recent times, the Italian government tried to simplify the decision-making process by further deconcentrating more competences based on the principle of subsidiarity. Particularly, in regard to transport and education the new local government Bassanini laws (59/97 and 127/97) established for the first time a united committee of state-regions and local governments (*conferenza unificata stato, regione e comuni*) that will lead to the abolishment of such partial bilateral coordinating mechanisms and making it more efficient and multilateral. This miniparliament will be consulted on legislative matters and particularly matters related to EU legislation. This opens a new first step toward a further federalization of the Italian Republic in view of a future revision of the constitution. Further devolution processes will completely change the relationship between center and the regions. More funding and competences shall give more autonomy to the regions according to the new laws agreed upon in 2000. The reform of the fifth title of the Constitution will grant more self-governnment powers to subnational government.[140] Italy is using the European integration process to become more hispanized in terms of the devolution process and reduce the inefficiencies in policy making by devolving more implementation powers in terms of European public policy, a normally chronic problem of Italian policy culture.

Greece

In Greece, the state was always highly centralized. Local government authorities always had limited powers. They were restricted to the implementation of infrastructures under the supervision of central government. The traditional centralistic tendency continued to prevail after the transition to democracy. Regional authorities were nonexistent in Greece. This situation is reinforced by a lack of interest in communal politics among citizens. First attempts to introduce regional governments were undertaken during the PASOK government between 1981 and 1989. The main reason was the need to monitor the implementation of EC Programs related to the European Regional Development Fund (ERDF) and the Integrated Mediterranean Programmes (IMPs). These monitoring regional institutions were established after 1986, but they were mere instruments of central government with almost no human and material resources. Its role was the monitoring and supervision of policies decided mainly at the central level. These regional councils had no legal identity outside the implementation of the IMPs. Thirteen administrative regions were created, which are more or less extended arms of the Greek central government (see Table 3.12). Like in the Portuguese case, the main intermediary tier between local and central government always has been the so-called *nomos* (prefecture). But even this tier awaited a more efficient provision with human and material resources. Law 1622 of 1986 provided for the council's transformation through the direct election of 75 percent of their members. The elections took place in autumn 1994, leading to an overwhelming majority of PASOK. In recent years, the regional councils have acquired more autonomy to shape the budget of the region. This is related to the growing pressure of the European Union to have more flexible and decentralized structures to implement policies.[141]

TABLE 3.12   Subnational Territorial Organization of Greece (1999)

Region	Counties	Municipalities (Demos)		Communities (Koinotites)	
	Number	Number	Population	Number	Population
Anatoliki Makedonia Thraki	5	47	554,630	8	15,866
Attici (Athens)	4	91	3,456,094	33	67,313
Voreio Aigaio	3	35	198,945	1	286
Dytiki Ellada	3	72	706,572	2	1,115
Dytiki Makedonia	4	44	283,501	17	9,514
Ipeiros	4	57	329,642	19	10,087
Thessalia	4	93	722,346	11	12,500
Ionia Nisia	4	33	191,783	6	1,952
Kentriki Makedonia (Thessaloniki)	7	126	1,699,858	8	9,119
Kriti	4	68	539,413	2	641
Notio Aigaio	2	45	252,208	13	5,273
Peloponnisos	5	100	601,950	7	5,478
Sterea Ellada	5	89	574,513	6	7,767
13	**54**	**900**	**10,111,455**	**133**	**146,911**

Source: http://www.eetaa.gr/statist_uk/perif_uk.html

Local Government

Portugal

Portugal's local government consists of 308 municipalities that are regularly exposed to the electoral process. This has naturally strengthened democracy at the grass roots. Local government in Portugal has gradually received more competences, nevertheless this has never been matched by an increase in financial resources. Financial difficulties is regarded as the major difficulty for local government. The ratio of government expenditure between central and local administration is 90 percent to 10 percent. This is naturally a major constraint for policy making at the local level. Another aspect is the lack of coordination between policy areas and other local government authorities. Local authorities had difficulties finding qualified personnel for some competences such as environmental policy. In the 1980s and 1990s, one could observe a growing recruitment of experts to deal with important policy areas for local government.[142]

On the whole, local government regained its place in Portuguese politics. The Association of Portuguese Local Government Authorities (*Associação Portuguesa de Autarcas Locais* [APAL]) has become an important powerful interest group always engaged in shifting boundaries of power from the center to the local government authorities.

Spain

In Spain, most of the 8,098 municipalities are underfunded. They have difficulties coping with the tasks allocated to them. The financial grants to local authorities are transferred from the central government via the intermediation of the regional governments. This naturally leads, in certain regions, to a renewed centralization of competences at the new level. A major problem for local government is the lack of cooperation between different municipalities. Another factor is the fact that over 7,000 municipalities have less than 5,000 inhabitants, leading to a dispersal of resources. The intermediary tier between regional and local government is the province. The fifty provinces of the Spanish state are still trying to find a place in the evolving political system. The growth and ascent of regional government are leading to the simultaneous decline of provincial government, a tier established in Spain during the nineteenth century. In some cases it is fighting with the local authorities to have autonomous communities with a low level of competence. Basically, the Spanish model of local government is following a similar to the German and Austrian one. The majority of the competences are shared between the three levels of government (central, regional, and local).[143]

Italy

Italian local government is presently in a period of transition. The presidentialization and personalization of most mayoral offices is transforming the whole system of accountability. Since the early 1990s, local government's financial situation has improved considerably, due to the decentralization of tax collection such as property tax and the ability to issue bonds.[144] According to the new Bassanini law, city managers will be contracted to supervise the whole policy-making process and strengthen the professionalism of local government administration.[145]

At the local level, it was attempted to found intermunicipal consortia so that the population can be provided with public services more efficiently. It is still to be seen if the growing deconcentration of the Italian government will lead to more fragmentation or, hopefully, more efficiency and citizen-friendly government.

Greece

Like in the Portuguese case, local government in Greece has been very restricted and very dependent on central government. Local government competences has been limited to street cleaning, rubbish collection, and the care and control of cemeteries. Local government authorities have been extremely limited in the field of social and welfare policy. Central control of the decision-making process prevented an autonomous role for the municipalities and communes (*demos* and *koinotites*). There are about 6,000 local government units. Aproximately 360 are municipalities and 5,560 communes. The former have to have at least 10,000 inhabitants, and the latter at least 1,000, but, as Susannah Verney argues, well over 3,000 of these units have less than 500 inhabitants. Although the PASOK government attempted to energize local government by giving more autonomy and competences to communes and municipalities, in reality the centralizing traditions prevented a change of political culture among local authorities. Moreover, a rationalization of local government through mergers between different communes or the creation of intermediary tiers was not successfully implemented.[146] In 1997, the "Kapodistrias Plan" was presented, which is designed to reduce the fragmentation of local government units to a more appropriate and efficient level.[147] In spite of that, local government in Greece continues to be dominated by central government. This is a major obstacle to democratization and decentralization of public policy-making. The European integration process is a major factor in promoting more decentralized structures in Greece, even though the political culture of centralization continues to prevail. Since the administrative regions were introduced the whole territorial organization was restructured so that some of the fragmentation could be overcome.

In sum, regional and local government are still evolving in southern Europe after decades of administrative centralization. One of the big challenges for southern European democracies is the ability to finally fulfill decentralizing and democratizing reform projects so that social capital and local civil society can be created in these highly centralized states.

CONCLUSIONS

Since joining the European Union, all four countries of southern Europe introduced major reforms and institution-building measures to make their political system more democratic, accountable, simplified, and transparent. This was particularly important in the process of decentralization and deconcentration of public administration, the introduction of elected local government, and reforms toward a regionalization of the political system. The central political system became somehow more stable in the second half of the 1990s. In spite of all that, a strengthening of the controlling institutions of government such as the parliament and judiciary is important so that cases of "political corruption," "bureaucratic clientelism" and *amiguismo* will become less likely in this new millennium. The European integration process is certainly a factor sustaining the modernization and further democratization of the political systems in southern Europe, but this has to be followed by an internalization of principles of accountability and transparency by the political elites and the populations alike.

NOTES

1. Victor Silva Lopes, *Constituição da Republica Portuguesa 1976* (anotada) (Lisboa: Editus, 1976); André Thomashausen, *Verfassung and Verfassungswirklichkeit in Portugal* (Berlin: Duncker und Humblot, 1981).
2. Thomas C. Bruneau, *Nationhood and Politics in Postrevolutionary Portugal* (New York; Praeger, 1984); Thomas Bruneau and Alex Macleod, *Politics in Contemporary Portugal: Parties and the Consolidation of Democracy* (Boulder, CO: Lynne Rienner, 1986); Ben Pimlott, "Portugal: Two Battles in the War of the Constitution," *West European Politics* (1980): 286–96.
3. José M. Magone, "The Assembleia da Republica: Discovering Europe," in *National Parliaments and the European Union*, ed. Philip Norton (London: Frank Cass, 1996), 151-165, particularly p. 157.
4. Manuel Braga da Cruz, "A revisão falhada do sistema eleitoral," in *Análise Social* 35 (154–155): 45–53.
5. Manuel Ramirez, *Partidos Politicos y Constitución (Un Estudio de las Actitudes Parlamentarias Durante el Proceso de Creación Constitucional* (Madrid: Centro de Estudios Constitucionales, 1989), 69–70.
6. Andrea Bonime-Blanc, *Spain's Transition to Democracy: The Politics of Constitution-Making* (Boulder, CO: Westview Press, 1987).
7. Jorge de Esteban, "El Proceso Constituyente Espanol 1977–78," in *La Transición Democratica Española*, ed. Felix Tezanos, Ramon Cotarelo, and Andres de Blas (Madrid: Editorial Sistema, 1993), 277–315.
8. A. Baldassare and C. Mezzanotte, *Introduzione alla Constituzione* (Roma-Bari: Editori Laterza, 1994), 63–64
9. Paul Ginsbourg, *The History of Society and Politics in Contemporary Italy* (Harmondsworth: Penguin, 1989), 100.
10. Ibid., 101
11. Gianfranco Pasquino, "Autopsia della Bicamerale," in *Politica in Italia. I Fatti dell'Anno e le Interpretazioni. Edizione 99*, ed. David Hine and Salvatore Vassalo (Bologna: Il Mulino, 1999), 117–18.
12. House of Parliament, Constitution of Greece voted by the fifth revisionary Parliament of the Hellenes on the 9th of June 1975 and entered into force on the 11th of June 1975 (Athens: House of Parliament, 1975).
13. Prodromos Dagtoglou, "Verfassung and Verwaltung," in *Südost Europa Handbuch, Bd. III: Griechenland*, ed. Klaus Detlev Grothusen (Göttingen: Vandenhoeck and Ruprecht, 1980), 13–53; particularly pp. 35–36.
14. José M. Magone, "Portugal: The Logics of Democratic Regime Building," in *Coalition Government in Western Europe*, ed. Wolfgang C. Müller and Kaare Strom (Oxford: Oxford University Press, 2000), 529–58.
15. Ibid., 555–56.
16. An autobiographical account of each of the prime ministers can be found in Victoria Prego, *Presidentes: Veinticinco anos de historia narrada por los cuatro jefes de Gobierno de la democracia* (Barcelona: Plaza Janés, 2000).
17. Paul Heywood, "Governing a New Democracy in Spain: The Power of the Prime Minister in Spain," *West European Politics* 14 (1991): 97–115.
18. A very good detailed study of Parliament-Government relations between 1993 and 1996 is Enrique Guerrero Salom, *Crisis y Cambios en las Relaciones Parlamento-Gobierno (1993–1996)* (Madrid: Tecnos, 2000).

19. Antonio Bar, "Spain," in *Cabinets in Western Europe*, ed. Jean Blondel and Ferdinand Muller-Rommel (London: Macmillan, 1988), 102–19, particularly p. 117.

20. El Pais, *Anuario* 2001, p. 150.

21. Paloma Román Marugán, "El Gobierno," in *Sistema Politico Español*, ed. Paloma Román (Madrid: McGraw-Hill, 2002), 235–58; particularly, p. 241.

22. Donatella Della Porta, *Lo Scambio Occulto: Casi di Corruzione Politica in Italia* (Bologna: Societá Editrice Il Mulino, 1992); Donatella Della Porta and Alberto Vannucci, *Un Paese Anormale: Come la Classe Politica ha perso l'Occasione di Mani Pulite* (Roma: Editori Laterza, 1999).

23. Gianfranco Pasquino, "Italy: A Democratic Regime under Reform," in *Political Institutions in Europe*, ed. Josep M. Colomer (London: Routledge, 1995), 138–69, particularly p. 162.

24. Geoffrey Pridham, *Political Parties and Coalitional Behaviour in Italy* (London, New York: Routledge, 1988), 80.

25. Donald Sassoon, *Contemporary Italy: Politics, Economics and Society since 1945* (London: Longman, 1986), 180–183.

26. Mark Gilbert, *The Italian Revolution* (Boulder: Westview Press, 1995); Sergio Fabbrini, "Dal Governo Prodi al Governo D'Alema: Continuitá o Discontinuitá?" In *Politica in Italia: I Fatti dell'Anno e le Interpretazioni*, ed. David Hine and Salvatore Vassalo (Bologna: Il Mulino, 1999), 139–59.

27. Maurizio Cotta, "Italy: A Fragmented Government," in *Cabinets in Western Europe*, ed. Jean Blondel and Ferdinand Müller-Rommel (Basingstoke, U.K.: Macmillan, 1988), 120–37, particularly p. 131.

28. Ibid., 128.

29. Ibid., 33.

30. Ibid., 135.

31. David Hine, *Governing Italy: The Politics of Bargained Pluralism* (Oxford: Oxford University Press, 1993), 222.

32. Geoffrey Pridham and Susannah Verney, "The Coalition of 1989–90: Inter-party Relations and Democratic Consolidation," *West European Politics* 14, no. 4 (1991): 42–69, particularly pp. 49–50.

33. Stephanos Pezmazoglou, "The 1980s in the Looking-Glass: PASOK and the Media," in *PASOK: A Decade of Populism*, ed. Richard Clogg (Basingstoke, U.K.: Macmillan, 1993), 94–112; George Mavrogordatos, "Civil Society under Populism," in *Greece 1981–1989: The Populist Decade*, ed. Richard Clogg (New York: St. Martin's Press, 1993), 46–63, particularly pp. 49–52.

34. Calliope Spanou, "Penelope's Suitors: Administrative Modernisation and Party Competition in Greece," *West European Politics* 19, no. 1 (1996): 97–124.

35. European Commission, *Greece—Common Support Framework 1994–99* (Office of the Official Publications of the European Communities, 1994).

36. Christos Lyrintzis, "Political Parties in Post-Junta Greece: A Case of 'Bureaucratic Clientelism'?" *West European Politics* 7, no. 2 (1984): 99–118.

37. George Mavrogordatos, "Greece," in European Political Data Yearbook 1992, *European Journal for Political Research* 22, (1992): 417–19, particularly p. 419; George Mavrogordatos, "Greece," in Political Data Yearbook 1994, *European Journal for Political Research* 26 (1994): 313–18, particularly pp. 315–16. Kostas Mitsotakis had to answer for corruption allegations coming from the parliament in 1994. Some cases related to telephone tapping affecting members of his own party as well as PASOK members including Andreas Papandreou, undertaken by Nikos Gryllakis, the security chief under Mitsotakis and phone company

employee Christos Mavrikis were later dropped by the Courts. The trial scheduled for January 1994 never took place. Finally, the Supreme Court dropped the charges against Mitsotakis, Gryllakis and Mavrikis (Balkans News International, April 23–29, 1995, p. 23).

38. *New Europe*, August 13–19, 1995, p. 33.

39. This happened only in January 1996 (*New Europe*, December 3–9, 1995, p. 23; *New Europe*, January 21–27, 1996, p. 24.

40. Simitis replaced Papandreou and was elected president of PASOK by the congress on June 30. In August 1996, he called for early elections scheduled for September 22, 1996, which he won with an absolute majority (*New Europe*, July 7–13, 1996, p. 31, and *New Europe*, August 25–31, 1996, p. 24).

41. Prodromos Dagtoglou, "Verfassung und Verwaltung," in *Südost Europa Handbuch, Bd. III: Griechenland*, ed. Klau Detlev Grothusen (Göttingen: Vandenhoeck and Ruprecht, 1980), 13–53, particularly pp. 37–38; Peter Zervakis, "Das Politische System Griechenlands," in *Die Politischen Systeme Westeuropas*, ed. Wolfgang Ismayr (Opladen: Leske and Budrich, 1997), 619–53, particularly p. 630.

42. José M. Magone, "Political Recruitment and Elite Transformation in Modern Portugal 1870–1999: The Late Arrival of Mass Representation," in *Parliamentary Representatives in Europe 1848–2000: Legislative Recruitment and Careers in Eleven European Countries*, ed. Heinrich Best and Maurizio Cotta (Oxford: Oxford University Press, 2000), 340–70, particularly pp. 354–64.

43. Cristina Leston Bandeira, "A Assembleia da Republica de 1976 a 1999," *Analise Social*, no. 154–55, 2000, pp. 175–205; Cristina Leston Bandeira,"O impacto das maiorias absolutas na actividade e na imagem do parlamento portugues," *Análise Social* 31, no. 135 (1996): 151–81.

44. Cristina Leston Bandeira, "The Role of the Portuguese Parliament Based on a Case-Study: The Discussion of the Budget, 1983–95," *Journal of Legislative Studies* 5, no. 2 (1999): 46–73.

45. Jordi Capo Giol, "Oposición y Minorias en las Legislaturas Socialistas," *Revista Española de Investigaciones Sociologicas*, no. 66, (1994): 91–113; Enrique Guerrero, "La Actividad del Congreso: Una Evaluación," *El Congreso de los Diputados en Espana: Funciones y Rendimiento*, ed. Antonia Martinez (Madrid: Tecnos, 2000), 141–71, particularly pp. 156–60.

46. A more detailed study can be found in Antonio Rubio and Manuel Cerdan, *El Origen del GAL: "Guerra Sucia" y Crimen del Estado* (Madrid: Temas de Hoy, 1997), and in Enrique Guerrero Salom, *Crisis y cambios*, 170–94.

47. *El Pais*, November 13, 2000, p. 25.

48. *El Pais*, December 16, 2001, p. 26.

49. Irene Delgado Sotillos, "Elites Politicas y Vida Parlamentaria: Actividades y Motivaciones de los Diputados Espanoles," in *El Congreso de los Diputados en Espana: Funciones y Rendimiento*, ed. Antonia Martinez (Madrid: Tecnos, 2000), 295–340, particularly pp. 315–19. According to a study, the Spanish Parliament is well regarded in public opinion, but citizens do not see it as a major locus of power. See Irene Delgado, Antonia Martinez, and Pablo Onate, *Parlamento y Opinion Publica en Espana* (Madrid: Centro de Investigaciones Sociologicas, Opiniones y Actitudes no. 19, 1998).

50. Maurizio Cotta, "The Rise and Fall of the 'Centrality' of the Italian Parliament: Transformation of the Executive-Legislative Subsystem after the Second World War," in *Parliaments in the Modern World: Changing Institutions*, ed. Gary W. Copeland and Samuel C. Patterson (Ann Arbor: The University of Michigan Press, 1994), 59–84.

51. Jack Brand and Thomas Mackie, "The 1994 Elections," in *Italian Politics: The Year of the Tycoon*, ed. Richard S. Katz and Piero Ignazi (Boulder, CO: Westview, 1995), 97–114, particularly pp. 100–103; Stefano Bartolini and Roberto D'Alimonte, "Les Elections Parlamentaires de 1994 en Italie: Competition Majoritaire et Realignment Partisan," *Revue Française de Science Politique* (1995): 915–53.

52. Luca Verzichelli, "The New Members of Parliament," in *Italian Politics: The Year of the Tycoon*, ed. Richard S. Katz and Piero Ignazi (Boulder: Westview, 1995), 115–34, particularly p. 118; Verzichelli, "The Uncertain Parliament: The Instability of Party Groups in Italy after 1994," *Polichange* 2 (1999): 4–6.

53. Vincent Della Sala, "Hollowing Out and Hardening the State: European Integration and the Italian Economy," *West European Politics* 20, no. 1 (1997): 14–33; *The Economist*, January 5, 2002, p. 26; *The Economist*, August 3, 2002, p. 32.

54. Vincent Della Sala, "The Relationship between the Italian Parliament and Government," in *Parliaments and Governments in Western Europe*, ed. Philip Norton (London: Frank Cass, 1998), 73–96; Paul Furlong, "Parliament in Italian Politics," in *Parliaments in Western Europe*, ed. Philip Norton (London: Frank Cass, 1991), 53–67; Mark Kesselman, Joel Krieger, Christopher S. Allen, David Ost, Stephen Hellman, and George Ross, *European Politics in Transition* (Boston: Houghton Mifflin Company, 2002), pp. 459, 477–478.

55. According to Jens Borchert, "Politik als Beruf: Die Politische Klasse in Westlichen Demokratien," in *Politik als Beruf: Die Politische Klasse in Westlichen Demokratien*, ed. Jens Borchert, in cooperation with Jürgen Zeiß (Opladen: Leske and Budrich, 1999), 29, Greek MPs receive L 17,000 per year, which clearly forces them to pursue their own careers. Most of them are lawyers.

56. Zervakis, "Das Politische," in Ismayr, 627–28.

57. Dyonissios G. Dimitrakopoulos, "Incrementalism and Path Dependence: European Integration and Institutional Change in National Parliaments," *Journal for Common Market Studies* 39, no. 3 (September 2001): 405–22, particularly p. 415.

58. Thomas Kurian, "Greece," in *World Encyclopedia of Parliaments and Legislatures*, vol. 1, ed. Thomas Kurian (Washington: Congress Books, 1999), 288; Nicos Alivizatos, "The Difficulties of Rationalization in a Polarized Political System: The Greek Chamber of Deputies," in *Parliament and Democratic Consolidation in Southern Europe: Greece, Italy, Portugal, Spain and Turkey*, ed. Ulrike Liebert and Maurizio Cotta (London, New York: Pinter Publishers, 1990), 131–60; Alivizatos, "The Presidency, Parliament and the Courts in the 1980s," in *PASOK 1981–89: The Populist Decade*, ed. Richard Clogg (New York: St. Martin's Press, 1993), 65–77.

59. Manuel da Braga Cruz , "O Presidente da República na Génese e Evoluçao do Sistema de Governo Português," *Análise Social* 29 (125–126): 237–65.

60. Maritheresa Frain, "Relações entre of Presidente e o Primeiro Ministro em Portugal: 1985–1995," *Analise Social* 30, no. 133 (1995): 653–77.

61. *Expresso*, December 22, 2001; *Expresso*, December 29, 2001; *Expresso*, January 4, 2002; *Expresso*, January 11, 2002.

62. Charles T. Powell, *Juan Carlos of Spain: Self-Made Monarch* (Basingstoke, U.K.: Macmillan, 1996); Michael T. Newton and Peter J. Donaghy, *Institutions of Modern Spain: A Political and Economic Guide* (Cambridge: Cambridge University Press, 1997), 31–44.

63. Enzo Balboni, "The President of the Republic, Judges, and Superior Council of the Judiciary: Chronicle of a Bitter Constitutional Battle," in *Italian Politics: A Review,* Vol. 7, ed. Stephen Hellmann and Gianfranco Pasquino (London: Pinter Publishers, 1992), 49–67.

64. Sondra Z. Koff and Stephen P. Koff, *Italy: From the First to the Second Republic* (London: Routledge, 2000), 144.

65. José M. Magone, *European Portugal: The Difficult Road to Sustainable Democrac.* (New York: St. Martin's Press, 1997), 52.

66. Ibid., 53

67. Pedro Coutinho Magalhães, "Democratização e Independencia Judicial em Portugal," *Análise Social* 30, no. 130 (1995): 51–90; Boaventura de Sousa Santos, Maria Manuel Leitão Marques, João Pedroso, and Pedro Lopes Ferreira, *Os Tribunais nas Sociedades Contemporaneas: O Caso Portugues* (Porto: Edicões Afrontamento, 1995), 403; José Magalhães, "Constituicao E As Suas Revisoes, A Lei e a Justiça," in *Portugal: 20 Anos de Democracia*, ed. Antonio Reis (Lisboa: Temas e Debates, 1996), 114–35.

68. Luis Lignau da Silveira, "O Provedor da Justica," in *Portugal: O Sistema Politico e Constitucional, 1974–1987*, ed. Mário Baptista Coelho (Lisboa: Instituto de Ciencias Sociais, 1989), 701–36.

69. *Die Zeit*, December 13, 2001, p. 2: In recent times, Garzón dealt with the request for extradition of General Pinochet, and now he is trying to bring Italian Prime Minister Silvio Berlusconi to trial in Spain, facing to allegations of fraud and corruption in relation to his television channel Telecinco.

70. *El Pais*, Anuario, 2001, p. 201

71. Ibid.,182; *El Pais*, July 23, 2000, p. 6; *El Pais*, Anuario, 2001, p. 201.

72. Ramon Arango, *Spain: From Repression to Renewal* (Boulder, CO: Westview Press, 1995), 170.

73. *El Pais*, Anuario, 1996, p. 184.

74. *El Pais*, Domingo, December 16, 2001, pp. 1–2.

75. David Nelken, "Stopping the Judges," in *Italian Politics: The Stalled Transition*, ed. Mario Caciagli and David I. Kertzer (Boulder, CO: Westview Press, 1996), 187–204; Della Porta and Vannucci, *Un Paese Anormale*, 56–57.

76. *La Repubblica*, March 10, 2000, p. 14.

77. Donatella Della Porta, "A Judges' Revolution? Political Corruption and the Judiciary in Italy," *European Journal for Political Research* 39, no. 1 (2000): 1–21. This is confirmed by the difficulties the judiciary has in dealing with several of the pending processes of Prime Minister Silvio Berlusconi. The obstruction shown by *Il Cavaliere* has undermined the credibility of the judiciary once again. See *Corriere della Sera*, January 9, 2002, pp. 7–8.

78. George Mavrogordatos, "Greece," in *European Journal for Political Research* 22, p. 418.

79. Prodromos Dagtoglou, "Verfassung," p. 31; Alivizatos, "The Presidency," in Clogg, *PASOK*, 70–72; Zervakis, "Das Politische," in Ismayr, 647–48.

80. Walter C. Opello, Portugal's Political Development: A Comparative Approach (Boulder, CO: Westview Press, 1985); António Costa Pinto, "Dealing with the Legacy of Authoritarianism: Political and Radical Right Movements in Portugal's Transition to Democracy, 1974-1980s," in *Modern Europe after Fascism*, ed. Stein Ugelvik Larsen, with assistance of Bernt Hagtvet (New York: Columbia University Press, 1998), 1679–1717.

81. Fernando Farelo Lopes, "Partisanship and Political Clientelism in Portugal (1983–1993)," *South European Society and Politics* 2, no. 3 (1997): 27–51, particularly pp. 38–49.

82. Lawrence Graham, *The Portuguese Military and the State: Rethinking Transitions in Europe and Latin America* (Boulder, CO: Westview Press, 1993).

83. Alvaro Xosé López Mira, "Portugal: The Resistance to Change in the State Model," *Regional and Federal Studies* 9, no. 2 (1999): 98–115.

84. Directorate-General for Public Administration (DGAP), *The Profile of the Portuguese Public Administration* (Lisbon: DGAP, 2000), 17; Magone, *European Portugal*, p. 55.

85. *The Economist*, "Survey on Portugal," December 2, 2000, pp. 10–11; *The Economist*, July 21, 2001, p. 36–37.

86. *O Publico*, December 17, 2001; *O Publico*, December 18, 2001.

87. Jaime Ferri Durá, "Las Administraciones Públicas" in *Sistema Politico Espanol,* coord. Paloma Roman (Madrid: McGraw-Hill, 1995), pp.160-181, particularly pp. 166-167.

88. Jeanie Bukowski, "Decentralization in Spain: A Re-evaluation of Causal Factors," *South European Society and Politics* 2, no. 3 (1997): 80–102, particularly p. 82.

89. Ibid., 86; José M. Magone, "EU Territorial Governance and National Politics: Reshaping Marginality in Spain and Portugal," in *Margins in European Integration*, ed. Noel Parker and Bill Armstrong (Basingstoke, U.K.: Macmillan, 2000), 155–77, particularly pp. 163–69.

90. *El Pais*, March 1, 2000, p. 28.

91. Della Porta and Vannucci, *Un Paese Anormale*, pp. 92–99.

92. Ibid, p. 100.

93. Sabino Cassese, "Hypotheses on the Italian Administrative System," *West European Politics* 16, no. 3 (1993): 316–28, particularly pp. 322–23.

94. *Eurobarometer* no. 56 (Autumn 2001), pp. 16–17; Leonardo Morlino and Mario Tarchi, "The Dissatisfied Society: The Roots of Political Change in Italy," *European Journal for Political Research* (July 30, 1996): 41–63.

95. Cassese, 324; Sabino Cassese, "Italy's Senior Civil Service: An Ossified World," in *Bureaucratic Elites in Western European States*, ed. Edward C. Page and Vincent Wright (Oxford: Oxford University Press, 1999), 55–64, particularly p. 56.

96. Hilary Partridge, "Can the Leopard Change Its Spots? Sleaze in Italy," *Parliamentary Affairs* 48, no. 4 (October 1995): 711–25, particularly p. 713.

97. Hine, *Governing Italy*, 236–38.

98. Mark Gilbert, "Le Leggi Bassanini: Una Tappa Intermedia Nella Riforma Dello Governo Locale," in *Politica in Italia: I Fatti dell'Anno e le Interpretazioni*, ed. David Hine and Salvatore Vassalo (Bologna: Il Mulino, 1999), 161–80, particularly p. 161.

99. R. E. Spence, "Italy," in *Comparative Public Administration*, ed. J. A. Chandler (London: Routledge, 2000), 126–46, particularly pp. 140–42. Two important taxes were introduced at regional and local levels, the so-called Regional Tax on Productive Activity (IRAP) and the local property tax (ICI). The principle of subsidiarity is a big buzzword in these reforms.

100. George T. Mavrogordatos, "From Traditional Clientelism to Machine Politics: The Impact of PASOK Populism in Greece," *South European Politics and Society* 2, no. 3 (1997): 1–26, particularly pp. 17–18.

101. Dimitri A. Sotiropoulos, "Description of the Greek Higher Civil Service," in *Bureaucratic Elites in Western European States*, ed. Edward G. Page and Vincent Wright (Oxford: Oxford University Press, 1999), 13–21.

102. Spanou, "Penelope's Suitors," 101–14; Dimitri A. Sotiropoulos, *Populism and Bureaucracy: The Case of Greece under PASOK, 1981-1989* (Notre Dame, London: University of Notre Dame, 1996), 79–108; Sotiropoulos, "Description," in Page and Wright, pp. 18–19.

103. P. C. Ioakimidis, "The EC and the Greek Political System: An Overview," in *Greece and EC Membership Evaluated*, ed. Stavros Theophanides (London: Pinter

1994), 139–53, particularly pp. 148–49; Kevin Featherstone, "'Europeanization' and the Centre Periphery: The Case of Greece in the 1990s," *South European Society and Politics* 3, no. 1 (1998): 23–39; Secretariado Para A Modernizacao Administrativa (SMA), *1st Quality Conference for Public Administrations in the EU: Sharing Best Practices. Conference Working Papers* (Lisbon: SMA, 2000), 296–98.

104. SMA, *1st Quality Conference*, 57–62.

105. Wolfgang C. Müller and Vincent Wright, "Reshaping the State in Western Europe: The Limits of Retreat," in *The State in Western Europe*, ed. Wolfgang Müller and Vincent Wright. Special issue of *West European Politics* 1 (1994): 1–11.

106. William Wallace, "The Sharing of Sovereignty: The European Paradox," *Political Studies* 47 (1999): 503–21

107. José M. Magone, "The Assembleia," in Norton, 156–57.

108. Ibid., 161–62.

109. *O Independente*, August 2, 1996, p. 14.

110. Magone, *European Portugal*, pp. 764–70.

111. Joao Pedro da Silveira Carvalho, "Prioridades e resultados da presidencia do Conselho da UE," *Europa: Novas Fronteiras* 7 (2000): 14–23.

112. For further reading on policy coordination at the domestic level, see José M. Magone, "Portugal," in *The National Coordination of EU Policy*, ed. Hussein Kassim, Guy Peters, and Vincent Wright (Oxford: Oxford University Press 2000); Federiga Bindi Calussi, "O Processo de Tomada de Decisões em Politica Comunitária," *Análise Social* 35, nos. 154–155 (2000): 383–404.

113. Carlos Closa, "Spain: The Cortes and the EU-A Growing Together," in *National Parliaments and the European Union*, ed. Philip Norton (London: Frank Cass, 1996), 136–150, particularly p. 144.

114. *The European*, June 23–29, 1995, p. 11.

115. Catarina Garcia, "The Autonomous Communities and External Relations," in *Democratic Spain: Reshaping External Relations in a Changing World*, ed. Richard Gillespie, Fernando Rodrigo, and Jonathan Story (London: Routledge, 1995), 123–40, particularly pp. 123–125.

116. Francesc Morata, *La Unión Europea: Procesos, actores y politicas* (Barcelona: Ariel, 1998), 401.

117. Manuel Sanchez de Dios, "Executive Parliamentary Control," in *Spain and EC Membership Evaluated*, ed. Amparo Almarcha Barbado (London: Pinter 1992), 219–28, particularly pp. 223–26; J. Zabala Otegui, "La Participacion Regional en el Proceso de Integracion Europea," *Revista Vasca de Administracion Publica*, no. 35 (Enero–Abril, 1993): 167–223; Morata, *La Unión Europea*, 395–99; Ignacio Molina, "2000: Spain," in *The National Co-ordination of EU Policy: The Domestic Level*, ed. Hussein Kassim, Guy B. Peters, and Vincent Wright (Oxford: Oxford University Press, 2000), 114–40.

118. T.A. Börzel, "From Competitive Regionalism to Cooperative Federalism: The Europeanization of the Spanish State of Autonomies," *Publius, Journal of Federalism* 30, no. 2 (2000): 17–42.

119. Paul Furlong, "The Italian Parliament and European Integration—Responsibilities, Failures, and Sucesses," in *National Parliaments and the European Union*, ed. Philip Norton (London: Frank Cass, 1996), 35–45; particularly pp. 34-36; David Hine, "Italy and Europe: The 1990 Presidency and the Domestic Management of European Community Affairs," in *Italy, the European Community and the 1990 Presidency: Policy Trends and Policy Performance*, ed. Phil Daniels, David Hine, and Marinella Neri Gualdesi (Bristol: University of Bristol—Centre for Mediterranean Studies, 1991), Occasional Paper no. 3, pp.17–38, particularly pp. 22–23.

120. Furlong, "The Italian Parliament," in Norton 39–45.

121. Hine, *Governing Italy*, 290–92.

122. Ibid., 293-97; Hine, "Italy and Europe," in Daniels, Hine, and Gualdesi, 30–35; Giacomo Della Cananea, "Italy," in *The National Co-ordination of the EU Policy: The Domestic Level*, ed. Hussein Kassim, Guy B. Peters, and Vincent Wright (Oxford: Oxford University Press, 2000), 99–113; David Hine, "European Policy-Making and the Machinery of Italian Government," in *Europeanization and the Southern Periphery*, ed. Kevin Featherstone and George Kazamias (London: Frank Cass, 2001), 26–46.

123. Dionyssis Dimitrakopoulos, "National Policy Formulation on European Issues in the Mediterranean Member-States: The Cases of Italy and Greece," in *Contemporary Political Studies: Proceedings of the Annual Conference held at the University of York, April 18th–20th 1995*, ed. Joni Lovenduski and Jeffrey Stanyer (Belfast: PSA), 1486–97, particularly p. 1494.

124. Dionyssis G. Dimitrakopoulos, "Incrementalism and Path-Dependence: European Integration and Institutional Change in National Parliaments," *Journal of Common Market Studies* 39, no. 3 (September 2001): 405–22; particularly pp. 413–15.

125. Athens News Agency, October 15, 2001.

126. Michael Christakis, "Greece: Competing with Regional Priorities," in *Adapting to European Integration: Small States and the European Union*, ed. Kenneth Hanf and Ben Soetendorp (London: Longman, 1998), 84–99.

127. Calliope Spanou, "Greece," in *National Coordination of EU Policy: The Domestic Level*, ed. Hussein Kassim, Guy Peters, and Vincent Wright (Oxford: Oxford University Press, 2000), 161–81.

128. P. C. Ioakimidis Stelios Stavridis and Achilleas Mitsos, *The Greek Presidency of the European Union, 1994*, in Occasional Paper, no. 12, September 1995, Centre for Mediterranean Studies, University of Bristol.

129. See the insightful article by June Burnham and Moshe Maor, "Converging Administrative Systems: Recruitment and Training in EU Member-States," *Journal of European Public Policy* 2, no. 2 (June 1995): 185–204.

130. Evelyne Ritaine, *Hypothèses pour le Sud de l'Europe: Territoires et Médiations*. Badia Fiesolana, Firenze: European University Institute, 1996, working papers, no. 96/33; Richard Balme, Philippe Garraud, Vincent Hoffman-Martinot, and Evelyne Ritaine (in collaboration with Lawrence Bonnet and Stéphanie LeMay), "Les Politiques Territoriales en Europe de l'Ouest," *Revue Française de Science Politique*, 43 (June): 453–68.

131. Liesbet Hooghe and Gary Marks, *European Integration and Multilevel Governance* (Lanham, U.K.: Rowman and Littlefield, 2001).

132. Kepa Sodupe, "La Union Europea y la Cooperación Interregional," in *Nacionalidades y Regiones en la Unión Europea*, coord. Francisco Letamendia (Madrid: Fundamentos, 1999): 13–50.

133. Jordi Solé-Vilanova, "Spain: Developments in Regional and Local Government," in *Territory and Administration in Europe*, ed. Robert Bennett (London: Pinter, 1989), 205–29, particularly, pp. 209–13.

134. Audrey Brassloff, "Spain: Democracy and Decentralisation," in *European Insights: Postwar Politics, Society and Culture*, ed. A.M. Brassloff and W. Brassloff (Amsterdam: Elsevier Science Publishers, 1990), 57–68; Juan Luis Paniagua Soto (ed.), *Gobierno y Administración en las Comunidades Autonomas, Andalucia, Canarias, Cataluna, Galicia y Pais Vasco* (Madrid: Tecnos, 2000); Miquel Caminal Badia and Jordi Matas Dalmases, *El Sistema Politic de Catalunya* (Madrid: Tecnos, 1998); Adela Mesa, "La Politizacíon de las Estructuras Administrativas de las Comunidades Autónomas," *Revista Espanola de Ciencia Politica* 1, no. 2 (April 2000): 211–35; Fabiola Mota and Joan Subirats, "El Quinto Elemento: El Capital Social

de las Comunidades Autónomas: Su Impacto Sobre el Funcionamiento del Sistema politico Autonómico," *Revista Española de Ciencia Politica* 1, no. 2 (April 2000): 123–58.

135. *El Pais*, Anuario 2001, p. 446.

136. Dwayne Woods, "The Rise of Regional Leagues in Italian Politics," *West European Politics* 15, no. 2 (April 1992): 56–76; Carlo Ruzza and Oliver Schmidtke, "Roots of Success of the Lega Lombarda: Mobilization, Dynamics and Media," *West European Politics* 14, no. 1 (1993): 1–24; Dwayne Woods, "The Crisis of Center-Periphery Integration in Italy and the Rise of Regional Populism: The Lombard League," *Comparative Politics* 27, no. 2 (January 1995): 187–203; Tom Gallagher, "The Regional Dimension in Italy's Political Uphearsal: The Role of the Northern League 1984–1993," *Parliamentary Affairs* 47, no. 3 (July 1994): 456–68.

137. Robert Putnam, *Making Democracy Work: Civic Traditions in Italy* (Cambridge, MA: Harvard University Press, 1993).

138. Della Porta, *Lo Scambio Occulto*, 135–42.

139. Aldo di Virgilio, "The Regional and Administrative Regions: Bipolarization with Reserve," in *Italian Politics: The Stalled Transition*, ed. Mario Caciagli and David I. Kertzer (Boulder, CO: Westview Press, 1996), 41–68; particularly pp. 63–64

140. Gilbert, "Le Leggi Bassanini," 172–79; Andrea Ciaffi, "Multilevel Governance in Italy: The Case of Marche," *Regional and Federal Studies* 11, no. 2 (2001): 115–46, particularly pp. 120–21. Articles 121, 122, 123, and 126 of the Constitution were changed.

141. Susannah Verney, "Central State-Local Government Relations," in *Greece and EC Membership Evaluated*, ed. Stavros Theophanides (London: Pinter, 1994), 166–79, particularly pp. 171–74; Kevin Featherstone and George N. Yannopoulos, "The EC and Greece: Integration and the Challenge to Centralism," in *The European Union and the Regions*, ed. Barry Jones and Michael Keating (Oxford: Clarendon, 1995), 249–66.

142. Juan Mozzicafreddo, Isabel Guerra, Margarida Fernandes, and Joao Quintela, *Gestao e Legitimidade no Sistema Politico Local* (Lisbon: Escher, 1991); César Oliveira, "A Construção do Poder Local Democrático," in *História dos Municipios e do Poder Local*, ed. César Oliveira (Lisboa: Temas e Debates), 361–494, particularly the subsection written by Carlos Nunes da Silva, "O Financiamento dos Municipios," pp. 433–62; Although there was an instrument to rebalance central-local expenditure called the Financial Equilibration Fund (*Fundo de Equilibrio Financeiro*) in the 1990s, still today Portugal has been, along with Greece, at the bottom of the European Union in terms of receipts and expenditure, in contrast to Denmark, Finland, and Sweden, which were at the top (p. 451).

143. Ernesto Carrillo, "Los Gobiernos Locales," in *Sistema Politico Espanol*, ed. Paloma Román (Madrid: McGraw-Hill, 2002), 315–38, particularly pp. 324–25.

144. Bruno Dente, "Subnational Governments in the Long Italian Transition," *West European Politics* 20 (1): 176–90, particularly p. 188.

145. Gilbert, "Le Leggi Bassanini," 165–66.

146. Verney, "Central State-Local Government Relations," p. 169.

147. P.C. Ioakimidis, "The Europeanization of Greece: An Overall Assessment," in *Europeanization and the Southern Periphery*, ed. Kevin Featherstone and George Kazamias (London: Frank Cass, 2001), 73–94, particularly p. 85.

4

Party Politics in Southern Europe

THE LATECOMERS TO WEST EUROPEAN POLITICS

The genesis of modern political parties took a long time to materialize in most countries of Western Europe. The competitive nature through elections was the most salient feature of its modernity. The creation of modern mass parties in the nineteenth and early twentieth centuries was important because the size of the electorate was gradually enlarged. A universal secret suffrage became established in most west European democracies between 1900 and 1945. After World War II, mass parties were gradually replaced by catchall parties that were more interested in maximizing the number of votes in elections. Since the 1980s, the cartel party is steadily replacing the catchall party. This new kind of party is interested in keeping in power and is highly dependent on subventions from the state. It is basically an office-seeking party.[1]

The southern European countries were only latecomers to a process that has been going on since the establishment of the modern nation-state. The discontinuity of party system development is their main feature.

THE DECLINE OF IDEOLOGY AND THE AMERICANIZATION OF PARTIES IN SOUTHERN EUROPE

According to Klaus v. Beyme, an Americanization of European politics is taking place in this postmodern era. He wonders how the American system of patronage is becoming the model for postmodern politics. Klaus v. Beyme defines this new development as follows:

> "Americanisation" in this context rather means the development of functional equivalent of American parties with little ideological profile and strong orientation towards patronage. Mass parties of the era of classical modernity could no longer be developed in the latest waves of democratisation in South and East Europe. These developments were hardly deliberate choices of party leaders in postmodern democracies. They were rather the result of long-term changes in the political systems and the respective societies. Much of what was dubbed "decline of parties" has proceeded to be "change in party systems."[2]

The discontinuity of political systems (see Chapter 2) in southern Europe made it impossible for parties to develop from mass party to catchall party and later on to a cartel party. The new southern European party systems in Spain, Portugal, and Greece were challenged from the very start by these changes of electoral politics that were going on in other west European countries. The whole nature of party politics was an imported package, in which past legacies, if they were existent, played a minor role.

THE CREATION OF MODERN PARTIES AND THE INTERNATIONAL ENVIRONMENT

The creation of modern parties in the late twentieth century was particularly facilitated by a positive international environment toward democracy. Indeed, democratic parties in most west European democracies created political foundations to support the establishment of a democratic civil society in their respective countries or in other countries. Particularly two German foundations attached to the major German parties were and are global players in democracy assistance and contributed to the stabilization of all three new party systems. The Konrad Adenauer Foundation attached to the Christian Democratic Union (*Christlich-Demokratische Union* [CDU]) and the Friedrich Ebert Foundation attached to the German Socialdemocratic Party (*Sozialdemokratische Partei Deutschland* [SPD]) were major players in providing logistics and financial support to the new parties belonging to the respective political families in Spain, Portugal, and Greece. In this context, the Cold War was a further factor pushing these international foundations to support democratic parties against an eventual takeover by Communist or left-wing radical parties.

The best example continues to be the Portuguese case. The revolutionary process got out of hand in the summer 1975, so that under the leadership of Mário Soares the international Western community was asked to support the democratic forces against a threatening colonization of the state by the Portuguese Communist Party (PCP). The SPD with its Friedrich Ebert Foundation became a major player in ensuring the continuing process toward democratization in Portugal. The strong support of the German social democrats also targeted the trade union sector. Indeed, in cooperation with the liberal social-democratic party in Portugal a new trade union confederation called the General Union of Workers (*União Geral dos Trabalhadores* [UGT]) was created to fight against the dominant Communist General Confederation of Portuguese Workers (*Confederacão Geral dos Trabalhadores Portugueses Intersindical* [CGTP-In]) in 1978. This ideological struggle ended in the late 1980s.[3]

Similar logistical and financial support was granted to the Spanish Socialist Workers' Party (*Partido Socialista Obrero Espanol* [PSOE]) and the attached General Union of Workers (*Unión General de los Trabajadores* [UGT]) against the Spanish Communist Party and the dominant Workers' Commissions (*Comisiones Obreras* [CCOO]).[4]

In Greece, New Democracy was able to profit from its international linkages. The connections of leader Kostas Karamanlis were more oriented toward France. Until the mid-1980s the Socialist International had difficulties dealing with PASOK because of its verbal-radical ideology. This began to change in the second half of the 1980s and 1990s, when the party became more similar to its counterparts in Western Europe.

The experience of the political foundations with the southern European party systems was extremely valuable to deal with emerging new parties in Latin America and central and Eastern Europe. This naturally further enhances the necessity to study this new dimension of party system building more closely in future studies.[5]

PARTY FAMILIES: THE ATTACHMENT TO WESTERN EUROPE

The Socialist/Social Democratic Party Family

Portugal

The Portuguese Socialist Party was founded in April 1973 in Bad Münstereiffel with the support of the German SPD. One year later, it became the most important party during the revolutionary process. Its ideological makeup was more radical than that of the other west European social democratic parties. It proposed the establishment of a democratic Socialist society based on long-term cultural revolution, of which the central aim was the establishment of a strong education sector.[6]

The PS was targeted as a counterrevolutionary party by the Communist party and other left-wing parties during the revolution. After the revolutionary process, the PS headed two governments between 1976 and 1978. The lack of qualified personnel, the severity of the economic and social problems, the lack of cohesion inside the party, and the very scarce relative majority led to its downfall in 1978.[7] It returned to power in 1983. Throughout the 1980s and 1990s, the Socialist party was characterized by factionalism. The personality of Mário Soares tended to lead to factions inside the party against new leaders such as Vitor Constancio, Jorge Sampaio, or Antonio Guterres. Since the victory of the PS in 1995, such factionalism became less evident.[8] Antonio Guterres was able to unite the party around a modernization of the party. He repeated his victory in the elections of October 10, 1999. After losing in major cities such as Lisbon, Porto, and Coimbra in the local elections of December 16, 2001, Guterres resigned from office. The Socialist Party started the process of looking for a new leader. The new leader became Eduardo Ferro Rodrigues. In terms of membership the official figure is over 100,000, but this may be too high.[9]

Spain

In Spain, the Spanish Socialist Workers' Party (*Partito Socialista Obrero Español* [PSOE]) was founded in 1879 and already has a long history in Spanish politics. The most important leader in the early period of the PSOE was Pablo Iglesias. Historically, the climax of the PSOE was the Second Republic (1931–1936), when it became the most important party on the left. During the authoritarian dictatorship, the PSOE continued its existence inside the country, but it became only more active in the late phase of Francoism. Felipe Gonzalez, alias "Isidro," Alfonso Guerra, Nicolas Redondo, and Enrique Mugica belonged to this leadership group. The Andalusian Gonzalez and Alfonso Guerra later became the uncontested leaders of the party. Felipe Gonzalez established himself as uncontested secretary-general in the party conference of 1979, one hundred years after the foundation of the party. Since then he remained secretary-general of the party until 1996. The party organization is federal, but with strong centralistic tendencies. In 1997 the PSOE had 373,030 members. Meanwhile, membership declined to 200,000 in 2001. In 1993, they were mainly from the working classes (39.7 percent), different groups of the middle classes, and the self-employed (16 percent).[10] In terms of historical geography, the PSOE is strong in Andalusia, Extremadura, and other southern regions as well as Euzkadi and the region of Madrid.[11]

The Socialist party was able to capture an absolute majority in 1982, 1986, and 1989 and a strong relative majority in 1993. It remained in power for fourteen years. In terms of policies the Socialist government recognized from early on the need to develop a realistic economic policy. Therefore, the very radical verbal rhetoric of the PSOE in 1982 was soon replaced by a more moderate one, emphasizing the need to modernize the economy via a stronger integration in global economic circuits. The party intended to achieve a stronger welfare policy focusing mainly on redistribution after a legislature that would lead to a flexibilization of the labor market and the reconversion of the public sector. It was hoped that the opening of the Spanish economy would lead to the conquest of new markets in Latin America and other parts of the world. The minister of finances Carlos Solchaga, and later on Miguel Boyer, clearly followed a liberalist-monetarist program to modernize the Spanish economy. The policies of the PSOE were supported by both trade union confederations until 1985. But in 1985, the PSOE wanted to further flexibilization of the economy without improving the condition of workers, leading to a final breakup of the trade union confederations with the party.[12]

The longevity of government led to the establishment of what James Petras called "patrimonial socialism." He meant that the Socialist government allied with the "beautiful people" of the financial and industrial elite to build up a ruling oligarchy solely interested in staying in power. Among the most prominent economists and bankers related to the Socialist government were Mário Conde, Juan Abelló, Alberto Alcocer, and Miguel Boyer. Personal enrichment and corruption were intertwined with the PSOE government. According to Petras, many senior positions in the administration were allocated to Socialists and their family members.[13] Inside the party, factionalism and discontentment began to be more pronounced after 1986. The more leftwing factions of the party wanted the PSOE to move toward more socially oriented policies. In spite of the fact that Alfonso Guerra, the deputy prime minister up until 1992, had built up a clientelistic network on behalf of *Felipismo*, which was devised to control the party. After a corruption scandal related to the abuse of public facilities by his brother Juan in Andalusia, Guerra instrumentalized his clientelistic network to fight against the *renovadores* (the moderate leaders of the party who wanted a renewal of the party). Factionalism became more visible after 1992.[14] Between 1989 and 1996 the public was confronted with several corruption scandals such as Filesa, the Luis Roldan Affair, the GAL affair, the Juan Guerra affair, and the collapse of Mário Conde's Banesto. It created a negative atmosphere inside the party. In 1994, the different regional party organizations were split between the left-wing *Guerristas* and centrist *renovadores*. Although it ended with the victory of Gonzalez's *renovadores*, the party was weakened by internal dissent. In the sixteen years of Socialist rule, the party moved ideologically from a verbal-radical Marxist-socialist ideological makeup to a more liberal democratic one. Public opinion labeled PSOE as *Corrupsoe* (corruption + PSOE), or the *Spanish Socialist Enterpreneurial Party* made a reference to close link of the Socialist party to the business sector.[15]

After defeat in the elections of 1996, PSOE became the main opposition party. Joaquin Almunia resigned after the March 2000 elections. His strategy to forge an electoral coalition with the communist United Left (*Izquierda Unida* [IU]) was rejected by the electorate. After a long process of selection, José Luis Zapatero, a thirty-nine-year-old lawyer, became the new leader of the PSOE in the thirty-fifth party conference in Madrid on July 21–23, 2000. This was regarded as an important step for the renewal of the party. This was reinforced by the rejection of Felipe Gonzalez to be elected president of the party. Zapatero has been engaged in a constructive opposition role. The new Socialist leader introduced a new document called *The Necessary Party for Spain of the 21st Century* (*El Partido Necessario para España del Siglo XXI*), which wants to democratize the party by limiting public office incumbency to three times in a row as well as party offices. Primaries are to be introduced for a large number of positions at the regional, local, and party levels.[16] Moreover, throughout 2001 Zapatero presented proposals for a reform of the ideology of the PSOE toward the center using the concept of a *liberal socialism*.[17]

Italy

In Italy the socialdemocratic space is represented today by the Party of Democratic Left (*Partito Democratico della Sinistra* [PDS]), originally the Italian Communist Party (*Partito Comunista Italiano* [PCI]). Since then, the PDS has been the major supporter of the reform of the Italian political system. The big moment of the PDS was when former leader Massimo d'Alema achieved a victory for the left-center coalition Olive Tree (*Ulivo*) in the elections of March 1996. This was a historical turning point in Italian politics, because until 1992, the Communist Party was ostracized from the political system. The main reason for the occupation of the social democratic space by a former reformed Communist Party is the fact that the Italian Socialist Party collapsed after the *tangentopoli* affair.[18]

The Italian Socialist Party was the oldest party in the political system until its demise after the *tangentopoli* affair in 1992. Ironically, the party was founded in August 1892 in Genova and was the dominant party on the left until the rise of the Fascists to power. In 1921, the party was affected by a split and subsequently by the emergence of a new party on the left side of the party system spectrum: the Communist Party of Italy (*Partito Comunista d'Italia* [PCdI]). After World War II, the PSI began to approach the DC and to take part in the center-left coalition. Although the PSI remained only the third largest party before 1992, it was able to play a pivotal role in coalition formation. This became evident in the 1980s when a five-party coalition had to be formed because the DC's electoral support was declining steadily. Party leader Bettino Craxi became prime minister between 1983 and 1987. Nevertheless, power-sharing with the DC led after 1992 to the collapse of the party, which was one of the most affected by the *tangentopoli* affair.[19] After 1992, the PSI collapsed because many of its leaders were involved in the web of systemic corruption with members of the DC. The electoral space was then occupied by the transformed PCI/PDS, which clearly became a social democratic party and is affiliated to the Socialist International. In recent elections, the son of Bettino Craxi, Bobo Craxi, tried unsuccessfully to relaunch his father's party by calling it New Socialist Party (*Nuovo PSI*). It was one of the allies of Silvio Berlusconi's House of Freedoms. It reached 1 percent of the vote, but no seats.[20]

Greece

PASOK was founded on September 3, 1974. From the beginning, leader Andreas Papandreou suppressed all attempts of internal diversity within the party. The party was dominated by its leader. He himself chose about ten out of the seventy-five members of the Central Committee; he also streamlined the youth movement of PASOK, the Panhellenic Camp of Militant Students (PASP). Between 1975 and 1977, several members decided to leave the party. The "charismatic" organization was highly dependent on the leader; but the new leader, Kostas Simitis, was able to initiate a smooth transition within the party structures after his takeover in 1995.[21] In terms of ideology, the party started as a radical party that sympathized with revolutionary ideologies or movement in the Third World. Indeed, the original ideological makeup particularly targeted the need to overcome the dependency of the Greek economy on foreign capital. The party intended to introduce a planned economy. After its victory in 1981, the party slowly gave up its original ideology and became more moderate. Now it resembles most social-democratic parties in other west European countries. In 1996, the party had a membership of approximately 155,642.[22] The new leader Kostas Simitis was able to moderate the party toward the center, in spite of the fact that many of the recent cuts in public spending related to the social security system have met resistance inside the more left-wing sections of the party. He had to justify the reforms to a two-day Central Committee meeting in early June 2001, and after massive protests of the population, he had to drop it. It shows that the radical socialist legacy is still vivid in PASOK.[23] In the four-day sixth PASOK party conference between October 10 and 14, 2001, Kostas Simitis was elected with 71.16 percent of the vote by the 6,439 delegates. This naturally strengthens his position inside the party. It is the third time that Simitis was elected president of PASOK after the death of Andreas Papandreou in 1996. He was able to stand against his main adversary, Defense Minister Akis Tsohatzopoulos, who represents the ideological left within the party.[24]

Southern European socialism began as quite radical in all four countries and moved in the past 25 years toward a less ideological and more pragmatic approach similar to the other countries of Western Europe. In all four countries, the socialist parties tend to be very close to French socialism, which emphasizes the importance of social welfare and social policy. After decades of logistic and financial support by the west European social democratic party family, southern European socialism is taking the lead in shaping the Socialist International.

The Conservative/Liberal Party Family

Whereas the Socialist party family remained extremely cohesive and well integrated internationally, the right and right-center parties had difficulties finding a common ground. Indeed, the diversity of ideological background is the most evident aspect of parties on the right. We may find Christian-democratic, liberal, and conservative elements integrated into certain catchall parties, which in the end give leeway for a high level of factionalism within the party structures. In all four countries one can find a fast decline of the original ideological sources of the party and development toward pragmatic Americanized politics.

Portugal

In Portugal, two parties are competing on the right and center of the party spectrum: the People's Democratic Party/Social Democratic party (*Partido Popular Democratico/Partido Social Democrata* [PPD/PSD]) and the Social Democratic Center/People's Party (*Centro Democrático Social-Partido Popular* [CDS/PP]). The PPD/PSD is a national modernizing party with a liberal-social makeup. It was founded on May 1, 1974, by Francisco Sá Carneiro and other liberal opponents of the regime. The new party remained extremely vague in ideological terms. Indeed, it had difficulties finding a political home among the west European democracies. Initially, it tried to become member of the Socialist International, but this was blocked by the Socialist party. After a long period in the liberal party family, it decided recently to become part of the European People's Party (EPP) in the European Parliament to achieve more influence. The uncontested leader was Francisco Sá Carneiro during the transition and the early consolidation period. This charismatic figure was able to unite the different factions inside the party. During the transition period it was an ally of PS and CDS to prevent the Communist Party and the MFA from achieving full control of the provisional political system. In 1978–1979 Sá Carneiro adopted a strategy of polarization against the PS, which led to the establishment of a

coalition alliance called Democratic Alliance (*Alianca Democrática* [AD])
with the CDS and the People's Monarchic Party (*Partido Popular
Monárquico* [PPM]). In spite of the unfortunate sudden death of Sá
Carneiro in December 1980 in an airplane crash, the AD strategy was
continued until 1983.[25] The party consists of so-called *baronatos*, which
refers to the influence of regional leaders with strong regional or local
electoral support. Factionalism tends to appear when the party leader
is not a strong, charismatic personality.

The decade of *Cavaquismo*[26] was characterized by strong party leadership and sense of direction. The technocratic-modernizing approach
of Cavaco Silva contributed to the decline of factionalism inside the
party. Party strategies and structure became very Americanized. After
the resignation of Cavaco Silva from the party leadership in February
1995, factionalism again became a major feature of the party. Meanwhile, the PSD had three leaders from 1995 to 2002.[27] The present party
leader, Manuel Durão Barroso, was not able to change this situation up
until now. The PSD is presently the main government party. Since the
summer of 1996, the PSD introduced major reforms to downsize the
party structures and adopted drastic measures to control the finance
deficit.[28] In 1996, it was estimated that the party had over 183,000
members.[29]

The conservative spectrum is covered by the CDS-PP. The party was
founded on July 19, 1974. Originally the party was inspired by Christian
democratic principles. It was founded by personalities connected in
some way to the former authoritarian regime, such as Diogo Freitas do
Amaral, Amaro da Costa, or Adriano Moreira. Soon it found its international political home in the supranational EPP and the International
Christian Democratic Union. The party had difficulties establishing
itself during the revolutionary period. It was targeted as the party of
the former authoritarian regime. This small party became quite important in the early phase of the constitutional period. Afterward the party
declined steadily from 12 to 14 percent to 5 percent. Only in 1992 did
new party leader, Manuel Monteiro, make an unexpected change to this
path of decline of the party, by engaging in anti-Maastricht discourse.
He targeted mainly losers of the European integration process, such as
fishermen and farmers. In 1995, he was able to more than double the
party's share of the vote from 4.44 percent to 9.05 percent. He changed
the party's name from CDS to People's Party (*Partido Popular* [PP]).
Internally as well as externally, Monteiro had to deal with resistance
against his populist approach. Former leaders such as Diogo Freitas do
Amaral decided to leave the party, and the EPP expelled the PP from
their EP-parliamentary group. The PP had to join the Union for Europe
(UFE/UPE), which comprises all the parties that are against Maastricht
and the Amsterdam Treaties. Monteiro's success came to a halt in 1997,

due to growing resistance inside the party and a poor result in the local elections of December 1997, in which the share of the vote of the party declined to slightly over 4 percent. He was replaced by Paulo Portas, who was more moderate than Monteiro, in spite of pursuing the same Euroskeptic line. In the general elections of October 1999, the party recovered to over 8 percent in spite of the predictions that it may collapse. PP is the third largest party of the party system, and in 1992 it had 23,860 members; this figure may still be accurate.[30] In the last local elections, the party was not able to impress—it declined in terms of votes and percentage share.[31] Paulo Portas is continuously being challenged by Manuel Monteiro, the previous populist leader of the CDS-PP.

Spain

In Spain, three main parties were representatives of the right-center. The Union of Democratic Center (*Union del Centro Democratico* [UCD]), which consisted of several social-democratic, Christian-democratic, and liberal parties, was quite crucial during the transition to democracy. The heterogenous composition prevented a consolidation of the party. The UCD consisted of eleven parties and was founded in 1977, shortly before the elections to the Constituent Assembly.

This heterogenous party was quite strong in Castilla La Mancha, Castilla-Leon, Valencia, and Andalusia in terms of membership. In the elections of 1977 and 1979, the party scored 34 percent and 31 percent respectively.

The party of transition, as it was subsequently called, was the major broker of the constitution in the *Cortes*. Although most of its members were involved in the former political system, they represented the more progressive elements of the Francoist elites. Nevertheless the heterogeneity of the political groups prevented the establishment of a cohesive structure. Though the UCD under the leadership of Adolfo Suarez was able to play a role of broker during transition, it lost initiative after adoption of the constitution. The barones, the main leaders of the different factions, tended to have ideological fights among themselves.[32]

The UCD had difficulties creating an overarching ideology. The coalition of parties collapsed during and after the general elections of 1982. Adolfo Suarez was able to found a new party which he thereafter called the Democratic Social Center (*Centro Democratico y Social* [CDS]). The party was quite as successful as the four largest national parties between 1986 and 1989. The party disappeared completely in the 1990s. Most of the voters were absorbed by the modernizing and more dynamic People's Party (PP) under José Maria Aznar. PP is the only conservative/Christian democratic party that survived until today. The People's Alliance/People's Party (*Alianza Popular-Partito Popular*

[AP/PP]) was founded shortly before the general elections of 1977. The party was a political-ideological home for the more conservative representatives of the Francoist elite. Until 1979, the party remained small and quite isolated from the new political system. The main leader was the former information minister Manuel Fraga Iribarne, who wanted to establish a right-wing party. He hoped to win parts of the population who still sympathized with the Francoist regime. The AP was farther to the right than the UCD and was never able to occupy the center-right of the spectrum. It remained marginal to the political process. Between 1977 and 1979, it tried to change its image by integrating smaller Christian-democratic and liberal parties as well as conservative notables who were not integrated in the UCD. The AP/PP had to go through a difficult period of party reorganization and establishment in the party system. Between 1979 and 1986, the party became the second largest party, but it was not able to challenge the PSOE. In the second half of the 1980s, there were several attempts to modernize the party. The main problem was the overdominance of the autocratic leader Manuel Fraga Iribarne. The party was also heavily in debt. In the extradionary congress celebrated in February 1987, a new president, Antonio Hernandez Mancha, was elected, who wanted to transform the party into a modern European right-wing party. Unfortunately, inner disputes prevented a consolidation of the party. By mid-1988, electoral surveys showed that support for the party was declining. This led to the return of Manuel Fraga Iribarne as party president and to the refoundation of the AP into the People's Party (*Partito Popular* [PP]). He appointed a new party leader, José Maria Aznar, who was able to change the image of the PP. Aznar started his reform plan in 1990. The decline of the electoral support of the PSOE to below 40 percent in 1989 showed that PP was slowly emerging as a second major force. In 1996, PP finally surpassed the PSOE by 1.3 percent. According to party figures, PP can count on over 600,000 members.

José Maria Aznar was able to transform the PP into a modern catchall party with a Christian-democratic agenda. The party is member of the EPP in the European Parliament. Aznar was successful in overcoming the original antiregionalist position of the party and in 1996 it signed a pact with all regionalist parties in view of reforming the State of Autonomies.[33] In the recent elections of March 12, 2000, PP was able to achieve an absolute majority, thus consolidating the position of the party within Spanish politics.[34] Aznar's position is quite consolidated inside the party. The 14th party conference in January 2002 endorsed the policies of Aznarismo. There is a lack of dissent and criticism inside the party. The ambitious agenda of Aznar is to restore the right balance between central state and the autonomous communities. Controversial policies such as the foreigners' law (*ley de extrajeria*) and the recent imposition of the reform of the Higher Education system only marginally affected his popularity. In the weeks before the party conference, his supporters asked him to reconsider his decision to step down after two legislature periods as prime minister. Aznar continued to stand by his decision throughout the period.[35]

Italy

By far one of the most important parties of the second half of the twentieth century was Christian Democracy (*Democrazia Cristiana* [DC]) in Italy. DC was founded after the war within the tradition of political Catholicism. It restored the tradition of the PPI of Don Luigi Sturzo founded in 1919 and subsequently destroyed by the Fascists. In the interwar period, some of the members and leaders of the PPI were employed in the Vatican. The most famous case is Alcide de Gasperi, the leader of DC throughout the 1950s, who was a librarian in the Vatican between 1929 and 1943.[36] Although DC was always a hetero-genous *mixtum compositum* integrating different currents, its cohesion was achieved by a fierce anticommunism. The Catholic social doctrine was the main element of Christian-democratic ideology. This was rein-forced by a strong religious faith and obedience to Church authority. DC remained the strongest party throughout the postwar period. It organized its power basis through clientelism and patronage or some-times even coercion. After forty years in government, DC became the main piece in a web of systemic corruption. After *tangentopoli*, the DC fragmented into three main parties: the Italian People's Party (*Partito Popolare Italiano* [PPI]), which was under the leadership of Romano Prodi; the conservative Christian Democratic Centre-United Christian Democrats (*Centro Cristiano Democratico-Cristiani Democratici* [CDU]); and the Christian Social Party (*Partito Cristiano Sociale* [CS]). The latter disappeared completely and joined the other parties. All parties are small and in different electoral coalitions. Whereas PPI is in a left-center coalition with the PDS, the CCD-CDU remained in the center-right coalition under the leadership of Silvio Berlusconis *Forza Italia* and Gianfrancos National Alliance (*Alleanza Nazionale* [AN]). Other factions within DC chose to join other parties.[37]

In March 1994, a new party was established within three months. In this period, the media tycoon Silvio Berlusconi set up a new party called *Forza Italia* (Go forth Italy). Using modern marketing techniques, Berlusconi used his marketing firm *Publitalia* to set up a party structure across Italy. The structure consisted of clubs spread out across the Italian territory. By March 1994, there were 12,000 such clubs consisting of five or more persons and comprising more than 1 million members. The new party addressed small and medium-sized businesspeople and the poorer segments of the population.[38] In good populist manner it promised jobs for the unemployed. Berlusconi used his television empire as well as his football club AC Milan to promote the new party. Actually, *Forza Italia* was a chanting slogan used by football fans to fire up the Italian national team. Marketing studies led to the creation of an "electoral package" for voters on the right-center spectrum. *Forza Italia* occupied space left by DC after its collapse.[39] FI came into crisis after the judiciary began to investigate the finances of Berlusconi's firms *Fininvest* and *Publitalia*. His brother Paolo Berlusconi was involved in a corruption scandal, which brought problems for Berlusconi. Later in 1994, Berlusconi himself had to face investigations by the judges related to falsified accounts of *Publitalia*. Silvio Berlusconi's government had to step down after a motion of censure tabled by the Lega Nord on December 21, 1994. FI tried to present itself as the heir of the Christian-democratic tradition, which led to the first congress of the new party in May 1998. Presently, FI is a member of the European People's Party. In 1999 and 2000, Silvio Berlusconi was again investigated by the judiciary because of irregularities related to the television sector, but he was acquitted. In preparation for the 2001 elections, Berlusconi set up an umbrella electoral coalition called the House of Freedoms (*Casa delle Libertá*), which wants to integrate FI, AN, and LN. Several legal processes of false accounting and corruption are still going on in Spain and Italy. In spite of that Berlusconi was able to win the elections of May 13, 2001, and form a government with the weakened coalition partners rightwing extremist AN and the regionalist-separatist LN.[40] Berlusconi's party is extremely autocratic, because it was established around the personality of *Il Cavaliere*. This naturally creates a major problem for democracy inside the party. Between 1996 and 2001 a fragmentation of the parties of the Olive Tree coalition took place. Several new party formations began to appear, which did not feel close to the Democrats of the Left. They decided to form a center alliance called *La Margherita* which comprised all center-right parties inside the coalition. Apart from the PPI, it consists of Italian Renewal (*Rinnovamento Italiano* [RI]), Democratic Union for the Republic (*Unione Democratica per la Repubblica* [UDR]), and Democratic People's Party (*Popolari Democratici* [PD]). The leader of La Margherita became Francesco Rutelli, who was also leader of the Olive Tree Coalition. La Margherita was able to get 14.5 percent of the vote, while the democrats of the Left got 16.6 percent.

Greece

New Democracy (*Nea Dimokratia* [ND]) started as a party of notables. It was founded by Kostas Karamanlis. The party advocated the establishment of a liberal market economy. During the first years, ND had difficulties building up a modern party structure, because it was in power. Karamanlis gave priority to the integration of the country into the European Community. After Karamanlis became president in 1980, support for the party declined. The leadership decided to strengthen the party structures and modernize the party in spite of a stronger tendency toward notabilism. The party strategy is based on catchallism, and in terms of ideology it is a pragmatic liberal-conservative party. The dependency of ND on state subsidies shows that in Greece the "cartelization" is becoming more and more of a reality. After the controversial style of Kostas Mitsotakis, the ND experienced two more moderate leaders: Miltiades Evert and Kostas Karamanlis.[41] Kostas Karamanlis has a more consensual style in opposition to ruling PASOK. He was elected new leader of ND in the fourth party conference on March 21, 1997. Forty one percent of the 3,600 delegates voted for him on the first ballot against Evert and Souflias. On the second ballot Evert finally decided to back Karamanlis, and he was able to get 69 percent of the vote. Karamanlis is the nephew of former prime minister and president Kostas Karamanlis. Although he is doing intensive opposition work against Simitis, it seems that ND still has difficulties challenging PASOK.[42] According to party figures, the membership is about 400,000 followers, but only 200,000 are actual activists.[43]

The ideologies of Christian democracy, conservatism, and liberalism have become less relevant at the beginning of the new millennium. Indeed, political marketing, catchallism, and charismatic personalities have been the major factors in the electoral context.

The Communist Party Family

Communist parties in Western Europe had to change considerably after the fall of the wall. Most of them chose the road to reform and moved toward social democracy. In southern Europe, communism is still characterised by orthodoxy and based on Marxist-Leninist ideology. In spite of these characteristics the parties were able to successfully fight off complete extinction and remain vital forces of the southern European political systems.

Portugal

The Portuguese Communist Party (*Partito Comunista Português* [PCP]) was founded on March 6, 1921. It was the main party resisting Salazar's dictatorship. During the transition period, it tried to colonize the state structures and reduce the influence of the other parties by working closely with the left-wing military Movement of Armed Forces (*Movimento de Forcas Armadas* [MFA]). This almost led to a civil war between the conservative north and the left-wing south.[44] Therefore, in the constitutional period it was ostracized from central government.

The party was and is, in a certain sense, dominated by the old Alvaro Cunhal. It based its organization on democratic centralism, and it can be regarded as a membership party. Membership estimations indicate that the PCP has 100,000 members.[45]

In electoral terms, the party has been in a coalition with smaller parties since 1976. The Democratic Unitary Coalition (*Coligacao Democrática Unitária* [CDU]) founded after 1987 did not change the steady decline of the party very much. While until 1985 the party was able to reach, at some stage, more than 15 percent of the vote in general elections, afterward it declined to 8 to 10 percent of the vote in the elections of October 1999. The secretary-general, Carlos Carvalhas, is still in the shadow of Alvaro Cunhal. Indeed, in autumn 2000 more prominent party members resigned from party offices due to the feeling that there is a lack of democracy within the party.[46] The party continues to be an orthodox communist party based on subcultural Marxist-Leninist identity. One of the main problems of the party is that is not able to attract young members and its membership is quite old.[47]

Spain

The Spanish Communist Party (*Partido Comunista Español* [PCE]) was regarded as the best organized party and as having the best chance to achieve a large share of the vote in the elections of June 1977. Nevertheless, the late legalization of the PCE and the general historical memory of the population in relation to the dubious role played by the Communists in destroying the other left-wing parties (Socialists and Anarchists) in the Republican zone during the Civil War years led to a poor showing of only 9.2 percent in 1977. Although communism was quite popular between 1976 and 1979, it declined thereafter to a less significant force in Spain. Its strength was related to the success of the trade union confederation Workers' Commissions (*Comisiones Obreras* [CCOO]).[48]

One the major factors in the decline of the PCE was internal factionalism, which lasted until 1986. Santiago Carrillo openly criticized Gerardo Iglesias. As a consequence, Carrillo left the party in 1986, and Iglesias formed a coalition with other left-wing parties. The so-called United Left (*Izquierda Unida* [IU]) was able to reverse the process of decline. The new political formation was able to capitalize on the growing discontentment of the left-wing vote within the PSOE. It remained critical of the PSOE until 1996. After the defeat of the PSOE in the general elections of March 3, 1996, party leader Julio Anguita tried to achieve a common platform with the PSOE against the minority government led by PP and supported by the regionalist parties. This approach only became successful under the new leader Francisco Frutos before the elections of March 12, 2000. In spite of that, the vote of the IU was cut in half in the elections, and divisions inside the communist coalition became evident. Financially the result was an organizational catastrophy for IU, which had to cut their costs substantially. In the 6th General Assembly of the IU on October 28–29, 2000, Gaspar Llamazares successfully challenged Francisco Frutos: 42.59 percent to 39.38 percent. The third candidate, Angeles Maestro, was a distant third with 18.02 percent. The seventy-five members of the Political Council voted for Llamazares, by only one vote against Frutos. IU is highly divided between supporters of Frutos and those of Llamazares, and this is not the best way to start a renewal of the party.[49] Llamazares wants to reactivate IU as a movement of the left, which may find alliances with the antiglobalization movement, the antiwar movement (from Kosovo to Afghanistan), and other new social movements. The overall idea is to broaden the electorate of the IU among the new social movements. The divisions inside the coalition, the debt of 1.2 million euros, and the near disappearance of the party from the media after the general elections are major problems for Llamazares.[50]

Italy

The Italian Communist Party (*Partito Comunista Italiano* [PCI]) was founded in Livorno in 1921 after a split from the Italian Socialist Party. In the 1970s, it became the second largest party, well integrated into the regional political system, and started to achieve some access to central government. The dominant hierarchical principle until the 1970s was democratic centralism, but growing moderation of the party led to a change of attitudes. Nevertheless, in the 1980s the electoral support for the PCI declined considerably, reaching a historical low point of about 16 percent in 1992. A change of the social structure, the declining attraction of communism, and the collapse of the Soviet Union had their impact upon the PCI.[51] In terms of membership, the party declined from over 2 million in 1980 to just over 1.3 million in 1990. Under the leadership of Achille Occhetto a reform of party program and structure was accomplished between 1987 and the twenty-first party conference in 1991, in spite of strong resistance of the orthodox communist faction. The PCI changed its name to Party of Democratic Left (*Partito Democratico della Sinistra* [PDS]). The new party tried to respond to the decline in party membership and electoral support. The victory of Achille Occhetto led to the emergence of a splinter group of party members who wanted to preserve the Communist identity. Communist Refoundation (*Rifondazione Comunista* [RC]) consisted of the more orthodox members of the postwar subcultural communist tradition. In the 1994 and 1996 elections, the new PDS was able to improve its share of the vote to over 20 percent, being now the largest party on the left of the party system and the present senior partner in the Ulivo government coalition. The Communist Refoundation led by Fausto Bertinotti, a prominent trade unionist, was able to improve its share of the vote in relation to 1992.[52] It was an important ally of the Ulivo coaltition, but in 1998, in view of more austerity measures presented by the government, it decided to no longer support the Ulivo government. This naturally created major difficulties for L'Ulivo to sustain in government. The PDS tries today to be a umbrella party for all left-wing voters and create an American-style broad-based light structure. This naturally contributes to a further erosion of the left-wing traditions of the PDS. In the 2001 elections the Communist Refoundation experienced an erosion of its voters. It lost almost 4 percent of the popular vote and was reduced to 5 percent and eleven seats (1996: 20) and 3 seats in the Senate.

Greece

In Greece the Communist movement is split into two main parties: the orthodox KKE and the Eurocommunist *Synaspismos/Hellenic Left* (EAR). Both parties are against membership in NATO and they led the opposition against the Kosovo war in 1999. In spite of all that, the two parties have different strategies. The Communist Party of Greece (*Kommunistikó Kómma Elládas* [KKE]) was founded in 1924. It was always stricken by internal factionalism, but it has remained intact even until today. It was the major force in resisting against the German occupation during World War II and was regarded as a threat by the establishment afterward. Until the coup d'état of the Colonels' junta in 1967, Communism and any left-wing party were negatively regarded by the establishment. The Communist leadership remained in exile and kept its orthodox position.

In 1968, the Communist representatives inside the country decided to break away from the main party and form the Greek Communist Party of the Interior (*Kommunistikó Kómma Elládas-esouterikou* [KKE-es]), which pursued a parliamentary democratic route to achieve its policies. This Eurocommunist position should remain the main difference between the two parties. Occasionally both parties may join forces and contest elections together, such as was the case in 1974 with the electoral coalition United Left (*Enoméni Aristerá* [EA]) when it achieved 9.47 percent and eight seats or in 1989–1990 with the Left Alliance (*Synaspismos tis Aristerás kai tis Prodou* [SAP]), which led to 10.9/10.3 percent of the vote and twenty-one seats. Afterward both parties continued to run separately. Both parties are extremely critical toward NATO membership, but in terms of EU membership only the KKE continues to have a Euroskeptic view. During the 1980s and 1990s, the KKE under the leadership of Aleka Papariga remained the only party opposed to EU membership, even when PASOK and *Synaspismos*/KKE-es moved toward a more reconciliatory position.[53] The KKE continues to promote a conflictual approach toward politics by organizing political strikes and political demonstrations against all kinds of issues.[54] The bombing campaign of NATO in the Kosovo war led to violent demonstrations organized by the KKE throughout 1999 and 2000. In 2001, KKE organized an antiwar campaign against involvement of the United States in Afghanistan and traditionally co-organized a remembrance of the National Polytechnic demonstration of November 13. The main characteristics of the party are antiwar, anti-Americanism, Marxist-Leninist orthodoxy, and resistance against foreign powers (including the EU).[55] *Synaspismos* was founded in 1992 and comprises a broader alliance of antiglobalization protest, feminism, and other social movements. It pursues an ideology based on democratic socialism, ecology, feminism, and antimilitarism. Since 1993, the main leader is Nicos Constantopoulos, a lawyer and human rights activist. In the last elections, both KKE and *Synaspismos* were able to achieve a remarkable representation.[56] KKE got 5.5 percent and eleven seats and *Synaspismos* 3.2 percent and six seats. They are respectively the third and fourth largest parties of the Greek political system.

Communist parties still play an important opposition role in Portugal, Spain, and Greece. The continuing support of a small part of the population allows some of the parties to remain orthodox Marxist-Leninist.

Other Parties

One special feature of southern Europe is that all four party systems are ultrastable. New parties have difficulties to changing the party system format.

Portugal

In Portugal, small parties tend to survive only one or two parliamentary legislatures. On the left, this was the case for the People's Democratic Union (*Uniao Democratica Popular* [UDP]), which was represented between 1975 and 1985 with one deputy in parliament. This small group was a Maoist-Albanist party, which remained critical to the established parties. In the elections of October 1999 and March 2002, the Block of the Left (*Bloco da Esquerda* [BE]), a coalition of several extreme left-wing groups, was able to achieve over 2.4 percent and two seats and 2.8 percent and three seats, respectively. It remains to be seen if their critical performance in the parliament will enthuse their supporters. Other smaller parties such as the Maoist Movement for the Reorganization of the Party of the Proletariat (*Movimento para a Reorganizacão do Partido do Proletariado* [MRPP]), or the Trotskyite Revolutionary Socialist Party

(*Partido Socialista Revolucionario* [PSR]) did not independently achieve representation in the Assembly of the Republic. Between 1985 and 1991 a presidentialist party called the Democratic Renewal Party (*Partido Renovador Democratico* [PRD]) around president General Ramalho Eanes was quite successful. It achieved over 17 percent in 1985 and then steadily disappeared soon afterward. A small pensioneers' party called the Party of National Solidarity (*Partito de Solidariedade Nacional* [PSN]) was able to gain a seat in parliament in 1991, but disappeared soon afterward.

Spain

In Spain, the most successful small parties come from the regions. The number of regionalist parties has increased over the past two and a half decades. From the Basque Country, there are three parties that achieve regular parliamentary representation in the *Cortes*. The Basque National Party (*Partito Nacionalista Vasco* [PNV]) was founded in 1879 by Sabino Arana and is a nationalist-regionalist party recently advocating the unification of the French and the Spanish Basque regions and independence from Spain. Herri Batasuna is the political arm of the terrorist organization ETA (*Euskadi ta Askatasuna* [Basque Country and Freedom]). It demands full independence. Since 1986, Basque Left (*Eusko Ezquerra* [EE]) has become a successful challenger of these two other party organizations. It was founded by former *lehendekari*[57] Carlos Garaikoetchea. It is a more moderate party asking for more autonomy.

In Catalonia, the main party is the fourth largest national party. Convergence and Union (*Convergencia i Unió* [CiU]) is dominated by the charismatic Jordi Pujol. It advocates autonomy for Catalonia and tends to be verbal-radical in terms of creating a dual nation comprising Catalonia and Spain. The left republican vote is represented by the Republican Left of Catalonia (*Esquerra Republicana di Catalunya* [ERC]). Their demands for autonomy are more radical than those of CiU. After the recent elections of Catalonia, CiU had to compromise with ERC to achieve a stable regional government.

In Galicia, in recent years the nationalist-regionalist vote rallied around the Galician Nationalist Block (*Bloque Nacionalista Gallego* [BNG]), which is a left-wing party requesting more autonomy for this region. In other parts of the country, similar small and smallish parties established themselves in the particular region and at the national level.

Italy

Before *tangentopoli* three parties regularly shared government with DC. They lost significance or disappeared completely after 1992. The Italian Republican Party *(Partito Repubblicano Italiano* [PRI]) was founded in 1895; it followed an antisystemic position until 1945, appealing particularly to the higher educated segments of the population. The PRI was an important actor of the coalition game until 1992.[58]

The Italian Liberal Party (*Partito Liberale Italiano* [PLI]) has its roots in the post-Risorgimento. In terms of organization only after the establishment of universal male suffrage in 1919 and the rise of Fascism did the PLI develop modern party structures. A National Union was founded in 1924, but it was forbidden two years later. The party was refounded in 1943–1944. It took part in most center and pentapartito coalitions.[59]

The third smaller party in the coalition game was the Italian Social Democratic Party (*Partito Social Democratico Italiano* [PSDI]), founded in November 1947. It was a splinter group of the PSI that did not agree with the union between PSI and PCI after the war. It pursued the objective of a democratic socialism against totalitarianism.[60] All three parties disappeared after 1992.

More important in electoral terms is the neo-fascist Italian Social Movement (*Movimento Sociale Italiano* [MSI]), which was founded by Giorgio Almirante, former propaganda minister of the fascist Republic of Salò. The MSI remained ostracized from the political system until 1994. The party was able to create parallel organizations of support. The party is quite strong in the south and the regions of central Italy. It established clientelistic and patronage structures to keep the loyalty of its electorate. Indeed, the MSI was able to increase its share of the vote in the 1970s in a context of rising left-wing social movements, terrorism, and a difficult financial crisis. Although the MSI achieved 8 to 7 percent of the vote in 1976, its average share during this period was always between 4 and 5 percent.[61] The neo-Fascist MSI also underwent a transformation. The new leader Gianfranco Fini made efforts to present a respectable image for the right. Although he paid lip service to the resistance movement during the fiftieth anniversary celebration of Italy's liberation from Fascism and defined his party as post-Fascist by dismissing Mussolini-style Fascism as a thing of the past, the AN/MSI still includes neo-Fascist radical groups. Nevertheless, Fini was successful in overcoming the exclusion of the right from the political system. The participation of the AN/MSI in Berlusconi's Good Government coalition ended the long phase of political ostracism. As Leonardo Morlino wrote, in 1994 the last antisystemic party was integrated in the political system.[62] In terms of the vote the AN achieved 13.4 percent of the vote in 1994, a substantial increase. Reasons for this rise of electoral success have to do with the corruption scandals in Italian government.[63] Gianfranco Fini became the vice prime minister in Berlusconi's coalition. This naturally creates the possibility that Fini and AN may gain more power in the political system.

A regionalist phenomenon is the emergence of the Northern League (*Lega Nord* [LN]). The history of LN goes back to the early 1980s. Umberto Bossi first founded the so-called Lombardy League (*Lega Lombarda*) in 1982. It was inspired by a small North Italian independence movement called the Union Valdotaine. The success of the Lombardy League began with the local elections of 1985. Two years later it achieved 2.7 percent of the vote in the Lombardy regional elections. In the European elections of 1989, the Lombardy League gathered 6.5 percent of the vote; it got 16.4 percent in the regional elections of 1992. The establishment of the LN in the 1990s, bringing together Lega Veneta and the Lombardy League, led to a campaign for a split of Italy in three macro-regions, one of them being the North. The LN mainly targeted the inefficient state sector and the south. It defined the north as a "community of interests" that was different from the south. It criticized the level of political corruption practiced by politicians, the inefficient political system based on an excessive bureaucracy, the waste of public resources due to poor management, and the inadequacy of state services. Moreover, LN expressed racist tendencies toward the southerners of Italy, whom they perceived to belong to a different Mediterranean culture. The industrious and hardworking north was contrasted to the "lazy" south. According to Carlo Ruzza and Oliver Schmidtke, the mobilization dynamics of the Lega particularly targeted youth peer groups of northern Italian villages and small towns. They are normally young, relatively uneducated, and disproportionately male. The recruitment pattern is mainly informal in casual places such as bowling halls, bars, parishes, video clubs, even stadiums. Discussion roundtables in pubs were a common way to activate and recruit new members. LN tends to use symbolic acts to emphasize the common heritage.[64] Other small regionalist parties exist in Alto Adige, also known as South Tyrol, and in the Val d'Aosta region. In the former case, it represents the German minority in the region, in the latter the French minority. In the elections of May 2001, the LN experienced a setback. It was not able to secure any MP in the elections and is dependent on the allocation of seats defined in the right-center coalition House of Freedoms. In spite of all that, LN is for the second time in a Berlusconi government and it was allocated three ministries: Labor and Health (Roberto Maroni, no. 2 of Lega); State Reform (Umberto Bossi, no. 1 of Lega), and Justice (Roberto Castelli).[65]

One of the main characteristics of Italian politics is the proliferation and personalization of politics. In the May 2001, elections several new parties emerged that were not able to achieve a high level of representation. This is the case for the New PSI of Bobo Craxi (1 percent), *Democrazia Europea* led by former prime minister Giulio Andreotti (2.4 percent), and the Panella-Bonnino list (2.2 percent). The 4 percent hurdle forces most of the parties to join one of the big coalitions to get allocation of seats in a coalition agreement as it happened in the case of *Democrazia Europea*, which performed strongly in Sicily.

Greece

In Greece, small parties have a very short life span. Back in 1974, the Center Union (*Enosis Kentrou* [EK]) and in 1977 the renamed Union of Democratic Center (*Enosis Dimokratiki Kentrou* [EDIK]) disappeared completely after being the second largest party. A splinter group of ND was able to get 6.8 percent of the vote and five seats, but it disappeared in the following elections of 1981. In the 1990s, Antonis Samaras' Political Spring (*Politiki Anixi* [POLAN]), which achieved 4.9 percent and ten seats in 1993, was a complete surprise. It campaigned particularly on the question of Macedonia and the dispute with the neighboring former Republic of Yugoslavia Macedonia (FYROM). It was not able to gain representation in 1996. Back in 1996 a left-wing splinter group from PASOK called Democratic Social Movement (*Dimokratiko Koinoniko Kinima* [DIKKI]) under the populist former finance minister Kostas Tsovoulas was able to gather 4.4 percent of the vote and nine seats, but it lost all seats in the recent elections of April 12, 2000, in spite of achieving 2.7 percent. The very complicated election system is the major reason for the stability of the Greek party system. New parties have to overcome several hurdles before they can achieve representation.[66]

COMPETING IN A MULTILEVEL ARENA

Legislative Elections

The electoral systems in southern Europe are all different from each other. Nevertheless, all of them are proportional representation systems. Only Italy deviated from this pattern, when it introduced, in 1993, a mixed electoral system of which 25 percent of MPs are elected by a proportional representation system, but the vast majority (75 percent) are elected by a simple majority system. The main reason for the change was the hope that the majoritarian system would create a more stable, less fragmented Parliament. In spite of the proportional representation systems, bipolarized party systems have emerged in Portugal, Spain, and Greece. This applies now to Italy as well. In this sense, one can say that in these four countries party systems have become more stable. The proportional representation system in Greece, Portugal, and Spain is favorable to the larger parties and detrimental to the smaller parties, while in Italy the only way small parties can survive now is to join one of the two major electoral alliances on the left and the right. One negative aspect of electoral systems and party systems in southern Europe is that the political elite is perceived as being quite distant from the electorate and that the mechanisms of candidate selection clearly reinforce this tendency toward a closed political class. In spite of this fact, one has to acknowledge that the electoral systems have produced stable party systems that are conducive to stable government (see Table 4.1).

Portugal

The Portuguese party system was able to achieve stability in its founding elections of April 25, 1974. Indeed, from the start, the party system remained constrained to two main parties (PS, PSD) and two small parties (CDS, PCP). Though the party system has been characterized as ultrastable, simultaneously it is also extremely fluid. These characteristics continue to play a major role in shaping the political system.

On April 25, 1975, elections to the Constituent Assembly were held, which led to the establishment of a mainly four-party system. This continues to persist until today: PS, PSD, CDS-PP, and the PCP/CDU.

In the elections to the Constituent Assembly on April 25, 1975, the PS was able to win a confortable majority (see Table 4.2), followed by the PPD/PSD, the PCP, and CDS. From the very start, the new party system was dominated by the two main parties with 64.1 percent of the vote in 1978. Internally, the party system should remain stable, but ultrafluid and volatile. This means that outside challengers have difficulties establishing themselves within the party system, at least for a lengthier period of time. The Portuguese electorate is extremely volatile in the center.[67] This first period can be defined as a period of political learning and governmental experiment. The party system was quite fragmented, and no party was able to win a clear-cut strong majority. Until 1979 the party system was dominated by the PS, which formed the first two governments. This was replaced by the dominance of the PPD/PSD, which forged a coalition government with the CDS and the PPM until 1983. After a victory of the PS in October 1983 and the subsequent coalition government with the PSD, the relationship between the two main parties became even more tense. This was due to the emergence of a new leader in the PSD: Anibal Cavaco Silva. His conflictual charismatic leadership style led to the break up of the coalition and the call for early elections in 1985. Cavaco Silva won the elections and formed a minority government. The PSD was able to gather 29 percent, and the PS declined to 20.77 percent, losing 15 percent relative to the results obtained in the 1983 elections. A new presidentialist party, Democratic Renewal Party (*Partito Renovador Democratico* [PRD]), founded by president Antonio Ramalho Eanes, was successful in capturing 17.92 per-

TABLE 4.1 Electoral Systems in Southern Europe

Country	Legislative Chamber	Electoral System	Constituencies	Period of Time	Party System	Voting Elegibility
Portugal	Unicameral (Assembleia da Republica) 230 MPs	PR-System D'Hondt Party list	22 constitu-encies: 18 in the continent (216); 2 in islands of Acores and Madeira (10); 2 Europe and outside Europe (4)	4 years	4-party system	18 years noncompulsory
Spain	Bicameral (Cortes) Lower House (Congreso de Deputados— 350 MPs)	PR-System Party list D'Hondt Party list + 3 percent of overall vote. Limited vote	52 provinces	4 years	3-party system + regionalist parties	18 years noncompulsory
	Upper House (Senado— 257 senators)	Limited vote + appointment by regional assemblies	52 provinces			
Italy	Bicameral Lower House (Camera die Deputati— 630 MPs; Upper House Senato—325 directly elected, 8 appointed, 2 ex officio)	**Pre-1993** D'Hondt PR system, party list + preferential voting	20 regions	5 years	Bipolar loose electoral coalitions	Chamber of Deputies: 18 years and Senate: 25 years
		After 1993 Mixed System Chamber of Deputies and Senate: 75 percent are elected by a majority system in uninominal constituencies and 25 percent by a PR system at district level	Uninominal constituencies in districts of the 20 regions			noncompulsory
Greece	Unicameral (Vouli) 300 MPs (288 MPs + 12 MPs of the state)	Reinforced PR-System Party list + Preferential voting Hagenbach-Bischoff	Three stages of electoral process	4 years	4-party system	18 years compulsory

TABLE 4.2   General Election Results in Portugal (1975-2002)

	General Elections (1975–1985)										
	1975		1976		1979		1980		1983		1985	
	%	Seats	%	Seats	%	Seats	%	Seats	%	Seats	%	Seats
PS	37.7	115	27.33	107	27.33	74	26.65	74	36.12	101	20.77	57
PPD/PSD	26.4	80	24.40	73					27	75	29.87	88
CDS	7.65	16	16	42					12.56	30	9.96	22
AD					42.52	128	44.91	134				
PCP/FEPU/ APU	12.5	30	14.35	40	18.80	47	16.75	41	18.07	44	15.49	38
UDP	0.79	1	1.35	1	1.38	1	1.38	1				
PRD											17.92	45
Other	15	5	16.60		9.97		10.30		6.30		5.99	
		247		263		250		250		250		250

	General Elections (1987–2002)									
	1987		1991		1995		1999		2002	
	%	Seats	%	Seats	%	Seats	%	Seats	%	Seats
PS	22.24	60	29.3	72	43.76	112	44	115	40.2	105
PPD/PSD	50.22	148	50.4	135	34.17	88	32.3	81	37.8	96
CDS-PP	4.44	4	4.4	5	9.08	15	8.4	15	8.8	14
CDU(PCP/PEV)	12.14	31	8.8	17	8.65	15	9	17	6.9	12
PRD	4.91	7								
PSN			1.7	1	0.21					
BE							2.5	2	2.8	3
Other	6.07		5.4		4.13		3.8		3.5	-
		250		230		230		230		230

Source: Comissão Nacional de Eleicões, http://www.cne.pt

cent of the vote in the 1985 election. Cavaco Silva's dominance in the political systems should last for the next decade.

This surprising result transformed the four-party system into a five-party system until 1991, when the PRD disappeared completely. The Eanist party was very critical and obstructive in the Assembly of the Republic. After a motion of censure was tabled in Parliament in March 1987, early elections were called. Almost all PRD voters decided to vote for the PSD, so the brand-new party almost collapsed, from 17.92 percent to 4.91 percent within two years. This major swing led to the absolute majority victory of the PSD. The main reason for its success was related to the personality of prime minister Anibal Cavaco Silva, who presented himself as a strong leader able to make the best out of the recent accession to the EC. This realigment of the electorate would remain a source of stability for the absolute majority government of Cavaco Silva.[68] He was able to repeat the same result in the general elections of 1991. Only after the resignation of Cavaco Silva as prime minister did a new realignment take place, now toward the PS. In the general elections of 1995 and 1999, the PS was able to win a strong relative majority under the leadership of Antonio Guterres. The PSD was stricken by factionalism throughout this period. The other small parties were able to recover slightly. Under the populist leadership of Manuel Monteiro and Paulo Portas, the CDS/PP was able to double its electoral support to over 9 percent in 1995 and keep it at over 8 percent in 1999. The continuing major factor of instability in the party system is the vote of the highly volatile and heterogenous new middle classes, which seem to shift opportunistically between the two main parties, whereas the fringe vote of the two small parties is more or less stable. Another negative aspect of elections in Portugal is that the level of abstention has increased steadily in the past twenty years from 20 percent to 40 percent.[69] It shows that there is a danger that any further increase of the abstention rate may lead to a widening of the gulf between the political elite and the population. Moreover, the concentration of vote among the two main parties that together are able to attract 76 to 80 percent of voters and the decline for the smaller parties shows that this gulf may widen even more in the future. The recent elections of March 17, 2002, just confirmed this trend. The two main parties were able to concentrate 78 percent of the valid votes. Both parties share a similar electorate consisting of the new middle classes, which this time split their vote between these two main parties. New Socialist leader Eduardo Ferro Rodrigues was able to keep the losses of the PS to an absolute minimum, achieving 37.2 percent, while Barroso's PSD was not about to become hegemonic by achieving only 40.2 percent. Barroso had to form a coalition with the People's Party, which was able to improve slightly to 8.8 percent. The big loser was the Communist Party, losing heavily and achieving only 6.9 percent, a historical low result. It led to dissent and divisions inside the party over the need to organize an extraordinary party conference. The tiny new Block of the Left was able to improve slightly to 2.8 percent and in getting an additional MP elected. In sum, Portuguese party politics shows a long-term tendency toward bipolarization and simultaneous decline of the smaller parties.

Spain: From Imperfect to Perfect Bipolarism
The Spanish party system can be divided into three main periods. The first period comprises the first elections up until 1982. The main pivotal party is the UCD. This coalition of parties has been labeled as the "party of transition" because it collapsed in 1982 and its supporters joined either the PSOE or the more conservative AP/PP. The second period can be characterized as the period of "patrimonial socialism," meaning that the strong absolute majority of the PSOE up until 1993 led to a so-called Mexicanization of society.[70] By 1996 the former AP/PP became a credi-

ble alternative to the PSOE, which was embroiled in a web of political corruption scandals, clientelism, and patronage after sixteen years in government. The election of 1996 is only the climax of the transition to the third period of the party system, in which a perfect bipartyism seems to be the outcome.[71] (See Table 4.3 and Table 4.4)

TABLE 4.3   General Elections in Spain (1977–2000)

	1977		1979		1982	
	%	Seats	%	Seats	%	Seats
PSOE	29.3	118	30.5	121	48.4	202
AP/PP	8.8	16	6.1	9	26.5	106
UCD	34.6	166	35	168	6.5	12
PCE	9.4	20	10.8	23	4	4
CDS					2.9	2
CiU	2.8	11	2.7	8	3.7	12
PNV	1.7	8	1.5	7	1.9	8
HB			1	3	1	2
ERC			0.7	1	0.7	1
EE	0.3	1	0.5	1	0.5	1
Others	13.1	10	11.2	9	3.9	-
TOTAL	100	350	100	350	100	350

	1986		1989	
	%	Seats	%	Seats
PSOE	44.1	184	39.90	175
AP/PP	26	106	25.90	107
IU	4.61	7	9.10	17
CDS	9.20	19	7.91	4
CiU	5	18	5	18
PNV	1.53	6	1.24	5
HB	1.15	5	1.10	5
ERC	0.42	-	-	-
EE	0.53	2	0.51	2
PAR	0.40	1	0.30	1
PA	-	-	1	2
PNG	0.40	1	0.40	1
EA			0.70	1
UV	0.30	1	0.70	2
Other	6.51	3	6.24	0
Seats	100	350	100	350

	1993		1996		2000	
	%	Seats	%	Seats	%	Seats
PSOE	38.70	159	37.50	141	34.1	125
PP	34.80	141	38.90	157	44.6	183
IU	9.57	18	10.60	21	5.5	8
NATIONAL PARTIES	83.07	318	87	319	84.2	316
CiU	4.95	17	4.64	16	4.2	15
NV	1.24	5	1.28	5	1.5	7
HB	0.88	2	0.70	2		

TABLE 4.3 *(continued)*

	1993		1996		2000	
	%	Seats	%	Seats	%	Seats
ERC	0.80	1	0.70	1	0.8	1
EE	0.54	-				
EA	0.55	1	0.46	1	0.4	1
UV	0.48	1	0.37			
CC	0.88	4	0.90	4	1.1	4
PA	0.48				0.89	1
PAR	0.61	1				
CHA			0.20		0.30	1
BNG	0.54		0.90	2	1.30	3
REGIONALIST PARTIES	11.95	32	10.15	31	10.49	33
Other	4.98		2.85	-	5.31	1
Seats	100	350	100	350	100	350

Source: José Ramon Montero, "Sobre las preferencias electorales en España: fragmentacíon y polarizacíon (1977-1993), in Pilar del Castillo (ed.), *Comportamiento Politico y Electoral* (Madrid: CIS 1998), 62–63; *El Pais,* Anuario 1987:70; *El Pais,* Anuario 1990:60; *El Pais,* Anuario 1994:78; *El Pais,* Anuario 2001:94.

TABLE 4.4 Distribution of Directly Elected Seats in the Spanish Senate (1989–2000)

	1989	1993	1996	2000
PP	77	93	111	126
PSOE	108	96	81	62
IU	1			
CiU	10	10	8	8
CDS	1			
PNV	4	3	4	6
CC	1	5	2	5
HB	3	1		
Agrupacion de Lectores "Eivissa i Formentera al Senat"			1	
Partido de Independientes Lanzarote	1		1	1
Independent Group Herrena	1			
Asamblea Majorera	1			
Seats	208	208	208	208

Source: El Pais, Anuario, 1990, p. 60; *El Pais,* Anuario, 1994, p. 78; *El Pais,* Anuario, 2001, p. 94.

The new party system that emerged after 1977 remained quite stable for the next two decades.

Most of the parties lacked a political structure due to the longevity of the Francoist political regime. Only two parties engaged in fighting against Franco's dictatorship: PCE and PSOE. Indeed, the modernizing Francoist elites embodied in the heterogenous UCD were able to capture most of the votes and play a broker role between the authoritarian elites and the new democratic—most of them left-wing—forces. In 1977 and 1979, the UCD was able to gather most of the votes, whereas the PSOE remained the second largest force. The electorate was very keen to vote for the moderate political parties. PCE and AP/PP remained on the fringes of the political system. After the constitutional settlement in 1978, the electorate became more daring, shifting their votes to the PSOE. Indeed, this is reinforced by the fact that Adolfo Suarez left the leadership of the UCD and was replaced by Calvo Sotelo. The heterogenous party failed to build up a party organization and collapsed in the elections of 1982.

The victory of the PSOE in 1982 was possible, because the UCD collapsed and there was no alternative in the center, center-left, and center-right to replace it. AP/PP and PCE were too marginal and connected to political models that were perceived negatively by the electorate.

Between 1982 and 1989, no other party had a cohesive structure similar to that of the PSOE. Felipe Gonzalez was an uncontested leader. *Felipismo* became a personalistic electoral phenomenon. The second largest party AP/PP was more than twenty percentage points behind the PSOE in all elections of the 1980s. On the left, the revitalization of the PCE by creating a coalition with other left-wing parties called United Left (*Izquierda Unida* [IU]) contributed to an increase of the electoral share, but far away from the two main parties. Such dominant power was consolidated by the PSOE through clientelistic and patronage structures. A close relationship to the business community made it possible to ensure the support of the economic establishment. The integration into the European Union and the flow of structural funds further strengthened the position of the PSOE. The lack of internal reform within the AP/PP made it impossible to challenge the PSOE. Until 1989, AP/PP was connected with the former authoritarian regime, and the PSOE did not shy away from using this in its campaign, declaring that by electing the AP/PP there was the danger of a return to an authoritarian dictatorship.[72]

The election of new party leader José Maria Aznar by the PP led to an internal reform and modernization of the party. Aznar was able to change the odds of the right-center PP in Spain. The moderation of the discourse from a rigid rejection of the autonomies in Spain to a more flexible one was the main feature of the new politics of PP.

Between 1989 and 1996, he was able to increase the vote of the PP by over fifteen percentage points finally achieving a victory in the March 3, 1996, elections. Such a change was already expected after the victories of the PP in the European elections of June 1994 and the regional elections of 1995. The electorate was quite cautious and gave PP only a tiny majority. Aznar was able to broker a deal with the regionalist parties and so create a working majority for the sixth legislature. Indeed, the cooperative style throughout the second half of the 1990s led to successes in the economy and the political climate after sixteen years of Socialist dominance. After Gonzalez's resignation, the PSOE was unable to find a suitable successor as party leader. Joaquin Almunia became the new leader. He tried to form a pact with the United Left against Aznar. This naturally strengthened the position of Aznar. Following the trend and due to the disarray in the Socialist camp, PP was able to gain an absolute majority in the March 12, 2000, elections.[73]

According to Pradeep Chiheeb and Mariano Torcal, PP is trying to be a party for everyone, whereas the PSOE clearly addresses the waged electorate. This very vague catchall construction of party strategies is accompanied by the general organizational development toward cartel parties. Both parties are extremely dependent on the subsidies of the state. Political marketing has become a major feature of Spanish party politics to attract the highest number of voters.[74]

The most salient cleavage of the Spanish party system has been between regionalist and centralist parties. Indeed, over the years the number of regionalist parties and their share of the vote increased considerably in the *Cortes*. The Catalan Convergence and Union (*Convergencia i Unió*) became quite pivotal in the 1990s as a kingmaker. Being the fourth largest party and given the avoidance of IU as a coalition partner by both main parties, the regionalist parties gain in importance in periods of minority governments.

Italy: From Imperfect Bipolarism to Polarized Bipolarism

The Italian party system can be divided into two main periods. The first period, between 1945 and 1992, was characterized by imperfect bipartyism. The second period, after 1992, saw the rise of a new party system with a new electoral system. The latter period can be characterised as one of polarized bipolarism.

The postwar Italian party system was established after the elections of April 18, 1948. The campaign of April 18, 1948, was conducted under the motto "Church against Communism" and established DC as the strongest party of the political system. Its main aim was to prevent that the second largest party, the PCI, from coming to governmental power.

The Cold War was a welcome supporter for the electoral fortunes of party leader Alcide de Gasperi. This fierce anticommunism character-ized the Italian political system until the early 1970s. Between 1948 and 1976 the DC kept in power by forming coalitions with other smaller parties. The Italian party system until 1992 was dominated by the ability to form coalitions against the PCI. This so-called imperfect bipolarism (*bipolarismo imperfetto*) or blocked democracy (*democrazia bloccatta*) pre-vented the establishment of genuine competitive politics. (See Table 4.5.) In its early stages, the DC used illicit methods—sometimes even using the Mafia—to fabricate electoral results. This was widespread in the southern regions of Italy.[75] The DC tended to form coalitions with three small secular parties, PRI, PLI, and PSDI. Occasionally it formed coalitions with the PSI. Between 1948 and 1962 a kind of centrism around the DC prevailed in the political system. Afterward, the DC experimented with coalition government with the PSI in conjunction with PRI and PSDI. A crucial turning point was the change in leadership in the PCI. New leader Enrico Berlinguer together with DC-leader Aldo Moro devised the formula of a "historical compromise" (*compromesso storico)* between right and left. Such a rapprochement between both parties started in 1973 and ended in 1978. The DC was declining in electoral terms and the PCI was able to gain more credibility as an alternative. There was its eventual possibility that the PCI would sur-pass DC. One of the factors that made the PCI more credible was its good administrative record as the party of regional governments since the 1970s.

The murder of Aldo Moro, leader of DC, on May 9, 1978, led to a breakup of the government of national solidarity comprising DC, PCI and PSI. Between 1979 and 1992, a five-party coalition government (*pentapartito government*) consisting of PSI, DC, PRI, PLI, and PSDI was the dominant form of government. After 1987, the party system became more fragmented.

In 1990, an electoral reform was introduced to reduce the number of preferential votings in elections from four to one. This was a way to reduce the widespread phenomenon of clientelism and patronage re-lated to abuse of preferential voting by local MPs. The last elections in 1992 (see Table 4.6) showed the continuing erosion and fragmentation of the DC-dominated party system. The *tangentopoli* affair gave the final blow to the political system. The *tangentopoli* affair targeted particularly DC and PSI. Both parties were depleted of their leaders within a very short period.

Within months, the main parties, DC and PSI, collapsed. The former second largest party, PCI/PDS, was the only major party to survive from the previous party system. In March 1994, a new party was established within three months. In this period, the media tycoon Silvio

TABLE 4.5 General Election Results in Italy (1948-1987)

	General Elections (1948–1968)									
	1948		1953		1958		1963		1968	
	%	Seats	%	Seats	%	Seats	%	Seats	%	Seats
DC	48.5	305	40.1	263	42.3	273	38.3	260	39.1	266
FP (PCI+PSI)	31.0	183	-	-	-	-	-	-		
United Socialists (PSI+PSDI)									14.5	91
PSI	-	-	12.7	75	14.2	84	13.8	87	-	-
PCI	-	-	22.6	143	22.7	140	25.3	166	26.9	177
PSDI	7.1	33	4.5	19	4.6	22	6.1	33	-	-
MSI	2.0	6	5.8	29	4.8	24	5.1	27	4.5	24
PDIUM/PNM	2.8	14	6.9	40	4.8	25	1.7	8	1.3	6
PRI	2.5	9	1.6	5	1.4	6	1.4	6	2.0	9
PLI	3.8	19	3.0	13	3.5	17	7.0	39	5.8	31
SVP	0.5	3	0.5	3	0.5	3	0.4	3	0.5	3
Comm. Val D'Aosta	-	-	-	-	0.6	1	0.1	1	-	-
PSIUP									4.4	23
Trieste List					0.1	1				
Peasants	0.3	1	-	-	-	-	-			
Sardinians	0.2	1	-	-	-	-	-	-		
Others	1.3	-	2.3	-	0.5	-	0.8	-	1	
	100	574	100	590	100	596	100	630	100	630

	General Elections (1972–1987)									
	1972		1976		1979		1983		1987	
	%	Seats	%	Seats	%	Seats	%	Seats	%	Seats
DC	38.7	266	38.7	263	38.3	262	32.9	225	34.3	234
PSI	9.6	61	9.6	57	9.8	62	11.4	73	14.3	94
PCI	271	179	34.4	227	30.4	201	29.9	198	26.6	177
PSDI	5.1	29	3.4	15	3.8	20	4.1	23	2.9	17
MSI	8.7	56	6.1	35	5.3	30	6.8	42	5.9	35
PIUM/PNM	-	-	-	-	-	-	-	-		
PRI	2.9	15	3.1	14	3.0	16	5.1	29	3.7	21
PLI	3.9	20	1.3	5	1.9	9	2.9	16	2.1	11
SVP	0.5	3	0.5	3	0.5	4	0.5	3	0.5	3
LN							-	-	0.5	1
Comm. Val D'Aosta	-	-	0.1	1	0.1	1	0.1	1	0.1	1
Sardinian	-	-	-	-	-	-	0.3	1	0.4	2
Venetian League							0.3	1	-	-
Trieste List	-	-	-	-	0.2	1				
DP	-	-	1.5	6	-	-	1.5	7	1.7	8
PDUP	-	-	-	-	1.4	6	-	-		
Green List	-	-	-	-	-	-	-	-	2.5	13
Progressive Group	0.1	1	-	-	-	-				
P. Radicale	-	-	1.1	4	3.5	18	2.2	11	2.6	13
Others	3.4	-	0.2	-	1.8	-	0.2	-	1.9	-
	100	630	100	630	100	630	100	630	100	630

Source: Data compiled from official results announced by Ministry of Interior, Ministero dell'Interno: http://cedweb.mininterno.it and http://www.cattaneo.org.

TABLE 4.6   The Last General Elections under the Old Italian Electoral System in 1992

Parties	1992	
	%	Seats
DC	29.7	206
PSI	13.6	92
PCI/PDS	16.1	107
PSDI	2.7	16
MSI	5.4	34
PRI	4.4	27
PLI	2.8	17
SVP	0.5	3
Lega Lombarda/Lega Nord	8.7	55
Communist Refoundation (RC)	5.6	35
Other Leagues	1.2	1
La Rete	1.9	12
Green List	3.0	16
Panella List	1.2	7
Pensioneers Federation	0.4	1
Com. Val D'Aosta	0.1	1
Others	2.7	-

Source: Data compiled from official results of Ministero dell'Interno: http://cedweb. mininterno.it and http://www.cattareo.org.

Berlusconi launched his new party *Forza Italia* (FI). This highly populist party won the elections of 1994 under the new mixed electoral system.

The new party system, based on a quota of 75 percent MPs elected in uninominal constituencies by a majority electoral system and 25 percent by proportional representation system suited well the needs of FI and its coalition partners AN and LN, which were parties based on personal politics. The PDS had difficulties adjusting to the new party system. The use of television and modern marketing strategies by Silvio Berlusconi changed the nature of electoral campaigns in Italy. The victory of Silvio Berlusconi in March 1994 filled the vacuum left by DC and PSI. The PDS became only the second largest party. The party system was now polarized between two different electoral coalitions. On the one hand, the right-center coalition of FI, AN, and LN was successful in attracting votes from all the regions of Italy. It campaigned in the north as the Pole of Freedom (*Polo della Libertá*) and in the south as the Pole of Good Government (*Polo del Buon Governo*). On the other hand, the left-center coalition led by PDS comprised several small parties and was called the Progressive Alliance.[76] (See Table 4.7 and Table 4.8.)

TABLE 4.7 The General Elections under the New Electoral System, 1994–2001 (Chamber of Deputies)

Parties	1994			
		Seats		
	%	PR	SM	Total
POLO DELLA LIBERTÀ/POLO DEL BUON GOVERNO	46.4	64	302	366
FI	21.0	30	74	104
AN/MSI	13.6	23	87	110
Lega Nord	8.4	11	107	118
CCD			22	22
UMC			4	4
Pannella			6	8
Liberal Democratic Pole			2	2
PROGRESSISTI	34.4	49	164	213
Independent Left			11	11
PDS	20.4	38	72	110
RC	6.0	11	27	38
Verdi	2.7		11	11
La Rete	1.9		6	6
PSI	2.2		14	14
AD	1.2		18	18
CS			4	4
Socialist Renewal			1	1
PATTO PER L'ITALIA	15.7	42	4	46
Segni	4.6	13		13
PPI/DC	11.1	29	4	33
OTHERS	3.5		5	5

Parties	1996			
		Seats		
	%	PR	SM	Total
OLIVE TREE	43.2	58	265	323
PDS	21.1	26	145	171
PPI/Prodi List	6.8	4	71	75
Dini-Italian Renewal List	4.3	8	18	26
Greens	2.3	0	16	16
Sardinian Action Party	0.1	-	-	-
Communist Refoundation (RC)	8.6	20	15	35
FREEDOM ALLIANCE	42.5	77	169	246
CDU/CCD	5.8	12	18	30
FI	21.0	37	86	123
AN	15.7	28	65	93

TABLE 4.7   *(continued)*

Parties	1996			
		Seats		
	%	PR	SM	Total
LN	10.1	20	39	59
Lista Aosta valley/Lista Valle d'Aosta	-	-	1	1
Southern League	0.2	-	1	1
Social Movement Tricolor Flame	0.9	-	-	-
Socialists	0.4	-	-	-
Others	2.7	-	-	-
SUM	100	155	475	630

Parties	2001			
		Seats		
	%	PR	SM	Total
OLIVE TREE (RUTELLI)	35.0	58	189	247
DS	16.6	31		
La Margherita	14.5	27		
Girasole (Greens)	2.2	-		
Comunisti Italiani	1.7	-		
HOUSE OF FREEDOMS (BERLUSCONI)	49.5	86	282	368
FI	29.5	62		
LN	3.9	0		
AN	12.0	24		
Biancofiore (CCD-CDU)	3.2	0		
New Socialist Party	1.0	0		
Fiamma Tricolore	0.4	-		
Lista Di Pietro	4.0	-		
Panella-Bonino List	2.2	0		-
Democrazia Europea	2.4	-	-	
RC	5.0	11		11
Others	1.6		4	4
SUM	100	155	475	630

Source: data compiled from official results presented by Ministero dell'Interno, http://cedweb.mininterno.it; and http://www.cattaneo.org.

After a long technical government by Lamberto Dini, new elections were called in May 1996, in which the left-center Olive Tree coalition under the leadership of Romano Prodi won against the right-center coalition dominated by Berlusconi's FI and Fini's AN. After the 1994 government experience with the right-center coalition, the population

TABLE 4.8 General Elections under the New Electoral System (Senate)

Parties	1994 Seats	1996 Seats	2001 Seats
Progressives (1994)/Olive Tree (1996; 2001)	122	157	128
Freedom Pole/Good Government Pole (1994)/Freedom Alliance (1996)/House of Freedoms (2001)	155	116	177
Pact for Italy (1994)	31		
LN (1996)	-	27	
RC	-	10	3
Fiamma	-	1	
Pannella List	1	1	
Others	6	3	7
	315	315	315

Source: Data compiled according to official results of Ministero dell'Interno, http://cedweb.mininterno.it; Inter-Parliamentary Union http://www.ipu.org/parline-e/ and http://www.cattaneo.org.

voted for Olive Tree. This historical win of the left clearly increased the expectations of the population.[77]

In spite of this victory, government in Italy continues to be unstable due to the fact that the electoral coalitions are very loose and majorities very weak. The former prime minister Massimo d'Alema was faced with a coalition crisis at the end of 1999. A similar situation happened to Romano Prodi when he was in government between 1996 and 1998. He failed to win a vote of no confidence in the Italian Parliament, which led to the collapse of the cooperation of the Olive Tree coalition with the Communist Refoundation party.

The March 13, 2001, elections consolidated the polarized bipolarism. In spite of pending trials, Silvio Berlusconi was able to once more rally the parties of the right under a loose coalition umbrella called the House of Freedoms (*Casa delle Libertá*). The whole approach of Berlusconi was very interesting, because he tried to create a catchall alliance including parties on the left and right. Particularly interesting is the comeback of the Socialists under the leadership of Bobo Craxi, who supported Berlusconi's coalition. Another supporter was the new party of Giulio Andreotti, *Democrazia Europea*. The present coalition was more stable than that of 1994. Berlusconi's *Forza Italia* was able to improve the electoral share and to play a pivotal role in keeping both Gianfranco Fini's AN and Umberto Bossi's LN under control. Both parties lost electoral support to FI in the last elections. Berlusconi was able to profit from a fragmented divided Olive Tree coalition. The population opted for change, disappointed with the performance of the leaders of Olive Tree. Berlusconi presented himself as a stable alternative, and he used modern marketing techniques such as message polling to win the elections. This naturally shows that elections in Italy are being affected by the phenomena of presidentialization and Americanization. The main posters of Berlusconi and Rutelli were accompanied by the word "presidente," meaning that the prime minister called in Italian *Il Presidente del Governo* became the focus of the electoral process. Although both parties had their party manifesto, in the end Berlusconi's populist agenda of cutting taxes, increasing the pensions for pensioneers, and modernization of public administration by using the new technologies such as the Internet were better presented to the public. A lesson from the Italian elections is that both the electorate as well as the parties have become flexible in their relations. The electorate has become more individualistic and approaches politics along consumerist lines, while the parties have become light and umbrella-like so that they can integrate larger followings. This naturally is leading to a decline of substance in political campaigning.[78]

In sum, the most salient feature of Italian politics is its Americanization. The formation of two coalitions of parties on the left and right created a similar system to that of Anglo-Saxon democracies. Modern marketing strategies and reorganization of parties further confirm this transformation. Presently the electoral law is under discussion. The left-center coalition wants to change it to a mixed system that again will give more importance to proportional representation. The Olive Tree coalition is calling for a change toward a 50:50 mixed system. This is opposed by the right-center coalition under the leadership of Silvio Berlusconi, which was able to profit from the predominance of the simple majority system in the present electoral system. One positive aspect of the May 2001 elections is that more than 80 percent of the population went to the polls and cast their vote. This is quite amazing, because the Olive Tree government had cut resources for the staging of the elections. Many election stations were closed, so that voters had to wait long to cast their votes. The last vote was cast at 5:00 a.m. the next day.[79]

Greece

The Greek party system has been quite stable from the outset. It can be divided into two main periods. The first period is dominated by New Democracy, the second, apart from a short exceptional period between 1989 and 1993, by PASOK. The party system has remained a two-and-a-half party system.

The Greek political system achieved its stability in the first founding elections of November 17, 1974. The dominance of ND and PASOK remained the main feature of the Greek party system.

The absolute majority of PASOK and the collapse of the Center Union in 1981 due to internal factionalism and the growing attractiveness of PASOK led to the final establishment of a four-party system.[80]

The two main parties became PASOK and ND, which benefited from the reinforced proportional representation electoral system while smaller parties were discriminated against, particularly the two small communist parties. ND lost against the emerging radical populist PASOK in 1981. The victory of PASOK marked the beginning of a new phase in the Greek party system. This phase of "patrimonial socialism" lasted two legislature periods until 1989. In this period, Papandreou's PASOK used its power to establish what Christos Lyrintzis called *bureaucratic clientelism*.[81] The abuse of power led to the manipulation of the electoral law. A change of the electoral law shortly before the June 1989 general elections prevented an absolute majority for ND.[82]

In 1989–1990, ND and the two communist parties conducted several parliamentary inquiries about corruption scandals during the PASOK tenure. Parliament became the central stage of the political system. The inquiries on political corruption were dropped or shelved after a while. Between June 1989 and April 1990 there were three elections because ND was not able to win a clear-cut absolute majority to form a government. Only in November 1990 did ND gather 47 percent of vote and 50 percent of the 300 seats (see Table 4.9).

Nevertheless the scarce parliamentary majority was subsequently eroded by defection of some MPs from ND. Prime Minister Kostas Mitsotakis had difficulties keeping his parliamentary group and government together and implementing the required public policies for the modernization of the country. His personal dislike of Andreas Papandreou also created a bad atmosphere between opposition and the ruling party. By 1993, Mitsotakis had to call for early elections.[83]

After 1993 PASOK returned to power under Andreas Papandreou. Two years later, Papandreou died and was replaced by the moderate Kostas Simitis, who is still leader of the party.[84] He introduced a more moderate style in politics. After the political scandals related to the former ND prime minister Kostas Mitsotakis, a new leader took over the leadership of the party. Miltiades Evert moderated its discourse, so that Greek politics became less conflictual between the two parties. In 1997, Miltiades Evert was replaced by Kostas Karamanlis, the nephew of former president Karamanlis, who was directly elected in the 4th ND party conference on March 21.

In the legislative elections of May 2000, PASOK repeated its absolute majority for the third consecutive time, but Karamanlis's ND became a strong second. The third largest party remains the KKE, which continues to have a strong support among intellectuals, the young, and blue-collar workers. *Synaspismos* now has a reduced electoral basis of

TABLE 4.9 General Election Results in Greece (1974–2000)

	GENERAL ELECTIONS (1974–1981)					
	1974		*1977*		*1981*	
	%	*Seats*	*%*	*Seats*	*%*	*Seats*
ND	54.4	220	41.9	171	35.9	115
EK-EDIK	20.4	60	12	16		
PASOK	13.6	12	25.3	93	48.1	172
EA	9.5	8				
KKE			9.4	11	10.9	13
SAP			2.7	2		
EP			6.8	5		
Others	2.1	-	1.9	2	5.1	-
SUM	100	300	100	300	100	300

	GENERAL ELECTIONS (1985–2000)													
	1985		*1989a*		*1989b*		*1990*		*1993*		*1996*		*2000*	
	%	*Seats*	*%*	*Seats*	*%*	*Seats*	*%*	*Seats*	*%*	*Seats*	*%*	*Seats*	*%*	*Seats*
ND	40.9	126	44.3	145	46.2	148	46.9	150	46.9	170	38.1	108	42.7	125
PASOK	45.8	161	39.2	125	40.6	128	38.6	125	39.3	111	41.5	162	43.8	158
KKE	9.9	12	13.1	28					4.54	9	5.6	11	5.5	11
KKE-es	1.8	1							-				3.2	6
SYN			13.0	28	10.9	21	10.3	21			5.1	10		
POLAN									4.90	10	2.3			
Greens							1.1	1						
DIKKI							1.1	1			4.4	9	2.7	-
Independents					2.3	3	2.1	2						
Moslem Minority Party							2.1	2						
Others	1.6	-	1.5	2			0.6	2	4.36		3	-	2.1	
SUM	100	300	100	300	100	300	100	300	100	300	100	300	100	300

Source: Own compilation based on the following sources: Keith R. Legg and John M. Roberts, *Modern Greece. A Civilization on the Periphery* (Boulder, CO: Westview Press, 1997), 142–143; George Mavrogordatos, "Greece" in *Political Data Yearbook 1997*. Special Issue of *European Journal for Political Research* 32, no. 3–4 (1997): 375; George Mavrogordatos, "Greece" in *Political Data Yearbook 2001*. Special Issue of *European Journal for Political Research* 40, no. 3–4, 313.

over 3 percent. It is too early to say if the two small left-wing parties will ever be able to challenge the two main parties. On the contrary, *Synaspismos* is probably interested in surviving the high threshold from election to election.

On the whole, the party system is extremely stable. It is essentially a four-party system although PASOK so far has been the dominant party. In the past twenty-five years of democracy, PASOK was in power for fourteen years and ND for nine years. In the other two years, coalition governments led to the inclusion of the Progressive Left Coalition in governmental responsibility.

The main cleavage remains ideological. The continuing existence of two communist parties in Greece shows how important ideology still is. In a survey, MPs expressed that political ideology is important or very important in Greek politics. About 25 percent of ND respondents tended to believe that it is less important. Nevertheless, MPs from the two main parties and *Synaspismos* believe that the Greek political system will undergo major changes in the future.[85] According to Hammann and Sgouraki-Kinsey, the Greek party system showed more stability in the predictatorship party system than did the Iberian countries. In terms of ideology, electoral geography, and social change there is a stronger continuity than in Spain and Portugal. The main reason is that the ideological reputation of certain parties represented by the political families remained almost intact, in spite of the dictatorship. In the case of Spain and Portugal, the long dictatorship eased the continuity of the democratic ideological reputation before and after the dictatorship; it allowed for the creation of absolute new party systems, in spite of the fact that some parties were present before and during the dictatorship.[86] This naturally explains the rigidity of the Greek electoral market, in spite of the major socioeconomic changes happening since 1974.

Regional Elections in Spain and Italy

Spain

The introduction of autonomous communities (*comunidades autonomas* [CCAA]) in Spain between 1979 and 1983 led to the creation of a new area of electoral competition. Seventeen autonomous communities produced seventeen regional electoral arenas with seventeen different party systems. Until the late 1980s, the two levels of electoral competition did not interact. This changed in 1993, when the PSOE was not able to gain a clear majority in the Congress of Deputies and asked CiU for support in parliament. This support was granted by Jordi Pujol until 1995. Afterward the main Catalan party realized that support for the PSOE was affecting their chances in the forthcoming Catalan elections. Most of the autonomous communities reproduce the party system at the national level. They are mere copies of national politics.[87] This is particularly the case in the regions of Castilla La Mancha, Castilla-León, Extremadura, Comunidad Madrid, Andalucia, Asturias, Baleares, Murcia, La Rioja, Navarra, Comunidad Valenciana, Cantabria, and Aragon. Only in four of the CCAA can one find strong regionalist-nationalist parties. The most evident case is Catalonia, where the CiU under the leadership of the charismatic Jordi Pujol was able to achieve a strong majority until today. In the elections of October 1999, the

Catalan Socialists under the leadership of the mayor Pascual Maragall of Barcelona was able to break the absolute majority of the CiU. (See Table 4.10.) Maragall is regarded as a potential successor for Jordi Pujol in the next elections. This would be an extradionary success for the PSOE in regional elections. Therefore, it is assumed that Pujol may step down before the end of the legislature and be replaced by Artur Más so that the success of Maragall in the next elections can be contained.

In the Basque Country, PNV has been the strongest party, but it always has failed to win an absolute majority. This party formed a coalition government with the Basque socialist party throughout this period. The PNV has also been able to compete successfully with other nationalist-regionalist parties such as HB and EA for the Basque electorate. In recent times, it demands a unification of all Basque regions in France and Spain. This verbal radicalism has been criticized by the major parties due to the return of the terrorist organization ETA to violence. In the elections of May 13, 2001, the PNV in coalition with EE emerged stronger against the national parties. Indeed, although the Basque PP chaired by the charismatic Mayor Oreja wanted to reduce the importance of the regionalist parties, the moderate nationalist parties were able to achieve almost an absolute majority. In these elections the Basque electorate rejected the politics of violence of the ETA separatist movement. Indeed, *Herri Batasuna/Eusko Herritarok*'s vote was reduced almost by half, and they lost half of their seats in comparison to the 1998 elections. This is due to the politics of moderation pursued by lehendekari. José Ibarretxe and the high voter turnout of 80 percent. Aznar was quite disappointed with the result. The outcome, indeed, has increased the polarization between regionalism and *españolismo* (non-Basque nationalism) in the Basque country.[88]

In Galicia, the nationalist-regionalist vote was very fragmented in the 1980s. Only in the 1990s did a major party begin to emerge that was

TABLE 4.10 Government Composition in the Spanish Autonomous Communities (1983–2001)

	1983	1987	1991	1995	1999
PSOE	12	10	8	3	4
AP/PP	3	4	3	8	10
Coalition Government	1	2	2	4	1
Regionalist Party	1	1	4	2	2
SUM	17	17	17	17	17

Source: Own compilation based on information from individual chapters in Manuel Alcantara and Antoina Martinez (eds.), *Las Elecciones Autonómicas en Espana, 1980-1997* (Madrid: CIS, 1998), and *El Pais*, June 15, 1999, p. 27.

able to play a role in the Galician party system. In 1997, The Nationalist Galician Bloc (*Bloque Nacionalista Gallego* [BNG]) was able to win over 25 percent and surpass the PSG and the IU in the regionalist elections. The main leader is Xosé Maria Beiras, a left-wing intellectual who wants to challenge the overdominance of the PP in regional government chaired by the former Francoist minister and former leader of the PP, Manuel Fraga Iribarne.[89] The popular Manuel Fraga was able to win the regional elections in Galicia in October 2001 with a renewed absolute majority. Indeed, the socialists were able to improve their results and are a major challenger to Xosé Maria Beiras. The big losers in Galicia are the communists, who almost disappeared from this region.[90] In recent times Manuel Fraga and Xosé Maria Beiras decided to overcome their differences and animosities and work more constructively on behalf of Galicia.[91]

A similar process happened in the Canary islands. In the 1990s the regionalist-nationalist party rallied behind the Canary Coalition (see Table 4.11), which has been successful in challenging the two main parties since the regional elections of 1995.

Italy

In Italy, there are regional elections in the fifteen regions and five special regions. Regional elections became more interesting with the decline of the former party system. The emergence of LN considerably changed the nature of electoral competition. The LN was able to gain a strong foothold in the northern regions of Italy. This is only contested by *Forza Italia*, which inherited the vote of DC. In the south, a party emerged in the 1990s called *La Rete* led by Leoluca Orlando who was a former member of DC. His party was able to capture the majority of the vote in Sicily in 1990s. The main platform is to fight against the Mafia.

In Val D'Aosta, the *Union Valdotaine* is the dominant party; it represents the interests of the French minority in this region. The same can be said about the South Tyrolian People's Party (*Südtiroler Volkspartei* [SVP]), which is the main representation of the German minority in Trentino-Alto Adige. The electoral system is similar to that at the national level. It reinforces alliances and personalization of politics. Since the elections of April 16, 2000, one can recognize a similar trend as it exists at the national level, the creation of bipolar alliances along left-right categories. At the same time, fragmentation and volatility within the coalitions have increased in the past six to seven years.[92] Therefore it was possible to declare a winner and loser of the April 16, 2000, elections and interpret them as a sign of the population against the government. It led to the immediate resignation of Massimo D'Alema as prime minister and the nomination of Giulio D'Amato to form a transitional technocratic government until the legislative elections of 2001.

TABLE 4.11 Regionalist-Nationalist Parties in the Spanish Autonomous Communities (2000)

Autonomous Community	Party	Significance
Andalucia	Andalucian Party/Partido Andaluz (PA)	Small party
Aragón	Aragonian Regionalist Party (Partido Regionalista Aragón)	Third largest party
Asturias	Asturian Party-Asturian Coalition (Partido Asturianista-Coalicion Asturianista-PAS-CA)	Small party
Baleares	Mallorcan Union (Unió Mallorquina-UM)	Small party
Canarias	Canarian Coalition (Coalición Canaria-CC)	Major party
Cantabria	Union for the Progress of Cantabria (Union para el Progreso de Cantabria-UPCA)	Fourth largest party
Castilla y León	None	
Castilla-La Mancha	None	
Catalonia	Convergence and Union (Convergencia i Unió-CiU) Other parties: Republican	Major party
	Left of Catalonia (Esquerra Republicana de Catalunya-ERC)	Small party
Extremadura	United Extremadura (Extremadura Unida-EU)	Small party
Galicia	National Galician Block (Bloque Nacional Gallego-BNG)	Second largest party
Madrid	None	
Murcia	None	
Navarra	Union of the Navarran People (Unión del Pueblo de Navarra-UPN) Other parties: Herri Batasuna and Partido Nacionalista Vasco (PNV)	Second largest party
Pais Vasco	Nationalist Basque Party (Partido Nacionalista Vasco-PNV);	Major party
	Other parties: Herri Batasuna (-HB and Eusko Askartasuna (-EA)	Small parties
Rioja	Party of Rioja (Partido de Rioja-PR)	Small party
Comunidad Valenciana	Valencian Union (Unió Valenciana-UV)	Small party

Source: Own compilation based on information from individual chapters of Manuel Alcantara and Antonia Martinez (eds.), *Las Elecciones Autonómicas en Espana, 1980-1997* (Madrid: CIS, 1998).

Second Order Elections: Local and European Parliament Elections

Local and European Parliament elections have been defined as second order elections. They have less significance than general elections. In some way they function as a political barometer for the governing party.

Portugal

In Portugal, local elections have taken place since 1976. There are 308 municipalities, which led to a similar result to that in general elections. Meanwhile, after two decades of local elections, one can say that the two main parties are the PS and the PSD. Whereas the PS was quite successful in the urban centers, the PSD was more successful in middle-range towns and in the rural areas of northern Portugal. The CDU has achieved a remarkably good reputation as a local government party. It is very strong in the suburban regions of Lisbon and in the Alentejo. The CDS-PP has lost in significance over the years.[93] In the elections of December 16, 2001, the PS lost control of most Portuguese cities. Indeed, Lisbon, Oporto, and Coimbra are now dominated by the PSD. The Socialists were more successful in the interior and middle-sized towns. This is naturally an interesting reversal of a two-decade-long trend. Moreover, in these recent elections, citizens' groups were successful in challenging the main parties in the smaller communities.[94] The impact of the local results led to the resignation of Prime Minister Guterres and the call for early elections by President Sampaio.

Spain

In Spain, local elections are a mirror of national politics and regional politics. Over 8,000 municipalities have to elect their representatives every four years. In the regions where regionalist-nationalist parties are strong the main parties are less successful, whereas in regions with no regionalist-nationalist parties, one can find a crucial barometer of how the government is performing. Apart from Galicia, Catalonia, Andalucia, and Basque Country, municipal elections seem to reflect national aspects of electoral choice. This became quite evident in the 1990s with the establishment of the PP as a credible challenger of the PSOE. Such a tendency toward a nationalization of local elections started in 1991 and became quite evident in 1995. This trend is certainly reinforced by the fact that local government is still extremely underfunded within the new democratic state. Presently the main party of local government is the PP, after twelve years of dominance by the PSOE.[95]

Italy

There are elections to the communes and provinces in Italy. There are about 8,000 communes, which more or less reproduce the results at the national level. The same can be said about the provinces. The big surprises are more related to the elections in the larger towns. The direct election of the mayor led to a stronger personalization of politics at the local level. In 1997 most of the larger towns were in the hand of the center-left coalition. Quite a surprise was the victory of FI in Milan against the center-left candidate. A turnover of the political class after *tangentopoli* happened only after 1995.[96]

Greece

In Greece, there are about 6,000 local government units (5,700 communes and 300 municipalities), which are directly elected. Local government in Greece continues to be dominated by central government. This is a major obstacle to democratization and decentralization of public policy-making. During the 1980s, local government was extremely politicized. PASOK made all efforts to place PASOK candidates as mayors of the major cities of Thessaloniki and Athens. A certain depoliticization took place during the 1990s leading to some reform of the local level known as the Capodistrias Reform, named after the founder of the first Greek Republic in the early nineteenth century. The main plan was to reduce the number of localities from over 5,600 to 809. In spite of resistance, the reform was undertaken (see Chapter 3). In the 1998 local elections, PASOK had to concede defeat to ND. The independent Dimitris Avramopoulos backed by New Democracy won the local elections in Athens with 57 percent of the vote on the first ballot on October 11, 1998. PASOK's Kostas Papadopoulos could claim only the narrowest of victories over the New Democracy candidate in Thessaloniki on the second ballot on October 18. PASOK was successfully challenged by ND at the different levels of the subnational system. ND won twenty-seven prefectures out of fifty-four against twenty-five by PASOK; at municipal level, PASOK carried 433 candidates, ND 368, KKE 24, SYN 12, DIKKI 5, Political Spring 3, and Independents 55. The abstention rate was over 30 percent. This shows that these elections are considered second order elections. These results are quite interesting, because they show that independents and citizens' groups are successfully challenging the larger parties at the local level. Recently, Mayor Avramopoulos of Athens founded a new political group called the Free Citizens' Movement, which intends to break the hegemony of the two main parties in the next legislative elections of 2004. The founding conference was in October 2001. Some surveys suggest that the charismatic Avramopoulos may reach up to 14 percent and become kingmaker of the next government.[97]

Like local elections, European Parliament elections have to be considered second order elections. The high levels of abstention across Europe suggest that there is no awareness of a European dimension of politics. The participation in European elections declined to an all-time low of 49.4 percent in 1999. Among the southern European countries, Portugal has the lowest participation rate of 40 percent; Greece has the highest at 70.8 percent, which is due to the fact that voting is compulsory. Spain's participation rate of 64.3 percent is quite good in the European context. Campaigning in these countries still does not touch European issues, but is more about national politics. In all countries one can see a strong dependency of this second order election on the results of general elections. Indeed, the results in Portugal were almost identical to that of the subsequent general elections in October 1999. The same can be said about the elections in Spain and Greece. Presently, the social democratic parties dominate in Portugal and Greece; in Spain the Christian-democratic PP continues to attract most of the voters. Whereas PSOE, PS, PDS and PASOK were involved in Euro-wide campaigning of the European Socialist Party (ESP), PP, ND, FI, and PSD joined the campaign strategy of the EPP. This naturally is symbolic politics. Most of the issues remain national. An exception to the rule may be the Italian case, where campaigns are more European and results may bring new personalities into the national political game. This was the case of the list of Emma Bonnino, former Commissioner of the Santer European Commission, who was able to win some seats in the new European parliament in the last elections. The Italian group is quite fragmented. FI emerged as the largest group with twenty-two out of eighty-seven seats. The Democrats of the Left were able to achieve 15. In Spain, the main party remained the PP with twenty-two out of sixty. Some regionalist parties returned to the European Parliament, and the PSOE was able to make a gain of two seats. The D'Hondt system used at European Parliament elections in Greece allowed for a broader representation. Indeed, the smaller parties Political Spring and the two left-wing parties were able to achieve seats in the new European Parliament.[98]

CONCLUSIONS

Modern political parties in southern Europe only became a concrete reality after World War II. Through in Italy a modern party system with all its failures was established after World War I for a short period of time, Portugal, Spain, and Greece had to wait until the 1970s to establish a genuine party system based on universal, secret suffrage. Manipulations of electoral systems took place throughout the twentieth century. In Greece, it lasted until 1989 when PASOK changed the electoral system shortly before the elections to prevent main rival ND from winning the elections. In spite of all these deficiencies, the four-party systems were to achieve a remarkable level of stability.

NOTES

1. Richard Katz and Peter Mair, "Changing Models of Party Organisation and Party Democracy: The Emergence of the Cartel Party," *Party Politics* (1995): 5–28.

For a critique from the Italian perspective, see Francesco Raniolo, "Miti e Realtà del Cartel Party: Le Transformazioni dei Partiti alla Fine del Ventesimo Secolo," *Rivista Italiana di Scienza Politica* 30, no. 3 (2000): 553–81.

2. Klaus v. Beyme, "Party Leadership and Change in Party Systems: Towards a Postmodern Party State?," *Government and Opposition* 31, no. 2 (1996): 135–59, particularly p. 140. According to Manuel Castells, Americanization can be observed in three main processes: the decline of political parties and of their role in selecting candidates; the emergence of a complex media system, anchored in television, but with an increasing diversity of flexible media, electronically interconnected; the development of political marketing, with constant opinion polling, feedback systems between polling and politicking, media spinning, computerized direct mailing and phone banks, and real time adjustments of candidates and issues to the format that can win. See *The Power of Identity*, vol. 2 of *The Information Age: Economy, Society and Culture* (London: Blackwell, 1997), 317–18. Here is not the place to discuss the growing importance of political marketing. For further reading, see Bruce I. Newman, *The Mass Marketing of Politics: Democracy in an Age of Manufactured Images* (London: Sage, 1999).

3. Rainer Eisfeld, *Sozialistischer Pluralismus in Europa: Ansätze und Scheitern and Beispiel Portugal* (Köln: Wissenschaft und Politik, 1984); Juliet Antunes Sablovsky, "The Portuguese Socialist Party," in *Political Parties and Democracy in Portugal: Organizations, Elections, and Public Opinion*, ed. Thomas C. Bruneau (Boulder, CO: Westview Press, 1997), 55–76, particularly pp. 64–66.

4. Ilse Marie Führer, *Los Sindicatos en España: De la Lucha de Clases a Estrátegias de Cooperación* (Madrid: Consejo Economico y Social, 1996).

5. According to *El Pais* (Febuary 1, 2000), p. 6, quoting the *Süddeutsche Zeitung* estimates, 30 to 40 million German marks were transferred from the social democratic government of Helmut Schmidt to political actions in Portugal and Spain. They were used to strengthen the democratic parties in southern Europe.

6. José M. Magone, "The Portuguese Socialist Party," in *Social Democratic Parties in the European Union*, ed. Robert Ladrech and Philippe Marliére (Basingstoke: Macmillan, 1999), 166–75, particularly pp. 166–69.

7. Bernd Rother, *Der verhinderte Übergang zum Sozialismus: Die sozialistische Partei Portugals im Zentrum der Macht (1974–1978)* (Frankfurt: Materialis, 1985).

8. Manuel Braga da Cruz, *Instituições Politicas e Processos Sociais* (Lisboa: Bertrand, 1995), 143–47; Tom Gallagher, "The Portuguese Socialist Party: The Pitfalls of Being First," in *Southern European Socialism*, ed. Tom Gallagher and Allan Williams (Manchester: Manchester University Press, 1990), 12–32.

9. Partido Socialista, *25 Anos em Documentos e Imagens: Fontes para a História do Partito: Fontes Para a História do PS 1*, CD-ROM, 1999.

10. Paul Kennedy, "The Spanish Socialist Workers' Party," in *Social Democratic Parties in the European Union*, ed. Robert Ladrech and Philippe Marliére (Basingstoke: Macmillan, 1999), 176–88, particularly p. 183. The best study on the organizational strategy of the PSOE since 1975 is Monica Mendez, *La Estrategia Organizativa del Partito Socialista Obrero Espanol (1975-1996)* (Madrid: Centro de Investigaciones Sociologicas, 2000).

11. Richard Gunther, Giacomo Sani, and Goldie Shabad, *Spain after Franco: The Making of a Competitive Party System* (Los Angeles: University of California Press, 1988), 72.

12. Wolfgang Merkel, "Sozialdemokratische Politik in einer post-Keynesianischen Ära? Das Beispiel der sozialistischen Regierung Spaniens (1982–

1988)," *Politisches Vierteljahresschrift* 30 (1989): 629–54; Wolfgang Merkel, *Ende der Sozialdemokratie? Machtresourcen und Regierungspolitik im westeuropaeischen Vergleich* (Frankfurt a.: M. Campus, 1993); Richard Gillespie, "The Break-Up of the 'Socialist Family': Party Union Relations in Spain, 1982–89," *West European Politics* 13 (1990): 47–62.

13. James F. Petras, "Spanish Socialism: On the Road to Marbella," *Contemporary Crises: Law, Crime and Social Policy* 14, no. 3 (1990): 189–217; Petras, "Spanish Socialism: The Politics of Neoliberalism," in *Mediterranean Paradoxes: The Political and Social Structures of Southern Europe*, ed. James Kurth and James Petras (Providence, RI: Berg Publishers, 1993), 95–127.

14. Richard Gillespie, "The Resurgence of Factionalism in the Spanish Socialist Workers' Party," in *Conflict and Cohesion in Western European Social Democratic Parties*, ed. David S. Bell and Eric Shaw (London: Pinter, 1994), 50–69.

15. Paul Heywood, "Political Corruption in Modern Spain," in *Distorting Democracy: Political Corruption in Spain, Italy and Malta*, ed. Paul Heywood (Bristol: Centre for Mediterranean Studies- University of Bristol, 1994), Occasional Paper no. 10, pp. 1–14; Heywood, "Sleaze in Spain," *Parliamentary Affairs* 48, no. 4 (October 1995): 726–37.

16. *El Pais*, July 22, 2000, pp. 15–22; *El Pais*, July 24, 2000, pp. 15–26; *El Pais*, May 16, 2001, p. 22.

17. *El Pais*, July 1, 2001, p. 22.

18. Francesco Gozzano, "Italian Politics after 'Kickback City,'" *Italian Socialism: Between Politics and History*, ed. Spencer Di Scala (Amherst: University of Massachusetts Press, 1996), 202–13.

19. David Hine, *Governing Italy: The Politics of Bargained Pluralism*.(Oxford: Oxford University Press, 1993), 114, 120–22.

20. Ministero dell'Interno, May 18, 2001, http://ced.web.mininterno.it:8890/camera/C000000.htm

21. Michalis Spourdalakis, *The Rise of the Greek Socialist Party* (London: Routledge, 1988); George Mavrogordatos, *Rise of the Green Sun: The Greek Election of 1981* (London: Centre of Contemporary Greek Studies, King's College, 1983), Occasional Paper, no. 1; José M. Magone, "Party Factionalism in New Small Southern European Democracies: Some Comparative Findings from Portuguese and Greek Experiences (1974–82)," in *Factional Politics and Democratization*, ed. Richard Gillespie, Michael Waller, and Lourdes López Nieto (London: Frank Cass, 1995), 91–101.

22. Gerassimos Moschomas, "The Panhellenic Socialist Movement," in *Social Democratic Parties in the European Union: History, Organization, Policies*, ed. Robert Ladrech and Philippe Marliére (Basingstoke, U.K.: Macmillan, 1999), 110–22, particularly p. 114.

23. Athens News Agency, June 2, 2001.

24. Ibid., October 15, 2001.

25. David Corkill, "Party Factionalism and Democratization in Portugal," *Democratization* 2, no. 2 (1995): 64–76, particularly pp. 70–72.

26. This is named after the dominant charismatic leader Anibal Cavaco Silva, who was leader between 1985 and 1995.

27. Fernando Nogueira (1995), Marcelo Rebelo Sousa (1996–1999), and presently former Minister of Foreign Affairs Manuel Durão Barroso (1999–).

28. *Expresso*, August 10, 1996.

29. Maritheresa Frain, "The Right in Portugal: The PSD and the CDS/PP," *Political Parties and Democracy in Portugal. Organizations, Elections, and Public Opinion*, ed. Thomas C. Bruneau (Boulder, CO: Westview Press, 1997), 76–111,

particularly p. 94; Frain, *PPD/PSD e a Consolidação do Regime Democrático* (Lisboa: Editorial Noticias, 1998). With the resurgence of the Socialist party, the party membership may have declined to below 100,000.

30. Frain, "The Right in Portugal," 97.

31. *Expresso, Revista*, December 22, 2001.

32. Jonathan Hopkin, *La Desintegración de la Union de Centro Democratico: Una Interpretacion Organizativa* (Madrid: Centro de Estudios Constitucionales, 1993); Hopkin, "Political Parties in a Young Democracy," in *Changing Party Systems in Western Europe*, ed. David Broughton and Mark Donovan (London: Pinter, 1999), 207–31; Mario Caciagli, "La Parabola de la Unión del Centro Democrático," in *La Transición Democrática Espanola*, ed. José Felix Tezanos, Ramon Cotarelo, and Andres de Blas (Madrid: Editorial Sistema, 1993), 389–413, particularly pp. 412–25; Carlos Huneeus, *La Unión del Centro Democrático y la Transicion a la Democracia* (Madrid: Centro de Investigaciones Sociologicas, 1985).

33. Sebastian Balfour, "'Bitter Victory, Sweet Defeat':" The March 1996 General Elections and the New Government in Spain," *Government and Opposition* 31, no. 3 (Summer 1996): 275–87, particularly pp. 281–85.

34. *El Pais*, March 13, 2000, p. 15.

35. *El Pais*, November 12, 2001, p. 21; *El Pais*, November 13, 2001, p. 30.

36. Richard Webster, *The Cross and the Fascist: Christian Democracy and Fascism in Italy* (Stanford: Stanford University Press, 1960).

37. Leonardo Morlino, *Which Democracies in Southern Europe?* (Barcelona: Institut de Ciencies Politiques i Socials, (Barcelona: UAB, 1996), working paper no. 113.

38. Leonardo Morlino, "Crises of Parties and Change of Party System in Italy," *Party Politics*, 2, no. 1 (1995): 5–10.

39. Jörg Seisselberg, "Conditions of Success and Political Problems of a 'Media-Mediated Personality Party': The Case of Forza Italia," *West European Politics* 29, no. 4 (October 1996): 715–43.

40. Particularly, the conservative British weekly magazine *The Economist*, April 28, 2001, pp. 23–25, made people aware of the pending legal processes against Berlusconi and his firms. Moreover allegations of close links to the Mafia were quite dominant during the campaign. (See also *El Pais*, May 20, 2001, pp. 4–5.) One of the reasons he went to politics was probably the fear of being prosecuted due to his former relations with his personal friend Bettino Craxi, who was one of the main protagonists in the *tangentopoli* affair of the 1980s. See Elisabeth Fix, *Italiens Parteiensystem im Wandel: Von der Ersten zur Zweiten Republik* (Frankfurt: Campus, 1999), 190–210.

41. Richard Clogg, *Parties and Elections in Greece: The Search for Legitimacy* (London: Hurst Company, 1987); Dimitrios K. Katsoudas, "The Conservative Movement and New Democracy: From Past to Present," in *Political Change in Greece: Before and After the Colonels*, ed. Kevin Featherstone and Dimitrios K. Katsoudas (London, Sydney: Croom Helm, 1987), 85–111; Keith R. Legg and John M. Roberts, *Modern Greece: A Civilization on the Periphery* (Boulder: Westview Press, 1997), 140–41; Takis S. Pappas, *Making Party Democracy in Greece* (Basingstoke, U.K.: Macmillan, 1999).

42. George Mavrogordatos, "Greece," in European Political Data Yearbook 1998, special issue of *European Journal for Political Research* 34, no. 3-4 (December 1998): 409–11; particularly p. 410.

43. Yannis Papadopoulos, "Gréce," in *Les Partis Politiques en Europe del'Ouest*, ed. Guy Hermet, Julian Thomas Hottinger, and Daniel-Louis Seiler (Paris: Economica, 1998), 241–45; particularly pp. 252–55.

44. José Medeiros Ferreira, *Ensaio Histórico sobre a Revolução de 25 de Abril* (Lisboa: Casa da Moeda, 1983).

45. Carlos Cunha, "The Portuguese Communist Party," in *Political Parties and Democracy in Portugal: Organizations, Elections, and Public Opinion*, ed. Thomas C. Bruneau (Boulder, CO: Westview Press, 1997), 23–54, particularly p. 35.

46. Diario de Noticias, November 9, 2000, p. 4; *Diario de Noticias*, November 10, 2000, p. 4.

47. Maria Theresa Patricio and Alan Stoleroff, "Portuguese Communist Party: Perestrojka and Its Aftermath," in *West European Communist Parties and the Revolution of 1989*, ed. Martin J. Bull and Paul Heywood (Basingstoke, U.K.: Macmillan, 1994), 90–118; Vinicio Alves da Costa e Sousa, "O Partido Comunista Portugues (Subsidios para um Estudo Sobre os Seus Adeptos)," *Estudos Politicos e Sociais* 11, no. 3-4 (1983): 497–543.

48. Paul Heywood, "The Spanish Left towards a 'Common Home'?," in *West European Communist Parties and the Revolution of 1989*, ed. Martin J. Bull and Paul Heywood (Basingstoke, U.K.: Macmillan, 1994), 56–89.

49. *El Pais*, October 18, 2000, p. 32; October 31, 2000, p. 31; *El Pais*, Anuario 2001, p. 89.

50. *El Pais*, November 26, 2001, p. 27.

51. Martin Bull, "Social Democracy's Newest Recruit? Conflict and Cohesion in the Italian Democratic Party of the Left," in *Conflict and Cohesion in Contemporary Social Democracy*, ed. David Bell and Eric Shaw (London: Pinter, 1994), 31–49.

52. John M. Foot, "The 'Left' Opposition and the Crisis: Rifondazione Comunista and La Rete," in *The New Italian Republic: From the Fall of the Berlin Wall to Berlusconi*, ed. Stephen Gundle and Simon Parker (London: Routledge, 1995), 173–88, particularly pp. 174–178.

53. Berta Alvarez-Miranda, *El Sur de Europa y la adhésion a la Comunidad: Los debates politicos* (Madrid: CIS, 1996), 45–48.

54. George Mavrogordatos, "Greece," in European Political Data Yearbook 1997, January 1, 1996 to January 1, 1997, *European Journal for Political Research* 32, no. 3-4 (December 1997): 379–81, particularly p. 381.

55. http://www.kke.gr

56. http://www.syn.gr/en/

57. Basque official title of the president of regional government.

58. Mark Donovan, "The Fate of the Secular Center: The Liberals, Republicans and Socialdemocrats," *The New Italian Republic: From the Fall of the Berlin Wall to Berlusconi*, ed. Stephen Gundle and Simon Parker (London: Routledge, 1995), 99–109, particularly p. 100.

59. Ibid.

60. Ibid., 101.

61. Piero Ignazi, *Il Polo Escluso: Profilo del Movimento Sociale Italiano*, 2nd ed. (Bologna: Il Mulino, 1998).

62. Morlino, "Crises," 5-10.

63. Piero Ignazi, "The Transformation of the MSI into the AN," *West European Politics* 29, no. 4 (October 1996): 693–714; Carlo Ruzza and Oliver Schmidtke, "Towards a Modern Right: Alleanza Nazionale and the 'Italian Revolution,'" in *The New Italian Republic: From the Fall of the Berlin Wall to Berlusconi*, ed. Stephen Gundle and Simon Parker (London: Routledge, 1995), 147–58.

64. Carlo Ruzza and Oliver Schmidtke, "Roots of Success of the Lega Lombarda: Mobilisation, Dynamics and Media," *West European Politics* 14, no. 1 (1993): 1–24; Dwayne Woods, "The Rise of Regional Leagues in Italian Politics," *West European Politics* 15, no. 2 (April 1992): 56–76; Woods, "The Crisis of

Center-Periphery Integration in Italy and the Rise of Regional Populism: The Lombard League," *Comparative Politics* 27, no. 2 (1995): 194–95. A very detailed study is Cesáreo R. Aguilera de Prat, *El Cambio Politico en Italia y la Lega Norte* (Madrid: CIS, 1999).

65. *La Repubblica*, June 11, 2001, p. 4.

66. For a more detailed study of the impact of the electoral system on small parties, see Yannis Papadopoulos, "The Decline of Small Parties and the Emergence of Two-Partyism in Greece," in *Small Parties in Western Europe: Comparative and National Perspectives*, ed. Ferdinand Müller-Rommel and Geoffrey Pridham (London: Sage, 1991): 174–202.

67. Joaquim Aguiar, "Portugal: The Hidden Fluidity in an Ultra-Stable Party System," in *Conflict and Change in Modern Portugal 1974-1984*, ed. Walter C. Opello and Eduardo de Sousa Ferreira (Lisboa: Teorema, 1985), 101–26; Aguiar, "Partidos, Eleicoes, Dinamica Politica (1974–1991)," *Análise Social* 29 (1994): 171–236; Aguiar, "Eleições, Configuracões e Clivagens: Os Resultados Eleitorais de 1995, *Análise Social*, no. 5, 154–55 (2000): 55–84; José M. Magone, "Party System: Installation and Consolidation," in *Changing Party System in Western Europe*, ed. David Broughton and Mark Donovan (London: Pinter, 1999), 232–34. See also the excellent study by Juan Carlos González Hernandez, *Desarollo Político y Consolidacíon Democrática en Portugal (1974-1998)* (Madrid: CIS, 1999), which clearly studied well the electoral geography of Portuguese politics. Last but not least, and influenced by the Alexandre Dumas novels of the Three Musketeers, see Yves Leonard, *Portugal: Vingt Ans aprés la Revolution des Ouillets* (Paris: La Documentation Française, 1994).

68. José Magone, *European Portugal: The Difficult Road to Sustainable Democracy* (Basingstoke, U.K.: Palgrave, 1997).

69. André Freire, "Participação e Abstenção nas Eleições Legislativas Portuguesas," *Análise Social* 35, no. 154–55 (2000): 115–45.

70. It refers to the overdominance of a party in the political system without any credible challenger. This may lead to corrupt practices and colonization of civil society by this main party—the Mexican Revolutionary Institutional Party (*Partito Revolucionario Institucional [PRI]*), which had ruled since the 1920s and tends to manipulate electoral processes.

71. On the Spanish party system, see Hopkin, "Political Parties in a Young Democracy," in Broughton and Donovan, 207–31. Quite crucial is Pilar Del Castillo (ed.), *Comportamiento Politico y Electoral* (Madrid: CIS, 1998). See also the classic by Richard Gunther, Giacomo Sani, and Goldie Shabad, *Spain after Franco: The Making of a Competitive Party System* (Los Angeles: California University Press, 1998); and José Ramon Montero, "Stabilising the Democratic Order: Electoral Behaviour in Spain," *West European Politics* 21, no. 4, (1998): 53–79.

72. On electoral behavior between 1977 and 1993, see José Ramon Montero, "Sobre las Preferencias Electorales en España: Fragmentación y Polarizacíon (1977–1993)," *Comportamiento Político y Electoral*, ed. Pilar del Castillo (Madrid: CIS, 1998), 51–124.

73. Elisa Roller, "The March 2000 General Elections in Spain," *Government and Opposition* 36, no. 2 (2001): 209–29; Raj S. Chari, "The March 2000 Spanish Election: A Critical Election?" *West European Politics* 23, no. 3 (July 2000): 207–14; Josep M. Vallés and Aida Diaz, "The March 2000 Spanish General Elections," *South European Society and Politics* 5, no. 3 (Winter 2000): 133–42.

74. Mariano Torcal and Pradeep Chhiber, "Elites, Cleavages y Sistema de Partidos en Una Democracia Consolidada, España (1986–1992)," *Revista Espanola de Investigaciones Sociologicas* 69 (1995): 7–38. On the relationship between political financing and party politics for the Spanish and Portuguese case, see Ingrid

van Biezen, "Party Financing in New Democracies: Spain and Portugal," *Party Politics* 6, 2001 no. 3, 329–42.

75. Mark Gilbert, *The Italian Revolution* (Boulder, CO: Westview Press, 1995); Norman Lewis, *The Honoured Society: The Mafia* (Harmondsworth, London, 1972).

76. Stefano Bartolini and Roberto D'Alimonte, "Plurality Competition and Party Realignment in Italy: The 1994 Parliamentary Elections," *European Journal for Political Research* 29 (January 1996): 105–42; Jack Brand and Thomas Mackie, "The 1994 Elections," in *Italian Politics: The Year of the Tycoon,* ed. Richard S. Katz and Piero Ignazi (Boulder, CO: Westview Press, 1996), 97–113.

77. On the 1996 elections, see the special issue of *European Journal for Political Research,* vol. 34 , 1998; James Newell and Martin Bull, "Party Organisation and Alliances in Italy in the 1990s: A Revolution of Sorts," *West European Politics* 1 (1997): 81–109; Roberto D'Alimonte and Stefano Bartolini, "'Electoral Transition' and Party System Change in Italy," *West European Politics* 1 (1997): 110–34; Sergio Fabbrini and Mark Gilbert, "When Cartels Fail: The Role of the Political Class in the Italian Democratic Transition," *Government and Opposition* 35, no. 1 (2000): 27–48; Vittorio Buffachi, "The Coming of Age of Italian Democracy," *Government and Opposition* 31, no. 3 (1996): 322–46.

78. Gianfranco Pasquino, "Berlusconi's Victory: The Italian General Elections of 2001," *South European Society and Politics* 6, no. 1 (Summer 2001): 125–37; Sergio Fabbrini and Mark Gilbert, "The Italian General Elections of 13 March 2001: Democratic Alternation or False Step?" *Government and Opposition* 36 (2001): 519–36; Mark Donovan, "A New Republic in Italy? The May 2001 Election," *West European Politics* 24, no. 4 (October 2001): 193–205.

79. *El Pais,* May 15, 2001, p. 3.

80. Clogg, *Parties and Elections in Greece,* 55–121.

81. See Chapter 3; Christos Lyrintzis, "Political Parties in Post-Junta Greece: A Case of 'Bureaucratic Clientelism'?" *West European Politics* 7, no. 2 (1984): 99–118; Christos Lyrintzis, "PASOK in Power: The Loss of the 'Third Road to Socialism,'" in *Southern European Socialism,* ed. Tom Gallagher and Allan Williams (Manchester: Manchester University Press, 1990), 34–55.

82. Geoffrey Pridham and Susannah Verney, "The Coalition of 1989–90: Inter-Party Relations and Democratic Consolidation," *West European Politics* 14, no. 4 (1991): 42–69.

83. George Mavrogordatos, "Greece," in Political Data Yearbook 1994, special issue of *European Journal for Political Research* 26 (1994): 313–18.

84. George Mavrogordatos, "Greece," in Political Data Yearbook 1996, special issue of *European Journal for Political Research* 30 (1996): 355–58; Mavrogordatos, "Greece," in European Political Data Yearbook 1997, January 1, 1996 to January 1, 1997, special issue of *European Journal for Political Research* 32, no. 3–4 (December 1997): 379–81.

85. D.E.M. Mihas, "New Political Formation in Greece: A Challenge to 1st Party System?" *Journal of Modern Greek Studies* 16 (1988): 49–72, particularly p. 51 and p. 57.

86. Kerstin Hammann and Barbara Sgouraki-Kinsey, "Re-entering Electoral Politics: Reputation and Party System Change in Spain and Greece," *Party Politics* 5, no. 1 (1999): 55–77, particularly pp. 64–70.

87. An elaborate analysis of the systemic nature of the regional party systems can be found in Kerstin Hammann, "Federalist Institutions, Voting Behaviour and Party Systems in Spain," *Publius* 29, no. 1 (1999): 111–37.

88. *ABC,* May 14, 2001, pp. 19–26; *El Pais,* May 15, 2001, pp. 15–18; *El Mundo,* May 15, 2001, pp. 2–8; *El Pais,* May 16, 2001, pp. 15–20.

89. José Manuel Rivera Otero, Neves Lagares Diez, Alfredo Castro Duarte, and Isabel Diz Otero, "Las Elecciones Autonomicas en Galicia," in *Las Elecciones Autonomicas en España 1980-1997*, ed. Manuel Alcantara and Antonia Martinez (Madrid: CIS, 1998), 285–307; Francesc Pallarés, "Las Elecciones Autonómicas en Espana:1980–1992," *Comportamiento Político y Electoral*, ed. Pilar del Castillo (Madrid: CIS, 1998), 151–220.

90. *El Pais*, October 22, 2001. The results were PP 50.9 percent/41 seats; BNG 23.3 percent/17 seats; PSOE 22 percent/17 seats; IU 0.7 percent /no seats.

91. *El Pais*, January 1, 2002.

92. See an excellent interpretation by Alessandro Chiaramonte, and Aldo di Virgilio, "Le Elezioni del 2000: Gli Frammentazione si Consolida, le Alleanze si Assestano," *Rivista Italiana di Scienza Politica* 30, no. 3, (December 2000): 513–42.

93. Magone, *European Portugal*, 59–79.

94. *O Publico*, December 17, 2000; *O Publico*, February 18, 2001; *Expresso, Revista*, December 22, 2001.

95. The most thorough study to date is Irene Delgado Sotillos, *El Comportamiento Electoral Municipal Español 1979–1995*. (Madrid: CIS 1997).

96. Aldo di Virgilio, "The Regional and Administrative Regions: Bipolarization with Reserve," in *Italian Politics: The Stalled Transition*, ed. Mario Caciagli and David I. Kertzer (Boulder: Westview Press, 1996), 41–68; Piero Ignazi, "Italy," European Political Data Yearbook 1998, special issue of *European Journal of Political Research* 34, no. 3-4 (December 1998): 447–51, particularly p. 450.

97. Greece Now: http://www.greece.gr/POLITICS/Internal Affairs/the-thirdman.stm; Athens News Agency, October 11, 1998; October 19, 1998.

98. Country reports can be found in Juliet Lodge (ed.), *The 1999 Elections to the European Parliament* (Basingstoke, U.K.: Palgrave, 2001); Lodge (ed.), *The 1994 Elections to the European Parliament* (London: Pinter, 1994); Lodge (ed.), *The 1989 Elections to the European Parliament* (Basingstoke, U.K.: Macmillan, 1990); Lodge (ed.), *Direct Elections to the European Parliament 1984* (Basingstroke: Macmillan, 1986); Juliet Lodge and Valentine Herman (eds.), *Direct Elections to the European Parliament: A Community Perspective* (Basingstoke, U.K.: Macmillan, 1982).

5

Interest Intermediation in Southern Europe

THE TRANSFORMATION OF INTEREST INTERMEDIATION IN SOUTHERN EUROPE

The Europeanization of national economic policies requires the southern European governments to create, within the framework of EMU, overall support from the relevant social and economic interest groups. Since 1997, all member-states have been implementing so-called stability pacts so that the economic policies of the government can be kept on target within the limits set up by the European Central Bank for each individual country. Moreover, the establishment of a successful SEM is putting pressure on national governments and economies to liberalize regulations and the labor market so that national economies can become more competitive. This naturally creates a problem for the establishment of a nationally autonomous economic policy. Deregulation of the labor market is increasing the precariousness of the predominantly cheap labor industries of Portugal, Spain, and Greece. A long-term chronic deficit in research and development investment makes it very difficult for these economies to improve their competitiveness, beyond the cheap labor-intensive industries. The same is valid for southern Italy, which has an economic structure closer to the other three southern European countries, whereas northern Italy represents a new kind of social capitalism based on high-technology small- and medium-sized enterprises.

After a decade of disorganized capitalism introduced by the neoliberalist policies of Margaret Thatcher and Ronald Reagan in the 1990s, the European Union has been at the forefront in reinventing

European capitalism by reorganizing it. The revived neocorporatist arrangement envisages the establishment of a more stable, flexible multilevel system of interest intermediation where social and economic agreements are discussed and formulated at the appropriate level (as shown in Table 5.1). Without returning to the rigidity of neocorporatist arrangements of the 1970s, where both the welfare state as well as the economies of Western Europe were becoming more and more inefficient. At the European level, framework agreements for all member-states of the European Union such as the directives on parental leave and the European works council are decided between the European-level social partners (ETUC, UNICE, and CEEP among others), which are then implemented in the different countries according to their social traditions. These minimalist agreements may be upgraded at a later stage transnationally or nationally.[1] Similarly, economic and social policies guidelines are set up at the European level and then implemented at the national level. Most of the collective bargaining takes place at the national or subnational level and is about wage-increase control so that the inflation targets can be kept at low levels.

The process is no longer interventionist and centralized as in the 1970s, but regulatory and decentralized. The multilevel collective bargaining structure that has been emerging since the mid-1990s gives discretion to the social partners at the local, regional, firm, and branch levels to adjust wage policies in relation to the overall framework set up at the national level.[2]

Portugal, Spain, Italy, and Greece had major difficulties coping with the transformation of interest intermediation and new economic condi-

TABLE 5.1   The Transformation of Capitalism since the 1970s

	Organized Capitalism	Disorganized Capitalism	Reorganized Capitalism
Production Organization	Fordism	Post-Fordism/ Lean production	Post-Fordism/ Lean production/ new technologies
Time Frame	1945–1970s	1980s	1990s–
Dominant Economic Unit	Large factories	Invisible firm	Invisible firm
Global Markets	National stock exchange	Global stock exchange	Global stock exchange
Collective Action	Collective identities	Individualization	Individualization/ Flexible collective identity/Multilevel
Interest Intermediation	Neocorporatism/ interventionist/ centralized	Pluralism/laissez-faire/collapse of neocorporatism	Light neocorporatism/ regulatory/multilevel interest intermediation
Political Organization	Nation-state	Nation-state/ Competition state	Post-nation-state/ Regional integration (EU)

tions at the European and global levels. In the 1970s and 1980s, most of the neocorporatist attempts were not very successful. Indeed, by the mid-1980s in all four countries the level of social conflict had reached a dramatic climax. Only in the 1990s within the framework of the convergence criteria toward EMU did all southern European countries engage in a thorough transformation of their institutional framework of interest intermediation so that they could adjust to the new macroeconomic reality defined at the supranational level. Since then, these countries have been able to introduce, more or less successfully, institutions and processes of genuine collective bargaining and interest intermediation. Only in the second half of the 1990s can we recognize a more genuine cooperation between interest groups and the government to comply with the economic prerequisites to take part successfully in the SEM and EMU.

THE ACTORS OF INTEREST INTERMEDIATION IN SOUTHERN EUROPE

The Business Associations

Portugal
The Confederation for Portuguese Industry (*Confederação de Industria Portuguesa* [CIP]) was founded in June 1974, which subsequently became the most important employers' association in postrevolutionary Portugal. It represents approximately 75 percent of enterprises (about 35,000 firms) in the private sector.

The competitors of CIP are the Industrial Association of Oporto (*Associação Industrial Portuense* [AIP]) and the Portuguese Industrial Association (*Associação Industrial Portuguesa* [AIP]). The former represents a large number of enterprises in the north of Portugal and recently has been working closely with the CIP. The latter comprises about 3,000 enterprises in the public sector, among the TNCs and other private enterprises.[3] A less important association is the Movement of Small- and Medium-Sized Trading and Industrial Firms (*Movimento de Pequenas e Medias Empresas do Comércio e Industria* [MPMCI]), which is closely linked to the Communist Party.

The Portuguese Confederation of Commerce (*Confederação do Comercio Portuguesa* [CCP]) was founded in November 1976. The CCP is the best-organized association with an extensive network of branches across the territory. Moreover, it is very active at the European level.[4]

The largest farmers' association, is the Confederation of Portuguese Farmers (*Confederação de Agricultores Portugueses* [CAP]), which represents more than 100,000 farmers. Its main rival is the communist-dominated National Confederation of Farmers (*Confederação Nacional de*

Agricultores [CAN]). Both are keen to get support from the Portuguese government for the agricultural sector.

Spain

Although several business organizations tried to achieve the position as a main national actor in tripartite negotiations in Spain, it was the Spanish Confederation of Entrepreneurial Organizations (*Confederación Española de Organizaciones Empresariales* [CEOE]) that became the main interest organization for the industrial sector. In the 1980s, it absorbed the main business organization for the small and medium enterprises, the Confederation for Small and Medium-Sized Enterprises (*Confederación para la Pequena y Mediana Empresa* [CEPYME]). It represented 1.3 million enterprises in the mid-1990s, comprising over 90 percent of all Spanish enterprises. It is organized in 165 regional and local branches. Such figures continue to be quoted as the approximate number of enterprises represented today.[5]

Eight associations represent Spanish farmers. Nevertheless, only the Confederation of Agricultural Organizations (*Confederación de Organizaciones de Agricultura* [COAG]) and the National Confederation of Agriculture (*Confederación Nacional de Agricultura* [CNAG]) are of organizational relevance.[6]

Italy

In Italy, the main employers' confederation in industry is the General Confederation for Italian Industry (*Confederazione Generale dell'Industria Italiana* [Confindustria]). It was founded in 1944. Its main objective was to regain employers the freedom to act within their factories as they liked and to prevent state planning from restraining their company strategies. The main employers' organization *Confindustria* was, therefore, very dependent on the DC system of power, and vice versa the state needed the expertise of the industrial confederation. As Joseph La Palombara found out in the 1960s, *Confindustria* had the Ministry of Commerce and Industry under its control. This so-called *clientela* relationship was related to the fact that certain departments inside the Ministry were underresourced in terms of experts and this was an opportunity for *Confindustria* to influence and shape policies by offering its expertise on issues related to the industrial sector.[7] Nevertheless, with the rise of the center-left governments, Confindustria was less and less able to influence policies at the governmental level. In 1970, Agnelli was elected president of Confindustria. He substantially changed the strategy of the confederation by moving toward a more independent position in relation to the state and DC. Indeed, Confindustria attempted to establish a new system of industrial relations with the trade unions. Agnelli reaffirmed the *centrality of the firm*, based on the principle of competitiveness and efficiency. The new approach to industrial relations established the highly complex multitiered system of interest intermediation in Italy. When Guido Carli, former president of the Italian National Bank, took over, he continued the same policy as Agnelli.[8] Nevertheless, the transformation of the consumer market, and subsequently, of the modes of production to respond to it, led to a less conciliatory approach toward industrial relations. Fiat initiated layoffs and dismissals in the first half of the 1980s; other firms soon followed suit. Simultaneously, the system of production became more decentralized. Subcontracting and reallocation of plants from the north to the south were strategies used to prevent a return of a situation of upheaval and permanent industrial action as happened in the 1970s.[8]

Today *Confindustria* has over 1 million firms as members, comprising a total of 3 million employees out of 11 million employers in all sectors of the private industry. In 1985, 44 percent of firms had less than 1,000 employers. A large number of firms have between 1 and 10 employees. Still today the larger multinationals FIAT, Montedison, Pirelli, and Olivetti dominate the policies of *Confindustria*, although channels to exert political influence have become more diversified. For example, a large majority of small- and medium-sized entreprises tried to support the *Leghe*. In terms of collective bargaining, *Confindustria* did not change policy. It has always taken part in collective bargaining.[9]

Other private business interest confederations are smaller. By far the most important is the Confederation for Small- and Medium-sized Enterprises (*Confederazione per le piccole e medie imprese* [CONFADI]) with 30,000 affiliated enterprises comprising 1 million employers. In the agricultural sector, by far the most important confederation is *Coldiretti* with 6,898 associations comprising 1.5 million employees.[10] In the past fifty years, the Italian economy was substantially dominated by the public sector. The two main public sector holdings established during Fascism are ENI and ERI. The National Agency for Hydrocarbons (*Ente Nazionale per Idrocarboni* [ENI]) was founded in the 1950s by the DC government for the energy sector, nevertheless it expanded to other industrial sectors. De Gasperi intended to strengthen the public ownership of industry to influence the economy. The Institute for Industrial Reconstruction (*Istituto per la Ricostruzione Industriale*) was founded in the 1930s during Fascism to save three banks from collapsing. The three banks were the Banco di Roma, Credito Italiano, and Banca Commerciale. This led to the acquisition of a large industrial sector. IRI founded its own interest representation organization called *Intersind* and left *Confindustria* in 1957. In view of privatization, these holdings were abolished by the Prodi government after 1996. The public enterprises are being privatized by the government. On the whole, the collapse of *partitocrazia* initiated a transition in the Italian system of

interest intermediation that was reinforced by Europeanization constraints. This is introducing new public management strategies based
on principles of privatization and decentralization in the public sector.
Overall, one can recognize a trend toward an Anglo-Saxonic form of
capitalism, which is affecting the private sector as well.[11]

Greece

In Greece, the employers' representation is split among three main
business organizations. By far the most important one is the Confederation of Greek Industries (SEV). It represents 550 affiliated companies and a number of regional associations representing over 2,000
firms. SEV was founded in 1917. It welcomed liberalism and the
pro-European integration position of ND. Nevertheless, ND's need
to forge a broader coalition to support democratic consolidation
prevented a closer relationship to SEV. In the first two years of PASOK
government, SEV had immense difficulties influencing policies.
PASOK's expansionary policies and pro-Labor position was a major
constraint to the development of a liberal market economy. PASOK
was essentially antibusiness. It wanted to introduce a planning
economy and strengthen the public sector. Most of the policies were
Keynesian demand-side oriented. The confrontation reached its peak
in 1984. The situation improved only in 1984 when PASOK became
more moderate and had to implement austerity measures to stabilize
the economy. In the 1990s, SEV was able to recover in terms of
membership and coverage. The relationship between government and
SEV became more moderate. SEV is recognized as an important
mediator in European policies related to the structural funds. On the
whole, Greek interest groups are strongly constrained by a state
corporatism that tends to support labor. The highly fragmented
business sector prevented a strengthening of SEV in relation to this
state corporatism. The General Confederation of Greek Artisans and
Handicrafts (GSEBEE) was founded in 1919 and has 131,548 members.
GSEBEE is characterized by political factionalism within a unitary
structure. The National Confederation of Greek Commerce (EESE)
was only established in 1961. It is a loose umbrella organization for
the commerce industry. It is highly dominated by the commerce
associations of the three largest urban centers of Athens, Piraeus, and
Thessaloniki. GSEBEE is also affected by political partisan infighting
inside the organization.[12] In general terms, one can say that business
groups in Greece are weak in relation to the dominance of state
paternalism.

On the whole, business interest groups in southern Europe are in a
process of modernization. The European integration process clearly

favored their reemergence as supporters of wealth creation and an essential part of the social dialogue.

Trade Unions

Portugal

The ideological polarization between the socialists / social-democrats and the communists led to the establishment of two separate trade union confederations in Portugal. The communist-dominated General Confederation of Portuguese Workers (*Confederação Geral de Trabalhadores Portugueses-Intersindical* [CGTP-In]) was founded at the end of the authoritarian regime. It was the only illegal trade union organization operating within the vertical syndicalist structure of the authoritarian regime. Therefore it had an organizational advantage in relation to the other interest groups in the first years of democracy. The CGTP-In has more or less 1 million members and is extremely close to the communist party. In some cases the leadership between party and trade union organization is interchangeable. The highly centralistic and communist-dominated structure led to the establishment of a separate socialist / social-democratic trade union confederation after negotiations between the leadership of the two main parties, PS and PSD.

The General Union of Workers (*União Geral dos Trabalhadores* [UGT]) was founded in 1979 and established itself among white-collar workers and the banking sector. The UGT has about 750 000 members, although the figures are unreliable and may have a component of propaganda for ideological purposes. The ideological polarization continued until the Cavaco Silva governments. Indeed, between 1987 and 1995 both trade union confederations tried to work closely together to prevent a further liberalization of the labor laws. The UGT has been very supportive of the Socialist government between1995 and 2001, whereas the CGTP-In expressed some reluctance to work within the stability pact framework. On the whole, Portuguese trade unionism is facing major economic difficulties. The move from an ideological to a professional approach of trade unionism is still in the making, although the European integration process helped to foster such inter–trade union cooperation.[13]

Spain

Trade unions existed before the transition to democracy in Spain. The General Union of Workers (*Union General de los Trabajadores* [UGT]) was established in 1870 as an organization linked to the Socialist party. This linkage continued to exist until today. The UGT today is a federal organization that was able to abandon the ideological warfare against the communist-dominated Workers' Commissions (*Comisiones Obreras* [CCOO]) in 1986. The level of unionization is very low. It is approximately between 9 and 15 percent of the working population. Although in 1994 CCOO had 656,167 members and UGT 684,040, this low level of unionization has to be seen in the context of the Spanish system of electoral trade unionism. Regular elections are held at the factory level, which in the end will say something about the strength of the trade union confederations. CCOO and UGT are more or less equal in their strength. All the other trade unions such as the Workers' Trade Unions (*Unión Sindical Obrera* [USO]), the Trotskyite General Confederation of Workers (*Confederación General de los Trabajadores* [CGT]), and the National Confederation of Labor (*Confederación Nacional del Trabajo* [CNT]) are very tiny. At the regional level, Solidarity of Basque Workers (*Euzko Langilleen Alkartasuna-Solidariedad de Trabajadores Vascos* [ELA/STV]) is strong in the Basque country, as is the Confederation of Galician Workers (*Intersindical Nacional de Traballadores Galegos/Confederacion Xeral de Traballadores Galegos* [INTG/CXTG]) in Galicia.[14] The regular trade union elections give almost equal strength to these two main trade union confederations. Spanish trade union confederations are entitled to receive some subsidies. This naturally eases some of the financial pressures trade union confederations are confronted with today. In spite of that, the main source of revenue is membership fees. The strategies of the two main trade union confederations are linked to the overall strategies of the European Trade Union Confederation (ETUC) and contributed to stability in Spain by supporting the stability pacts of the government since 1997.[15] Both trade union confederations experienced bitter struggles in the transformation from ideological to professional trade unionism in the late 1990s. The two leaders who made this transition possible were former CCOO secretary-general Antonio Gutierrez[16] and the present leader of UGT, Candido Mendez.

Italy

In Italy, the reconstruction years were characterized by authoritarian practices of employers against trade union activists. Formal industrial relations were practically absent at the workplace level. This was reinforced by the ideological fragmentation of the trade union movement into three main confederations.[17] The largest confederation was the General Confederation of Italian Workers (*Confederazione Generale Italiana del Lavoro* [CGIL]) founded after all parties signed the so-called Pact of Rome in 1944. The main ideology was anti-Fascism. The executive positions were distributed among the three main parties, PSI, PCI, and DC. This gave enormous strength to the working class, because two parties that represented their interests were in power. Indeed, in the first years of the unity coalition government trade unions had enormous power because the labor market was blocked, due to the fact that nobody could be dismissed. This was abolished in 1946, nevertheless

CGIL was able to influence collective bargaining and wage indexation. The emergence of the Cold War in 1947–1948 created tensions within the trade union confederation. In 1948 the Christian-democratic members decided to found the Italian Confederation of Workers' Trade Unions (*Confederazione Italiana dei Sindacati dei Lavoratori* [CISL]), and in 1950 the Socialists left the CGIL and established the Union of Italian Workers (*Unione dei Lavoratori Italiani* [UIL]). This ideological polarization and fragmentation led simultaneously to a decline of unionization and union activity.

In the second half of the 1980s, trade unionism was split, and its possibility of influence on political parties declined considerably. All parties were declining in membership and electoral support. In 1993, the level of unionization was 38.5 percent comprising 10.5 million members in the three trade unions. By far the largest confederation continued to be CGIL with 5.237 million, followed by CISL with 3.769 million and UIL with 1.588 million. Although in 1972, the three main trade union confederations set up a unitary structure and kept independent from party political influences, in the 1980s this cooperation broke down. This negative experience and the collapse of *partitocrazia* after 1992 led to a more moderate and cooperative policy approach of the trade union confederations. During the technocratic Ciampi government between May 1993 and May 1994, a tripartite agreement was signed by trade unions, *Confindustria* and the government. Such cooperative policy was continued with the technocratic government of Lamberto Dini. The trade union confederations supported the outgoing unstable left-center coalition government and the subsequent technocratic government of Giuliano D'Amato, which were and are committed to strict macro-economic measures so that Italy may continue on track toward successful participation in EMU.[18] Trade union confederations are extremely opposed to Berlusconi's government, which is under pressure to make substantial public expenditure cuts.[19]

Greece

In Greece the main trade union confederation, the General Confederation of Greek Workers (GSEE), has approximately 430,000 members, nevertheless it is quite fragmented in several small federations. This has to do with the fact that the Greek business structure consists predominantly of small- and medium-sized enterprises. The membership density is approximately 35 percent. Its monopoly of the labor representation is reinforced by a state corporatism introduced in 1931 that leads to compulsory membership of workers and employers organized by the Labor Home. The reemergence of GSEE after 1974 assured that labor continued to play the dominant role in a political economy which constrained liberal-economic efforts. GSEE is a unitary structure, but allows for party political factions to compete with each other for leadership positions. Moreover, GSEE is a recipient of state subsidies, which makes them almost independent from membership fees.[20] But GSEE, becomes thus extremely dependent on the dominant party in government. Civil servants are organized in the Highest Executive Committee of Workers in the the Civil Service (ADEDY), which comprises 200,000 members and is quite close to ND.[21] Indeed, Mavrogordatos asserts that trade unionism is the contagion gateway for clientelistic party politics in Greece.[22]

On the whole, trade union confederations in southern Europe are in a process of transformation. After decades of being instrumentalized by parties as transmission belts for the control of electoral clienteles, all of them are now moving toward a more professional approach based on a Europeanized rationale of social Europe.

THE NATIONAL SYSTEMS OF INTEREST INTERMEDIATION

In Portugal, Spain, and Greece economic and social committees were established to prepare long-term national strategies in convergence with the European guidelines. The inclusion of a chapter on employment in the Treaty of Amsterdam, which came into force in May 1999, clearly increased the role of the social partners in shaping economic policy making. The establishment of an open method of coordination (OMC) in employment since the Lisbon Extradionary European Council in March 2000 led to a strengthening of supranational coordination in this field in relation to the national countries. (See Figure 5.1.) The different member-states are under permanent scrutiny by the employment committee attached to the Council.

Portugal
In Portugal, major improvements of the system of industrial relations were achieved since the introduction of intermediation mechanisms in 1984. The so-called Permanent Council for Social Concertation (*Conselho Permanente para Concertação Social* [CPCS]) was able to gain more importance only after accession to the European Union, in spite of the resistance of the communist-dominated trade union confederation CGTP-In. The deregulation of the labor market led to considerable opposition of the trade union confederations, until 1995, against the Cavaco Silva governments. This contributed to an increase of strike activity and workplace disputes. The lack of compromise from the Cavaco Silva government created a highly tense

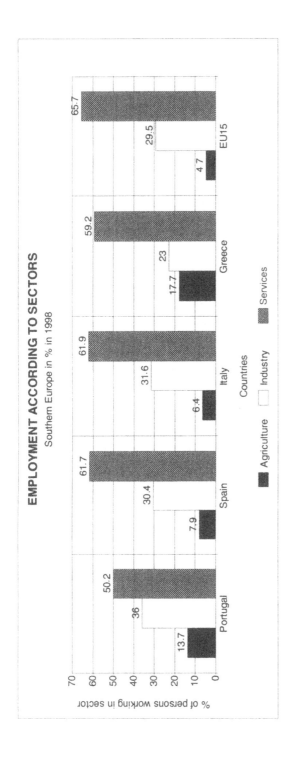

Figure 5.1 Employment Structure in Southern Europe (1998)
Source: Eurostat.

situation in 1993 and 1994.[23] This attitude changed considerably after 1995. The climate of industrial relations has improved considerably under the Socialist administration, although the communist CGTP-In continued to stay away from some important general agreements that would require the support of all social partners. Since 1993, the CPCS became part of the Economic and Social Council (*Conselho Economico e Social* [CES]). The reforms of the Portuguese government since the mid-1980s led to a situation of full employment, although it is expected that the recent need for the government to drastically reduce public spending and the rise of interest rates will probably slow down the growth of the Portuguese economy and lead to an increase of unemployment.

Spain

In Spain, after the election of José Maria Aznar's PP into government, a climate of social dialogue replaced decades of scarce dialogue between the Socialist government and the social partners. Since 1997, business and trade union organizations under the auspices of the government are working together to liberalize the labor market and make it more competitive. This ended the long *intermezzo* of one decade, in which the social dialogue between the social partners under the previous socialist government broke down. In spite of some social agreements between the social partners under the auspices of the Socialist government in 1992 and 1994 to reform the social security system, they were only finalized during the PP government. Moreover, PP built on the timid privatization plans of the Socialist government by being more radical. The overall strategy adopted by the Socialists in 1992, of Europeanization and globalization of the Spanish economy, was not changed under the PP, it became even more radical. The basic problem is that Spain, like Portugal and Greece, is sliding into a dilemma. Though the research and development ratio is still very low in international comparative terms and most of it is provided by foreign multinationals, the reforms clearly are designed to make labor cheaper and increase employment in labor-intensive industries. This naturally may solve the problem of the Spanish economy in the short term, but in the long term it does not clearly change its structure.[24]

Indeed, between 1996 and 2000 unemployment decreased from 24 percent to 13 percent due to the continuing flexibilization of the labor market, so that social peace was achieved and a positive climate set in. Spain is dominated by a provincial-sectoral–based collective bargaining system, which covers the majority workers; only a minority is covered at the national-sectoral level. There is also a strong fragmentation and uncoordination between lower- and higher-level agreements. Trade union confederations are also stronger in some regions, such as

Madrid, Catalonia, or Valencia, than others. This naturally shows that although Spain has a multilevel system of collective bargaining, a more efficient coordinated structure is still awaiting.[25] Similarly to Portugal and Greece, an economic and social committee (*consejo economico y social* [CES]) was established in 1993 so that the social partners could discuss issues related to social and economic policy. Social partners are requested to issue opinions on legislative proposals of the government. Trade union confederations have been more militant after the reelection of José Maria Aznar with an absolute majority in March 2000, due to the fact that in spite of an improvement of the unemployment figures, the precarious situation of the workforce continues to increase and make these short-term gains very unstable in the event of a return of a recession. In December 2001, a social pact including trade unions and business organizations was signed in a situation of a possible return of the recession.

Italy

In Italy, a system of interest intermediation has existed since the 1960s. Governments tended to work closely with the social partners to ensure social peace in the country. This naturally was partially successful. Social partners were entangled in party politics and highly politicized. Moreover, the governments tended to pay compensations through the budget to achieve some kind of settlement. By the mid-1980s, this kind of approach reached its limits due to a high budget deficit related to the practice of compensatory payoffs. Any kind of settlement collapsed in 1983 and 1984. Only in 1993 did the technocratic government of Giuliano D'Amato achieve a reform of the former system, which allowed for an automatic wage adjustment of workers' wages to the yearly inflation. This so-called *scala mobile* was a major problem for the competitiveness of the industry. The new system allowed for the beginning of a more regulatory multilevel system of collective bargaining, giving more room to maneuver for trade unions at local, branch, or firm levels.[26] In 1995, the technocratic government of Lamberto Dini initiated the beginning of a reform of the pensions system, which was supported by the trade union confederations but only tacitly tolerated by the main employers' organization *Confindustria*.[27] The collapse of the former political class around DC and the PSI led to a decline of party influence on major social partners. Moreover, this also implied a weakening of Confindustria and industrialists who were close to the DC oligarchy.[28] Indeed, one explanatory thesis for the emergence of Silvio Berlusconi in politics was the intention to defend the industrial class from complete exposure in relation to *tangentopoli*. All these developments triggered development toward a more professional approach on social and economic issues in the 1990s. The Prodi and D'Alema governments after 1996 clearly counted on the social partners to support their economic and social policies, so that Italy would achieve membership in the first wave of EMU. One of the factors that led to decline of the relationship between parties and social partners was the fact that the convergence criteria of EMU reduced the possibilities to return to past forms of clientelistic behavior of distributing state spoils or any spoils in exchange for policy support as was the case until 1992. The whole collective bargaining system became more multilevel and flexible in approach. This is probably the direction that all the other southern European countries will move toward in the long-term perspective.[29]

Greece

Among the four countries, the Greek system of interest intermediation is still awaiting development toward more efficient structures. The basic problem in Greece has been that the ideological polarization between the two main parties, PASOK and ND, is reflected also in terms of the main social partners. The highly militant trade union movement traditionally was able to count on the support of the governmental dominance of PASOK. This naturally led to establishment of ND-close trade unions and business organizations. The impasse between the two ideological groups was almost insurmountable. Greece had the highest level of strikes and workplace disputes of all OECD countries during the 1990s.[30] Nevertheless, since the mid-1990s the emergence of the highly pragmatic prime minister Kostas Simitis has improved the climate in the system of interest intermediation. The establishment of the economic and social committee in 1994 was regarded as a turning point in the culture of interest intermediation in Greece, although only time will show if this will contribute to more social peace for a highly conflictual polity.[31] Although collective bargaining is highly centralized and dominated by the wage policies in the public sector, some efforts at decentralization and flexibilization have been more promising in recent years in view of convergence with other European economies within the framework of EMU. Probably, one of the major obstacles to a transformation of the Greek economy is the strong dominance of the state in the economy, which tends to perpetuate the rigidities of the Greek market within the European Union. Such state paternalism has created a subaltern attitude of interest groups in the whole process of economic restructuring and transformation.[32] The recent plans to reform social security and social policy, which has been a huge burden for the budget of the Greek state, have been resisted by trade union confederations and left-wing factions within PASOK. In spite of that, Prime Minister Kostas Simitis is committed to transform the Greek state regardless of any negative impact on his electoral fortunes.

On the whole, the systems of interest intermediation in southern Europe are in transition toward a complete multilevel European system of interest intermediation. The emphasis of social partnership in developing long-term policies linked to European coordinating guidelines is forcing the governments of southern Europe to adjust and reorganize their political-economic structures.

THE IMPACT OF THE MULTILEVEL EU GOVERNANCE SYSTEM ON SOUTHERN EUROPE

Interest Representation at the EU Level

In comparison to the northern European countries, southern European national associations are underrepresented at the supranational level. A comparison between Spain and Italy on the one hand and Germany, France, and the United Kingdom on the other hand show that civil societies in the northern countries are more dynamic and interested in supranational representation than are the southern European countries. Regional representation in Portugal and Greece is nonexistent. This highlights the fact that southern European national associations still concentrate their activities at the national level. Since accession to the European Union, the number of represented national interest groups at the European level in Portugal, Spain, and Greece is proportionally smaller than the other European countries (as shown in Table 5.2).

Most of the relevant southern European national associations are integrated into the larger transnational confederations. This is the case for the employers' organizations CIP, CEOE, *Confindustria* and SEV, which are part of the Union of Confederations of Industry and Employers in Europe (*Union des Confederations de Industrie et des Employeurs d'Europe* [UNICE]).

UNICE has been characterized by a very fragmented, decentralized structure always requiring a long consultation period with its individual members. It still lacks a supranational decision autonomy. This is quite different from its counterpart, the European Trade Union Confederation (ETUC) which in spite of differences about the future design of the organization and the European Union, has more autonomy in decision making. Indeed, more coordinated action in so-called European days of labor among the national members has been achieved in the 1990s. ETUC is an ardent supporter of European integration, the social dialogue, EMU, and SEM. It has been successful in pushing the importance of a common European strategy toward employment, which has gained relevance since 1997. All main national trade union confederations, in spite of their ideological differences are members of ETUC. Cooperation at the supranational level has boosted cooperation among the trade union confederations with different ideological backgrounds

TABLE 5.2   Representation of National Interest Groups at the European Level (1999)

	Chambers of Trade, Industry and Agriculture	Employers' and Employees' Associations	Regional Representations and Associations	Other National Interest Group Representations	Total Number of Interest Groups	Percentage
Portugal	7	3		3	13	3.6
Spain	2	1	17		20	5.5
Italy	8	1	6	6	21	5.8
Greece	2	2			4	1.1
Germany	7	5	18	55	85	23.5
UK	5	2	29	6	42	11.6
France	16	2	25	41	84	23.2
Austria	4	2	10	5	21	5.8
Belgium	1	1	8		10	2.8
Luxembourg					-	-
Netherlands	4	2	2		8	2.2
Ireland	5		2		7	1.9
Sweden	2	2	9	2	15	8.3
Finland	1		6		7	4.2
Denmark	4	3	10	7	24	6.5
Total	68	26	142	125	361	100

Source: Calculations by the author based on data published in Euroconfidentiel, *The Directory of EU Information Sources* (Brussels, 1999), D33–D57.

at the national level. Only the Portuguese CGTP-In had difficulties moveing toward a position of compromise. Indeed, for many decades, CGTP-In's application for ETUC membership was blocked by the rival UGT. CGTP-In was only accepted in 1994. A more amicable relationship due to European integration and cooperation at the supranational level exists between the Spanish main confederations, UGT and CCOO. Indeed, both main trade unions subscribe completely to a European strategy of employment. The same can be said for the Italian CGIL, CISL, and UIL. The Greek GSEE joined ETUC in 1976 and is involved in the restructuring of the system of interest intermediation toward social dialogue and social concertation in Greece.

All these main interest groups are also integrated in the European Economic Social Committee (EESC), which is an advisory body within the institutional framework of the European Union and issues opinions on legislation proposed by the three main European institutions. The councillors are appointed by the national governments according to their importance in national civil societies. The ESC is organized in three main groups of interest groups: the employer's organizations (group 1), the workers' organizations (group 2), and diverse activities group (group 3). In group 1, one can find, for example, representatives of the Portuguese AIP and CIP, Spanish CEOE and CEPYME, Italian *Confindustria, Confagricultura,* and *Confcomercio,* and Greek Union of Greek Shipowners and SEV. The most cohesive of all groups is group 2 which comprises several workers' organizations such as the Portuguese CGTP-In and UGT, the Spanish UGT and CCOO, as well as the Basque ELA-STV, the Italian CGIL, UIL, and CISL, and naturally the Greek GSEE. In group 3 we find representatives from all possible professions and segments of civil society, including consumers' protection groups, environmental associations and other social groups. More concretely, one can find there representatives of the Portuguese Association for the Defense of the Consumer (DECO), the Union of Portuguese Charities or the National Council for the Liberal Professions, the Spanish Federation of Young Farmers or the Spanish National Federation of the Rural Woman, the Italian *Confartigianato,* the Greek General Confederation of Agricultural Associations as well as the Economic Chamber of Greece. The whole approach of the decision making is consensual so that representatives are embedded in a culture of compromise. Moreover, interest groups are also involved in a myriad of specialized consultative, decision-making, and monitoring committees (the so-called comitology) attached to the European Commission.

EMU, Stability Pacts, and Employment Policy Coordination

Since the Essen European Council summit of 1994, the modernization of the European economy has been at the forefront of European policymaking. An employment strategy was always attached to it. Indeed, since the extraordinary European Council in Luxembourg of November 1997, employment policy coordination has become part of the *acquis communautaire.* A chapter on employment policy coordination was enshrined in the Amsterdam Treaty,[33] which came into force in May 1999.[34] An employment committee was set up in January 2000 to monitor the implementation of the guidelines established by the Council of Ministers and make recommendations to the different countries.[35] Finally, in the Extraordinary European Council in Lisbon in March 2000, an open method of coordination (OMC) of employment policies was agreed among the member-states, which led to annual monitoring and benchmarking of labor market policies and their deficiencies in relation to the EU guidelines. The OMC is naturally based on decentralization and subsidiarity.[36] At the national level, the stability pacts for the implementation of macroeconomic policies set up by the European Central Bank and Ecofin are now complemented by National Employment Action Plans, which are based on the employment policy guidelines decided at the supranational level. In medium- to long-term perspective there is the intention to create a synergy among economic, monetary and employment policies. For this effect, member-states are requested to improve their data reliability and converge the methodologies of data gathering, so that a truly European database on employment availability can be created. The so-called European Employment Services (EURES) located in border regions can be regarded as a first step toward this network of employment services across the EU.[37] This creation of a European employment strategy naturally involves the use of new technologies and the preparation of the population for the knowledge-based information society. Part of the strategy is to reduce the gap of skills between jobseekers and the available employment. For this the upgrading of qualifications and deregulation of the labor market are essential to achieve the goal of creating sustainable employability and the return of full employment (as shown in Table 5.3). The

TABLE 5.3   Guidelines for Member-States' Employment Policies for the Year 2000

I. Improving Employability
*Tackling youth unemployment and preventing long-term unemployment
*Transition from passive to active measures
*Encouraging a partnership approach
*Easing the transition from school to work
*Promoting a labor market open to all

II. Developing Entrepreneurship
*Making it easier to start up and run businesses
*Exploiting new opportunities for job creation
*Making the taxation system more employment friendly

III. Encouraging Adaptability of Businesses and Their Employees
*Modernizing work organization
*Support adaptability in enterprise

IV. Strengthening Equal Opportunities Policies for Women and Men
*Gender mainstreaming approach
*Tackling gender gap
*Reconciling work and family life
*Facilitating reintegration in the labor market

Source: Council Decision of March 13, 2000, on guidelines for Member-States' employment policies for the year 2000. In O.J. L72, March 21, 2000, pp. 15–20.

Lisbon European Council intended to raise the EU average employment rate of the working population in relation to the whole population from 61 percent to 70 percent and enrolment of women from 51 percent to more than 60 percent by 2010.[38]

This naturally will be a major challenge to Portugal, Spain, Italy, and Greece. One positive aspect will be the standardization of methodologies, which will prevent statistical manipulation in such an important field as employment. Many unemployed are only partially covered by statistics in southern Europe. The informal economy in southern Europe may hide a substantial amount of workers who are in a situation of latent unemployment. The standardization of methodologies will allow for verification mechanisms and adequate measures of improvements within a European context. Another positive aspect will be the challenge to upgrade the qualifications of a work force that has been chronically underqualified in relation to northern European countries. This can only build on the efforts already made, which were partly financed by the European Social Fund. One basic deficit of southern European labor market policies is the dominance of passive policies to fight unemployment and the reduced share of investment in active original adequate measures when compared with northern European countries. Particularly Greece and Spain need to improve their approach to unemployment by raising the expenditure on active policies for labor market insertion.[39]

In the new European economy, Spain, Portugal, Greece, and Italy will need a revision of public-private partnership projects so that better conditions for the establishment of the information society can be created. Still today the number of people in Portugal, Spain, Greece, and Italy using the new technologies is lower than in the northern European countries, particularly in the Nordic countries. (See Figure 5.2.)

According to a major international study, these four countries will continue to be laggards in democratizing the Internet at least until 2004. E-commerce in southern Europe will remain behind the EU average. Particularly Greece and Portugal have a long way to go.[40] This is a unique opportunity to make a thorough reform of the welfare and employment policies of the southern European countries, which in the past have been characterized by a clientelistic pattern of organization.[41] This Europeanization will iron out the inefficiencies and contribute to a more integrated approach nationally and transnationally.

The big challenge for the southern European economies will be to improve the integration of women in the labor market. According to a recent study, such integration has only partly been achieved. Indeed, newcomers to the labor market are confronted with precarious jobs and sometimes continuing discrimination between male and female pay. In

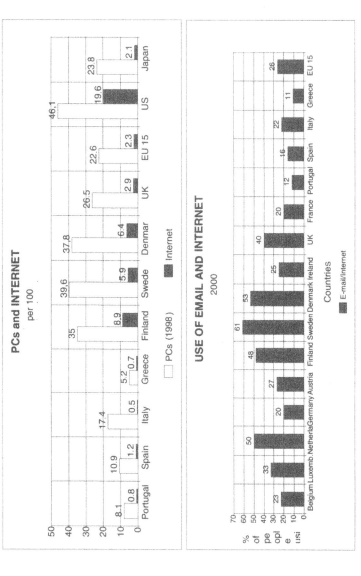

Figure 5.2 Information Society in Southern Europe

Source: Eurostat, Yearbook 2001, pp. 38–39; Eurobarometer 54 (Autumn).

spite of that, some progress has been made in attitudes and recognition of the problem by major policy makers. Mainstreaming gender equality will naturally be related to the overall modernization of southern European economies.[42]

CONCLUSIONS

At the present stage, we are witnessing a complete Europeanization of the systems of interest intermediation in southern Europe. Since the early 1990s, policy making has become a multilevel approach, which requires the support of the social partners from the supranational, over the national, to the subnational level. This reorganization of systems of interest intermediation led to a return of neocorporatism. The basic difference between today's neocorporatism and the past form is its regulatory nature. Policy making at the national level occurs more and more as a function of policy guidelines in the fields of the macroeconomy, monetary policy, and employment policy. The process of synergy of policy making at the supranational level started in 1993 and was reinforced after 1997. In short- and medium-term perspective, it is expected that southern European systems of intermediation will become more relevant in modernizing the structures of labor market policy and entrepreneurship.

NOTES

1. Gerda Falkner, "The Maastricht Protocol on Social Policy: Theory and Practice," *Journal of European Social Policy* 1, no. 6 (1996): 1–16; Falkner, "European Works Councils and the Maastricht Social Agreement: Towards A New Policy Style?," *Journal of European Public Policy* 3, no. 2 (June 1996): 192–208; Daniela Obradovic, "Prospects for Corporatist Decision-Making in the European Union: The Social Policy Agreement," *Journal of European Public Policy* 2, no. 2 (June 1995): 261–83; Henri Nadel and Robert Lindley, "Le Dialogue Social Europeen: Institutions et Economie," *Les Relations Sociales en Europe: Economie et Institutions*, ed. Henri Nadel and Robert Lindley (Paris: L'Harmattan, 1998), 7–18.

2. Marino Regini, "Still Engaging in Corporatism? Einige Lehren aus Jüngsten Italienischen Erfahrungen mit der Konzertierung," *Politische Vierteljahresschrift* 38, no. 2 (1997): 298–317; Juergen Grote and Philippe Schmitter, *The Corporatist Sysyphus: Past, Present, Future* (Florence: EUI Working Paper, SPS no. 97/4, 1997); Paul Teague, "Europe of the Regions and the Future of National Systems of Industrial Relations," in *Behind the Myth of European Union*, ed. Ash Amin and John Tomaney (London: Routledge, 1995), 149–73; particularly p. 161 and pp. 164–65; Teague, "Reconstructing Corporatism? Organized Decentralization and Other Paradoxes," in *Organized Industrial Relations in Europe: What Future?*, ed. Colin Crouch and Franz Traxler (Aldershot: Avebury, 1995), 311–30.

3. José Barreto and Reinhard Naumann, "Portugal: Industrial Relations under Democracy," in *Changing Industrial Relations in Europe*, ed. Anthony Ferner and Richard Hyman (London: Blackwell, 1998), 395–425, particularly pp. 407–8.

    4. Guilhermina Marques, "L'Integration des Groupes d'Interêt Portugais au Niveau Européen," in *L'Europe du Sud dans la Communauté Européenne. Analyse Comparative dans la Communauté Européenne*, ed. Dusan Sidjanski and Ural Ayberk (Paris: PUF, 1990), 165–84, particularly pp. 195–98; Marinús Pires de Lima, "A Europa Social: Questões e Desafios," *Análise Social* 28, no. 123-124 (1993): 835–67, particularly p. 852.
    5. Philippe Schmitter, "Organised Interests and Democratic Consolidation in Southern Europe," in *The Politics of Democratic Consolidation: Southern Europe in Comparative Perspective*, vol. 1 of *The New Southern Europe*, ed. Richard Gunther, Nikiforos P. Diamandouros, and Hans-Jurgen Puhle (Baltimore: Johns Hopkins University Press, 1995), 284–314; Jelle Visser, "A Truly Mixed Case: Industrial Relations in Italy," in *Industrial Relations in Europe: Traditions and Transitions*, ed. Joris van Ruysseveldt and Jelle Visser (London: Sage, 1996), 265–309, 321.
    6. Maria Esther del Campo Garcia, "Los Grupos de Presión en la Transicion y Consolidación Democratica," in *Sistema Politico Español*, ed. Paloma Roman (Madrid: McGraw-Hill, 1995), 201–22, particularly pp. 213–14.
    7. Joseph LaPalombara, *Interest Groups in Italian Politics* (Princeton: Princeton University Press, 1967).
    8. Alberto Martinelli, "Organised Business and Italian Politic: Confindustria and the Christian Democrats in the Post-War Period," *West European Politics* 2 (October 1979): 67–87, particularly p. 83; for a thorough multifactorial explanation, see Roberto Franzosi, *The Puzzle of Strikes: Class and State Strategies in Postwar Italy* (Cambridge: Cambridge University Press, 1995); Anna Giunta and Flavia Martinelli, "The Impact of Post-Fordist Corporate Restructuring in a Peripheral Region: The Mezzogiorno of Italy," in *Behind the Myth of European Union*, ed. Ash Amin and John Tomaney (London: Routledge, 1995), 221–62.
    9. Orazio Lanza, "Confindustria and the Party System in Italy," in *Contemporary Political Studies 1996*, Proceedings of the Annual Conference of the Political Studies Association (PSA) held at the University of Glasgow, April 10–12, 1996, ed. Hampshere Monk and Stanyer (Belfast: PSA, 1996), 1602–11.
    10. Schmitter, "Organised Interests," 301.
    11. Dermot McCann, "Economic Internationalization, Domestic Political Crisis and Corporate Governance Reform in Italy," *South European Society and Politics* 5, no. 1 (Summer 2000): 53–72, particularly pp. 62–69.
    12. Nicos D. Kritsantonis, "Greece: Maturing the System," in *Changing Industrial Relations in Europe*, ed. Anthony Ferner and Richard Hyman (London: Blackwell, 1998), 504–528, particularly pp. 509–11.
    13. José M. Magone, *Iberian Trade Unionism: Democratization under the Impact of the European Union* (New Brunswick, NJ: Transaction Publishers, 2001).
    14. Marc van der Meer, "Aspiring Corporatism? Industrial Relations in Spain," in *Industrial Relations in Europe: Traditions and Transitions*, ed. Joris van Ruysseveldt and Jelle Visser (London: Sage, 1996), 310–36, particularly p. 318.
    15. Wolfgang Lecher and Reinhardt Naumann, "The Current State of Trade Unions in EU Member States," in *Trade Unions in the European Community: A Handbook*, ed. Wolfgang Lecher (London: Lawrence and Wishart, 1994), pp. 3–126.
    16. In 2000, Antonio Gutierrez was succeeded by José Maria Fidalgo.
    17. Donald Sassoon, *Contemporary Italy: Politics, Economics and Society since 1945* (London: Longman, 1986), 15–26.
    18. Michael Braun, "The Confederated Trade Unions and the Dini Government: The Grand Return to Neocorporatism," in *Italian Politics: The Stalled Revolution*, ed. Mario Caciagli and David I. Kertzer (Boulder, CO: Westview Press, 1996), 205–21.

19. *The Economist*, October 6, 2001, pp. 41–42; *Die Zeit*, January 10, 2002, p. 19; *Frankfurter Allgemeine Zeitung*, January 14, 2002, p. 6.

20. Kritsantonis, "Greece," in Ferner and Hyman, 514–20.

21. Peter Zervakis, "Das Politische System Griechenlands," in *Die Politische Systeme Westeuropas*, ed. Wolfgang Ismayr (Opladen: Leske und Budrich, 1997), 619–53, particularly pp. 641–42; Gunnar Hering, George Demetriou, and M. Kelpanides, "Das Politische System," in *Südost Europa Handbuch*, Vol. 3: *Griechenland*, ed. Klaus-Detlef Grothusen (Göttingen: Vandenhoeck and Ruprecht, 1980), 54–120, particularly pp. 105–13.

22. George T. Mavrogordatos, "From Traditional Clientelism to Machine Politics: The Impact of PASOK Populism in Greece," *South European Politics and Society* 2, no. 3 (1997): 1–26, particularly p. 23.

23. Alan D. Stoleroff, "Between Corporatism and Class Struggle: The Portuguese Labour Movement and the Cavaco Silva Governments," *West European Politics* 15, no. 4 (1992): 118–50; Daniel Nataf, *Democratization and Social Settlements: The Politics of Change in Contemporary Portugal* (New York: New York State University, 1995).

24. Carles Boix, *Partidos Politicos, Crecimiento e Igualdad: Estrategias Economicas Conservadoras y Socialdemocratas en la Economia Mundial* (Madrid: Alianza Editorial, 1996); Wolfgang Merkel, *Ende der Sozialdemokratie? Machtresourcen und Regierungspolitik im westeuropaeischen Vergleich* (Frankfurt a. M.: Campus, 1993); Brendan Murphy, "European Integration and Liberalization: Political Change and Economic Policy Continuity in Spain," *Mediterranean Politics* 4, no. 1 (1999): 55–78; *El Pais*, October 25, 2000, pp. 1, 72; *El Pais*, October 17, 2000, p. 31.

25. Miguel Martinez Lucio, "Spain: Regulating Employment and Social Fragmentation," in *Changing Industrial Relations in Europe*, ed. Anthony Ferneran and Richard Hyman (London: Blackwell, 1998), 426–58, particularly pp. 438–49; Holm-Detlev Köhler, "Gewerkschaften und Arbeitsbeziehungen in der Demokratie," in *Spanien heute: Politik, Wirtschaft, Kultur*, ed. Walther L. Bernecker and Klaus Dirscherl (Frankfurt a. M.: Vervuert, 1998), 267–93; particularly pp. 279–89; van der Meer, "Aspiring Corporatism?," 322–29.

26. Jelle Visser, "A Truly Mixed Case," in van Ruysseveldt and Visser, 290–308.

27. Onorato Castellino, "Pension Reform: Perhaps Not the Last Round," in *Italian Politics: The Stalled Transition*, ed. Mario Caciagli and David I. Kertzer (Boulder, CO: Westview Press, 1996), 153–65, particularly pp. 163–65.

28. Regini, "Still Engaging in Corporatism?," particularly p. 314.

29. Vincent Della Sala, "Hollowing Out and Hardening the State: European Integration and the Italian Economy," *West European Politics* 20, no. 1 (1997): 14–33.

30. Kritsantonis, "Greece," 524–26.

31. Christos A. Ioannou, "Trade Unions in Greece: Change and Continuity," *Transfer* 3 (1996): 500–18, particularly pp. 515–18.

32. Keith R. Legg and John M. Roberts, *Modern Greece: A Civilization on the Periphery* (Boulder: Westview Press, 1997), particularly pp. 90–92; this was the case in the local elections of October 1998, which were a major defeat for PASOK; see the *Athens News Agency*, June 2, 2001.

33. This is the Treaty of Amsterdam, §109 N-S.

34. Jean-Luc Sauron, "Le Conseil Européen Extraordinaire de Luxembourg 20 et 21 Novembre 1997 pour l'Emploi: Synergie des politiques communautaires et integration des politiques nationales, ou la resurgence de la planification á la Française," *Revue du Marché Commun et de l'Union Europeenne* 3, no. 41 (Decembre 1997): 649–55; Reimut Jochimsen, "Europa 2000—Herausforderungen fur die EU nach dem Vertrag von Amsterdam," *Integration* 21, 1/98, (1998): 1–11.

35. The employment committee replaced the Employment and Labor Market Committee set up in 1997 (OJ L 6, January 10, 1997).

36. Conselho Europeu de Lisboa, March 23–24, 2000, "Conclusões da Presidencia," *Europa: Novas Fronteiras*, no. 7 (June 2000): pp.92–103, particularly pp. 100–101.

37. Meanwhile 38 EURES were already established across the European Union to help cross-border migrant workers.

38. *Bulletin of the European Union*, March 2000, p. 13.

39. Monica Threlfall, "Spain in Social Europe: A Laggard or Compliant Member State?," *South European Society and Politics* 2, no. 2 (1997): 1–33; Dimitris Demekas and Zenon Kontolemis, "Labour Market Performance and Institutions in Greece," *South European Society and Politics* 2 (Autumn 1997): 78–109. European Commission, *Social Protection in Europe 1997* (Luxembourg: Office of the Official Publications of the European Community, 1998), 112.

40. European Commission, *Managing Change: Final Report of the High Level Group on Economic and Social Implications of Industrial Change* (Luxembourg: Office of the Official Publications of the European Community, 1998), 15; *Expresso*, November 4, 2000, p. 23.

41. Maurizio Ferrera, "The 'Southern Model' of Welfare in Social Europe," *Journal of European Social Policy* 6, no. 1 (1996): 17–37; for Ferrera's recent consideration of the development of social policy and the welfare state in the future European Union, see, "Integrazione Europea e Sovranità Sociale dello Stato-Nazione: Dilemmi e Prospettive," *Rivista Italiana di Scienza Politica* 30, no. 3 (2000): 393–421.

42. Christine Cousins, "Women and Employment in Southern Europe: The Implications of Recent Policy and Labour Market Directions," *South European Society and Politics* 5, no. 1 (Summer 2000): 97–122.

6

Political Culture and Civil Society in Southern Europe

A CRITICAL REVIEW OF THE POLITICAL CULTURE CONCEPT

The introduction of the concept of political culture by Gabriel A. Almond[1] and his subsequent first systematic survey of political culture with Sidney Verba[2] transformed the approach toward democracy across the world. Their basic definition of political culture was the "subjective dimension of politics." These two authors believed that culture, essentially a qualitative category in anthropology studies, could be quantified and thus help identify how large the political support of a national population is for a political system. For this, Almond and Verba differentiated between cognitive, affective, and evaluative attitudes. The methodology used for the studies was based on opinion poll surveys, which had achieved some degree of institutionalization in American politics at that time. The more or less closed questionnaire allowed for a comparative approach of attitudes in different countries in spite of their past political traditions. Although this methodology was subject to criticisms after the results were published, this study can be characterized as pioneering in scope and character. Their main thesis was that political culture is not homogenous throughout any of the countries. Indeed, they created three ideal types of political culture for the study: parochial, subject, and participant. Parochial political culture is complete ignorance of the political system. Subject culture is one of alienation and deference to the political leaders and institutions. Last but not least, participant political culture is positive involvement in the political system. According to the authors, none of these ideal political cultures existed in a modern democratic political system. Instead a mixture of these three political cultures is the rule. The larger the number of people belonging to the participant political culture, the more civic it is. The stronger the other political cultures are in relation to the participant political culture, the less civic and more alienated and deferent is the country's political culture. Of the five countries studied the United States and the United Kingdom were regarded as civic, whereas West Germany, Italy, and Mexico were categorized as still progressing toward it. This ethnocentric bias led to major criticisms, particularly in Germany.[3]

Although all these criticisms are quite correct, the methodology of the civic culture has continued to be the predominant way of measuring political culture since the 1960s. Indeed, opinion poll surveys regularly observe how the political and economic performance of institutions and leaders are evaluated. The study of political culture in the emerging democracies of southern, central, and eastern Europe focused particularly on the aspect of performance of the economic and political systems. Once again, political stability, legitimacy, and accountability are the essential categories for most researchers:

> A newly introduced democracy can consolidate only if there is positive feedback from the experience of citizens with the performance of democracy to the structure and values of democracy. . . . What is decisive for this feedback, which is presumed to lead to the institutionalization of already implemented values and structure, is not any objectively ascertainable performance perceived by citizens.[4]

This stability is naturally related to the fact that modern democratic political systems are embedded in an international economic order and they do not need to have a political culture adjusted to the domestic arena, but as well as to the dominant world culture of capitalism.[5] Therefore, Gabriel Almond's first, intuitive definition of the requisites of the secular homogenous political culture in the United States is that it has the "atmosphere of the game" and it is multivalued, rational-calculating, bargaining, and experimental. In this sense it has to be congruent with a liberal market society. One of the criticisms of Almond in the mid-1950s was that continental European political culture was only partially secularized and therefore was thwarted in its potentiality for "political market behavior."[6] These naturally were the main elements of a marketization of political life. Such a structure and culture of politics existed in the United States for a long time, but in the European context they were only slowly emerging. Indeed, an Americanization of European politics became visible in the 1970s and 1980s. Cleavage class politics is slowly being replaced by a marketization of the political field. An exception to the rule was always the close special relationship of the United Kingdom and the United States. In spite of all that, the other EU member-states, including the southern European countries, are becoming more Americanized and closer to the marketization and individualization induced by the economy. The growing individualization is naturally a consequence of the colonization of the life-world by the market. In this sense, individual citizens become consumers of politics through the processes of political marketing and the media spectacle. Past stable collectivities such as the working class or Christian democratic subcultures have eroded and are being replaced by a market of individuals subject to the marketing strategies of economic and political actors. This naturally is becoming faster with the introduction of third generation phones, Internet, interactive television, and personal computers. Programs such as *Big Brother* make a mockery of the ideological fight between the United States and the Soviet Union by introducing the totalitarian experience as a television spectacle.[7] Also the celebrity industry has become more and more autoreferential, due to the fact that it is a creation of PR firms.[8] This led even the famous political scientist Giovanni Sartori to speak of today's man/woman as a *homo videns*, which is shaped and dominated by television.[9] Political culture can no longer be defined as restricted by the national sphere; more than that it is influenced and shaped by global television circuits and global economic trends. Since the 1970s, corporate global strategies clearly have become more flexible and have created more flexible market-oriented individuals, which in the end will affect the political culture of a country. The fall of public man/woman in terms of civic culture is being replaced by a more flexible man/woman that may have difficulties keeping going without neglecting social life. The rising number of divorces and neglected children further fosters this marketization of social life.[10] According to Richard Münch we already abandoned the class society and are moving very fast to the communication society, which clearly is no longer national but global. We live already in a virtual communicative society via Internet, mobile phones, and interactive television. The European integration process is bringing the nationally defined societies of the member-states slowly closer together and creating, slowly but with certainty, a European society compatible with the emerging single European market.[11] Southern European political cultures are not excluded from these global trends. On the contrary, they are among the most vulnerable citizens to be colonized by the market economy. Political culture has to be understood within this context of marketization of values in present liberal democratic societies. In this sense, the project Almond and Verba engaged in some forty years ago clearly has become more relevant viewed from the perspective of marketization of social and political life that is created via marketing strategies directed toward individuals as consumers of political phenomena.

INSTITUTIONS AND POLITICAL CULTURE IN SOUTHERN EUROPE

Based on the pioneering work of Almond and Verba are the regular surveys of the *Eurobarometer* carried out by the European Commission. Such *Eurobarometer* studies have been undertaken and published by the European Commission since 1973. In this section, we use these studies widely to show how the southern European countries perceive their national democracy and institutions in comparison to other member-states. The general assessment is that in the 1990s, all four countries tend to converge in their attitudes with those of other democracies.

The transformation of political culture in southern Europe from authoritarian, patrimonial-traditional political attitudes to democratic universalistic-modern ones is a long-term process. A civic culture can only be established after more than a generation of socialization and participation in the new political system. Even so, longevity of governance does not assure the establishment of a successful strong political culture. The performance of the institutions may be under constant crisis and subject to negative subjective evaluation by the population. Indeed, the Italian case belongs to this category. There is a permanent dissatisfaction with democracy in Italy, which in the 1970s led to the emergence of terrorism and of violent nonconventional forms of expression and, in the 1980s and 1990s to a growing alienation from the institutions of the first Republic.[12] Still today the population is the most dissatisfied with the national democracy of the European Union.[13] In contrast, in the other southern European democracies of Portugal, Spain, and Greece, satisfaction with the national democracy is still more widespread than dissatisfaction. Spain is clearly the country with the highest score of satisfaction of all countries. Compared with the survey of 1994, the degree of satisfaction with the national democracy has increased considerably. Although in Italy there was only a 9 percent improvement and in Portugal 10 percent, in Spain and Greece it was 31 percent.[14] The Spanish case is certainly related to the *desencanto* (disenchantment) with the longevity of the PSOE in government, which in 1994 was exposed to several cases of political corruption. Similarly, in Greece the negative economic situation and the introduction of austerity measures in view of the preparation for a potential membership of the second and third stage of EMU led to more dissatisfaction (as shown in Figure 6.1).

In terms of trust in the political system, only Italy of the four southern European countries remains below the EU average. The other three

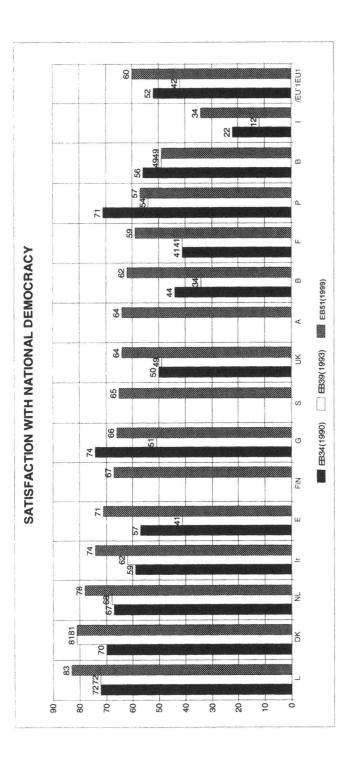

Figure 6.1 Satisfaction with National Democracy in the 1990s

Source: Eurobarometer 34 (December 1990): A-17; *Eurobarometer* 39 (June 1993): A-14; *Eurobarometer* 51 (Spring 1999): 6.

countries are above the very low EU average of 35 percent of respondents trusting the political system. This low trust of Europeans in their national political systems is less widespread in the Netherlands (56 percent) and lowest in Italy (25 percent). While the Portuguese respondents still rank among the four most trusting nationalities (44 percent), in Greece and Spain this figure is only 38 percent.[15]

In terms of trust toward institutions, Italian respondents do not like their institutions very much. The national government, national parliament, political parties, civil service, the justice system, and trade unions score low in terms of trust by their citizens. This naturally clearly shows that there is a persistent alienation of Italians toward their institutions even after the judiciary successfully prosecuted the political class of the First Republic. In spite of the fact that since 1992 major reforms were undertaken and new parties emerged on the scene, Italians continue to mistrust their institutions. Portugal, Spain, and Greece have clearly higher scores of trust in most of the institutions (even higher than the EU average), which shows that democratic consolidation and institutionalization have been quite successful in these countries The only institutions the Italians trust like their southern European counterparts are the church, the army, and the police. In similarity to their European counterparts, southern European respondents do not trust political parties. In Portugal, Spain, and Greece the low level of trust is slightly above the EU average of 18 percent. Very salient is the fact that Greece, has the highest trust scores in relation to the church and army. This is explained by the fact that the Greek Orthodox Church is part of the Greek identity and culture and has to be defined as more or less a national institution. Any new government in the Greek Parliament is blesssed by the Greek Patriarch, meaning that the religious aspect is still an important element in the definition of Greek political culture. The high scores of trust in the army are related to the fact that after independence of the Ottoman empire, the Greek army became the only guarantor for the preservation and defense of the Greek territory against potential foreign enemies (Turkey and the unstable new states of former Yugoslavia). Another factor is that the conscription in Greece is obligatory. All young men have to serve almost two years in the army, which naturally makes it a national institution supported by the whole population (as shown in Figure 6.2).

In retrospect, southern European democracies and institutions have improved their legitimacy since the early 1990s. Although there is still a "democratic cynicism" in relation to political parties and political leaders,[16] this is widely shared by all EU member-states apart from the Netherlands, which has a very high level of trust in its institutions, including political parties. This naturally shows that the southern European pattern is slowly diluting itself into the European context.

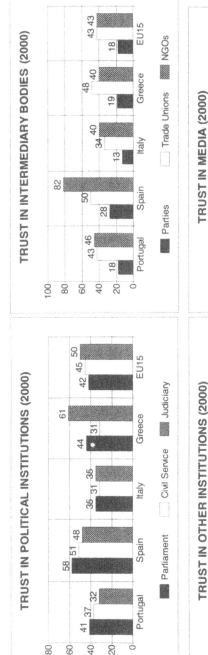

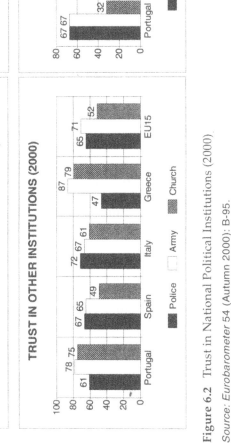

Figure 6.2 Trust in National Political Institutions (2000)

Source: Eurobarometer 54 (Autumn 2000): B-95.

Instead of speaking of a "crisis of democracy in Southern Europe,"[17] we really have to speak of a general crisis of "political parties" as adequate transmission belts in present democratic European societies. This again tells us a lot about the growing distancing between political parties and the national populations, including the United Kingdom, which may lead to further Americanization and presidentialization of party system to prevent a complete divorce between party politics and the citizens. On the way, we may find other forms of political expression, such as new social movements, non-governmental organizations, or nonconventional actions. The European integration process is certainly a factor that led to this convergence of attitudes and political culture with the other EU member-states.

SOCIAL REPRESENTATIONS OF DEMOCRATIC POLITICS AND CIVIL SOCIETY IN SOUTHERN EUROPE

Although the process of individualization in southern European democracies has continued to be the most salient feature of the transformation of the social basis of the political system, it is quite useful to look at the transformation of past social representations of politics and their replacement by new ones. In many ways, the conditions for civic culture are the effort toward collective action so that the political system can be influenced. If one looks at Portugal, Spain, Italy, and Greece, one can observe a fast process of erosion of traditional social representations of politics that tended to be dominated by a pattern of deference. All four countries have become more democratic in the past three decades. Indeed, in spite of the high level of dissatisfaction with national democracy, Italian civic culture has become stronger and more salient as seen in the struggle against terrorist violence back in the 1970s, in the fight against the Mafia in the south, and, last but not least, in support for new social movements such as the Northern League of Umberto Bossi. Although the ideological boundaries between left and right are becoming more blurred and the old allegiances are disappearing with the older generation, other cleavages are emerging with corresponding minimalist organizational flexible horizontal structure. The best example is naturally the so-called civic movement-party *La Rete* (The Network), which wants to become a national, loose horizontal structure without membership cards so that it avoids becoming a rigid party organization and is able to respond flexibly to the developments in Italian politics.[18] The emergence of a loose, flexible, light, almost virtual structure has become a characteristic of most new Italian political parties such as the Silvio Berlusconi's *Forza Italia*, Umberto Bossi's

Northern League, and the Olive Tree Coalition of Romano Prodi and Massimo D'Alema. These loose structures create opportunities for voters and political activists to cross boundaries and pragmatically seek the defenders of their interests. The Italian case clearly shows that the new generation is linked to a process of faster mobility in every sense. The flexible man/woman is part of the new politics. This naturally led to the emergence of the new middle classes and the disappearance of the working classes due to the transformation of the economic structure toward the new economy and information society. Indeed, as Manuel Castells found out, we are moving from the class society to a network society that clearly emphasizes individualization.[19] Portugal, Spain, Greece, and Italy are not exceptions to this rule. Most advanced economies are moving toward it, but some faster than others. Whereas Italy and Spain clearly moved very fast toward it in the past three decades, Portugal and Greece still have pockets of social resistance against the winds of modernity. In Italy and Spain, the main cleavage seems to be defined in territorial terms. The ongoing regionalization and regionalism in the two countries have become the most dynamic elements of their political culture.

Italy

In Italy, the collapse of *partitocrazia* of the First Republic led to the emergence of a more radical regionalism in northern Italy. According to Patrizia Messina, the former subcultures dominated by the DC and the PCI experienced major transformations in the 1990s. In the first constituent assembly elections in 1946, one could differentiate among four political subcultures: the white zone in the northeast of Italy, which was mainly dominated by DC and Catholic values; the lay zone of northwest Italy, in which the Italian socialist party was dominant; the red political territorial subculture, where the PCI was the strongest party in the regions of Emilia-Romagna, Tuscany, and Umbria, and the red class subculture to the south of the Po river, very strong among the land laborers.

It seems that since the 1970s, these subcultures were beginning to change considerably, creating major problems for the political parties. The decline of electoral support for the main parties between 1979 and 1992 is a reflection of the change in the subcultures. In the white zone, the DC was losing votes from election to election. The electorate became more mobile. This was related to individualization and the growing secularization of society. In the lay zone, PSI and DC were facing more and more the challenge of the regionalists leading to complete collapse in the early 1990s.

One of the reasons for the growing dissatisfaction of the northern electorate with DC was the fact that the DC was becoming more and more a party of the south. The meridionalization of DC led to this strong opposition by the northern league against the southernization of the administration. Indeed, the Northern League became the vehicle of discontentment of former DC voters against the southernization of the state.[20] The anti-statism even led to calls for secession. The whole civil religion of the Northern League is geared to create Padania (regions of northern Republic), which may be either part of a federal Italy partitioned in three macroregions or complete independence. After a radicalization of the Lega between 1995 and 1998 that led to initiatives such as the constitution of the Republic Padania by introducing symbolisms such as the Government, the Parliament, and the constitution of Padania, finally the party conference decided to return to moderation and seek devolution within the Italian state.[21]

The PCI/PDS was able to more successfully resist the changes that were taking place in the subcultures. One of the reasons is probably the fact that regional governments were very successful in keeping the social cohesion of the subculture intact due to their regional economic policies. The inherent civic culture has among its core values a sense of "moral familism" among the high-technology small- and medium-sized enterprises, which emphasizes social responsibility and participation in political life. Although the red political class subculture showed signs of erosion in the past three decades and is becoming slowly a competition field for all new political parties, it has shown also shown a strong ability to resist Berlusconi's populist discourse.

In spite of that, the signs of erosion affect the declining social group of blue-collar workers. For example, one of the centers of the red subculture, Sesto San Giovanni with a very strong traditional communist constituency, is being replaced by a dominance of *Forza Italia*. Apart from the fact that factories are closing down and the traditional working class is disappearing, the power of television and the media approach of Silvio Berlusconi is speeding up the erosion of the social basis of the PDS.[22] In spite of the inroads of Berlusconi's *Forza Italia*, the identity of central Italy continues to be overwhelmingly left-wing. Indeed, in spite of social change and different ways of interpreting identity between the older and younger generations, the former core regions of pre-1992 Italy continue to be resilient against a more conservative south and north. The nature of identity has become less concrete around the institutions of the Communist Party, becoming diffuse and undefined. This means that the gap between social and political organizations and the electorate is widening, making it more likely that Berlusconi's *Forza Italia* may find a formula to gain more support in these regions. One factor that may have prevented the overwhelming part of the population to vote for the right-center alliance is their reluctance, due to historical memory, to give their votes to the post-fascist National Alliance (*Alleanza Nazionale* [AN]).[23]

AN was able to improve its credibility by transforming itself into a post-fascist party eligible for the new generation. Also here one can find a party that defines itself territorially, emphasizing the need to keep the unity of the Italian nation against regionalism and separatist tendencies.[24]

Indeed, according to a survey, secessionism is not regarded as an option by most Italians. In spite of all that, the Northern League has, for economic or state failure reasons, introduced this question into the constitutional discussion.[25]

Quite important for a renewed Italian political culture or cultures is the fact that in the 1990s one could observe the strengthening of civil society in the southern regions of Italy, particularly in Sicily. The over-dominance of criminal organizations in the Mezzogiorno always created problems for the establishment of a virtuous circle of citizenship in Southern Italy. One of the factors for the underdevelopment of the south was the fact that criminal organizations tended to get hold of the public funding and divert for other purposes. The Mafia was an important element sustaining the postwar web of systemic corruption established by DC and discovered by the Milan judiciary during their *Mani Pulite* operations. In spite of that, in the 1980s and 1990s, both judiciary and police were very active in fighting against the Mafia.[26]

The courageous fight of several public figures, such as carabinieri Mario della Chiesa, judge Giovanni Falcone, magistrate Paolo Borsellino, and mayor Pio della Torre, led to the emergence of Anti-Mafia movements that clearly were designed to strengthen the role of the state in southern Italy.[27] The creation of the regional party *La Rete* (The Network) under the leadership of the mayor of Palermo, Leoluca Orlando, clearly helped improve the prospects of citizenship in Sicily. This movement was not able to expand to the Italian mainland, but it is quite popular in Sicily. The informal nature of *La Rete*, the lack of membership cards, and the importance of working together to improve living conditions are all features of a new kind of postmodern politics that is reshaping Italian politics after the collapse of the old party system.[28]

Women were particularly involved in social movements to create a more secure environment in Sicily. According to Alison Jamieson, the anti-Mafia movement was an important catalyst of associativism in southern Italy. After 1992 there was a boom of new associations against the Mafia or for other purposes so that today southern Italy has a level of associations (6,400 associations) similar to the level that exists in northern and central Italy. This naturally is quite promising. The members of the associations tend to be more educated than the average population, but what is important in this fact is that civil society and associativism have become sustainable in the Mezzogiorno.[29]

In spite of that, the Sicilian *Mafia*, the Reggio-Calabrian *N'Dranghetta*, the Neapolitan *Camorra* or rather *Camorre*, and the *Sacra Corona Unita* in Puglia are still successful in undermining the state authority. First of all, these organizations ceased to be mere local criminal organizations in the 1960s and 1970s and are now international organizations. Secondly, their decentralised structure allows them to reconstitute their leadership very fast. Thirdly, the activities of criminal organizations have diversified over the past thirty years, including today weapons trafficking, trafficking of nuclear material, smuggling of illegal immigrants, trafficking in women and children, trafficking in body parts, money laundering, and drug trafficking. Fourthly, the diversified nature of the business leads to more interdependent relationships among the global Mafias, making it more difficult for state-based police actions to be organized. In spite of that, the recent movements toward Europol, bilateral security cooperation between Spain and Italy, and other actions have contributed to successes against Italian criminal organizations.[30] The big achievement was the imprisonment of *capo di capi* Toto Riina who is now serving a life sentence. Less successful has been the capture of new *capo di capi* Bernardo Provenzano, who even at present is on the run.[31] In sum, in spite of emerging civil society in southern Italy, criminal organizations are still a major problem for the Italian authorities.

Spain

In Spain, regionalism and regionalization became important elements pushing forward the democratization and decentralization of the state. In spite of all those changes, Spaniards still today tend to identify themselves more with their locality than with the higher structures of administration at regional or national levels. This naturally shows that there is a sense of localism and moderate regionalism in Spain. Regional consciousness is strongest in Catalonia, Basque Country, Galicia, the Baleares, Andalucia, Valencia, and Canarias. This can be measured by the emergence of regionalist-nationalist parties in these regions (see Chapter 4). The centrality of Catalonia in creating this dominant cleavage of Spanish politics cannot be understimated. Most Catalans speak both Catalan and Spanish and belong to one of the richest regions of Spain. The strength of the main coalition of parties *Convergencia i Unió* may document this support for regionalist-nationalism even in national elections. The same can be said for Galicia since the mid-1990s. The so-called *Bloque Nacional Gallego* is representing a growing number of voters who want a more regionally and locally democratic citizenship. Galician, a language close to Portuguese, is widely spoken in Galicia.

The state of autonomies was a major factor in enhancing regional consciousness and accommodating the policies of moderate regionalist nationalism.[32]

The exception to the rule so far has been the Basque Country. In the northern regions, only one fifth to one third of the population can be said to have a strong Basque consciousness, which implies speaking and understanding Basque. This is actually the group that the Basque separatist movement Basque Country and Freedom (*Euskadi ta Askatasuma* [ETA]) has been targeting since its foundation on July 31, 1959.[33] Their killing campaigns started in 1968 during the Franco regime. Their assassinations and culture of terror intend to force the Spanish state to give independence to the Basque Country. Indeed, their ultimate aim is a unification with the French Basque regions and the creation of a Basque state. The Spanish government has so far rejected any negotiations with ETA. The terrorist organization declared a cease-fire, which lasted for fourteen months until December 1999.[34] Since then ETA has resumed its killings and assassinations of politicians, businessmen, and policemen and -women. Meanwhile, the number of killings in the recent campaign has risen to over twenty, and the total number of killings since 1968 has risen to almost 800 victims.[35] ETA clearly is rejected by the overall majority of the population and the political class, but their actions create splits among the nationalist regionalist parties in the Basque Country, which are more or less ambiguous on the question of independence. The political arm of ETA, Basque Nation (*Euskal Herritarok* [EH]),[36] although elected only by a minority, is interested in pushing the issue of independence on the agenda. According to a survey, most Basques are afraid to take part in politics: 70 percent of the respondents are very afraid to take part in politics; 71 percent feel that the present PP government was wrong in missing the opportunity to dialogue with ETA during the cease-fire. This is felt among the majority of both Basque nationalists and non-nationalists. It is quite important is that a substantial section of the population (15 percent) would like to leave the Basque country if they had the opportunity of similar employment conditions in another part of Spain. This is quite high among the young people, reaching 30 percent among those under twenty-five years of age.[37] Apart from a small minority in the Basque Country, secessionism became less relevant in Spain. This is naturally a great success for the constitution of 1978. The elections of May 13, 2001, led to a further polarization between Basque nationalists and the rest of the Spanish population living in the Basque Country.

Portugal

The small democracies of Portugal and Greece never experienced these regionalist tendencies. Apart from the regional governments of the Atlantic island archipelagos of Madeira and Acores, Portugal is characterized by a population who is comfortable with the unitary structure of the Portuguese Republic. In the November 8, 1998, referendum on regionalization, less than 50 percent of the electorate bothered to vote, and two thirds of those who did vote decided against the establishment of eight administrative regions proposed by the Socialist government under Antonio Guterres and enshrined in the constitution.[38] This shows that other cleavages are more salient in the Portuguese case. Portuguese and Greek political cultures are similar in some way because of the dominance of the family and the belated transition from traditionalism to modernity. Although the European integration process is contributing slowly to an expansion of a rational-legal universalistic structure of opportunities, patrimonial forms of behavior may still persist in a predominantly democratic culture. The carriers of this culture are among the younger generation, who are already socialized in a market-oriented contract culture and will in the end transform patterns of amoral familism of the older, less literate population. In some cases, such as in the inner regions of Alentejo, Trás-Os-Montes, and Beira Interior in Portugal, fatalism and parochialism of the older generation, in spite of television, may contribute to the persistence of subcultures of pre-modern ways of life. The pace of modernization in Portugal has been quite considerable since accession to the European Union. The structure of qualifications of the population and the structure of opportunities have improved, but the education sector still shows signs of inefficiency. The dropout rate from secondary school is still very high. Portugal has highest rate of early school dropouts of the EU with 43.1 percent of all enrolled children.[39] The continuing urbanization and declining agriculture sector are contributing to a homogenization of political culture toward the market culture Almond was speaking about. In this equation, the massive entrance of women in the labor market can be considered as an important factor in this transformation. This may also lead in the long term to an erosion of the land-laborer culture of Alentejo and the blue-collar workers of the industrial sector in Lisbon and Setubal, which votes predominantly communist.

Greece

In Greece, the European integration process is also regarded as an important factor in transforming the Greek political culture. In spite of all the reforms introduced by the political parties, Greek political culture today is still dominated by two main subcultures. One is nationalist, centered around Greek orthodoxy and influenced by the past experiences of a Greece permanently ruled by foreign power. The distrust of the political system among carriers of this political subculture goes back to the occupation of Greece by the Ottoman empire. The lack of a legal-rational universalistic political structure led to a constant avoidance of the political institutions as representatives of foreign rule. The consequence was amoral familism, meaning a family-centric behavior that distrusted political institutions. The Greek Orthodox Church clearly encouraged this behavior of introvertedness and struggle against foreign rule. This led to a solidly entrenched xenophobia that could erupt at any time in strong feelings against the West and of solidarity with populations who are oppressed by the West. Indeed, PASOK's Third Worldism of the late 1970s and early 1980s instrumentalized these feelings among the population. Today this subculture is dominated by the orthodox Greek Communist Party. The other subculture is more westernised and modern. It really is open-minded to new ideas and economic development. The carriers of this subculture are intellectuals, the modern economic and political elites. Democracy and the creation of functioning intermediation institutions are at the heart at this conception of democracy. Liberalism and open-mindedness are clearly the most salient elements of this culture.[40]

It seems that neither the Greek orthodox culture nor the modernizing liberal culture was able to gain hegemony in the 1990s. In reality both subcultures merged into one, in spite of the European integration process. According to Nicolas Demertzis, one cannot conceptualize the two subcultures as at the different ends of the process of transition from tradition to modernity. On the contrary, in the Greek case a kind of inverted syncretism happened—the liberal modernizing subculture was domesticated by the more ingrained Greek Orthodox culture.[41] In this sense, the political culture of democratic transition and consolidation is one of split personality. On certain occasions it may lead to an eruption of traditionalist regressive behavior that can come from conservative or left-wing parties. The ongoing Europeanization and marketization via the introduction of the EMU and deepening of the SEM will be the major factor in leading to a universalization of the rational-legal enlightened cultural framework. One aspect that seems to consolidate and reproduce the more ethnocentric worldview is the teaching of history in the school curriculum. From early on, pupils are taught, in an ethnocentric, repetitive way, about history. The study of history is a rigid exercise not allowing for alternative views. The textbooks are provided by the Ministry of Education, and it is all a highly centralized process. Such an approach to history has to be changed, so that the younger generation can be carriers of a new, more free-thinking political culture.[42] This will naturally take time to happen.

Indeed, a major European-wide study called the *History and Politics Youth Project*, carried out in 1995 and 1996, gives us an insight into the atittudes of school dropouts in all southern European countries. This is quite relevant, because these young people will shape the political cultures of tomorrow in the individual countries. In general terms, in all four countries democracy as a form of government is highly regarded. In their overwhelming majority, young people think that democracy is government of the people, by the people, and for the people; it favors the establishment of a welfare state; it implies obedience before law and justice; and it promotes equality of opportunities between men and women. There is also some critical view that the rich and powerful tend to dominate the political system. Regarding the question of the importance of religious faith for southern European youngsters, the Greek respondents single out religious faith as extremely important. In the other three countries, there is only a moderate reference to religion as important in their lives. In the end, the study finds that although the Greeks and the Portuguese have high scores in both ethnocentrism and global solidarity, Spanish youngsters are less ethnocentric and more solidarity minded. The Italians are balanced between two worldviews, although global solidarity seems to prevail slightly. On the whole, one can probably sum up that southern European youngsters are predominantly in support of democratization and they link it, in some way, to the fact that some responsibility has to be carried by the state to ensure this.[43]

The Future

Quite important is the further development of national civil societies that can foster these democratic attitudes in practice. In Portugal, Spain, and Greece the level of associationism is still the lowest of the European Union. It seems that in Spain, 22 to 31 percent of the population belongs to some kind of association, whereas only 25 percent in Portugal or Greece belongs. Membership in political parties and trade union confederations is quite low in Spain and Portugal,[44] whereas in Greece, political parties and trade unions have been dominated by state paternalism.[45] In these circumstances, the return of civil society in these three countries will be achieved only if new, unconventional, flexible forms of collective action are developed to assure a stronger participation of the population. It seems that Spain is a leader in this aspect. The importance of nongovernmental associations promoting all kinds of international and national issues finds its expression in the streets. A popular meeting place in Madrid is the *Plaza del Sol*, where hundreds of NGOs organize spontaneous meetings by attracting passersby to join them and making them aware of topics such as national contribution to aid to the Third World. According to Samuel H. Barnes, these new forms of spontaneous participation are an innovative element of a more flexible, less rigid civil society that tends to escape commitment to organization. He calls it cognitive mobilization in contrast to past social mobilization, meaning that the public is not only individualized but better informed due to exposure to television and other media.[46] In Greece and Portugal, there is the emergence of citizens' groups at the local level that compete successfully in local elections against the major parties. Indeed, recently the independent mayor of Athens, Dimitris Avramopoulos, decided to found a party—the Citizens' Forum— against the major parties. He is predicted to win at least 15 percent of vote. This is naturally a positive development in Greek politics (see Chapter 4).

ATTITUDES TOWARD THE EUROPEAN UNION

As already mentioned, the European integration process is one of the most important factors leading to a change of political attitudes in southern European states. Although the attachment to the European level is still weaker than to village/town, region, or country, southern Europeans score quite high in their attachment to Europe. If we look at the data in more detail, we can see that Portugal and Greece have a stronger attachment to their country than do Spain and Italy. This may be interpreted with the argument that small democracies tend to support their countries more strongly in relation to the European integration process. Another factor may be the fact that economic modernization is bringing both Italy and Spain closer to Europe, while Portugal and Greece are still trailing behind. This could be confirmed by the fact that Denmark and Sweden are fairly attached to the European level. Another explanation may be the fact that the nation-state continues to make it difficult for some countries to attach themselves to a higher level. Greece looks to be closer to the United Kingdom, Netherlands, and France than to its southern European counterparts in this respect (as shown in Table 6.1). (See also Figure 6.3.)

The question about identity is even more interesting. Meanwhile, most Europeans have several coexisting identities. In some countries such as Luxembourg, the European identity is stronger than the national one. Only a tiny minority think of themselves as having an exclusive European identity; most people have both a European and a national identity or vice versa. In all countries, there is still a strong group of people who have only national identity. It seems that the difference among the southern European countries becomes more salient here. Indeed, whereas Italy and Spain rank among the four countries with people perceiving themselves as in some way European, Greece and Portugal rank among the five countries with populations who perceive themselves as least European, along with Finland, Swe-

TABLE 6.1 Attachment to Different Levels of Governance

LEVEL OF ATTACHMENT	VERY + FAIRLY ATTACHED	NOT VERY + NOT AT ALL ATTACHED
THEIR VILLAGE/TOWN (EU average)	87	13
Portugal	93	7
Spain	95	5
Italy	90	10
Greece	94	6
THEIR REGION (EU average)	86	14
Portugal	95	5
Spain	95	5
Italy	87	13
Greece	96	4
THEIR COUNTRY (EU average)	89	10
Portugal	96	4
Spain	90	10
Italy	91	8
Greece	98	2
EUROPE (EU average)	56	40
Portugal	61	36
Spain	68	28
Italy	65	31
Greece	41	57

Source: European Commission, Eurobarometer 51 (Spring 1999): 8.

den and the United Kingdom. Whereas Greece and Portugal still hold to their national identity because they do not perceive the supranational level due to lack of information, in Finland, Sweden, and the UK it seems to be the democratic deficit that leads to their attitudes (as shown in Figure 6.4).

The southern European countries have persistently shown attitudes of support for EU membership. This happened even in periods of recession. This clearly shows that the southern European countries align with Luxembourg and the Netherlands and Ireland, the latter being one of the cohesion countries. In some way this group of countries has been supportive of the European Union throughout the past decade. They contrast heavily with Austria, Sweden, and the United Kingdom where most Euroskeptic support can be found. Finland is moving slowly toward the EU average (as shown in Table 6.2). This support naturally has to be seen together with the question of whether the country has benefited from EU membership. Here we can again find a

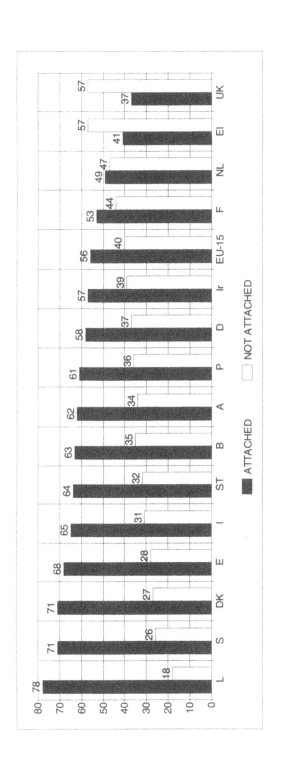

Figure 6.3 Attachment to Europe in Different Member-States

Source: European Commission, *Eurobarometer* 15 (Spring 1999): 9.

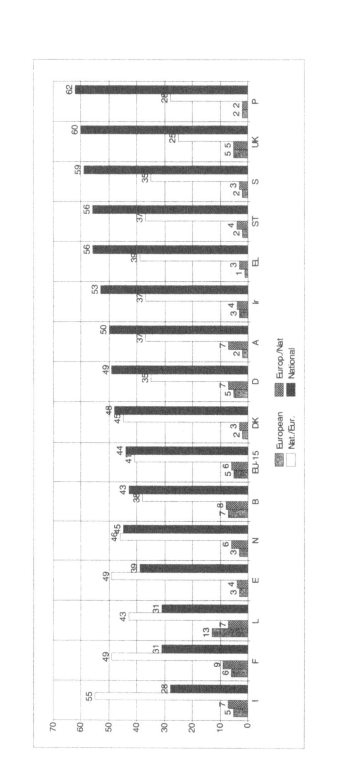

Figure 6.4 National and European Identity

Source: European Commission, *Eurobarometer 49* (1998): 42.

TABLE 6.2 Support for EU Membership

Member-State	Good Thing	Bad Thing
Luxembourg	72	3
Ireland	72	4
Netherlands	63	9
Italy	*57*	*7*
Spain	*57*	*7*
Portugal	*57*	*8*
Greece	*57*	*10*
Belgium	54	8
France	49	12
EU-15	*48*	*13*
Denmark	48	21
France	49	12
Germany	45	11
Finland	36	23
Austria	34	21
Sweden	33	37
UK	29	24

Source: European Commission, *Eurobarometer* 55 (April–May 2001): 2.

cleavage between Portugal/Greece and Italy/Spain. Although all countries have scores above the EU average of a positive assessment of their EU membership, Portugal and Greece along with Ireland are among the populations who feel that their countries benefited from EU membership. Spain and Italy are slightly above the EU average, but if we look diachronically, one can say that the positive scores of Italy and Spain in these two items have been declining since the early 1990s. The main reason is probably the austerity measures that both governments had to introduce to achieve membership in EMU. In the case of Spain, the perceived benefits by the populations have increased since the 1980s. The main reason is the increase in their share of structural funds flowing into the country, which is supporting the country to come closer to the EU average. Indeed, Spain has already achieved 80 percent of the GDP/per capita EU average; some regions are already above the EU average such as Catalonia and Baleares (as shown in Table 6.3).

Satisfaction with EU democracy in southern Europe is quite high. Only Greece is slightly below the EU average. Spain has the highest score of the EU along with Ireland and Luxembourg. Italy is the only country with a higher satisfaction with democracy in the European Union than with national democracy. In the most recent *Eurobarometer* survey (56, 2001) Portuguese and Italian respondents joined the cluster

TABLE 6.3 Benefit from European Union Membership

Member-State	Yes	No
Ireland	83	3
Greece	*69*	*19*
Portugal	*68*	*16*
Luxembourg	66	16
Netherlands	63	20
Denmark	61	24
Belgium	55	23
Spain	*54*	*21*
Italy	*49*	*24*
France	47	28
EU 15	*45*	*30*
Germany	39	37
Austria	38	42
Finland	38	44
UK	29	38
Sweden	27	55

Source: European Commission, *Eurobarometer* 55 (April–May 2001): 14.

of countries dissatisfied with democracy in the European Union. This is naturally a complete reversal of the long-term trend of positive assessment. Only the Spaniards continue to be very satisfied with democracy in the EU, whereas Greek respondents are divided in their opinion. Clearly, this contrasts heavily with the usual cluster of countries that are critical of democracy in the European Union: Austria, Finland, Denmark, Sweden, and the United Kingdom. Their main criticism is that there is a lack of democratic legitimacy in the European Union. The so-called "democratic deficit" argument continues to play a major role in shaping the attitudes of these northern democracies (as shown in Figure 6.5).

The southern European countries also tend to strongly trust the EU and the EU institutions. All four countries have scores above the EU average. The four countries are among the five (along with Luxembourg) that most trust the European Union and its institutions. On the other end of the spectrum are the United Kingdom, Sweden, Germany, Austria, and Denmark (as shown in Table 6.4). Southern Europeans are more or less above the EU average in terms of trusting individual institutions of the European Union (this is valid for the less known institutions such as the Committee of the Regions or the Economic and Social Committee of the European Union). There is still an ambiguous

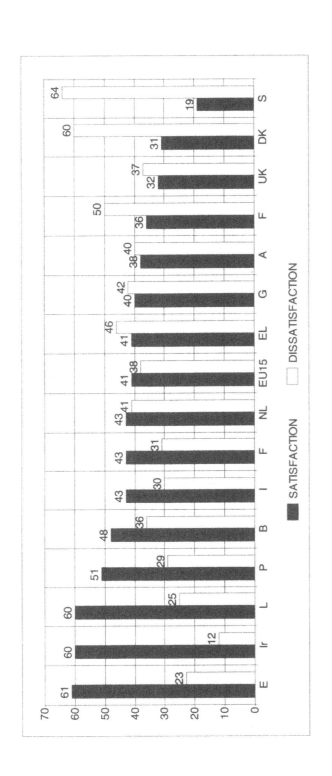

Figure 6.5 Satisfaction with Democracy in the European Union

Source: Eurobarometer 51 (Spring 1999): B-7.

TABLE 6.4   Trust or Distrust in European Institutions

	European Parliament		European Commission		Council of Ministers of the EU		Court of Justice of the EC		European Ombudsman		European Central Bank		European Court of Auditors		Committee of the Regions of the EU		Economic and Social Committe of the EU	
	+	-	+	-	+	-	+	-	+	-	+	-	+	-	+	-	+	-
Belgium	53	33	45	40	36	40	45	32	29	31	44	27	35	30	22	32	25	30
Denmark	48	42	23	65	39	36	64	22	28	23	43	25	17	22	15	26	23	27
Germany	43	34	28	45	31	36	50	23	15	25	50	24	39	27	19	30	21	30
Greece	55	28	43	33	38	34	45	29	24	30	36	26	24	29	24	27	28	28
Spain	59	17	51	18	45	20	38	21	39	17	37	24	32	23	33	19	33	19
France	54	31	44	35	39	36	39	32	24	30	41	32	36	30	23	30	26	30
Ireland	55	16	44	23	38	21	51	9	41	7	48	11	35	9	31	10	33	10
Italy	65	13	58	13	47	18	46	15	27	16	49	14	37	15	28	16	30	16
Luxembourg	68	18	60	24	54	21	63	15	27	21	61	12	55	15	34	16	42	17
Netherlands	51	35	46	36	50	26	62	16	33	17	68	12	51	14	19	19	24	17
Austria	48	32	35	42	35	36	45	27	25	27	44	27	38	29	23	31	26	31
Portugal	56	15	51	16	45	16	40	14	27	15	42	15	38	15	34	15	33	15
Finland	58	27	43	39	43	32	59	21	57	19	54	24	34	27	26	28	31	27
Sweden	38	39	23	52	28	43	45	26	14	27	37	29	14	26	10	26	12	26
UK	32	37	25	37	15	32	30	27	19	25	22	31	11	25	8	25	11	26
EU 15	50	28	40	33	36	30	44	23	24	23	42	24	32	24	22	25	24	25

Source: Eurobarometer 51 (Spring 1999): B-34.

relationship with the European Central Bank, particularly among Spaniards and Greeks. In Greece it is related to the fact that their membership of in the third stage of EMU was delayed for not meeting the convergence criteria until 2001. Apart from the European Ombudsman, the Economic Social Committee, and the Committee of the Regions, southern Europeans seem to be aware of the European institutions. The best known are naturally the European Parliament and the European Commission.[47]

In terms of perceived knowledge of the European Union, the Portuguese and Spaniards along with the British rank among the Europeans who know least about the European Union. In Spain and Portugal one third of the population perceives themselves as knowing nothing at all about the European Union; in Greece and Italy, it is only one fifth and half of the population respectively. At the bottom is the United Kingdo,m with almost 40 percent of respondents who perceive themselves as knowing nothing or little about the European Union. This contrasts heavily with the Danes and Austrians, with only a minority of slightly over 10 percent not knowing anything about the European Union.[48] This pattern has been quite constant throughout the past decade.

Last but not least, the southern Europeans desire a faster speed toward European integration. Indeed, their score indicates that they are in favor of European integration. They are on the top of the ranking, while Denmark, Finland, Sweden, and the United Kingdom are among the countries that have the lowest scores in the Eurodynamometer. This further confirms that European integration is positively regarded among southern Europeans—they even desire a faster pace. This future-oriented attitude of southern Europeans clearly shows that they expect the improvement of their life quality and democracy in the context of further European unification.[49]

In sum, the Europeanization of southern European political cultures will have to be accompanied by information campaigns so that European citizenship may arise from the already existing positive attitudes of southern Europeans toward the European integration project.

CONCLUSIONS

Southern European political cultures are being challenged by the European integration process and the growing marketization processes of the political field. The social representations of the political world are becoming more homogenous. Marketization and individualization are creating new more flexible forms of collective expression that materialize in very loose, sometimes virtual organizational structures. The European integration process and the modernizing rationale behind it are slowly sustaining a transition from national politics to a European-wide market. In this respect, southern European countries are all in the same boat with fellow Europeans, due to the fact that in spite of the implementation of the Single European Market program since 1986, a compatible culture has still to follow up. In terms of satisfaction with national democracy, Italy has to be singled out for having the highest scores of dissatisfaction. This pattern has been dominant for over thirty years now, leading to an escapist support to further European integration.

NOTES

1. Gabriel A. Almond, "Comparative Political Systems," *Journal of Politics* 13, no. 3 (1956): 391–409.

2. Gabriel A. Almond and Sidney Verba, *The Civic Culture. Attitudes On the Democracy in Five Countries* (Princeton, NJ: Princeton University Press, 1963); Gabriel A. Almond and Sidney Verba, *The Civic Culture Revisited* (Boston: Little Brown Company, 1980).

3. Peter Reichel, *Politische Kultur in der Bundesrepublik* (Opladen: Leske und Budrich, 1981); Peter Reichel (ed.), *Politische Kultur in Westeuropa: Bürger und Staaten in der Europäischen Gemeinschaft* (Frankfurt, New York: Campus, 1984); José Magone, *The Changing Architecture of Iberian Politics. An Investigation on the Structuring of Democratic Political Systemic Culture in Semiperipheral Southern European Societies* (Lewiston, NY: Mellen University Press, 1996), 47–52; Maria Luz Moran and Jorge Benedicto, *La Cultura Politica de los Españoles: Un Ensayo de Reinterpretación* (Madrid: CIS, 1995), particularly pp. 10–12.

4. Dieter Fuchs and Edeltraud Roller, "Cultural Conditions of Liberal Democracy in Central and Eastern Democracy," in *The Postcommunist Citizen*, ed. Samuel H. Barnes and Janos Simon (Budapest: Erasmus Foundation, 1998), 35–77, particularly p. 58.

5. Magone, *Changing Architecture*, 114–125.

6. Almond, "Comparative Political Systems," particularly pp. 398 and 406.

7. *El Pais*, July 23, 2000, p. 14. According to the report, this multimedia voyeurism was followed in Spain particularly by young kids between twelve and eighteen years of age. This media spectacle already has been seen in several countries in Europe and it will be presented in the United States. This will have the effect of pushing the boundaries reducing privacy. This will be reinforced by new forms of communication. In some way, George Orwell's *1984* came to us in a more subtle way. See also Manuel Castells, *The Power of Identity*, volume 2 of *The Information Age: Economy, Society and Culture* (London: Blackwell, 2000), pp. 324–28.

8. Channel 4 News, 7 p.m., August 9–10, 2000.

9. Giovanni Sartori, *Homo Videns: La Sociedad Teledirigida* (Madrid: Taurus, 1998).

10. Richard Sennett, *The Corrosion of Character* (New York: W.W. Norton, 1998); *Die Zeit*, August 3, 2000, pp. 11–14; *Die Zeit*, August 10, 2000, pp. 11–16; *Die Zeit*, August 17, 2000, pp. 11–14; *Die Zeit*, August 24, 2000, pp. 11–14; Manuel Castells, *The Power of Identity*, 138–56. The southern European family has been more resilient to the trend toward divorce, single-motherhood and other family forms, but it is following the same pattern. The highest levels can be found in Sweden, Denmark, and the United Kingdom.

11. Richard Münch, *Dialektik der Kommunikationsgesellschaft* (Frankfurt a. M.: Suhrkamp, 1992); Münch, *Das Projekt Europa: Zwischen Nationalstaat, Regionaler Autonomie und Weltgesellschaft* (Frankfurt a. M.: Suhrkamp, 1994).

12. Sidney Tarrow, *Democracy and Disorder: Protest and Politics in Italy, 1969–1973* (New Haven, CT: Yale University Press, 1989).

13. Leonardo Morlino and Mario Tarchi, "The Dissatisfied Society: The Roots of Political Change in Italy," *European Journal for Political Research* 30 (July 1996): 41–63; *Eurobarometer* 56 (Autumn 2001): 16–17.

14. Irene Delgado Sotillos, "Comportamiento y Valores: La Cultura Politica de los Europeos," *Revista Mexicana de Sociologia* 59, no. 1 (1997): 139–60, particularly p. 144; Leonardo Morlino and José Ramon Montero, "Legitimacy and Democracy in Southern Europe," in *The Politics of Democratic Consolidation: Southern Europe in Comparative Perspective*, ed. Richard Gunther, Nikiforos P. Diamandouros, and Hans-Jürgen Puhle (Baltimore and London: Johns Hopkins University Press, 1995), 231–60, particulatly p. 239. According to the *Eurobarometer* 56 (Autumn 2001), Portuguese, Greeks, and Italians form a cluster of dissatisfaction with national democracy (p. 16).

15. *Eurobarometer* 51 (December 1999): 7.

16. Morlino and Montero, "Legitimacy and Democracy," 256–58.

17. Leonardo Morlino, *Democracy between Consolidation and Crisis: Parties, Groups and Citizens in Southern Europe* (Oxford: Oxford University Press, 1998).

18. Elisabeth Fix, *Italiens Parteiensystem im Wandel: Von der Ersten zur Zweiten Republik* (Frankfurt a. M.: Campus, 1999), 178–90.

19. Manuel Castells, *The Rise of the Network Society*, volume 1 of *The Information Age: Economy, Society and Culture* (London: Blackwell, 2000).

20. Patrizia Messina, "Opposition in Italy in the 1990s: Local Political Cultures and the Northern League," *Government and Opposition* 30, no. 4 (1998): 462–78.

21. Margarita Gomez-Reino Cachafeiro, "A Territorial Cleavage in Italian Politics? Understanding the Rise of the Northern Question in the 1990s," *South European Society and Politics* 5, no. 3 (Winter 2000): 80–107, particularly pp. 99–100. The name Padania was taken from a cooperative agreement between the regions of the Po Valley in the 1970s (p. 86).

22. *Die Zeit*, July 20, 2000, p. 7.

23. Francesco Ramella, "Still a 'Red Culture'? Continuity and Change in Central Italy," *South European Society and Politics* 5, no. 1 (Summer 2000): 1–24, particularly pp. 8–18.

24. For a good summary on the transformation to post-Fascism as a new identity, see Ferran Gallego, *The Extreme Right in Italy: From the Italian Social Movement to Post-fascism* (Barcelona: Institu de Ciencies Politiques i Socials, Universitat Autonoma de Barcelona, 1999), working paper no. 199; see also Chapter 4.

25. M. Chiara Barlucchi, "Quale Secessione in Italia?," *Rivista Italiana di Scienza Politica* 27, no. 2 (August 1997): 345–71, particularly pp. 362–69.

26. Massimo Brutti, "Cosa Nostra nella Crisi del Sistema Politico Italiano," in *Mafia e Anti-Mafia: Rapporto '96*, ed. Luciano Violante (Roma: Laterza, 1996), 49–71; Nicola Tranfaglia, *Mafia: Politica e Affari, 1943-91* (Roma: Laterza, 1992); a very good account of the relationship between politics and Mafia in 1980s and early 1990s is Alfredo Galasso, *La Mafia Politica* (Milan: Baldini & Castoldi, 1993); Pino Arlacchi, "Mafia: The Sicilian Cosa Nostra," *South European Society and Politics* 1, no. 1 (Summer 1996): 74–94; Stefano Guzzini, "La Longue Nuit de la Premiére Republique: L'Implosion Clienteliste en Italie," *Revue Francaise de Science Politique* 44, no. 6 (December 1994): 979–1013.

27. An excellent account can be found in Alison Jamieson, *The Anti-Mafia: Italy's Fight against Organized Crime* (Basingstoke, U.K.: Macmillan, 2000); Filippo Sabetti, "The Mafia and Anti-Mafia: Moments in the Struggle for Justice and Self-governance in Sicily," in *Italian Politics*, vol. 3, ed. Robert Leonardi Corbetta (London: Pinter, 1989), 174–95.

28. Fix, *Italiens Parteiensystem*, 157–83.

29. Jamieson, *The Anti-Mafia*, 152–58.

30. Manuel Castells, *End of Millenium*, volume 3 of *The Information Age: Economy, Society and Culture* (London: Blackwell, 2000), 177–83; Isaia Sales, *La Camorra, le camorra* (Roma: Editori Riuniti, 1993); Enzo Ciconte, *N'Dranghetta: Dall Unitá a Oggi* (Roma: Laterza, 1992).

31. The state prosecutor of Palermo, Piero Grasso, believes that the Mafia is close to victory because it has become invisible again. This was always the main aim of the Mafia. The inability to capture Bernardo Provenzano seems to confirm his thesis (see *Corriere della Sera*, May 20, 2001, p. 12).

32. Manuel Garcia Ferrando, Eduardo Lopez-Aranguren, and Miguel Béltran, *La Conciencia Nacional y Regional en la España de las Autonomias*. (Madrid: CIS, 1994).

33. The ideology of ETA is based on the superiority of the Basque race over the Spanish race. It mixed itself with Marxist ideology in the 1970s. Basque revivalism goes back to the works of Sabino Arana in the nineteenth century. The key text for the ETA is Federico Krutwig's *Vasconia* (1963). He was the son of a German industrialist living in Bilbao. In the book, he presents a racialist interpretation of Basque superiority over the Spanish (Daniele Conversi, *The Basques, the Catalans and Spain: Alternative Routes to Nationalist Mobilisation* [London: Hurst, 1997], 92–95). The ETA uses its youth movement Jarrai to intimidate Basques who may want to protest against the organization. Industrialists in the Basque Country are blackmailed and have to pay a "revolutionary tax"(*Die Zeit*, August 17, 2000, p. 8). In the regional elections of May 13, 2001, *Euskal Herritarok* (EH), the political arm of ETA, lost almost half the votes, leading to a weakening of extremist nationalism in the Basque Country. EH lost particularly in the regions where ETA had carried out assassinations against PP and PSOE local councillors. The verdict was a complete support for moderate nationalism represented by PNV and a condemnation of terrorism and political violence (*El Pais*, May 15, 2001, p. 18). On the different political discourses of Basque nationalism, see José Manuel Mata, *Nationalism and Political Parties in the Autonomous Community of the Basque Country: Strategies and Tensions* (Barcelona: Institut de Ciencies Politiques i Socials, Universitat Autonoma de Barcelona, 1998), working paper no. 137. After the events of September 11, 2001, the European Union concerted their efforts against terrorism. Aznar, with support of main opposition leader Zapatero, included ETA and the political arm of ETA, Herri Batasuna, in the common list of terrorist organizations against which the European Union will fight to erradicate terrorism (*Die Zeit*, January 10, 2002, p. 2; *El Pais*, November 28, 2001, p. 17).

34. ETA was also a major problem for the previous Socialist government. The establishment by the former Ministry of the Interior of an illegal mercenary group called Anti-Terrorist Groups of Liberation (*Grupos Anti-Terroristas de Liberacion* [GAL]) led to outrage and political scandal in Spain. The GAL targeted the family members of known ETA terrorists to demoralize the organization. This so-called dirty war (*guerra sucia*) was condemned by the population and the media as "state terrorism" (see Antonio Rubio and Manuel Cerdan, *EL Origen der GAL: "Guerra Sucia" y Crimen del Estado* [Madrid: Temas de Hoy, 1997]).

35. *The Times*, August 21, 2000, p. 14; *El Pais*, October 31, 2000, p. 30.

36. Until 1998 it was called Homeland and Freedom (*Herri Batasuna* [HB]).

37. *El Pais*, July 28, 2000, p. 15; *El Pais*, November 3, 2000, p. 26.

38. Alvaro Xosé López Mira, "Portugal: The Resistance to Change in the State Model," *Regional and Federal Studies* 9, no. 2 (1999): 98–115. For a detailed analysis of the results, see the excellent study by Michael A. Baum and André Freire, "Political Parties, Cleavage Structures and Referendum Voting: Electoral Behaviour in the Portuguese Regionalization Referendum 1998," *South European Society and Politics* 6, no. 1 (Summer 2001): 1–26.

39. European Commission, *Recommendation for a Council Recommendation on the Implementation of Member States' Employment Policies* (presented by the Commission), Brussels, September 12, 2001, COM(2001), 512 final, p. 17.

40. P. Nikiforos Diamandouros, "Greek Political Culture in Transition: Historical Origins, Evolution, Current Trends," in *Greece in the 1980s*, ed. Richard Clogg (Basingstoke: Macmillan, 1985), 43–69; P. Nikiforos Diamandouros, "Politics and Culture in Greece, 1974–91: An Interpretation," in *Greece 1981-89: The Populist Decade*, ed. Richard Clogg (New York: St. Martin's Press, 1993), 1–25, particularly pp. 4–6.

41. Nicolas Demertzis, "Greece," in *European Political Cultures: Conflict or Convergence?*, ed. Roger Eatwell (London: Routledge, 1998), 107–21, particularly p. 119; see also the enlightening article by Constantine Tsoukalas, "European Modernity and Greek National Identity," *Journal of Southern Europe and the Balkans* 1, (1999): 7–14, particularly pp. 11–13.

42. Efi Avdela, "The Teaching of History in Greece, *Journal of Modern Greek Studies* 18 (2000): 239–53: "The basic purpose of the lesson becomes cultivation of patriotism and democratic ideals through the appropriate selection and interpretation of historical events. Knowledge of the past is subordinated to an agenda that lies outside the sphere of historical knowledge, an agenda that is explicitly didactic in the sense that its goal is to make sure students draw the 'proper'conclusions from history. Students do not learn how to distinguish between historical data and the interpretation of data; they do not learn how to discern opinions from facts. As a result they do not learn how to pose questions about the past, something that is a pre-requisite for the development of critical thinking" (241–42).

43. José Machado Pais, *Consciencia Histórica e Identidade. Os Jovens Portugueses Num Contexto Europeu* (Lisboa: Celta, 1999), 167, 172, 176; Anna Frangoudaki, "Reproduction of the Patterns of Interstate Power Relations in the Conceptions of 15-year-old Students in EU Countries: The Persistence of Prejudice," *Journal of Modern Greek Studies* 18 (2000): 355–74.

44. Maria Jesús Funes Rivas, "Evolución y Tendencias de las Asociaciones Voluntarias en España: Las Organizaciones No Gubernamentales como Nuevo Fenómeno en el Panorama Asociativo," in *Tendencias de Futuro en la Sociedad Espanola: Primer Foro sobre Tendencias Sociales*, ed. José Felix Tezanos, José Manuel Montero, and José Antonio Diaz (Madrid: Editorial Sistema, 1998), 511–31, particularly p. 516; Manuel Braga da Cruz, "A Participação Social e Politica," in *Portugal Hoje* (Oeiras: Instituto Nacional de Administração, 1996), 351–68.

45. George Mavrogordatos, "Civil Society under Populism," in *Greece 1981–1989: The Populist Decade*, ed. Richard Clogg (New York: St. Martin's Press, 1993), 46–63.

46. Samuel H. Barnes, "The Mobilization of Political Identity in New Democracies," in *The Postcommunist Citizen*, ed. Samuel H. Barnes and Janos Simon (Budapest: Erasmus Foundation, 1998), 117–37, particularly pp. 121, 125, and 127; see also the excellent comparative study of Spain with Brazil and South Korea by Peter McDonough, Samuel H. Barnes, and Antonio Lopez Pina, *The Cultural Dynamics of Democratization in Spain* (Ithaca, London: Cornell University Press, 1998), particularly pp. 122 and 166. It clearly comes to the conclusion that political participation and mobilization have changed from ideological to instrumental.

47. *Eurobarometer* 51 (1999): B-14.

48. *Eurobarometer* 51 (1999): B-13.

49. *Eurobarometer* 50 (1998): B-27.

7

European Public Policy
and Southern Europe

THE EMERGENCE OF EUROPEAN PUBLIC POLICY
SINCE THE 1980s

Since the southern enlargement of the EC/EU, which led to the membership of Greece in 1981 and Portugal and Spain in 1986, European public policy gained in relevance. The main trade-off for the acceptance of the SEM program and subsequently of EMU was the establishment of consistent and long-term structural policies devised to achieve more social and economic cohesion between northern and southern Europe within the SEM.[1] European public policy emerged in a period of economic restructuring in the most advanced member-states from the welfare state over the competition state to the multilevel governance system of the EU (see Chapter 5). Present member-states slowly transferred some powers to the European Union to achieve a more efficient economic and social space in Europe. The main rationale was naturally the ongoing competition with the United States and the Asia-Pacific rim. European public policy was not developed to replace the public policies of the individual member-states. On the contrary, European public policy was and is an important device to achieve more convergence of national public policies where it is possible so that the SEM is shaped by the same rationale across the European Union territory. But at the same time it allows for national diversity and traditions. Indeed, the end result is to create a level playing market that will not lead to disadvantages of certain less developed regions in relation to others. Although there is still a long way to go, the mere strategic choice and decision toward it is a qualitative step toward European integration and transnationalization of market relations.

Although originally the decision-making process was dominated by the tandem Council of Ministers of the European Union and the European Commission, today the decision-making process is also conducted by the European Parliament.[2] The Treaty of Amsterdam and the Treaty of Nice strengthened the co-legislator role of the European Parliament, which has to be consulted in the legislative process and also has co-decision rights in most European public policy areas.[3] In this sense, three institutions with different rationales are now involved in European public policy. The Council of Ministers is a chamber that is concerned with protecting national interests, the European commission is the guardian of the treaties that wants to further the European integration process, and the European Parliament represents the citizens of the European Union. The changing nature of the relationships also in the perspective of further enlargement are major factors affecting the efficiency and reform of the decision-making mechanisms of the European Union.[4] In this triangle of power, the relationship between European Commission and the European Parliament has become quite interesting in recent times. The fall of the Santer Commission after parliamentary enquiries into allegations of corruption and mismanagement of funds led to an enhancement of the role of the Parliament.[5] Indeed, the Prodi Commission had to be approved by the European Parliament, which naturally shows that some parliamentarization, in an American sense, is taking place.[6] Recent proposals by the Germans and French toward a direct election of the president of the Commission and a stronger linkage toward a parliamentary system of government at the European level further confirm this important discussion about the future of democracy in the European Union.[7] Finally, the Laeken European Council, during the Belgian presidency, on December 13–15, 2001, established a Constitutional Convention under the leadership of Giscard D'Estaing, which was in charge of transforming the treaties into a readable, simplified constitution for a more efficient working of the institutions and to reduce the democratic deficit between citizens and the political elites.[8] (See Table 7.1.)

Up until this point European public policy was guided by the principles of partnership, subsidiarity/appropriateness, and solidarity.

The principle of partnership envisages the cooperation among supranational, national and subnational actors so that policy formulation, making, and implementation are done in a consensual, negotiated way. Most policy areas also involve, apart from public institutions, the growing number of supranational, national, and subnational interest groups, which recently were labeled by the European Economic and Social Committee as organized civil society.[9] Several interest groups are in-

TABLE 7.1   Voting Rights in the Council of Ministers According to the Amsterdam Treaty of 1993 and Nice Treaty of 2000

Weighting after Amsterdam Treaty (1993) and Nordic + Austria Enlargement in 1995			
Country	Voting Weight	Country	Voting Weight
Germany	10	Portugal	5
France	10	Sweden	4
Italy	10	Austria	4
U.K.	10	Denmark	3
Spain	8	Finland	3
Belgium	5	Ireland	3
Netherlands	5	Luxembourg	2
Greece	5	Total	87
Qualified Majority	62 over 87	Blocking Minority	23 to 25/65
New Weighting after Nice Summit December 2000 (after Central and Eastern Enlargement 2003/4)			
Country	Voting Weight/ Share of EU Population in %	Country	Voting Weight/ Share of EU Populaton in %
Germany	29/17.04	Sweden	10/1.84
France	29/12.25	Bulgaria	10/1.71
Italy	29/11.97	Austria	10/1.67
U.K.	29/12.31	Slovakia	7/1.12
Spain	27/8.18	Denmark	7/1.10
Poland	27/8.05	Finland	7/1.07
Romania	14/4.67	Ireland	7/0.77
Netherlands	13/3.27	Lithuania	7/0.76
Greece	12/2.18	Latvia	4/0.5
Czech Republic	12/2.13	Slovenia	4/0.41
Belgium	12/2.12	Estonia	4/0.3
Hungary	12/2.09	Cyprus	4/0.15
Portugal	12/2.07	Luxembourg	4/0.08
Simple majority	14 over 27	Malta	3/0.07
Qualified Majority	255 over 345	Blocking Minority	91 over 345

volved in the advisory, monitoring, and regulatory committees—the so-called comitology, attached to the European Commission. A huge number of actors are traveling to and from Brussels to take part in such regular meetings so that future legislation is able to include the feedback of the most important political groups.[10] This naturally has been difficult to attain as it can be observed in the social policy sector. Any agreement is always a minimalist compromise between fifteen member-states in the Council of Ministers of the European Union, which may be upgraded at some later stage. Still today, some policy areas sensitive to member-states, such as asylum and immigration policy, have to be agreed upon by unanimous vote. A veto by a member-state may lead to a periodic crisis, but in the end all countries are bound to reach the same kind of *acquis communautaire*. Or using a metaphor by Jacques Santer, all member-states are bound to reach the same port, even if this means that some will be there sooner than others. This is naturally backed up by the treaties under the heading of flexibility.[11] Since the Single European Act (SEA), the unanimous vote has been replaced by a qualified majority vote or simple majority vote in many areas, making the process more efficient. It is quite important that after fifty years of European integration, structures of policy decision-making are in place that are designed to improve cooperation among the member-states and their administrations. At the EU level, national administrations are represented by Permanent Representations, which are working closely together with their national governments to ensure a fast response to decisions required by the Council of Ministers of the European Union. Most of the work is prepared by these national civil servants in the so-called Committee of Permanent Representatives (COREPER) represented by the Permanent Representatives (COREPER II), which deals with more political issues, and Deputy Permanent Representatives (COREPER I), which is in charge of technical policy issues. On the whole, a daily routine of these civil servants of the permanent representatives (created in the 1950s and improved in the 1960s) developed a network of experts who are socialized into a transnational administrative culture with an internalized European integration approach as well as national interest approach to come to a balanced position.[12] In this network, southern European countries have been peripheral in decision-making. They normally align with proposals made by Germany or France. Their ability to shape the discussion with their own proposals is limited.[13]

The smallness of Portugal and Greece is the main reason for the lack of visibility of their positions. Moreover, Portugal, Spain, and Greece are latecomers to a structure that has been in place since the 1960s and is dominated by Germany, France, and the United Kingdom. The case of Italy is quite striking. Although it was a founding member of the EC/EU, the inconsistent and disorganized way EU national policy coordination was conducted over the past fifty years prevented Italy from playing a pivotal role in the decision-making process in the European Union. Somehow, national EU policy coordination reflects the confusion of public administration that still exists domestically in Italy.[14]

Among the four southern member-states, Spain has been the most ambitious, always presenting new initiatives and ideas for the European integration process. Apart from the toughness in the negotiation of the Delors II package in the Edinburgh summit in 1992 and the Berlin summit in 1999, Spain was a major architect of the Euro-Mediterranean partnership that strengthened the relations between the European Union with the southern rim of the Mediterranean. The so-called Barcelona process was initiated in 1995 by the Spanish presidency of the Council of Ministers of the European Union, which wants to establish a Mediterranean Free Trade Area (MEFTA) by 2010 in the region.[15] Under José Maria Aznar, Spain acquired the reputation of being a hard-bargaining partner and extremely interested in pursuing its national interests. This became a salient feature during the last intergovernmental conference leading up to the Nice Treaty. The Spanish government demanded a leveling of its voting power with the larger member-states (Italy, the United Kingdom, France, and Germany) and the right to keep one commissioner in the reformed allocation of commissioners in the European Commission. This has been regarded both by France and Germany as problematic for their envisaged reform of the treaties.[16] Portugal and Greece are more concerned in keeping the right to nominate a representative for the Commission.

The southern European coalition always emerges in those aspects related to the regular negotiation of structural funds. In this they are supported by Germany and Ireland, which are quite keen to receive part of the funds for the Eastern Länder and the less developed areas respectively. After May 13, 2001, legislative elections in Italy, Aznar found an ally in Silvio Berlusconi, who is very keen to keep structural funds for the Mezzogiorno for the period after 2007. This alliance is still in the making but can be regarded as a new southern European approach to counteract the interests of Germany, France, and the United Kingdom. A pact of cooperation was sealed between the two countries. Regular meetings between Aznar and Berlusconi are designed to articulate the protection of national interests in the European Union. After the resignation of Italian foreign minister Ruggiero, Aznar was the only politician supporting Berlusconi's European position. This was widely publicized in the Italian and Spanish media.[17]

Subnational authorities have been more involved in other stages of the decision-making process, particularly in the implementation level, which may more directly affect the metropolitan areas or regions. In recent years, some countries such as Belgium, Austria, Germany, Spain and the United Kingdom have strengthened the participation of subnational governments in the EU policy-coordination process leading to a stronger cooperation within the multilevel governance system. Moreover, the Committee of the Regions and Local Authorities (CoR) has institutionalized the growing importance of the regions in the European Union project. Although the CoR has only advisory powers, it is an excellent forum to bring the different subnational actors together and foster integration at the third level of European integration. This is particularly important, because there are many cross-border projects going on in the European Union that require transnational and trans-regional networks of decision making. Due to the fact that all four countries are unitary, the role and importance of subnational govern-ment are not as extensive as in countries such as Germany, Belgium, and Austria. In spite of all that, the dynamics initiated around the concept of "Europe of the Regions" led to a strong presence of Spanish regional politicians in the Committee of the Regions, such as Pascual Maragall, the mayor of Barcelona, or Jordi Pujol, the president of the Catalan Generalitat.[18]

Since 1996, Italian northern regions have established representation offices in Brussels and are engaged in enhancing their role at the supranational level. In contrast, Portuguese and Greek regions are still dominated by their capitals and quite underdeveloped in terms of representation. Most of the decision-making process tends to ignore the subnational tiers, which are more or less extensive arms of central administration without any decision-making powers (see Chapter 3).

Complementary to the principle of partnership is the principle of subsidiarity/appropriateness. The concept of subsidiarity was intro-duced by the Treaty of the European Union after long debates among the different national governments to assure an appropriate involve-ment of the European Union in the member-states. This means that direct involvement of the European Union is permissible only if the member-state cannot fufill the task on its own. Meanwhile, the concept was extended to the principle of appropriateness, which means that policy formulation, making, and implementation have to take into account the appropriate level within the EU governance system. This is a more sophisticated and flexible approach in relation to the original rigid protectionist and defensive concept of subsidiarity. Still today, subsidiarity is connected to the defensive national policies of the John Major government, who wanted to prevent any kind of federalism or overdominance of the "European super-state" from diminishing the sovereignty of the United Kingdom. Meanwhile, the United Kingdom is moving toward a decentralized structure that has internalized the subsidiarity principle within the subnational governments of Scotland, Wales, and Northern Ireland.

The principle of subsidiarity was less discussed in southern Europe. Apart from Portugal under the government of Anibal Cavaco Silva (1985–1995) and the subsequent referendum on regionalization on No-vember 8, 1998, southern European countries have accepted European Union involvement without any problems. The liberal Cavaco Silva rejected any regionalization of Portugal, because this would lead to the disintegration of the country and diminish the bargaining power in the

European Union. In Greece, the financial and budgetary difficulties of the Greek government led in the 1980s and 1990s to an almost permanent monitoring of Greek financial, budgetary, and economic policies by EU officials in Athens.[19] Moreover, the monitoring structures related to the implementation of structural funds was reinforced and extended. It was the Mitsotakis government that asked Brussels for help to sort out their budgetary finances.[20]

Spain and Italy are almost unconditional supporters of further European integration, so that the subsidiarity/appropriateness discussion was only marginal in these countries. Although Berlusconi has used a rhetoric of national interest and his defense minister Antonio de Martino speaks of the need to establish a light European Union, the overwhelming support by the population for European integration has been a major characteristic of Italy (see Chapter 6).

All four countries absorb, more or less without defiance, the regulatory incremental and technocratic EU legislation. Parliamentary scrutiny is only pro forma and post facto (see Chapter 3).

The third principle of solidarity is probably the most important for the southern European countries. It became an important element in the overall rationale of European public policy, which is designed to establish an even, developed market. The southern European countries, particularly Portugal, Spain, and Greece, in this respect had to catch up in relation to more developed countries in northern Europe. Italy has in common with the other southern European countries the fact that their national territories are characterized by a dualist structure of development. In the Italian case the main cleavage is between north and south. Whereas the northern regions achieve a GDP/per capita above the EU average, southern Italian regions continue to have a GDP/per capita below it. The same can be said about Spain, which has some regions such as Catalonia, Madrid, the Basque Country, and the Baleares above it, but most of the other regions are still below it. Portugal and Greece are less developed in this respect. Most of the country apart from the larger towns of Lisbon, Oporto, Athens, and Thessaloniki are below the EU/GDP per capita. This naturally led to the coalition of southern European countries, Ireland, and Germany in relation to the negotiations for the structural funds. Today all member-states can make a case for solidarity with some of their regions that may face difficulties within the SEM.

Apart from this aspect of social and economic cohesion, the principle of solidarity has to be further extended to the concept of "shared sovereignty,"[21] meaning that the European Union is a device to strengthen the sovereignty of the individual member-states in relation to global processes. This becomes clear in negotiations within the World Trade Organization (WTO) with the United States or other parts of the world in relation to agricultural, industrial, services, or new economoic issues. Speaking with one voice is a way to gain more leverage in global negotiations. The rise of the oil price is leading to a mobilization of the EU member-states to work together and speak with one voice in relation to the Organization of Petroleum Exporting Countries (OPEC). Such "shared sovereignty" can also be applied to other fields such as police, military, and immigration policy.[22] This is still a new phenomenon, but the functional gains from it are strengthening cooperation among member-states. The southern European countries are quite interested in this aspect of the European integration process because it enhances their ability to influence and shape global negotiations or work in cooperation with supranational institutions to deal with aspects of illegal immigration coming from the southern Mediterranean rim or the growing international criminal activity spearheaded by the Italian, Russian, and Albanian Mafia, which is making these countries more vulnerable to criminal activities. Recent efforts to coordinate policing between Spain and Italy fits in the growing cooperation of national police forces within Europol.[23] This can be said about the recent initiative between Spain and France to combat Basque terrorism.[24]

On the whole, European public policy has become a dominant phenomenon in southern Europe. Whereas some policy areas profited from the involvement of the European Union, other clearly were sacrificed in this process.

EUROPEAN REGIONAL POLICY IN SOUTHERN EUROPE

It was Jacques Delors who reformed the budgetary planning of the EC/EU. The reform of the structural funds in 1988 was part of the overall reform of the policy process in the function of establishing an SEM and later on EMU. The Delors package I in 1988 and Delors package II in 1992 helped structure the overall long-term planning of the SEM and EMU. The territorial politics of the EU were and are an essential element in this respect.[25]

Competitiveness and social and economic cohesion were regarded as complementary and reinforcing each other. The SEM was informed by these territorial politics so that all citizens of the European Union had equal access to the market.[26] Since 1989, the EC/EU has been able to count on a more long-term planned budgetary approach that ensures a more ambitious territorial politics. In this respect, Portugal, Spain, and Greece clearly profited from this new rationale. In the past decade, these three countries were the main beneficiaries of the EU structural funds along with Ireland.

In Portugal and Greece the whole territory was declared eligible for structural funds. Both countries were substantially behind the EU average on GDP/per capita. Both populations apart from the larger cities were still 50 percent behind the EU average in the late 1980s. Spain, although more developed than Portugal and Greece, was also considerably behind the EU average. The Italian case is characterised by uneven development between the rich north and the poor south. For decades, the Italian government poured funds from the *Cassa per il Mezzogiorno* into the southern regions so that they could improve their economic structures, but this proved quite unsuccessful due to various factors related to poor regional government performance, lack of modernizing economic elites, and the big problem of criminal organizations that tended to divert funds for their own illicit activities.[27]

Since the reform of the structural funds in 1989, five objectives were agreed upon that would qualify regions to apply for structural funds. During the negotiations of the Nordic enlargement in the mid-1990s a sixth objective for the less populated areas of Sweden and Finland was added to the original five objectives. Since 1998, the Agenda 2000 document of the European Commission reduced the number of objectives from six to three. The basic idea is to make the use of structural funds more efficient and concentrated. Naturally this reform is based on continuity of previous programs.[28] After the settlement in the European Council in Berlin in March 1999, there was no big change of allocation of the funds among the member-states. On the contrary, most countries received the same amount as in the year before. In spite of all that, Spain clearly was able to improve its situation in relation to the past periods (as shown in Table 7.2).[29] This has to do with the hard-bargaining position of Aznar's government in all Council meetings.[30]

By far the most important objective is the first one, which targets lagging behind regions: 70 percent of all structural funds commitments for the period 1994–1999 was directed toward this objective (as shown in Table 7.3). Out of the € 153 billion, 73.6 percent was allocated to the southern European countries. Taking all the structural funds together Spain has profited most of all countries with 22.5 percent of available structural funds. In the period 2000–2006 almost 70 percent out of € 195 billion will go to objective 1 regions. The rest is split among objective 2, and community initiatives such as Interreg, Leader, and Urban (see Table 7.3). This means that southern European countries continue to profit heavily from the financial flows of the European Union, which make more or less 3–4 percent of the national GDP of the individual countries. This naturally gives an important strategic role to the structural funds in the modernization and transformation of these econo-

TABLE 7.2   Net Receivers and Net Payers (2000–2006) after the Berlin Summit of 1999 (Million Euro)

Member-State	Net Receiver/Net Payer
Belgium	1,127
Denmark	-512
Germany	-13,416
Finland	-277
France	-3,916
Greece	*5,005*
United Kingdom	-4,155
Ireland	1,605
Italy	*-3,113*
Luxembourg	997
Netherlands	-2,934
Austria	-1,142
Portugal	*2,818*
Sweden	-1,360
Spain	*7,544*
Sum EU-15	-11,731*

*Negative balance because of expenditure for central and eastern enlargement and EU foreign and security policy; positive net sums = receiver; negative net sums = payer.
Source: Based on Spanish Finance Ministry, *Die Zeit*, September 14, 2000, p. 13.

mies. Some regions were able to gain transitional objective 1 status in the budget negotiations leading up to the Berlin summit.[32] Portugal, Spain, Greece, and Ireland are also eligible to funds from the cohesion fund created for countries with less than 90 percent of average EU GDP per capita. Most projects are related to the Transeuropean Transport Networks and environmental projects. In the period 1994–1999 Spain was able to receive up to 52 to 58 percent of the funds, the largest share of the four countries. It was followed by Greece with 16 to 20 percent, Portugal 16 to 20 percent, and Ireland 7 to 10 percent (see Table 7.4).

The European integration process is a major factor in overcoming these national vices that prevented economic development in the poorer regions in the past. The modernizing element of the European Commission focused particularly on developing proper infrastructures that will lead in the long run to better access to the SEM. This is reinforced by investing in education and vocational training and the creation of small- and medium-sized enterprises so that in the long-term perspective these countries, including the southern regions of Italy, are able to play an active part in shaping the SEM. In the case of Portugal, Greece, and Spain, one of the major problems was the lower

TABLE 7.3   The Objectives of the Structural Funds before and after Agenda 2000 (Period 2000–2006)

Period 1994–1999		Period 2000–2006	
Objective	Target	Objective	Target
Objective 1 70%	Lagging behind regions (GDP/ per capita less than 75% of EU average)	Objective 1 69.7%	Lagging behind regions (GDP/per capita less than 75% of EU average)
Objective 2 10%	Areas in industrial decline		
Objective 3 5%	Long-term unemployed	Objective 2 11.5%	Economic and social restructuring of declining regions
Objective 4 5%	Workers whose employment situation is threatened by changes in industry and production		
Objective 5a 4.5%	Farmers, fishermen involved in processing and marketing of products from those sectors who are facing changes in the structure of production	Objective 3 12.3%	Investment in human resources
Objective 5b 4.48%	Vulnerable rural areas with a low level of socio-economic development that also meet two of the following criteria: high proportion of employment in agriculture, low level of agricultural incomes, low population density or high level of out-migration		
Objective 6 4.45%	Areas with an extremely low population density		
Community initiatives 9.18%	Leader II, Interreg II, Pesca, Urban, Adapt, Now; Horizon; Youthstart, Integra, Pyme	Community initiatives 5%	Interreg, Leader, Equal, and Urban
€ 153 billion		€ 195 billion	
Cohesion Fund € 15.5 billion	Member-states below 90% of EU GDP/per capita average Environmental projects, transnational transport networks	Cohesion Fund € 18 billion	Environmental projects, transnational transport networks

level of education of the work force in relation to those of the other member-states (see Chapter 5). This problem was only partly overcome in the past decade, nevertheless the European programs helped to mobilize these southern European populations in the effort to improve their skills by taking part in vocational training programs co-financed by the European social fund. Special programs were set up to improve

TABLE 7.4   Distribution of Structural Funds (%) According to Countries

Countries	Period 1993–1999	Period 2000–2006
Germany	14.2	14.82
Austria	1.03	0.76
Belgium	1.37	0.94
Denmark	0.55	0.38
Spain	22.5	22.10
Finland	1.07	0.94
France	9.76	7.5
Greece	9.9	10.74
Ireland	3.9	1.58
Italy	14.1	14.6
Luxembourg	0.746	0.04
Netherlands	1.71	1.35
Portugal	9.8	9.76
United Kingdom	8.6	8.02
Sweden	0.9	0.98
Total	∈ 153 billion	∈ 195 billion
Southern European countries (%) total	56.3	57.2

the basic and higher education sector. The best example regarded as a big success by the European Union is the Specific Program for Education in Portugal (*Programa Específico para a Educação em Portugal* [PRO-DEP]), which led to an improvement of the network of basic and higher education schools and universities across the country.[33] In spite of that, the joint employment report of the European Commission for the year 2000 clearly shows that the dropout rate in Portugal is still very high and problematic.[34]

A similar strategic choice was made by Greece in spite of early problems of implementation and adjustment. A major reform of the education and vocational training sector was approved in 1997 allowing for a simplification of the secondary level of basic education and increasing the number of vocational training places. One of the major difficulties for the Greek program of investment in human resources is due to the fact that up until 1993–1994, partisan politics and gaps in the monitoring system prevented a more consistent and successful implementation. Since 1994, under the supervision of monitoring committees, the whole process has improved considerably, even if there is some delay.[35] Vocational training programs were also relevant in both Spain[36] and Italy.

Another field in which the structural funds have made an impact is investment in infrastructures. Portugal, Spain, and Greece used the funds to build motorways and bridges, modernize and extend the railway system, and modernize public services such as the post office. Some of the innovations such as the high-speed train AVE between Madrid and Seville and the extension of the subway in Lisbon were related to ambitious projects of national projection such as the world expositions in the two countries in 1992 and 1998 respectively. The world exposition in Lisbon also led to the construction of a second bridge linking Lisbon to the southern part of Portugal and the extension of the railway system linking north and south Portugal, which until 1998 was nonexistent. Passengers could use the ferry to continue to travel by train only if they came from the north. Such infrastructure revolution can be observed in Greece as well. In spite of many difficulties in dealing with the implementation of structural funds until the mid-1990s, some projects such as the extension of the subway in Athens are regarded as positive. Similar to Portugal and Spain, Greece was chosen to host the Olympic Games in 2004, which will certainly boost the integrative approach in the use of structural funds. Similarly, EU funding is also changing ethnic relations between Greeks and the Turkish minority of Thrace. Decentralization, democratization, and dialogue are replacing rigid exclusionary relations that prevailed until the early 1990s. The structural funds give an opportunity to develop common projects that will help build trust between the two communities. This naturally will require decades to consolidate, but it shows the positive impact of the European integration process with a discourse of cooperation on previous rigid noncooperative relations.[37] In Italy, objective 1 funds targeted, among other projects, the Brindisi region in Puglia, which was in a permanent crisis. Four multiregional programs related to environment, airport infrastructure, industrial parks, and civil protection are contributing to a change of this region. Some of the funds were invested in creating supportive organizations in the agricultural sector.[38] The creation of modern infrastructures is an important pre-condition for these countries to be competitive in the SEM. After decades of geographical isolation, the past decade of coordinated and long-term investment has changed the face of these countries and had a mobilizing impact on economic actors in the individual countries.

The structural funds are also designed to restructure the political economy of these southern European countries. Based on the idea of social capitalism of the small- and medium-sized enterprises in northern Italy[39] that were able to develop high-technology capacities and compete very successfully in the world market, this became an important characteristic of the EU industrial policy. Recently this was naturally connected to the new technologies of information such as the

Internet or telecommunications. The flexibility of response of the northern Italian small- and medium-sized markets to a more complex and diverse market is a major feature of EU structural funds policy. The renewal of the economic fabric can be achieved only by creating incentives for new small- and medium-sized enterprises. Indeed, one salient feature of southern European industries is that they are dominated by SMEs in comparison to northern European countries (see Figure 7.1).[40]

In Portugal, this has led to the establishment of a Specific Program for the Development of the Portuguese Industry (*Programa Específico para o Desenvolvimento da Industria Portuguesa* [PEDIP]), which was dominated by multinational companies in the first period. In the second period, the government was proactive in strengthening the capability of new small- and medium-sized enterprises in applying for funds. This process has been slow, but nevertheless it is changing the culture of enterprises in Portugal.[41]

In Spain, a global grant of ∈ 56.2 million from the European Regional Development Fund (ERDF) was used for the establishment and modernization of SMEs in Castilla-Leon, one of the poorest regions of Spain. It also dedicated some of its funds to the establishment of technology parks such as the one in Malaga housing over forty high-technology SMEs. It brings together university high-technology laboratories such as the Andalusian Institute for Advanced Automation and Robotics and is naturally a way to create cooperation networks with north Africa and other member-states. Similar projects co-financed by the EU can be found in Murcia and Tarragona (Catalonia).[42]

In Italy, a national scheme co-financed by the ERDF is assisting SMEs in the areas of transport, the environment, RTD, and industry in the Mezzogiorno. The basic approach is to create network infrastructures so that SMEs are able to improve their marketing possibilities and training and research facilities. The jewelry industry in Naples may be cite as an example of undertaking major efforts to improve its competitiveness in a more complex and difficult world market.[43] EU funding has certainly mobilized economic actors across the Mezzogiorno to reconsider past forms of behavior and change the culture of organization.[44] In general terms, Italy adjusted their structures in the past decade to the multilevel governance system of the European Union. The ongoing decentralization of public policy has contributed to a considerable improvement of the absorption in the structural funds in the second half of the 1990s.[45]

In Greece a national program for industrial modernization is clearly supporting SME enterprises. One of the advantages of the Greek market is that it is very close to new emerging markets in Bulgaria, Romania, and the Balkan reconstruction process. The structural funds are supporting efforts of SMEs to gain access to these markets through a global

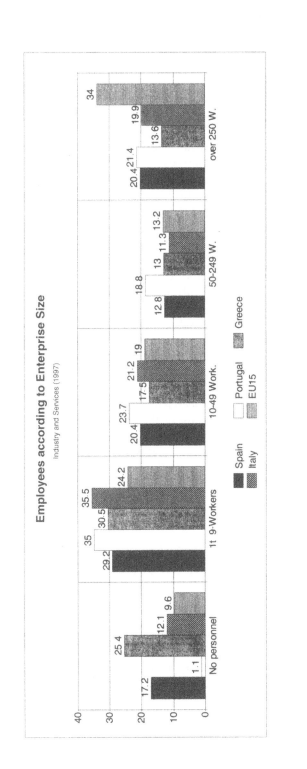

Figure 7.1 The Structure of Enterprises in Southern Europe (1997) in Percentage of the Total Work Force

Source: Author's graph based on Eurostat data.

grant made to economic and social actors in the north of Greece. A technology park in Heraklion, Crete, wants to contribute to a change in the economic structure of the island, which is dominated by agriculture and services. In comparison to the other three countries, Greek projects were affected by delay due to the lack of appropriate coordinating structures. Such problems were more or less overcome after 1995.[46]

Complementary to the structural funds, the European Commission also has several Community Initiatives such as Interreg, Rechar, Leader, or Retex. In the 1994–1999 period the southern European countries profited the most from the community initiatives with 35.1 percent of € 15 billion. Portugal profited particularly from the Retex program which is designed to modernize the textile industry in the community. Spain, Italy, and Greece are beneficiaries of the more industry-related initiatives and rural reconversion programs such as Adapt, Employment, and Leader as well as SMEs. All these countries are profiting as well from the cross-border cooperative initiative Interreg (e.g., between Spanish and Portuguese border regions)[47] and the recent project of Territorial Employment Pacts,[48] which envisages the introduction of enterprise innovation across the European Union.[49] Last but not least, additional funding from the cohesion fund for Portugal, Spain, Greece, and Ireland contributed to related national infrastructures projects taking into account environmental protection.

In sum, structural funds have been a major factor in restructuring the conditions of the political economy of these southern European countries. The outcome of this investment will be felt in generations to come. In spite of all that, the increase in social and individual mobility, the renewal of the industrial fabric, and the improvement of the pool of human resources will make southern Europe better able to shape the future of SEM.

COMMON AGRICULTURAL POLICY (CAP) AND COMMON FISHERIES POLICY (CFP) IN SOUTHERN EUROPE

Among the policy areas that southern European countries had to sacrifice in the process of European integration has been agriculture and fisheries. In all four countries, agriculture has been characterized by a low level of productivity and a large employment. The CAP was established in 1957 in the Rome Treaties and came into force in 1962. It was designed to stabilize the prices in the European Community, protect European products from foreign competition, ensure the security of supply in the Common Market, and support the export of agricultural products via subventions. When CAP came into force, agriculture still affected a large part of the population. The implementation of CAP led to a quite successful improvement of agriculture products, control mechanisms, and price stability. Nevertheless in the 1980s surplus production and a growing reduction of people employed in agriculture made a reform imperative. Major reforms were undertaken, which only partly solved the problem. Subsequently, governments prepared for the next reform of CAP based on the recommendations laid down in the Agenda 2000 document. The so-called medium-term review took place during 2002. More or less, the new reform emphasizes the need to develop toward a sustainable, environmentally friendly agriculture. The cases of bovine spongiform encephalopathy (BSE, also called mad cow disease) in beef production and among other livestock further strengthen the commitment to this reform of the agricultural sector. Parallel measures related to the creation of employment in rural areas as well as revitalization programs for regional economies in crisis are presented in the document. Indeed, the Commission also proposes that more flexibility shall apply in defining the ceilings for direct payments to farmers at the national level. In spite of all the good will, changes of CAP have been difficult, particularly due to resistance from the United Kingdom, France, and Germany. Most of the funding is going to these three economies. In spite of that, due to the growing concern about the quality of production, there is a stronger commitment to make substantial changes in the next decade. One begins to realize the importance and potential of organic farming and the role of farmers in taking care of the land. Until now, most of the funding has been going to larger agricultural enterprises and also as direct payment to farmers.[50] The 1999 Berlin Summit adopted the suggestions of the Agenda 2000 document to separate the financing for the present system of CAP on the one hand and measures for rural development and the rural economy on the other. In spite of the changes, the funding invested in the restructuring of the agricultural sector is still very small. Naturally, this has to be seen in context. The CAP is becoming more integrated into the structural policies of the European Union, so the funding available for restructuring the agricultural sector is to be found in actions of vocational training, industrial restructuring, and infrastructure projects.

After Agenda 2000, CAP main objectives are (1) to ensure the competitiveness of the European Union agricultural sector, both in the community market and on growing export markets; (2) to promote ways of farming that contribute to the maintenance and enhancement of rural environment and landscapes; and (3) to contribute to sustaining the livelihood of farmers while promoting the economic development of the wider rural economy.[51]

Since the 1980s the farmers of southern Europe have been under pressure to improve the productivity of their products and change mentalities. The recent proposals by EU Commissioner Franz Fischler are designed to reduce the amount in direct payments to European farmers and transfer saved funds to projects of rural development. The main intention is to reduce the amount paid directly to farmers by 20 percent over a longer period of time starting in 2005–2006. Most small farmers, those receiving up to 5,000 Euros in direct payments annually, will not be affected by the reform. Fischler set also a ceiling of payments of 330,000 Euros, which will affect only a small portion of farms across the EU. The reform is supported by the northern countries, led by Germany, that are net payers into the Common Agricultural Policy. Opposition has come from Spain, France, Portugal, Greece, Italy, and Ireland. In spite of these modest proposals by Fischler, it was difficult to find an efficient compromise overlooking national interests. The reform also envisages differentiated low payments to the farmers of the candidate countries when they join the European Union. In the past two decades, the agricultural sector in those countries had to cope with major transformations. (See Table 7.5.)

In Portugal, the agricultural sector had and continues to have major difficulties adjusting to the common regime of CAP. Sooner than expected, the protection measures for certain Portuguese products were abolished in 1993, when the SEM came into force. A real steep fall in prices led to major difficulties for the Portuguese agricultural sector. Moreover, the SEM led to difficulties in dealing with competition of products coming from other countries such as Spain. Structural funds organized under the umbrella of the Specific Program for Portuguese Agriculture (*Programa Específico para a Agricultura Portuguesa* [PEDAP]) was the only way to ease the transition of a very inefficient agriculture. The highly fragmented structure of agricultural units prevented a further rationalization and increase of efficiency in Portuguese agriculture. The low level of education and the dominance of traditional methods of farming prevented more efficiency. Until 1993, structural funds served as a net of survival for most farmers. A more progressive and future-oriented approach began to happen only after 1994. Like many other countries, Portuguese agriculture has been recently affected by the BSE beef crisis. This naturally contributed to a downfall of prices among livestock of Portuguese agriculture. Portuguese agriculture still has major difficulties adjusting to the growing competition of other countries. Younger farmers tend to look for seasonal jobs across the border or even in Switzerland.[52] Portugal, along with Finland and Luxembourg, is one of the countries with the lowest level of support from EU funding. Most of the subsidies go to the olive oil and wine sectors.

Already before membership, Spanish agriculture was the most difficult dossier tackled during the negotiations. Today, the Spanish share

TABLE 7.5 Some Indicators of the Agricultural Sector in the European Union

Country	Individual member-states' shares in final agricultural products (1998)	Number of persons per 100 ha agricultural land (1999)	Percent of people working in agriculture in the European Union, national share (1999)	Share of national GDP in percent (1999)
Sweden	1.5	5.4	1.7	2
Denmark	2.9	4.8	1.3	4
Finland	1	10.3	1.5	4
Netherlands	7.7	14.1	3.4	3
UK	8.4	3.9	6.2	2
Ireland	2.1	6.5	3.4	6
Belgium	2.9	8.4	1.4	1
France	21.7	5	14	2.4
Portugal	1.8	28	9	4
Spain	12.4	9.7	14	3
Italy	16.5	31	16	3
Greece	4.2	45.6	9	11
Austria	1.7	15	3	1
Germany	15.1	7.2	15	1
Luxembourg	0.1	5.4	0.4	1

Sources: Own compilation out of data from the following publications: Eurostat, *Eurostat Yearbook 2001: The Statistical Guide to Europe Data 1989–99* (Brussels: Office of the Official Publications of the EC, 2001); *El Pais*, Anuario 2001, pp. 50–56; European Commission, *The Common Agricultural Policy—1999 Review* (Luxembourg: Office of the Official Publications of the European Union, 2000), 14.

of the EU's agriculture is 12.4 percent. Therefore, between 1986 and 1991 Spanish agriculture was in some way blocked by the major countries, particularly France. So-called transition regimes were devised which would delay the entrance of Spanish products in to the Common Market for seven to ten years. The implementation of the SEM directives led to an earlier entrance of these Spanish products and the eligibility for CAP funds through the European Agricultural Guidance and Guarantee Fund (EAGGF). (See Table 7.6.) CAP covers 95 percent of all Spanish production in terms of price support. It also supports modernization and rural development projects. Spain is presently the fourth largest recipient of CAP subsidies. Most of the subsidies are allocated to the olive oil and wine production sectors. Spanish agriculture has undergone major transformations since the 1950s. Apart from the diversity of production across the territory, it was very keen to improve productivity, marketing, and organization structures. Similar to the Portuguese case, the agricultural work force is aging, and the younger people tend

TABLE 7.6   Distribution of European Agricultural Guidance and Guarantee Fund (EAGGF) in 1999

Country	EAGGF (Guidance)		EAGGF (Guarantee)	
	Million ∈	Share of Funds (%)	Million ∈	Share of Funds (%)
Belgium	851.3	2.3	40.2	0.91
Denmark	1,154	3.2	27.4	0.62
Germany	5,553	15.2	839	19
Greece	*2,556.8*	*7*	*374.4*	*8.5*
Spain	*5,293.5*	*14.5*	*758.2*	*17.14*
France	9,007.12	25	800.3	18.1
Italy	*4,129.2*	*11.3*	*753.1*	*17.02*
Luxembourg	17.4	0.04	12.2	0.28
Netherlands	1,372.7	3.7	8.3	0.19
Austria	842.5	2.3	127.7	2.9
Portugal	*637.4*	*1.7*	*444.1*	*10.04*
Finland	575.7	1.6	98.8	2.23
Sweden	270.1	0.74	60.9	13.8
UK	4,314.2	11.8	75.2	1.7
EU	40.3	0.11	5.6	0.13
	36,615,220	100	4,425,400	100
Southern European Countries	*15,173,700*	*34.5*	*2,329,800*	*52.7*

Source: European Commission, *Common Agricultural Policy—1999 Review* (Luxembourg: Office of the Official Publications of the EC, 2000), 25.

to leave for the larger towns. This naturally led to a growing shortage in the work force. In Andalusia and Murcia, north Africans, seasonal workers (many of them in illegal status), are employed to overcome the labor shortage. The same happens in Extremadura, where Portuguese workers are employed.[53]

Italian agriculture has been entitled to CAP funding since its beginnings. Italy was a net receiver of funds related to the CAP up until the late 1990s. It is the third largest receiver of subsidies allocated mainly to the tobacco, wine, and olive oil sectors. In the past two decades, Italian agriculture underwent a major restructuring and modernization process. The reduction of enterprises between 1982 and 1997 was of 517,000 (18.7 percent). Like Spain, Italy is one of the countries receiving the largest amounts of EAGGF funds, directed particularly to the southern regions of Italy. Most of the funds are used for the restructuring agriculture in terms of creating alternative employment possibilities such as rural tourism. Between 1985 and 1998 the number of rural tourism enterprises has increased by 30 percent. The majority of these enterprises are located in the northern regions (70 percent). In terms of administration, CAP is slowly leading to a stronger decentralization of the EAGGF funds, although the pace of reform has been slow.[54]

Greek agriculture has many similar problems. The fragmentation of the land distribution, which was made worse by an archaic inheritance law, made it very difficult to improve the productivity of farming. Moreover, the working population in agriculture was not equipped with the most modern technologies or trained in new technologies.

A further point is that too many people are still working in agriculture compared to other EU countries. Over one fifth of the population is working in the agricultural sector. Another major problem is that, internationally, Greece faces competition from other Mediterranean countries that produce the same products. All this is reinforced by an institutional setting that needs an overall reform. The CAP was directed mainly to support the income of the farmers, but also for the modernization of the agriculture. Greece is the fifth largest receiver of subsidies directed mainly to the tobacco and olive oil sectors. Similar to Portugal, an integrated national program for agricultural modernization has been implemented, which is designed to improve productivity, create marketing and distribution networks, and invest in rural development projects.[55]

Quite encouraging is the progress made in organic farming. Greece, Spain, and Italy have increased their number of organic farming enterprises substantially. Portugal is still lagging behind. In spite of that, southern European agriculture accounts for more than half of organic enterprises in the EU (see Table 7.7).

CFP

The Common Fisheries Policy (CFP) has been a major constraining factor for the fishery industries in all four countries. The new CFP defined in 1983 and reviewed in 1993 clearly attempted to develop a global approach to the problem of overfishing in the Community waters. Although there is the principle of free access enshrined in the CFP, there is also more strict control of fish catch quota regulations at the national level. At the same time, efforts were made to restructure the regions affected by a decline of the fishing industry. One further aspect is the improvement of marketing and negotiations with third countries to ensure the livelihood of the fishermen. In recent years the conservation of some fish species such as cod, whiting, and the Nordic hake become a priority of the EU policies. Indeed, the so-called Total Admissible Catches (TAC) negotiated by the EU member-states every year is only partly working well. The monitoring mechanisms are still too lax in dealing with overfishing issues. The decline of income of fishermen and the whole industry is not only a European specific problem, but a

TABLE 7.7　Organic Farming in the European Union (1998)

Country	Number of organic farming enterprises	Percent of the whole in the EU
Belgium	400	0.38
Denmark	2,272	2.15
Germany	9,209	8.7
Greece	*4,231*	*4*
Spain	*7,782*	*7.4*
France	6,139	5.8
Ireland	1,121	1.1
Italy	*43,698*	*41.36*
Luxembourg	28	0.027
The Netherlands	970	0.92
Austria	20,000	18.93
Portugal	*510*	*0.48*
Finland	4,975	4.71
Sweden	2,860	2.71
UK	1,462	1.38
Total	105,657	100
Southern Europe	*56,221*	*53.24*

Source: European Commision, *Common Agricultural Policy—1999 Review* (Luxembourg: Office of the Official Publications of the EC, 2000), 22.

world wide one, so that the European Union has to play an active role in the major international institutions to create the conditions for a worldwide sustainable fisheries industry. At the moment, the European Commission is consulting the public over the future of the fisheries policies in the European Union. A *Green Paper on the Common Fisheries Policy* after 2002 clearly acknowledges the failure of the present CFP. One of the main points is that the different multiannual programs established since 1983 did not lead to the progress they were intended to achieve. Reluctance of the member-states to introduce the needed reforms was clearly the major factor in this failure of the CFP. The *Green Paper* was written as a document for the mid-term review in 2002.[56] Commissioner Franz Fischler is also in charge of reforming the Common Fisheries Policy. This naturally will affect predominantly southern European countries. The main aim of the reform is to reduce substantially the number of vessels working in the sector, so that the fisheries industries becomes more sustainable. Indeed, over 8,500 vessels are to be scrapped over the period of 2003 to 2006. This will be financed by the structural funds and additional funding of the Commission, which amounts to 272 million Euros over the three year period. Further measures want to strengthen the position of the European Commission vis-à-vis the national governments in terms of scientific evidence and sustainability of long term measures. In spite of constant interventions by Spain, such reform is very important to make fisheries more sustainable. Fischlers' reform has been opposed mainly by Spain, which has the largest fisheries fleet in the European Union.

The Iberian accession further pushed the issue of proper organization and policing of fishing in the European Union.[57] The Spanish fishing fleet is still the largest and clearly was able to profit from the CFP in relation to exploiting fishing zones of other EU countries. The controversy with British fishermen in 1996 may be reported as one incident related to this access of Spanish vessels to Community waters.

The Portuguese fishing fleet had to learn to deal with the fact that certain distant fishing zones where they used to fish were no longer available to them because of negotiations with third countries. The Greek fishery industry was and is regarded as quite inefficient. In spite of a substantial fishing fleet, the productivity is quite low. In the Italian case, still too many people are working in the fishery industry. (See Table 7.8 and Table 7.9.)

The main strategy in relation to the four countries is one of reconversion of the fishery industries. Apart from a reduction of people and vessels working in the fisheries sector, the CFP is designed to create alternative forms of employment for those who may become unemployed as a consequence of sectoral restructuring. This process is an ongoing process, which is being reviewed in 2002 (See Table 7.10).

TABLE 7.8   Distribution of EU Fleet According to Countries (1998)

Country	Vessels	KW	Tonnage
Belgium	0.1	0.8	1.1
Denmark	4.4	4.7	4.9
Germany	2.3	2	3.4
Greece	*20.4*	*8.2*	5.3
Spain	*17.5*	*18*	27.9
Finland	3.9	2.7	1.1
France	8.5	14.4	10.6
Ireland	1.2	2.4	2.9
Italy	*18.9*	*19.4*	12.5
Netherlands	1.1	8.1	8.9
Portugal	*11.2*	*5*	6
Sweden	2.1	3	2.4
UK	8.4	13.1	12.9
European Union	100,106	236,514	1,986,230
Southern Europe	*68*	*50.6*	51.7

Source: http://www.europa.eu.int/comm/fisheries

TABLE 7.9   Working Population in Fisheries Sector and Share of Catches

Country	Population Working in Fisheries Sector (1995)	%	Fish Catches in 1,000 Tons (1998) Share of EU total
Austria	0		0
Belgium	624	0.23	0.46
Denmark	5,055	1.9	23.11
Germany	4,979	1.8	4
Greece	*40,164*	*15.27*	*1.9*
Spain	*75,009*	*28.52*	*18.04*
France	26,879	10.22	8.7
Ireland	5,500	2.09	5.4
Italy	*45,000*	*17.11*	*4.7*
Luxembourg	0		0
Netherlands	2,752	1.05	8.02
Portugal	*30,937*	*11.76*	*3.4*
Finland	2,792	1.06	2.5
Sweden	3,400	0.94	6.1
UK	19,928	7.58	13.73
Total	263,019	100	6,736
Southern Europe	*191,110*	*72.66*	*28.04*

Source: http://www.europa.eu.int/comm/fisheries/

In sum, CAP and CFP are quite relevant for the southern European countries. In spite of progress made, these countries are still characterized by inefficiencies and low productivity, if we consider the human and material resources put into the effort. These two policies are also highly problematic in the European Union and will have to be reformed radically to achieve better results.

PROBLEMS OF ADJUSTMENT TOWARD SEM AND EMU

All four countries regarded participation in SEM and EMU as quite essential for economic well-being. One can really extrapolate the findings by Kenneth Dyson and Kevin Featherstone in relation to the Italian approach toward EMU as the overall rationale of all southern European governments in the 1990s. Participation in EMU was used to externally impose economic discipline and economic reform. This so-called *vincolo externo* (external link) is still today an important factor in shaping domestic economic policy in these countries.[58] Participation in the highest levels of European integration is a question

TABLE 7.10   Distribution of Funding from the Financial Instrument for Fisheries Guidance (1990–1999)

Country	Aid for Markets	Aid for Structures	Total	
Austria	0	2,000	2,000	0.05
Belgium	1,828	45,428	47,255	1.22
Denmark	32,504	202,177	234,681	6.06
Germany	3,446	217,289	220,734	5.7
Greece	*5,015*	*264,424*	*280,430*	*6.96*
Spain	*75,163*	*1,314,386*	*1,393,548*	*35.97*
Finland	0	29,211	29,211	0.75
France	85,769	291,211	376,979	9.73
Ireland	10,059	99,795	107,955	2.78
Italy	*7,657*	*448,422*	*456,0791*	*1.77*
Luxembourg	0	910	990	0.025
Netherlands	854	74,126	74,980	1.94
Portugal	*20,912*	*366,789*	*387,601*	*10.01*
Sweden	3,450	45,354	49,924	1.29
UK	19,245	201,839	221,084	5.71
EU-15	0	1,840	1,840	0.05
Total	277,810	3,596,210	3,974,020	100
Southern Europe	*108,027*	*2,394,061*	*2,517,658*	*64.71*

Source: http://www.europa.eu.int/comm/fisheries/

of prestige. The recent success of the Greek government in joining EMU in January 2001 and adopting the Euro as currency simultaneously with the other eleven European countries may be fit in this category. All these countries tried either through raising of indirect taxes (Italy) or through the use of privatization windfalls (Portugal) to achieve an early participation in EMU.[59] In the end, Italy achieved participation in EMU in spite of a huge public debt deficit that clearly surpassed the allowed 60-percent-of-GDP limit set up in the Treaty of European Union. This naturally may lead after the full implementation of the EMU to asymmetrical shocks in the southern European countries—in particular in Portugal, Spain, and Greece, which have weaker economic structures. The latter is still struggling with a huge public debt deficit of over 100 percent of the national GDP, which increased in 2000 to 11 billion drachma due to the declining value of the Euro. In spite of all that, interest rates, inflation, and the budget deficit are more or less convergent to the rest of the European Union countries, and Greece stayed on track for the full implementation of the Eurozone in January 2002.

In the past two years, the Simitis government applied a very strict fiscal discipline and prepared the move toward liberalization of the telecommunications and energy sectors. Further efforts are being made to change the culture of state expenditure from public consumption to more productive fields such as research and development or education and training. Stability in the Balkans and consensus between the two main parties ND and PASOK contributed to this improvement in the Greek economy. Greece aims at being the "anchor of stability" in a troubled region.[60] In spite of the positive signs coming from Athens, Simitis was not able to achieve a reform of the pension systems. The opposition from trade union confederations and other interest groups led to a delay of the needed reform. This seems to follow a pattern of nonreform, in spite of reports and plans for reform for two decades.[61] It was also Simitis who initiated major reforms in the field of public procurement policy. After long negotiations with the European Commission, the pattern of behavior of the Greek authorities became more reform-friendly. This is now having spillover effects on other, adjacent subpolicy areas. In spite of that, this process of transformation is taking longer than expected. Particularly, the implementation side is quite problematic.[62]

Implementation of the directives is the main problem of adjustment of southern European countries. Some countries such as Portugal were quite successful in transposing most of the directives into national legislation, but the lack of real implementation clearly prevented a real effect on the national economy concerned. These kinds of discrepancies were slowly overcome in the 1990s. Italy even has difficulties implementing most of the SEM legislation on time, so that it had to develop a fast-track procedure and reform its complex administrative structure to respond faster to the incremental pressure of the EU. Nevertheless, one has to acknowledge that there is some policy learning going on that improves over time the way Italy has improved its implementation rate.[63]

The southern European economies are quite vulnerable to economic shocks deriving from the workings of the SEM and EMU. Portugal still needs to implement major public sector reforms to achieve a better position within the EU. After months of waiting the new government under Durão Barroso was confronted with a higher figure for the 2001 budget deficit than expected. Indeed, it was expected that the budget deficit would remain slightly below the 3 percent of GDP ceiling allowed by the Maastricht criteria. Instead, in July 2002 the Statistical Office of the European Union came with a revised figure of 4.1 percent, well above the allowed ceiling. This will lead to the payment of a huge fine by the Portuguese government, if it does not manage to turn around the present difficult financial situation by 2004. Moreover, the low-skilled, low-paid economy may be affected by competitive products coming from Southeast Asia.[64]

The Spanish economy is more affected by a high level of unemployment, which is still the highest in the European Union. In the case of a continuing recession, it may create problems for the Spanish economy (see Table 7.11).

In sum, the European integration process clearly reduced the scope for expenditure in these southern European countries. It clearly introduced new forms of behavior related to economic discipline and reform. Moreover, it clearly had an impact upon the relationship between government and social partners to assure that long-term planning linked to the policies of the European Central Bank and the European Commission is kept on course for the establishment of the SEM. There was a considerable policy learning over these past two decades. According to a study undertaken by Tanja Börzel, the picture of non-compliance with EU legislation is not a southern European problem. In a more differentiated diachronical analysis and taking into account all stages of the process of noncompliance, only Italy and Greece can be considered as laggards within the southern European group, whereas Portugal and Spain have improved their capacity of complying with EU legislation.[65]

CONCLUSIONS

The growing domestication of European public policy contributed to an improvement of the efficiency of governance in southern European countries. The interdependent integration within the European Union

TABLE 7.11   Selected Macroeconomic Data for Eurozone 2000–2002 (Estimates in %)

	GDP-Growth			Unemployment			Budget Deficit/Surplus		
	2000	2001	2002	2000	2001	2002	2000	2001	2002
D	3	0.7	1.3	7.9	7.8	7.8	-1.3	-2.5	-2
F	3.4	1.8	1.9	9.5	8.6	8.5	-1.3	-2	-2.5
I	2.9	1.7	1.6	10.5	9.6	9.6	-1.5	-2.7	-2.3
E	4.1	2.5	2.2	14.1	13.1	12.7	-0.4	-0.2	-0.5
NL	3.9	1.3	2	3	2.5	2.8	1.5	0.2	-0.3
B	4	1.4	2	7	6.8	6.8	0.1	-0.1	-0.2
A	3.4	1.4	2	3.7	3.8	3.9	-1.5	1.3	-1.1
FIN	5.7	-0.5	1.5	9.8	9.2	9.4	6.9	3.2	1
Gr.	4	2.4	2.7	11.1	10.8	10.5	-1.1	-1	-0.7
P	3.3	1.5	2	4.1	4.3	4.5	-1.8	-2	-1.9
Irl.	11	8	4.5	4.2	3.9	4	4.5	3	2
L	8.5	4.5	4.5	2.4	2.4	2.4	6.1	3.83	

Source: Die Zeit, October 25, 2001, 22.

transformed patrimonial rationales of policy making into more democratic and technocratic ones that emphasize transparency and accountability of procedures.

In the past fifteen years, southern European countries were and are major recipients of structural funds designed to enhance the conditions of competitiveness. This overall aim is being gradually achieved, because the structural funds are strategically placed in the sectors of human resources enhancement, modernization and creation of infrastructures, and support of small- and medium-sized enterprises.

Farmers and fishermen have been regarded as the losers of European integration. In the case of southern Europe, CAP and CFP have been an opportunity to introduce major reforms of the ailing and in some cases unproductive sectors of the economy. It is expected that in a long-term perspective both sectors will be downsized and become more efficient within the EU. Last but not least, one has to emphasize the growing importance of interdependent economic policy-making that offered southern European governments an escape from the vicious circle of clientelistic overspending, inflation, and devaluation of currency toward a virtuous circle of monetary and price stability. For the southern European countries, it is a matter of prestige to be at the forefront of SEM and EMU. This naturally leaves some doubts about the strategy to achieve these aims. In spite of all that, this strategy had a positive, stable impact in these countries so far. This may be a sufficient reason for endorsing the past integration efforts of southern European countries.

NOTES

1. Lord F.A. Cockfield, *The European Union: Creating the Single Market* (Chichester: Wiley Chancery Law, 1994).

2. Helen Wallace, "The Policy Process: A Moving Pendulum," in *Policy-Making in the European Union*, ed. Helen Wallace and William Wallace (Oxford: Oxford University Press, 2000), 39–64; a more challenging and suggestive book is Svein S. Andersen and Kjell Eliassen (eds.), *Making Policy in Europe* (London: Sage, 2000).

3. Christine Neuhold, "Into the New Millenium: The Evolution of the European Parliament from Consultative Assembly to Co-Legislator," *Eipascope* 1 (2000): 3–11; Renaud Dehousse, "An I du Parlementarisme Européen?," *Pouvoirs* 93 (2000): 197–207.

4. Jonathan Golub, "In the Shadow of the Vote? Decision Making in the European Community," *International Organization* 53, no. 4 (Autumn 1999): 733–64.

5. Andrew Macmullen, "Fraud, Mismanagement and Nepotism: The Committee of Independent Experts and the Fall of the European Commission 1999," *Crime, Law and Social Change* 31, no. 3 (1999): 193–208.

6. Fulvio Attiná, "Integrazione e Democrazia: Un'Analisi Evoluzionista dell'Unione Europea," *Rivista Italiana di Scienza Politica* 30, no. 2, pp. 226–56, particularly pp. 230–39.

7. Frank Decker, "Mehr Demokratie Wagen: Die Europäische Union Braucht Einen Institutionellen Sprung Nach Vorn," *Aus Politik und Zeitgeschichte* B5 (2001): 33–37; Beate Kohler-Koch, "Regieren in der Europäischen Union: Auf der Suche Nach Demokratischer Legitimität," *Aus Politik und Zeitgeschichte* B6 (2000): 30–38, particularly 31–32; *El Pais*, Domingo, May 20, 2001, p. 9.

8. *Die Zeit*, December 13, 2001, p. 7; "El Futuro de la Unión Europea: Declaración de Laeken," *El Pais*, December 18, 2001, p. 4.

9. José M. Magone, "La Costruzione di Una Societá Civile Europea: Legami a Più Livelli Tra Comitati Economici e Sociali," in *Il Comitato Economico e Sociale nella Construzione Europea*, ed. Antonio Varsori (Venice: Marsilio, 2000), 222–242, particularly pp. 231–32.

10. Maurizio Bach, *Die Bürokratisierung Europas: Verwaltungseliten, Experten und Politische Legitimation in Europa* (Frankfurt, New York: Campus, 1999), particularly pp. 96–106.

11. "What we are happy with is that several countries, a majority of countries, that is, can go ahead faster in the integration process, so long as they accept the same destination as everyone else. The final port must be the same for all the ships in the convoy. The target must be the same. If there are different speeds that is OK. But these countries that are speeding ahead cannot be permitted to form an exclusive inner core. They must be open to newcomers. They must be a magnet to other member states which cannot follow quite yet" (*The European*, February 13, 1997, p. 11). The flexibility provision was included in the Amsterdam Treaty.

12. Vincent Wright, "The National Coordination of National European Policy-making: Negotiating the Quagmire," in *European Union: Power and Policy-Making*, ed. Jeremy Richardson (London and New York: Routledge, 1996), 148–69; Jaap W. Zwaan, *The Permanent Representatives Committee: Its Role in European Union Decision-Making* (Amsterdam: Elsevier, 1995); Michael Mentler, *Der Ausschuss der Ständigen Vertreter bei den Europäischen Gemeinschaften* (Baden-Baden: Nomos Verlagsgesellschaft, 1995); Vincent Wright, "La Coordination Nationale de la Politique Européenne: Le Bourbier de la Négociation," *Revue Française d'Administration Publique*, no. 93 (2000): 103–24.

13. Jan Beyers and Guido Dierickx, "The Working Groups of the Council of the European Union: Supranational or Intergovernmental Negotiations?," *Journal of Common Market Studies* 36, no. 3 (1998): 289–317, particularly pp. 305–6.

14. David Hine, *Governing Italy: The Politics of Bargained Pluralism* (Oxford: Oxford University Press, 1993), 287–99; Giacomo Della Cananea, "Italy," in *The National Co-ordination of the EU Policy: The Domestic Level*, ed. Hussein Kassim, B. Guy Peters, and Vincent Wright (Oxford: Oxford University Press, 2000), 99–113, particularly pp. 107–11; David Hine, "European Policy Making and the Machinery of Italian Government," in *Europeanization and the Southern Periphery*, ed. Kevin Featherstone and George Kazamias (London: Frank Cass, 2001), 25–46, particularly pp. 37–41.

15. Richard Gillespie, "Spanish Protagonismo and the Euro-Med Partnership Initiative," in *The Euro-Mediterranean Partnership: Political and Economic Perspectives*, ed. Richard Gillespie (London: Frank Cass, 1997), 33–48.

16. *Die Zeit*, September 14, 2000, pp. 12–13; *El Pais*, September 27, 2000, p. 4; see, for a first assessment, Cécile Barbier, La Répartition des Pouvoirs dans l'Union Européenne aprés Nice," *Notabene* no. 119 (Février 2001): 11–17.

17. *El Pais*, May 19, 2001, p. 4. This can be observed in the position position taken by Aznar and Berlusconi in relation to the new defense initiative of the

United States against France and Germany. See *El Pais*, June 14, 2001, p. 3; see also the Italo-Spanish bilateral meeting in Granada on November 13, 2001(*El Pais*, November 14, 2001, p. 26); *Corriere della Sera*, January 9, 2002, p. 2.

18. John Loughlin, "Representing the Regions in Europe: The Committee of the Regions," *Regional and Federal Studies* 6 (1996): 147–65; Federiga Bindi Calussi, The Committee of the Regions: An Atypical Influential Committee?" in *EU Committees as Influential Policy-makers*, ed. M.P.C.M. Van Schendelen (Aldershot: Ashgate, 1999), 225–49; José Maria Munoa, "El Comité de las Regiones y la Democracia Regional y Local en Europa," in *Nacionalidades y Regiones en la Unión Europea*, ed. Francisco Letamendia (Madrid: Fundamentos, 1998), 51–68.

19. George Pagoulatos, "Economic Adjustment and Financial Reform: Greece's Europeanization and the Emergence of a Stabilization State," in *Europeanization and the Southern Periphery*, ed. Kevin Featherstone and George Kazamias (London: Frank Cass 2001), 191–214, particularly pp. 204–10.

20. Yannis G. Valinakis, "Southern Europe between Détente and New Threats: The View from Greece," in *Southern European Security in the 1990s*, ed. Roberto Aliboni (London: Frank Cass, 1992), 40–51; Kevin Featherstone, Georgios Kazamias, and Dimitris Papadimitriou, "Greece and the Negotiation of Economic and Monetary Union: Preferences, Strategies, and Institutions," *Journal of Modern Greek Studies* 18 (2000): 393–414, particularly p. 396; The amount of the loan requested was ECU 2.2 billion to help overcome its immediate difficulties. Tough conditions were attached to it. Greece's credibility in negotiating EMU was impaired by this fact.

21. William Wallace, "The Sharing of Sovereignty: The European Paradox," *Political Studies* 47 (1999): 503–23, particularly pp. 509–12.

22. *Frankfurter Allgemeine Zeitung*, September 25, 2000, p. 5; September 29, 2000, p. 7.

23. *El Pais*, July 21, 2000, p. 30; *El Pais*, November 5, 2000, p. 26.

24. *El Pais*, September 27, 2000, p. 8.

25. Ian Bache, *The Politics of EU Regional Policy: Multi-level Governance or Flexible Gatekeeping?* (Sheffield: Sheffield Academic Press, 1998); Liesbet Hooghe and Michael Keating, "The Politics of European Union Regional Policy," *Journal of European Public Policy* 3, no. 3 (1996): 367–93.

26. F.P. Belloni, *The Single Market and Socio-Economic Cohesion in the EC: Implications for the Southern and Western Peripheries*, Centre for Mediterranean Studies, Occasional Paper no. 8, 1994; Liesbet Hooghe, "EU Cohesion Policy and Competing Models of European Capitalism," *Journal of Common Market Studies* 36, no. 4 (1998): 457–77.

27. P.A. Allum, *Italy: Republic without Government?* (London: Weidenfeld and Nicolson, 1973), 23–25; Fiorella Padoa-Scioppa, *Italy: The Sheltered Economy* (Oxford: Oxford University Press, 1993).

28. European Commission, "Agenda 2000: For a Stronger and Wider Union," *Bulletin of the European Union*, Supplement no. 5, 1997, pp. 21–26.

29. Jean-Pierre Chevalier, "L'Accord Interinstitutionnel du 6 Mai 1999 et les Perspectives Financières 2000–2006: De Nouvelles Ambitions pour l'Union Européenne?," *Revue du Marché Commun et de l'Union Européenne* (part 1), no. 440 (July, August 2000) 441–60, and (part 2), no. 441 (September 2000): 524–32; Herbert Jakoby, "Reform der EU-Strukturfonds: Handlungsbedarf in den Ländern für die Neue Programmperiode 2000–2006," *WSI-Mitteilungen* 6 (1999): 407–14; J. Christoph Jessen, "Agenda 2000: Das Reformpaket von Berlin, ein Erfolg für Gesamteuropa," *Integration* 22, 3/99 (1999): 167–75.

30. *Die Zeit*, September 14, 2000, 12–13.

31. Spain received 28 percent of this sum, Italy 16 percent, Portugal and Greece 14 percent each (European Commission, *Europe at the Service of Regional Development* Luxembourg: Office of the Official Publications of the EC, 199]).

32. European Commission, "Agenda 2000," 21–26.

33. José M. Magone, "The Transformation of the Portuguese Political System: European Regional Policy and Democratization in a Small EU Member-State," *South European Society and Politics* 5, no. 2 (2000): 121–40, particularly p. 138.

34. European Commission, *Recommendation for a Council Recommendation on the Implementation of Member States' Employment Policies,* presented by the Commission, Brussels, September 12, 2001, COM(2001), 512 final, p. 17.

35. European Commission, *The Structural Funds in 1997: Ninth Annual Report* (Brussels: Office of the Official Publications of the EC, 1999), 66.

36. Cases of funding for nonexisting vocational training courses by the Autonomous Community of Madrid came to the fore recently, which will lead to a reimbursement of the European Union (*El Pais,* January 9, 2002).

37. Dia Anagnostou, "Breaking the Cycle of Nationalism: The EU, Regional Policy and the Minority of Western Thrace, Greece," *South European Society and Politics* 6, no. 1 (Summer 2001): 99–124, particularly pp. 113–18.

38. *Inforegio,* December 17, 1998, p. 12.

39. Rafaella Y. Nanetti, *Growth and Territorial Policies: The Italian Model of Social Capitalism* (London: Pinter, 1988).

40. *Frontier-Free Europe,* no. 4 (April 1999).

41. Magone, "The Transformation of the Portuguese Political System," 130–32.

42. *Inforegio,* December 17, 1998, p. 10.

43. Ibid., 12; European Commission, *Structural Funds in 1997,* 81.

44. Pietro Evangelista, "International Competitiveness and Inter-Firm Cooperation in the Footwear Industry in Southern Italy," *Journal of Southern Europe and the Balkans* 2, no. 1 (May 2000): 57–73.

45. Andrea Ciaffi, "Multilevel Governance in Italy: The Case of Marché," *Regional and Federal Studies* 11, no. 2 (Summer 2001): 115–46, particularly pp. 128–29.

46. European Commission, *Structural Funds in 1997,* 65.

47. José M. Magone, *Iberian Trade Unionism: Democratization under the Impact of the European Union* (New Brunswick, NJ: Transaction Publishers, 2001), 259–80.

48. Meanwhile eighty-nine pacts exist across the European Union. Twenty-six of them are in southern Europe (Italy 11.1 percent, Greece 7.8 percent, Spain 6.3 percent, and Portugal 3.3 percent).

49. *Inforegio,* December 17, 1998, p. 4; European Commission, *Sixth Periodic Report on the Social and Economic Situation and Development of the Regions of the European Union* (Luxembourg: Office of the Official Publications of the EC, 1999).

50. European Commission, *The Common Agricultural Policy—1999 Review* (Luxembourg: Office of the Official Publications of the EC, 2000), 1, 22.

51. A more detailed study can be found in Albert Massot Martin, "La Politica Agricola Comun," in *Politicas Publicas en la Unión Europea,* ed. Francesc Morata (Barcelona: Ariel, 2000), 87–120.

52. Francisco Avillez, "The Portuguese Agriculture and the Common Agricultural Policy," in *Portugal and EC Membership Evaluated,* ed. José da Silva Lopes (London: Pinter, 1994), 30–50; José da Silva Lopes, "A Economia Portuguesa desde 1960," in *A Situacão Social em Portugal, 1960-1995,* ed. Antonio Barreto (Lisboa: Instituto de Ciencias Sociais, Universidade de Lisboa, 1996), 233–364, particularly pp. 258–62.

53. Carlos San Juan Mesonada, "Agricultural Policy," in *Spain and EC Membership Evaluated*, ed. Amparo Almarcha Barbado (London: Pinter, 1992), 49–59; Keith Salmon, *The Modern Spanish Economy:Transformation and Integration into Europe* (London: Pinter, 1995), 87–90. This naturally led to major problems with the authorities, which under Aznar made it more difficult for illegal immigrants to get work in Spain (see *El Pais,* January 1, 2002, p. 18).

54. Giuseppe Ieracci, "European Integration and the Relationship between State and Regions in Italy: The Interplay between National and Common Agricultural Policies," *Regional and Federal Studies* 8, no. 3 (1998): 21–33, particularly pp. 28–31; Istat, *Rapporto sull'Italia,"* Edizione 1999 (Bologna: Il Mulino, 1998), 49–53; Elisabetta Croci-Angelini, "Agricultural Policy," in *Italy and EC Membership Evaluated,* ed. Francesco Francioni (London: Pinter, 1992), 31–50.

55. N. Maraveyas, "The Common Agricultural Policy and Greek Agriculture," in *Greece and EC Membership Evaluated,* ed. Panos Kazakos and P.C. Iokamidis (London: Pinter, 1994), 57–73; European Commission, *Structural Funds in 1997,* 66; Alain Buzelay, "Le Financement Structurel Communautaire Face aux Difficultés de l'Èconomie Grecque," *Revue du Marché Commun et de l'Union européenne,* no. 424 (January 1999): 46–52.

56. European Commission, *Green Paper on The Common Fisheries Policy after 2002.* Brussels, 20.3.2001, COM (2001), 135 final (Luxembourg: Office of the Official Publications of the European Union, 2001). There were four multi-annual guidance program (MAGP): MAGP I (1983–1986) led to maintaining capacity, but no increase; MAGP II (1986–1991) led to a modest reduction; MAPG III (1992–1996) no progress made; MAPG IV (1996–2001) modest progress made; see also Carlos Closa, "La Politica Pesquera Comun," in *Politicas Publicas en la Unión Europea,* ed. Francesc Morata (Barcelona: Ariel, 2000), 121–42.

57. European Commission, *The New Common Fisheries Policy* (Luxembourg: Office of the Official Publications of the EC, 1994).

58. Kenneth Dyson and Kevin Featherstone. "Italy and EMU as a 'Vincolo Esterno' Empowering the Technocrats, Transforming the State." *South European Society and Politics* 1, no. 2 (Autumn 1996): 272–99.

59. Claudio Radaelli and Marcello G. Bruni. "Beyond Charlemagne's Europe: A Sub-National Examination of Italy within EMU." *Regional and Federal Studies* 8, no. 2 (Summer 1998): 34–51. David Corkill, *The Development of the Portuguese Economy: A Case of Europeanization* (London: Routledge, 1999).

60. *Frankfurter Allgemeine Zeitung,* September 29, 2000, p. 26; Bernhard Herz and Angelos Kotios, "Coming Home to Europe: Greece and the Euro," *Intereconomics* (July/August 2000): 170–76; Kostas Karamanlis, "Greece: The EU's Anchor of Stability in a Troubled Region," *The Washington Quarterly* 23, no. 3 (2000): 7–11, particularly p. 7.

61. Kevin Featherstone, Georgios Kazamias, and Dimitris Papadimitriou, "The Limits of External Empowerment: EMU, Technocracy and Reform of the Greek Pension System," *Political Studies* 49 (2001): 462–480; *The Economist,* January 6, 2002, p. 45.

62. Dionyssis Dimitrakopoulos, "Learning and Steering: Changing Implementation Patterns and the Greek Central Government," *Journal of European Public Policy* 8, no. 4 (August 2001): 604–22, particularly p. 615.

63. Hine, *Governing Italy,* 286–97; Marco Giuliani, "Europeanization and Italy: A Bottom-Up Process?," in *Europeanization and the Southern Periphery,* ed. Kevin Feathersone and George Kazamias (London: Frank Cass, 2001): 47–72.

64. M. Emerson and D. Gros, *Impact of Enlargement, Agenda 2000 and EMU on Poorer Regions: The Case of Portugal* (Brussels: Center for European Policy Studies), working document 125.

65. Tanja Börzel, "Non-compliance in the European Union: Pathology or Statistical Artefact?" *Journal of European Public Policy* 8, no. 5 (2001): 803–824; particularly p. 819. The leaders are Denmark, Ireland, the United Kingdom, Luxembourg, and Netherlands. The laggards are Italy (a class of its own), Greece, Belgium, and France. Portugal is quite responsive to any claims of non-compliance. Spain and Germany are in the middle. One thing that one has to take into account is that the data from the European Commission are incomplete and inconsistent (p. 810); see also Tanja Börzel's excellent work on environmental policy, "Why There Is No 'Southern Problem': On environmental Leaders and Laggards in the EU," *Journal of European Public Policy* 7(1): 141–62.

8

The International Politics of Southern Europe

THE SYNERGY OF NATIONAL FOREIGN POLICIES AND THE COMMON FOREIGN AND SECURITY POLICY (CFSP)

The post–Cold War redefinition of the system of international relations gave a new meaning to national foreign policies in the European Union. The transitions to democracy in central and eastern Europe, socio-economic, political, and military instability in the southern fringe of the Mediterranean, and the necessity of the European Union to speak with one voice at the global level led to a growing integration and synergy of national foreign policies of the member-states and the European Union. Although there are always problems of adjustment to this new reality, these collective efforts toward a common foreign and security policy (CFSP) can be regarded as a positive development in terms of establishing a pan-European and Mediterranean zone of peace and democracy. Portuguese, Spanish, Italian, and Greek foreign policymakers are among the most ardent supporters of such collective efforts, in spite of their different national foreign policy identities.

This ambitious challenge can be achieved only by strengthening democracy and economic well-being in the central and eastern European countries as well as the southern Mediterranean countries. The 1990s can be considered the decade of reinventing collective security and democratization in the European context. The new southern European democracies of Portugal, Spain, and Greece, and Italy had no difficulties integrating themselves in these collective efforts. In spite of original hesitancy in relation to North Atlantic Treaty Organization

(NATO) membership in Greece (1981) and Spain (1984–1986), this changed in the 1990s. At the same time, southern Europeans were prominent in pushing the European CFSP project, the second pillar of the Maastricht Treaty, and the Amsterdam Treaty. Until the Kosovo War of 1999, CFSP was regarded as an excellent car, but one without an engine. This changed considerably after the NATO intervention and the adoption of the Amsterdam Treaty. The Amsterdam Treaty introduced several innovations to the CFSP. The most important one is the creation of a high representative of CFSP, the so-called Mr./Mrs. CFSP. The first appointed Mr. CFSP is the Spaniard Javier Solana, who was general secretary of NATO and led the war campaign against Yugoslavia. His function is to restructure the military structures of the member-states within CFSP and strengthen the capacity of fast response to eventual political and military crisis. At the moment, this restructuring led to the establishment of an interim political and defense committee that was agreed to in the European Council of Helsinki in December 1999. This transition committee is in charge of creating a military committee with an appropriate integration of the military leaders of the individual member-states. There were already some controversies in March 2000 between the French and the other members of the European Union about allowing the United States to take part in the military committee. In the end, this discussion was postponed until a later stage, when the military committee would be ready for action.[1] It seems that the West European Union (WEU) will become, in the long-term perspective, the European arm of NATO and the central institution to create, along with the military committee, a European Foreign and Security Identity (ESDI), which is still in the making. Although since the late 1980s there were attempts to create a European army through the 60,000 troops-strong Eurocorps consisting of battalions coming from Germany, France, Belgium, Netherlands, Luxembourg, Italy, and Spain as well as the rapid intervention troops Medcorps with their headquarters in Florence for Mediterranean military crisis, these efforts were not very well coordinated and still nationally divided. After the Amsterdam Treaty and the Council at Feira in June 2000, new guidelines and principles were agreed upon to establish a transnational European intervention troop by 2003. Although France is still worried about the relationship between NATO and the new intervention troop, it is extremely supportive of this European initiative. In a meeting of the defense ministers in September 2000, a fifty-page working paper with a detailed timetable and resource analysis for the establishment of the European intervention troop was discussed and finalized. The European intervention troop shall consist of 60,000 to 80,000 men. According to a more realistic estimation, taking into account rotation of soldiers in intervention of up to one year, thrice that number of these soldiers will be needed for the European intervention troop. The European intervention troop will also have a spillover effect on the creation of common arms procurement policy and a European military-industrial complex that will lead to the manufacture of 300 to 350 air fighters and eighty warships.[2] The basis for the intervention is the Petersberg declaration agreed between the defense and foreign ministers of the member-states in June 1992. The so-called Petersberg tasks and missions comprise humanitarian, catastrophe, conflict prevention, peacekeeping, and, after the Kosovo War, peace-restoring operations. They were fully integrated into the CFSP pillar in the recent Treaty of Amsterdam.

This restructuring of the military security architecture is only one aspect of the CFSP. Indeed, in the European Commission the Commissioner for External Relations, Chris Patten, is in charge of coordinating the nonmilitary, diplomatic dimension of CFSP. This may be regarded as a transitional phase toward the full integration of all the different military bodies into the new architecture. Indeed, High Representative Javier Solana almost resigned from office when it became known that it was proposed at the Laeken European Council in December 2001 to merge his office with that of the Commissioner of External Relations, and include it in the Declaration of Laeken on the future reforms of the European Union. A crisis in the European Union was prevented at the last moment when Chancellor Schröder and Prime Minister Blair changed the text. The main reason for the original proposal was to achieve a higher level of synergy in the field of external relations. This was counteracted by Solana, Blair, and Schröder claiming that the relations between Solana and Chris Patten are excellent. In the end, such synergy and merging of the two offices is an inevitable fact, particularly in 2003 when Solana's term as High Representative of CFSP is over.[3] The establishment of the new Balkans led to the death of WEU as a separate organization. It was agreed in May 1999 in Bremen during the German presidency that the WEU would merge with the EU.[4] Military intervention is only the last resort in the instrumentarium of the European Union to create what is now known as "democratic peace." The synergy between democracy and peace clearly defines the CFSP along United Nations terms. This means that the European Union is interested in creating stable democracies based on sound economies. This is why the financial efforts to support new democracies and democratization processes has increased from 200,000 Euros in 1987 to 100 million Euros in 2000.[5] This democracy-aid is a genuine attempt to construct or reconstruct democratic states and civil societies after periods of war (Bosnia-Herzegovina, Croatia, Kosovo) and/or authoritarian/totalitarian regimes (central and eastern Europe). In this context, the southern European democratization experiences of the 1970s up to EU membership are regarded as crucial successful experiences of this approach. The very complex CFSP also involves speaking with one voice in the major international fora such as the World Trade Organization. Moreover, it is more and more involved in coordination work in relation to humanitarian aid organization, the clearing of mines, and the protection of human rights across the world.[6] In this context, the Mediterranean is a laboratory for CFSP, which is still trying to find an identity of its own.

THE PURSUIT OF COMPLEMENTARY NATIONAL FOREIGN POLICY IDENTITIES

The growing complexity in cooperation networks related to the emergence of a more efficient CFSP has eased in many ways the main threats that Spain, Italy, and Greece were facing in the Mediterranean. Portuguese foreign policy was only indirectly vulnerable to Mediterranean threats. In spite of all that, in the recent decade, through NATO, WEU, and CFSP, one could witness a Mediterraneization of Portuguese foreign policy. The intertwinedness of national and supranational foreign policy ambitions leaves space for the individual countries to pursue additional projects that are complementary to the overall CFSP. Special postcolonial ties or direct interest in a particular strategic constellation led to the pursuit of these complementary projects.

Portugal: The Community of Portuguese-Speaking Countries

Since Portugal joined the European Union in 1986, there was a major restructuring of Portuguese foreign policy. Until 1985, foreign policy lacked consistency and coherence. The main reason was the fact that the political system was quite unstable. The political elites concentrated on achieving political and economic consolidation domestically and creating the conditions to join the EC as soon as possible. During the revolutionary period, the Portuguese colonies of Angola, Mozambique, Guinea-Bissau, Sao Tomé e Principe, and Cape Verde Islands became independent and were taken over by liberation movements. The whole process was very chaotic and disorganized. The occupation of East Timor by Indonesia in 1975 fell in this period of transition to democracy in Portugal. East Timor would remain one of the main issues of Portuguese foreign policy from 1975 onward, but particularly since joining the European Community. The EC was used as an amplifier to make the Portuguese position heard and put pressure on the Indonesian government. This became quite successful in 1999, when East Timorese voted for independence under UN protection.

Between 1986 and 1992, Portuguese foreign policy was very keen to adjust adequately to the European Political Cooperation (EPC) system, the origins of CFSP. This also meant creating the appropriate channels to communicate within the EC/EU and among their foreign representations across the world. Only during the first presidency of the Council of Ministers of the EC in 1992 was Portuguese foreign policy ready to take the challenge. A further restructuring of the ministry of foreign affairs by Manuel Durão Barroso in 1994 further helped to improve coordination between the EU institutions and Portuguese foreign policy.[7]

Portugal is one of the most loyal members of NATO. The air bases in the Azores are extremely important to American foreign policy in relation to their Near East and Mediterranean security policy. In spite of this overall unproblematic Portuguese position toward NATO, there was always a veto in allowing Spanish senior military to take over responsibility over the Portuguese soil. This led to a separation of commandos so that Portuguese and Spanish responsibilities remained separated. In the 1990s, the Mediterraneization of Portuguese foreign policy, particularly in their engagement in Bosnia-Herzegovina and Kosovo, led to a synergetic less problematic approach to Spain.[8]

Although since the 1980s, Portuguese foreign policy tried to regain the confidence of the African Lusophone countries, such efforts did only lead to success in 1996. The Community of Portuguese-speaking countries (*Comunidade de Paises de Lingua Portuguesa* [CPLP]) comprises seven members: Mozambique, Angola, Cape Verde, Sao Tomé e Principe, Guinea-Bissau, Portugal, and Brazil. East Timor has observer status as long as it is under UN protection. The CPLP wants to have a role similar to those of the French Community (*Communauté Française*) and the British Commonwealth. Since 1997 the meetings among the members have increased. The main priority is to strengthen Portuguese presence through the establishment of education, television, and culture. One of the last meetings in Maputo, Mozambique, July 17–19, 2000, focused on overcoming a mere rhetoric of Lusophony and moving on to concrete deeds. The declaration of Maputo on "Cooperation, Development and Democracy in the Globalization Era" focuses on creating institutions across the lusophone space and improving living conditions among the African members by pleading for a reduction of external debt, by supporting economic initiatives to eradicate poverty and to promote sustainable development. In this context, the fight against AIDS is the main priority. Brazil is regarded in this respect as the main source of inspiration to its own approach to the problem. The development of an internal complex of research laboratories and free distribution of medicaments as well as preventive programs is regarded as a way forward to fight against AIDS, which is a major problem in Africa. The presence of Brazil in the CPLP is probably one of the strengths of the project, due to the fact that this country is the fifth largest in the world. Although the CPLP comprises only 3 percent of the world population in comparison to 8 percent in the French Community and 25 percent in the Commonwealth, it is regarded by Portuguese foreign policy as a major success that in long-term perspective may enhance the role of the Portuguese-speaking world in international institutions such as the EU-ACP agreements, Mercosur, or the United Nations. The declaration of Maputo also wanted to prepare a contribution on peace, human rights, development aid, international trade, and social justice to the UN millennium conference of 2001. Again, this project is clearly complementary to the emerging CFSP and the UN principles, which clearly are moving toward an overall comprising strategy of democratic peace around the world.[9] Some of the plans of the CPLP such as double citizenship and free movement of people are less realistic because they are in contradiction to the Schengen agreement. Moreover some of the countries did not wait for the Portuguese initiative to join other international organizations. Mozambique joined the British Commonwealth and along with Angola is a member of the South African Development Community (SADC) spearheaded by South Africa. São Tomé e Principe and Cape Verde joined the French Community and are members of the Monetary Community of Western Africa (*Union Monetaire de Ouest Africaine* [UMOA]). Brazil is engaged in the development of the economic regional integration of the southern cone of South America through the Mercosur. Last but not least, most of the populations in Africa do not speak Portuguese, due to the fact that the Portuguese failed during their colonial empire to socialize the vast majority of the population into the Portuguese structures and Brazil is successfully introducing Spanish in the education curriculum to facilitate communication in the Mercosur. All this shows that the CPLP has still a long way to go to achieve more influence at world stage. Projects such as gaining a permanent seat on the Security Council of the United Nations are still a long way from becoming a reality.[10]

Spain: Ibero-American Summits and EU-Mercosur Cooperation

After transition to democracy, Spanish foreign policy became an important issue among political elites. Already under the premiership of Calvo Sotelo and his minority UCD government, the issue of NATO membership became quite relevant. Although in 1982 Spain remained a NATO member, the new Socialist government used this issue to define themselves in relation to the United States. The involvement of the United States in supporting Franco's dictatorship since the 1950s clearly led to some anti-Americanism in Spain. Between 1982 and 1986, the Socialist party wanted withdrawal from NATO. Nevertheless, in a referendum in 1986, Prime Minister Felipe Gonzalez finally expressed his positive opinion of remaining in the NATO alliance. This led to Spain's yes to NATO membership. Like France, Spain tried to keep some of its military structures outside the alliance. This naturally changed over time. Today the membership of Spain in NATO is uncontested, particularly since Javier Solana became general secretary of the organization in the second half of the 1990s and led a more or less successful war campaign against the Milosevic government. Spain has remained at the forefront of the initiatives of CFSP. It supports most of the initiatives related to a European armament industry. Spain seeks to become a world superpower, similar to the United Kingdom, Italy, France, and Germany. The latest hope is to become part of the G-8 group and get a permanent seat on the Security Council of the UN. This foreign policy projection of present prime minister José Maria Aznar shows continuity with the previous Socialist administration. In the Mediterranean, Spain was quite successful in pushing through the Barcelona process, which led to the establishment of the Euro-Mediterranean partnership in 1995. Beyond that, it continued its confidence-building policies toward Morocco and Algeria. Whereas the interest in Morocco is related to the security of the two enclaves of Ceuta and Melilla, Spain receives over 46 percent of its energy gas supplies from the Algerian pipelines. Islamic fundamentalist terrorism and political instability are factors that may affect these Spanish interests. After some hope that Mohammed VI of Morocco would introduce reforms toward democratization, one had to accept that he wanted to keep the patrimonial-oligarchical rule as it is. Problems related to fisheries and other issues led to a growing diplomatic standstill between Spain and Morocco.[11] The interest of Spain to keep the southern fringe of the Mediterranean as stable as possible was one of the possible motivations for becoming the chief architect of the Euro-Mediterranean partnership.[12] Spain also contributes to the 50,000 troops-strong fast reaction forces Eurofor and Euromarfor, founded in 1992, which have their headquarters in Florence and are designed as fast reaction forces in the Mediterranean within WEU. It naturally follows the rationale of the Petersberg declaration of 1992 enshrined in the Amsterdam Treaty.[13]

Although Spain has some postcolonial ties with Equatorial Guinea and former Spanish Sahara, it actually never developed any initiative in this region, in spite of the fact that Spanish administration has some concerns about the security of the Canary islands. Even the question of Gibraltar is on the way to its solution after negotiations between the United Kingdom and Spain. The establishment of joint sovereignty over the enclave after consultation with the population is the main idea behind the proposal. First reactions from Gibraltar were quite negative. The main minister, Peter Caruana, boycotted the negotiations that took place in Barcelona.[14]

Most interest of Spanish foreign policy after 1982 was given to the improvement of the relationships with the Spanish-speaking South and Central American countries. One particular reason was the fact that Spanish is becoming the second most important diplomatic language in the world after English, slowly replacing French in that regard. Moreover, all these countries developed toward democratic regimes in the 1980s and 1990s, and the new Spanish democracy hoped to contribute to a strengthening of democracy in the region. Efforts started within the *Contadora* group in the 1980s and moved on the establishment of the informal Ibero-American summits (*Cumbres Ibero-Americanas*) in 1990. Although Portugal resisted, until 1998, becoming part of this Spanish project, in the end it also became a member of this informal institution. Annual summits of the heads of states and prime ministers take place to discuss issues of mutual interest. Meanwhile twenty countries (Argentina, Bolivia, Brasil, Colombia, Costa Rica, Cuba, Chile, Equador, El Salvador, Spain, Guatemala, Honduras, Mexico, Nicaragua, Panama, Peru, Portugal, Dominican Republic, Uruguay, and Venezuela) have joined the initiative. Since the founding summit of July 1991 in Guadalajara, Mexico, ten summits have taken place. In 2000, the summit took place in Havana, Cuba, which created major tensions among the members and between the organization and the United States. Some differences of opinion were also registered between King Juan Carlos and Prime Minister Aznar. The latter was against the meeting in La Havana and Castro's regime. The summits are designed to exchange information on aspects related to poverty; external debt; economic, social, technological, and cultural development; childhood; health; narcotraffic; marginalization; underdevelopment; and cooperation.[15] The eleventh Ibero-American summit in Lima, Peru, on November 24, 2001, was dedicated to the fight against terrorism after the September 11 events. Moreover, the crisis in Argentina became a major concern for all participants.[16] Spain is also strongly involved in strengthening the linkage between EU and the emerging Mercosur, a Common Market project carried on by Brazil, Argentina, Chile, Paraguay, and Uruguay. It was founded in 1995, but is still developing its institutions and identity within South America and the global arena.[17] Another Spanish initiative was the setting up of a Mexico-EU forum on 22 November 2001, which is designed to reactivate economic relations between Mexico and the EU.[18] A further attempt to strengthen the Euro-Mediterranean partnership by introducing a Euro-Mediterranean Development Bank and a conference in Valencia and the connections between EU and Latin America were on the agenda of the Spanish presidency for the first half of 2002. Certainly, the crisis in Argentina, which is badly affecting the Spanish economy due to their high amount of investments was part of this agenda.[19]

In sum, Spanish foreign policy became ambitious after membership in the European Union. In spite of a gap between the weak political economy and the overambitious foreign policy, there is a tacit understanding among the Spanish foreign policy makers, that Spain has to increase its active role in global affairs.

Italy: Tacit Global Player and the Primacy of Mediterranean Security

In comparison to Spain and Portugal, Italy is a long-established superpower in global politics. Since the 1980s it has belonged to the G7/8 group. Through this international forum, Italy carries responsibility for global governance in economic, political, and military questions. The Kosovo war clearly recurred to the decision-making processes in this forum. Italian foreign policy grew in importance since the mid-1970s through the commitment of the Italian political class to play an active role in stabilizing global politics. Italy actively took part in the Gulf War and was one of the architects of the Euro-Mediterranean partnership along with Spain. The majority of their efforts were related to the creation of a Conference for Security and Cooperation in the Mediterranean (CSCM), which did not materialize in spite of strong commitments of Italian foreign policy makers. Libya is regarded as the major threat to Italy, due to the past history of Italian involvement in Libya in the beginning of the twentieth century and due to the dominance of the difficult Arab leader colonel Mu'ammar Gadhafi. During the 1980s, terrorist attacks were carried out on Italian soil. In spite of this direct danger, Italy is one of the most loyal supporters of NATO. At the same time, it is constructively involved in the creation of CFSP.[20]

Italy is also extremely committed to reducing the external debt of and to increasing the amount of development aid to developing countries. This became even more salient since the Olive Tree government came to power.

During the Polo government of 1994 under the leadership of Silvio Berlusconi and the inclusion of the post-Fascism National Alliance, there was some fear across the world that Italian foreign policy may change. In reality, foreign minister Antonio De Martino assured that continuity of Italian foreign policy based on loyalty to the NATO alliance, CFSP, and international responsibility would prevail. In spite of that, some irredentist demands were made to Slovenia and Croatia in relation to the Treaty of Osimo of 1975, which was designed to normalize the relations between Italy and former Yugoslavia. The main demands were (a) more protection for Italian minorities in Slovenia and (b) the return of property lost by Italians after the formation of Yugoslavia after World War II. This was rejected by Slovenia, and the Italian government blocked the proposed association status for prospective members of the European Union.[21] The collapse of Berlusconi's government during December 1994 led to a return to a more pragmatic and tacit foreign policy. Internationally, Italian foreign policy is regarded as weak. This is naturally related to the fact that domestic political instability before and during the 1990s prevented the development of a stronger engagement of Italy at the global level. The recent appointment of Emma Bonino as representative of the United Nations in 2000 was regarded as a big success for Italian foreign policy, but in the same month Italy's ambition to become a member of the UN Security Council for the period of 2000-2002 was shredded to pieces when the smaller European countries Norway and Ireland were chosen instead. A series of recriminations and accusations among members of the political class were made in public.[22] This naturally shows the problems of projection of Italian foreign policy within the country and internationally. The new Berlusconi government is trying to establish a new Italian foreign policy around their national interest. The growing dissent of Italian foreign policy in relation to the European Union is showing signs of a "Berlusconization" of Italian foreign policy. This became clear in the opposition of Berlusconi's government to comply with the Euro-wide warrant in the context of the fight against terrorism and in the cancellation of participation in the European project for the construction of a military transport aircraft A-400-M. The forced resignation of foreign minister Renato Ruggiero in early January and Berlusconi's takeover of foreign policy further confirms the growing dominance of Silvio Berlusconi of Italian foreign policy. This naturally has to be seen in the context of the continuing judicial trials in Italy and abroad that further demonstrate his inability to resolve his conflict of interests. This is naturally quite negative for Italian foreign policy within the European Union.[23]

Greece: The New Balkans, Turkey, and the Black Sea Economic Cooperation Group

The determinants of Greek foreign policy are related to the geopolitical position within Europe. On one hand, Turkey and Turkish foreign and security policy ambition have shaped foreign policy priorities in Greece. On the other hand, the volatile Balkans have created and still create major concerns for Greek foreign policy makers. Moreover, until 1974 Greece had been subject to regular foreign interference or intervention in domestic affairs since the nineteenth century.[24] Only after the establishment of democracy in 1974 and membership in the EU in 1981 did Greece begin to slowly develop its own more proactive foreign policy within the west, Turkey, and the Balkans. This was quite evident during the Kosovo war, in which the Greeks did not take part. The majority of the population condemned the intervention and people were mobilized to protest in demonstrations against the bombardment of Serbia.

During and after transition to democracy, Greeks were fierce anti-Americans, due to the fact that the U.S. administration was supportive of the military Greek junta between 1967 and 1974. This anti-American-ism is still virulent among the Greek population and may be reactivated by the strong Communist party in the country. The emergence of PASOK to power in 1981 under the leadership of the charismatic An-dreas Papandreou further strengthened this independence of Greek foreign policy. Papandreou propagated an illusionary Third Worldism of non-alignment and rejected membership in NATO. In spite of this radical rhetoric, Papandreou continued the membership in NATO after negotiating good conditions in the leasing of air bases to the Americans. Greek foreign policy also has been very friendly toward the Arab world, due to the fact that Greece is very close to the Near East.[25]

The main determinant of Greek foreign policy is naturally Turkey. Membership in the EU played a card against Turkish ambitions to join the European Union. Only recently did the very pragmatic and lucid foreign minister George Papandreou, the son of Andreas Papandreou, contribute to an improvement of relations with Turkey. The rapproche-ment between Greece and Turkey started in the early 1990s. It reached a climax with the solidarity act of the two governments helping each other after earthquakes that happened in 1999 in both countries. More-over, there is a will of Greek foreign policy makers to overcome the long years of distrust between the two countries and move toward a new, more prosperous era. Therefore, the Greek veto for Turkish membership in the EU was lifted in 1999. During the Finnish presidency, Turkey was accepted as an official candidate to join the European Union. Although, in financial terms, Greece cannot play an important role in the region, the ambitions exceed the possibilities. The most concrete example is the ambition of Greece to gain access to the new markets of Bulgaria, Romania, Albania, and the new Balkans. This wish also led to economic and political cooperation with Ankara to establish a Black Sea Economic Cooperation Group. It was founded in June 1992 in Istanbul, and it comprises the eleven countries of Albania, Armenia, Azerbaijan, Bul-garia, Georgia, Greece, Moldova, Romania, Russia, Turkey, and the Ukraine. The main difficulty is to find the financial means to establish the basic institutions of this new regional integration group. Turkey, Greece, and Russia, as leaders, all have major financial difficulties. Although originally a Turkish project, Greece was able to increase the influence in the region. After many years of difficulties the Black Sea Development Bank was finally founded with the seat in Thessaloniki, which emulates the European Bank for Reconstruction of Development designed to finance projects in central and eastern Europe. The over-ambitious project is hampered by the fact that most of the member-countries are very unstable, particularly Azerbaijan and Georgia. In spite of that, it is a way forward to stabilize a region that is crucial to the security of Greek foreign policy, even if economically it is still insignificant.[26]

THE BREAKDOWN OF FORMER YUGOSLAVIA AND THE EMERGENCE OF THE NEW BALKANS: THE ROLE OF THE EUROPEAN UNION

One of the most important geopolitical settings of southern Europe is the Balkans. Both Greece and Italy are affected by instability in the region. The Balkans have been throughout history a region of permanent instability due to the struggle between the southern Slavic nations such as Croats, Serbs, and Albanians as well as international intervention and dominance such as the Ottoman Empire and the Habsburg empire. Before World War I, several Balkan Wars led to interventions by the powers of the time, Russia and the Austro-Hungarian Monarchy. In the interwar period, an artificial kingdom of the Slovenes, Croats, and Serbs was established that was characterized by a growing fear of Serbian dominance. During World War II, the Balkans were occupied by the Axis powers. In Croatia, a German-dominated regime of Croat national-ists under the leadership of Ante Pavlević was established that pursued policies of ethnic cleansing of the Serb orthodox population. These im-ages of war should coin postwar policies in Yugoslavia.

After a fierce guerrilla war with the monarchist-loyalist fighters Četniki, Communist partisans under the leadership of Tito created the Socialist Republic of Yugoslavia. Tito, as a Croat, worked hard to unite the southern Slavs and overcome former national differences. One integrating force was the struggle for independence from Stalin after World War II. Yugoslavia became a champion of the nonaligned move-ment. Some arrangements were made to include all the different na-tional representatives into the Yugoslav system. Kosovans were able to gain a similar privilege in the 1974 constitution.[27] After the death of Tito in 1980, it was difficult to create the same kind of cohesiveness that Tito had achieved for thirty-five years. Nationalism began to be a virulent force related to the distribution of resources within the Yugoslavian federation. Particularly Slovenes and Croats no longer wanted to fi-nance the development in the poorer Republics of Montenegro and Macedonia. Nationalism broke out in Kosovo, Macedonia, and Monte-negro, which led to protests and violent clashes.

The autonomy of Kosovo and Vojvodina was suspended in the late 1980s. The final collapse of the Socialist People's Republic of Yugoslavia came in December 1990, when nationalist communist Slobodan Milosevic was elected president of the Serbian Republic. In 1991, he blocked a collective leadership of Yugoslavia under a Croat—which led to the proclamation of independence of Slovenia and Croatia. After ten days and seven months of war in Slovenia and Croatia respectively, Slobodan Milosević had to give up on these two Republics. Macedonia proclaimed its independence in the same year.[28]

From 1992 on Slobodan Milosević started a war campaign against Bosnia-Herzegovina, which led to the late intervention of NATO and the United Nations. Bosnia-Herzegovina was and is quite difficult for the international community, because it comprised Serbian, Croat, and Muslim ethnic groups. The politics of ethnic cleansing by Serbians and Croats became a major issue in the Bosnian war. The Serbs decided to proclaim their own Republic, the *Srspka Republika*, in which they protected several Serbian leaders who were accused of crimes against humanity. This still remains unresolved. Only in 1994 did the United States and the Contact Group related to the G-7 (France, Germany, Russia, United Kingdom, United States) and Slobodan Milosević agree to the Dayton Agreement, which would allow for a multiethnic Bosnia to exist. In spite of the Dayton Agreement, the relationship among the ethnic groups continues to be one of distrust, particularly in the divided city of Mostar, where Croats and Muslims are still separated from each other. The establishment of a multinational military force called Ifor in 1994, comprising 60,000 troops, was reduced to a multinational stabilization force of 31,000 in 1998. The United Nations established a High Representative for Bosnia-Herzegovina, which is in charge of building the new political system in all its aspects. The Spanish diplomat Carlos Westendorp was the first such High Representative; he was replaced by Wolfgang Petritsch in 1999. The process of reconciliation and the return of refugees have been difficult, nevertheless it is slowly becoming more stable. Spanish, Italians, Portuguese, and Greeks have sent military personnel for this mission.[29]

Between 1996 and 1999 the situation in Kosovo became quite problematic. The ethnic tensions between the Albanian majority and the Serbian minority increased. In spite of the presence of OSCE representatives, the Yugoslav army was regarded as acting on behalf of the Serbs against the Albanian Kosovars. In December 1998, the UN Security Council demanded a retreat of the Yugoslav army from Kosovo. The increasing success of the Kosovo Liberation Army (KLA) with logistical support in Albania further destabilised the situation. Reports of ethnic cleansing and attacks against Kosovar Albanians by the Yugoslav Army further exacerbated the situation. The threat of NATO intervention was used throughout 1998, but only in January 1999 did NATO achieve agreement to go ahead with a possible intervention. In February and March 1999 in Rambouillet, negotiations were undertaken to overcome the crisis, in which, after several warnings and the ultimatum of NATO's secretary-general Javier Solana, a bombardment campaign was started against Serbia and Kosovo to force Milosević to withdraw the army from Kosovo. Whereas Italy supported the air campaign, Greece remained neutral. The main reason is that public opinion was against Greek participation and the Greek government, being a neighboring country, felt that this was the wrong strategy to solve the problem. This policy led to ethnic cleansing en masse of Serbs against Kosovar Albanians. Albanians were forced to leave the country by force. They were driven to the borders of Macedonia and Albania. Only in June did negotiations with Milosevic restart after a peace mission of Finnish president Matti Ahtisaari and Russian foreign minister Tschernomyrdin. Since then, Kosovo is under the protectorate of the United Nations. A 50,000 troops-strong multinational KFOR military troop is deployed in Kosovo. In the same month the European Union decided to create a "stability pact for the Balkans" during the German presidency in Cologne. The coordinator is Bodo Hombach from the Chancellor's Office of German Chancellor Schröder. Moreover, the United Nations nominated Bernard Kouchner as the High Representative of the United Nations civil transition government for Kosovo. In spite of the contribution of the EU to reconstruct Kosovo, the relationship between the two ethnic groups is characterized by tension and separation. After more than one year of UN civil transition government, killings between the two communities continued to happen.[30] The collapse of the Milosević regime in October 2000 after a mass uprising against the falsification of the electoral results and the restoration of the rule of law and democracy by new president Kostunica, created the conditions for a reintegration of Serbia in the international community. Meanwhile Slobodan Milosević was arrested by the new government and sent to the International War Crimes Tribunal in Former Yugoslavia in 2001. The recent conflicts on Macedonian borders between Albanian rebels and the Macedonian army clearly indicated that the volatility and instability of the Balkans is far from over. The delicate ethnic composition of Macedonia, in which one third of the population is Albanian and two thirds Macedonian Slavs, indicates further danger of destabilization in the region. This is reinforced by a Montenegro that is split between pro-Yugoslavia supporters and independence supporters. Intervention by the European Union in the summer 2001 led to a decline of conflict between the two ethnic groups. Constitutional change will allow a better integration of the ethnic Albanians in Macedonia. On the whole, the Balkanization process continues to be a major concern for the European Union.[31]

The Stability Pact for Southeastern Europe coordinated by Bodo Hombach on behalf of the European Union wants to transform the region into a peace, democracy, and prosperity zone by promoting political and economic integration into the European Union. In the long-term perspective, it is hoped that these countries will fulfil the criteria for membership set up in Copenhagen in 1992: (i) stability, democracy, rule of law, and respect of human rights and minorities; (ii) a functioning market economy and ability to compete in the European market; (iii) the ability to fulfill the duties of a member-state as well as to support the aims and objectives of the political union and economic and monetary union; and (iv) the adaptation of administrative structures so that it is able to absorb the *acquis communautaire*. Meanwhile, since 1991 the European Union has allocated ∈ 4.5 billion for aid programs within Phare and the Obnova humanitarian program. Further, ∈ 5.5 billion will be invested in southeastern Europe over the next six years. During the Portuguese presidency, the whole project became more concrete. The European Union established a European agency for Reconstruction in Thessaloniki to contribute to the reconstruction of Kosovo. Several regional and European institutions such as the Black Sea Economic Cooperation Group, the Central European Initiative, the Southeastern Cooperation initiative, the American-sponsored Cooperation Process in Southeastern Europe and the Royaumont-process, the European Bank for Reconstruction and Development, and the Organization for Economic Cooperation and Development are taking part in the project.[32]

In sum, after American leadership in NATO, which led to intervention in Bosnia-Herzegovina and Kosovo, the European Union slowly became the dominant actor in coordinating the economic and humanitarian aid needed in the period of reconstruction. The southern European countries were active partners in this process, even if the whole policy-making process was dominated by the Balkan contact group.

SOME NOTES ON EVENTUAL FURTHER SOUTHERN EUROPEAN ENLARGEMENT

The prospects of membership for the new Balkan countries are still distant due to existing ethnic divisions, the lack of economic infrastructures after the wars of the 1990s, and the unsettled situation in relation to the final territorial outlook of the Balkans. More concrete are the prospects of the Mediterranean islands and the other southeastern countries, Slovenia, Romania, and Bulgaria. Whereas Cyprus, Slovenia, and Malta are expected to join the European Union by 2003, Romania and Bulgaria belong to the second wave of membership candidates. Turkey is regarded as a special case, even if it received membership candidate status in the Helsinki European Council in December 1999.

The first wave candidates, Slovenia, Cyprus, and Malta, are regarded as unproblematic in terms of political criteria, economic convergence, and the adoption of the *acquis communautaire*. Moreover, these countries have small populations that are easily absorbed into the European Union. Their economic structure is also quite similar to that of southern European countries such as Portugal and Spain. Also, in terms of GDP per capita in relation to the EU average, they show similarities to the southern European countries. Negotiations with the European Union started jointly with the Czech Republic, Hungary, Poland, and Estonia in the Helsinki European Council.

The Slovenian political class represented in Parliament is across the board pro-integrationist both toward the EU as well as NATO. Moreover, the popular commitment to European integration is quite widespread. Membership of EU is regarded as quite unproblematic, it stands even a better chance than in the cases of the Czech Republic, Hungary, and Poland.[33] The only problem in the case of Cyprus is that the island is divided into a democratic Republic of Cyprus and a semidemocratic Turkish Northern Republic of Cyprus (TNRC) led by Turkish leader Rauf Denktasch. TNRC is not recognized by the international community, only by Turkey. It was established after a coup d'état of the Greek military junta in July 1974 against president Archbishop Makarios. The unsuccessful coup attempt led to the intervention of Turkey on behalf of the Turkish cypriots. Since then the island is divided into two parts. Two thirds belong to the Republic of Cyprus with 650,000 inhabitants and one third to the TNRC with 200,000 inhabitants. Attempts to bring the two communities together since the 1970s failed, due to resistance of the TNRC. It opposed a single federalist constitution for both parts of the island. Denktash proposed a confederal solution with two separate constitutions. Since the early 1990s, the European Union was engaged in offering a solution for the unification of the island, but in 1997 the TNRC broke the thin relations with the EU. The strong commitment of Turkey to protect the TNRC is the basic problem of the integration of the Republic of Cyprus into the European Union. Therefore since 1998 the European Union attempted to improve relations with Turkey, which led to the granting of membership candidate in the Helsinki European Council. Recently, negotiations between Denktasch and the Greek Cypriot President Clerides started again. It is still too early to say if they will lead to a rapprochement of the two countries. In spite of the fact that integration of the Republic of Cyprus may damage the relations with Turkey, the European Union may solve the crisis much more easily if there are mechanisms for conflict solution.[34]

The other Mediterranean island, Malta, was also supposed to join in the first wave of new members. The prime minister of the pro-European Nationalist Party (*Partit Nazzionalista* [PN]) government, Adam Fenech, submitted the membership application in 1991. In 1996, under the leadership of Adam Sant, the Maltese Labor Party won the elections and decided to freeze the membership application. Sant presented the alternative project that Malta could become the "Switzerland of the Mediterranean." Within two years, the Sant government lost the support of its backbenchers, which were elected directly by a Single Transferable Voting System (STV). In 1998, new elections were called which led to the victory of the pro-European PN. Prime Minister Adam Fenech again normalized the membership application of Malta, and it seems that it will be included in the first wave. In spite of that, negotiations with the second wave countries were started in 2000 parallel to the first wave ones. Although Malta is quite an unproblematic candidate, the main problems raised by the opinion of the European Commission are the extremely statist and clientelistic outlook of the Maltese economy. The small population of 375,000 inhabitants is very easy to absorb. The economic structure is dominated by services. The only problem is the high level of foreign debt. In spite of all that, the renewal of the application clearly has to be regarded as very positive within the Euro-Mediterranean partnership, of which the PN is extremely supportive.[35]

The most problematic southeastern candidates to EU membership are Romania and Bulgaria. Romania has been stricken by political and economic instability since its development toward democracy. In 1999, it had to implement an austerity plan of the International Monetary Fund to overcome the economic crisis. The continuing unhappiness of miners and the closure of several pits created a difficult period for the Romanian government. Living conditions in Romania are still very poor in comparison to other candidates, particularly Slovenia. The large agricultural sector will also be one of the problems with which the negotiations with the EU must deal. Moreover, the 22.5 million inhabitants will be more difficult to absorb than the small populations of the previously mentioned countries. Last but not least, the relationship to the ethnic Hungarian and Roma minorities still need to improve even further to achieve convergence to the European Union. Present prime minister Adrian Nastase is pushing forward with reform, although inflation is still around 45 percent. The main problem will be overcoming corruption and inertia. Many reforms in all policy areas have to be undertaken before Romania can qualify for membership. This may last until the end of the decade.[36]

The Bulgarian political system is more consolidated than the Romanian one. In spite of all that, the economic structure still has a large agricultural sector, which will remain a key issue for negotiations. Recently the record of relations with ethnic minority rights such as the Macedonians and Turks living in Bulgaria has improved. The relationship with neighboring Macedonia has also improved considerably. In terms of the population, 8.4 million are probably easy to absorb into the European Union. In spite of that, corruption, delays in reforming the political and judicial system, and the delay in privatization of the public sector will certainly continue to be major factors preventing Bulgaria's early entry.[37]

Quite problematic is the recent granting of member-candidate status to Turkey in the Helsinki European Council. This country of 63 million inhabitants is expected to increase its population to 90.9 million by 2025.[38] This naturally will create major problems of integration. All sectors of the Turkish economy have to be reformed and administrative structures adjusted so that it can stand competitiveness in the SEM. The recent establishment of Customs Union in 1996 may be regarded as a first step in this direction.[39] It has been quite positive for the European Union, which was able to have a trade surplus of 60 billion Euros between 1996 and 2000.[40] The main problem of Turkish ambitions to become member of the European Union is political. The continuing persecution of minorities such as the Kurds in eastern Turkey and the poor human rights record clearly make it difficult to accept this large country into the European Union. Moreover, civil-military relations are still not settled.[41] The role of the military in political life is still too unsettled. Last but not least, the political party system is very fragile, fragmented, and volatile, creating problems for long-term policies. Although the political class is supportive of European Union membership, they seem to ignore the main issues that are actually preventing it from happening. Infringement of human rights and the Cyprus question are not mentioned by the political elites in Ankara.[42] It does not seem very realistic that Turkey can become a member for the next fifteen to twenty years.[43] Although recently, the Turkish government established an independent Council to deal with religious questions and thus depoliticize religion and weaken the position of political Islamists,[44] there is still the question of European identity, which may erupt in the next two decades when enlargement in the European continent has reached its limits. Beyond the fact that one may be against or for the integration of Turkey, an eventual membership will change completely the nature of the European Union toward a Eurasian or Euro-Mediterranean Community, giving leeway to further expansion to other non-European countries. This may create major problems for the already difficult process of continental European integration. A more promising

scenario is to integrate Turkey through the Euro-Mediterranean partnership without granting full EU membership status.[45]

THE MAKING OF A MEDITERRANEAN SECURITY
AND COOPERATION AREA

During the 1990s the southern member-states were confronted with
a new post–Cold War security agenda. The main perceived problems
were the increase in south-north illegal immigration, the rise of political
Islamism leading to civil war in Algeria since 1992, and the unstable
political and economic situations in the Maghreb, which may lead to
disruptions in gas and oil supplies. The growing political, economic,
social, and military instability in the southern fringe of the Mediterranean led to the pursuit of dialogue by Italian and Spanish diplomacy
with Maghreb and Mashreq member-state representatives. The intention was to create a Conference for Security and Cooperation in the
Mediterranean (CSCM), which should fulfil the same integrating task
as the Organization for Security and Cooperation in Europe (OSCE) has
done since the mid-1970s in the European context. Several meetings of
the "4+5" latter on "5+5" group of member-states comprising the southern member-states, Turkey, Mauritania, the Maghreb countries (Morocco, Algeria, and Tunisia), and Egypt wanted to move in this
direction. In spite of several meetings and declarations, the CSCM never
became reality. Instead, the European Union through the European
Commission proposed the establishment of a Mediterranean Free Trade
Area (MEFTA), which should be established by 2010 and should comprise the member-states, Turkey, Malta, Cyprus, the Maghreb (Morocco,
Algeria, and Tunisia), Mashreq (Egypt, Jordan, Syria), and the Middle
East (Israel, Palestine Authority, Lebanon). In total twenty-seven members take part in this project. The so-called Barcelona process was sealed
during the Spanish presidency in the second half of 1995. On November
25–26, a large conference with parallel events on other issues such as
trade union cooperation or civil society organizations was held and the
protocol signed by all members. The whole project naturally has a
long-term goal of creating the conditions for economic, social, and
political convergence between the northern and southern fringe of the
Mediterranean through political dialogue, economic exchange, and
promotion of social, cultural, and human development.[46]

Quite crucial for the success of the project is the ability to transform
present patrimonial, semidemocratic states into genuine sustainable
democracies, that clearly focus on improving the living conditions of
the population. One of the main reasons for political Islamism is clearly
the fact that a large share of the populations in all these countries live

below the poverty line. One of the reasons for the success of the the Islamic Salvation Front (*Front Islamique de Salut* [FIS]) and their continuing terrorist campaign in the 1990s is the fact that two thirds of the population are under thirty and more than 40 percent of young people are unemployed. It is very easy to recruit new people for terrorist actions in Algeria. Moreover, the political class tends to be involved in a web of corruption to get special access to revenues related to oil or gas exports. The poor living conditions clearly make the population quite radical. The denial of the victory of FIS in 1992 is not the best way to promote the idea of democracy.[47] Although in other countries such as Tunisia, Morocco, and Egypt political Islamism is quite strong, more or less existing democratic structures allowed for integration of these political movements into the political system.[48]

The present situation shows that the southern fringe of the Mediterranean has still a long way to go before they can achieve full convergence within MEFTA. Most of the GDP per capita averages are less than one third of the European Union average. The human index figures are at the bottom of the category of countries with an average human development index figure, whereas all EU countries are in the top category of countries with a high level of human development.[49] Education, employment, decentralization, and deconcentration of public administration, democratization of local authorities, and the emergence of civil societies are essential conditions for the creation of more efficient markets. Economic liberalization alone will not transform these societies.

Economically, both national intramarket integration as well as subregional market integration are first steps toward the larger MEFTA. One basic problem is that south-south trade is very limited still. Neither the Maghreb, nor the Mashreq, nor the Middle East are integrated units, due to distrust, warfare, or lack of interest in creating larger markets. The recent eruption of war in the Middle East shows the problems that lie ahead in the process of creating MEFTA. It may take at least thirty years until MEFTA becomes a reality.[50]

In the past five years, first efforts to create a civil society and strengthen nongovernmental organizations in these countries through Euro-Mediterranean partnership devices at the local level that would bypass the government and achieve a direct relationship with economic actors did not lead to overwhelming success. The basic problem is that funding for the support of civil society initiatives is still insignificant. Some projects collapse when the money runs out. Moreover, without genuine commitment to democratization and liberalization, any efforts at reform will be halted when they may lead to any change in the status quo.[51] Although it is crucial that the Euro-Mediterranean partnership continues to progress, the successes will come only in long-term perspective. Five years after the launching of the Euro-Mediterranean partnership, the fourth meeting of the Euro-Mediterranean council of ministers was quite disappointed about the progress made to that point.[52]

CONCLUSIONS

In the past decades, southern European countries had to restructure their national foreign policies according to the synergetic elements created by the ambition of a CFSP. Southern European countries always were and continue to be strong supporters of a CFSP. One could witness a Mediterraneization of the national foreign policies and their integration into NATO, WEU, and EU structures. This synergy led to the prospect of new zones of democracy, peace, and prosperity in the Mediterranean. The Euro-Mediterranean partnership and the Stability Pact for Southeastern Europe are examples of the complementarity and complex definition of security. Such projects may pay off only in the next twenty or thirty years, but they symbolize an increasing self-confidence of the European Union to speak with one voice in foreign and security questions. Spanish and Italian diplomacy were the forerunners of the Euro-Mediterranean partnership, and Greece plays a role in shaping stability in the New Balkans. Beyond the CFSP, Portugal, Spain, Italy, and Greece pursue their individual complementary projects. The experience of CFSP is extrapolated to Latin America, Africa, the southern fringe of the Eurasian geopolitical region, and the global stage. The contribution of southern European diplomacy to more stability in the world can be only measured in years to come. In spite of that, southern European foreign policies have gained more momentum than ever before as part of European security and foreign policy architecture.

NOTES

1. Peter Van Ham, "The Prospects for a European Security and Defence Identity," *European Security* 4, no. 4 (Winter 1995): 523–45; Peter Van Ham, "Europe's Precarious Centre: Franco-German Co-operation and the CFSP," *European Security* 8, no. 4 (1999): 1–26; Trine Flockhart, "The Dynamics of Expansion: NATO, WEU, and EU," *European Security* 5, no. 2 (Summer 1996): 196–218; Javier Solana, "Die Gemeinsame Europäische Sicherheits—und Verteidigungspolitik—Die Integrationsprojekt der nächsten Dekade," *Integration* 23, no. 1 (2000): 1–6, particularly p. 3.

2. *Frankfurter Allgemeine Zeitung*, September 25, 2000, p. 5.

3. *El Pais*, December 19, 2001, p. 2.

4. Van Ham, "Europe's Precarious Center," 16.

5. Christopher Patten, "Die Zukunft der Europäischen und Verteidigungspolitik und die Rolle der Europäischen Kommission," *Integration* 23, no. 1 (2000): 7–17, particularly p. 13; see Aidan Cox and Jenny Chapman, *The*

European Community: External Cooperation Programmes: Policies, Management and Distribution, Report prepared by the Overseas Development Institute for the European Commission (Brussels: Office of the Official Publications of the European Union, 2000), p. 23; for a list of the projects on democratization and human rights financed by the EU, see European Commission, *European Initiative for Democracy and Human Rights (EIDHR), Compendium 2000* (European Commission, 2001).

6. Patten, "Die Zukunft," 13–14.

7. José M. Magone, "Portugal," in *The Foreign Policies of the Member-States in the European Union*, ed. Ian Manners and Richard Whitman (Manchester: Manchester University Press, 2001), 162–73.

8. This is related to Portugal's fear of being dominated by neighboring Spain. This goes back to the annexation of Portugal by Spain 1580–1640 after King Sebastian died in Africa in 1578. For sixty years, Portugal was in personal union with the Spanish Hapsburg empire; Maritheresa Frain, "A Peninsula Ibérica e a Europa: Uma Convergencia nas Politicas de Defesa Espanhola e Portuguesa no pós-Guerra Fria?," *Politica Internacional* 1, no.15/16 (Outono-Inverno, 1997): 249–282; Herminio Santos, "The Portuguese National Security Policy," in *Southern European Security in the 1990s*, ed. Roberto Aliboni (London: Pinter, 1992), 86–98.

9. *O Publico*, July 19, 2000, pp. 4–5.

10. Manfred Wöhlke, "Die Gemeinschaft Portugiesisch-sprachiger Staaten und die EU," *Aus Politik und Zeitgeschichte*, B29–30 (2000): pp.14–21, particularly pp.17–18.

11. *El Pais*, October 30, 2001, p. 29; *El Pais*, October 31, 2001, p. 28; *El Pais*, November 20, 2001, p. 27. The crisis started on Saturday, October 17, 2001. Spanish Diplomacy was not clear what the reasons were for the diplomatic standstill. It causes major problems for the ongoing, now interrupted cooperation between Andalusia and Morocco financed by the European Union (*El Pais*, January 8, 2002, p. 20).

12. Richard Gillespie, *Spain and the Mediterranean: Developing a European Policy towards the South* (Basingstoke, U.K.: Macmillan, 1999), 66–77, 90–99, 161–64.

13. Christophe Degryse, *Dictionnaire de l'Union Européenne: Politiques, Institutions, Programmes* (Brussels: De Boeck Université, 1998), 315–16.

14. *El Pais*, November 20, 2001, p. 27.

15. Nancy Gomes, "As Relacões Externas de América Latina," *Janus 98: Anuário de Relacões Exteriors* (Lisboa: Publico, Universidade Autonoma de Lisboa, 1999), 130–31; Jean Grugel, "Spain and Latin America," in *Democratic Spain: Reshaping External Relations in a Changing World*, ed. Richard Gillespie, Fernando Rodrigo, and Jonathan Story (London: Routledge, 1995), 141–158; particularly pp. 144–47; Paul Kennedy, "Spain," in *The Foreign Policies of the Member-States in the European Union*, eds. Ian Mannery and Richard G. Whitman (Manchester: Manchester University Press, 2001), 105–27, particularly pp. 123–24.

16. *El Pais*, November 23, 2001, p. 15.

17. Paulo Borba Casella and Eduardo Lorenzetti Marques, "European Union-MERCOSUR Relations: A Critical Overview," *European Foreign Affairs Review* 2, no. 4 (1997): 455–64; Felix Pena, "Sobre o Futuro do Mercosul," *Politica Externa* 8, no. 3 (2000): 3–14.

18. *El Pais*, November 23, 2001, p. 30.

19. *El Pais*, January 9, 2002.

20. Ettore Greco and Laura Guazzone, "Continuity and Change in Italy's Security Policy," in *Southern European Security in the 1990s*, ed. Roberto Aliboni (London: Pinter, 1992), 69–85.

21. Pernilla M. Neal, "The New Foreign Policy," in *Italian Politics: The Year of the Tycoon*, ed. Richard S. Katz and Piero Ignazi (Boulder, CO: Westview Press, 1996), 159–68, particularly pp. 164–66.

22. *La Repubblica*, October 11, 2000.

23. *Die Zeit*, January 17, 2002, p. 2; *El Pais*, January 8, 2002, p. 6; *El Pais*, January 6, 2002, p. 8; *El Pais*, January 13, 2002, p. 15; *The Economist*, December 15, 2001, p. 34; *The Economist*, January 15, 2002, p. 37; *The Economist*, January 19, 2002.

24. Theodore A. Coulombis, Harry Petropoulos, and Harry J. Psomiades, *Foreign Interference in Greek Politics: An Historical Perspective* (New York: Pella Publishing Company, 1976).

25. Yannis G. Valinakis, "Southern Europe between Detente and New Threats: The View from Greece," in *Southern European Security in the 1990s*, ed. Roberto Aliboni (London: Frank Cass, 1992), 40–51.

26. Ekavi Athanassapolou, "Turkey and the Black Sea Initiative," in *Mediterranean Politics*, volume 1, ed. Richard Gillespie (London: Pinter, 1994), 130–37; Athanassapolou, "Greece, Turkey, Europe: Constantinos Simitis in Premiership Waters," *Mediterranean Politics* 1, no. 1 (1996): 113–17; Theodore A. Coulombis, "Prodromos Yannas: Greek Foreign Policy Priorities for the 1990s," in *Greece in a Changing Europe: Between European Integration and Balkan Desintegration*, ed. Kevin Featherstone and Kostas Ifantis (Manchester, New York: Manchester University Press, 1996), 160–75; Epstathios T. Fakiolas, "Greece in the New Balkans: A Neo-Realist Approach," *European Security* 6, no. 4 (1997): 130–56; Dimitrios Kavakas, "Greece," in *The Foreign Policies of the Member-States in the European Union*, ed. Ian Manners and Richard Whitman (Manchester: Manchester University Press, 2001), 144–61; Alexander Kazamias, "The Quest for Modernization in Greek Foreign Policy and Its Limitations," *Mediterranean Politics* 2, no. 2 (1997) 71–94.

27. Misha Glenny, *The Balkans, 1804–1999: Nationalism, War and the Great Powers*, London: Granta, 2000.

28. Misha Glenny, *The Fall of Yugoslavia: The Third Balkan War* (London: Penguin, 1996); Viktor Meier, *Yugoslavia: A History of Its Demise* (London: Routledge, 1999).

29. Robin Alison Remington, "Former Yugoslav Space: The 'Eastern Question' and European Security," *European Security* 8, no. 1 (1999): 43–63; Nebojsa Bjelakovic and Francesco Strazzari, "The Sack of Mostarm 1992–1994: The Politico-Military Connection" *European Security* 8, no. 2 (1999): 73–102; Tom Gallagher, "'This Farrago of Anomalies': The European Response to the War in Bosnia-Herzegovina, 1992–95," *Mediterranean Politics* 1, no. 1 (1996): 76–94.

30. Viktor Meier, "Aus dem Kosovo ist Ein Irrgarten Geworden: Der Internationale Beistand Ist Ohne Perspektive und Lässt die Berücksichtigung Historischer Gegebenheiten Vermissen," *Frankfurter Allgemeine Zeitung*, February 24, 2000, p. 10.

31. *The Economist*, April 28, 2001, pp. 43–44; *La Repubblica*, June 11, 2001; p. 17.

32. Andreas Wittkowski, "Der Stabilitätspakt für Südosteuropa und die 'Führende Rolle' der Europäische Union," *Aus Politik und Zeitgeschichte*, B29–30, 2000, pp. 3–13, particularly pp. 5 and 9; Marie Janine Calic, "Der Stabilitätspakt für Südosteuropa. Eine erste Bilanz," *Aus Politik und Zeitgeschichte*, B13–14, 2001, pp. 9–16. Over forty organizations are involved in the reconstruction of this

region (p.10); Magarditsch Hatschikjan, "Die 'großen Fragen' in Südosteuropa: Ein Balkan-Locarno für Stabile Strukturen," *Aus Politik und Zeitgeschichte*, B13–14, 2001, pp. 17–26; see also the more detailed volume by Thanos Veremis and Daniel Daianu (eds.), "Balkan Reconstruction," special issue of *Journal of Southeast European and Black Sea Studies* 1, no. 1 (January 2001).

33. Anton Bebler, "Slovenia and the Second Round of NATO Enlargement," *European Security* 9, no. 1, (2000): 105–12.

34. Stavros Panteli, *The Making of Modern Cyprus: From Obscurity to Statehood* (New Barnet: Interworld, 1990); *The European*, July 9, 1997; John Redmond, The *Next Mediterranean Enlargement of the Community: Turkey, Cyprus and Malta* (Aldershot: Datsmouth, 1993), 70–88; Neill Nugent, "EU Enlargement and the 'Cyprus Problem,'" *Journal of Common Market Studies* 38, no. 1 (March 2000): 131–50; Kevin Featherstone, "Cyprus and the Onset of Democratization: Strategic Usage, Structural Transformation and Institutional Adaptation," in *Europeanization of the Southern Periphery*, ed. Kevin Featherstone and George Kazamias (London: Frank Cass, 2001), 141–62.

35. Dominic Fenech, "Malta," in European Political Data Yearbook 1992," special issue of *European Journal for Political Research* 22 (1992): 471–74; Fenech, "Malta," in *European Political Data Yearbook 1993*, special issue of European Journal for Political Research 24, no. 4 (1993): 495–500; Fenech, "Malta," in *European Political Data Yearbook 1994*, special issue of European Journal for Political Research 26 (1994): 365–68; Fenech, "Malta," in *European Political Data Yearbook 1995*, special issue of European Journal for Political Research 28 (1995): 421–25; Fenech, "Malta," in *European Political Data Yearbook 1996*, special issue of European Journal for Political Research 30, no. 3–4 (1996): 411–14; Fenech, "Malta," in *European Political Data Yearbook 1997*, special issue of European Journal for Political Research 32, no. 3–4 (1997): 439–45; Fenech, "Malta," in *European Political Data Yearbook 1998*, special issue of *European Journal for Political Research* 34, no. 34 (1998): 465–70; David M. Boswell, "Clientelism, Patronage and Accusations of Corruption in Malta in the 1970s and 1980s," in *Distorting Democracy: Political Corruption in Spain, Italy and Malta*, ed. Paul Heywood (Bristol: Centre for Mediterranean Studies, University of Bristol), occasional paper no. 10, 1994, pp. 27–39; Stephen C. Calleya, "Early Elections in Malta," *Mediterranean Politics* 4, no. 1 (1999): 113–18; Michelle Cini, "The Europeanization of Malta: Adaptation, Identity and Party Politics," in *Europeanization and the Southern Periphery*, ed. Kevin Featherstone and George Kazamias (London: Frank Cass, 2001), 261–76.

36. *The Economist*, December 1, 2001, p. 45; Daniel Daianu, "Romania," *Journal of Southeast European and Black Sea Studies* 1, no. 1 (2001): 203–18; Philippe Deloire, *Vers L'Europe des 30: Le Processus d'Elargissement de l'Union Européenne* (Paris: Gualino Editeur, 1998), 60–61.

37. *El Pais*, November 14, 2001, p. 14; Krassen Stanchev, "Bulgaria," *Journal of Southeast European and Black Sea Studies* 1, no. 1 (2001): 140–47; Philippe Deloire, *Vers L'Europe des 30*, 46–47.

38. Adam S. Jacobs, "Die Beziehungen der Türkei zur Europäischen Union und die Frage des Türkischen EU-Beitritts," *Aus Politik und Zeitgeschichte*, B29–30, 2000, pp. 22–28, particularly pp. 26–27.

39. Heinz Kramer, "The EU-Turkey Customs Union: Economic Integration amidst Political Turmoil," *Mediterranean Politics* 1, no. 1 (1996): 60–75.

40. Faruk Sen, "Die Türkei zu Beginn der EU Beitrittspartnerschaft: Politik, Wirtschaft und Gesellschaft im Wandel," *Aus Politik und Zeitgeschichte*, B13–14, 2001, pp. 27–38, particularly p. 34. For more on the economy, see Mehmet Ugur,

"Europeanization and Convergence via Incomplete Contracts? The Case of Turkey," in *Europeanization and the Southern Periphery*, ed. Kevin Featherstone and George Kazamias (London: Frank Cass, 2001), 217–42.

41. *Economist*, September 9, 2000, p. 62.

42. Lauren McClaren, "Turkey's Eventual Membership of the EU: Turkish Perspectives on the Issue," *Journal of Common Market Studies* 38, no. 1 (March 2000): 117–29, particularly p.124.

43. Carl Cavanagh Hodge, "Turkey and the Pale Light of European Democracy," *Mediterranean Politics* 4, no. 3 (1999): 56–68, particularly p. 65.

44. *The Economist*, June 8, 2000, p. 56.

45. Werner Weidenfeld, "Erweiterung Ohne Ende? Europa als Stabilitätsraum strukturieren," *Internationale Politik* 8 (2000): 1–9, particularly p. 5; Helmut Schmidt, "Wer Nicht zu Europa Gehört: Türkei, Rußland, Ukraine, Weißrußland: Sie Alle Sind Große Nationen und wichtige Partner der EU. Aber Keine Geeigneten Kandidaten für die Erweiterung," *Die Zeit*, October 5, 2000, pp. 12–13, particularly p.13; Philippe Durteste, "La Turquie Doit-Elle Etre en Europe?," *Défense Nationale* (March 2000): 71–76.

46. Jean Pierre Derisbourg, "The Euro-Mediterranean Partnership since Barcelona," in *The Euro-Mediterranean Partnership: Political and Economic Perspectives*, ed. Richard Gillespie (London: Frank Cass, 1997), 9–11, particularly pp. 10–11.

47. Gema Martin-Muñoz, "Political Reform and Social Change in the Maghreb," ed. Alvaro Vasconcelos and George Joffé, in *The Barcelona Process: Building a Euro-Mediterranean Regional Community*, special issue of *Mediterranean Politics* 5, no. 1 (2000): 96–130, particularly pp. 114–126.

48. Mustafa Hamarneh, "Democratization in the Mashreq: The Role of External Factors," ed. Alvaro Vasconcelos and George Joffé, *The Barcelona Process: Building a Euro-Mediterranean Regional Community*, special issue of *Mediterranean Politics* 5, no. 1 (2000): 77–95.

49. United Nations Development Programme, *Human Development Report, 2000* (New York: UNDP, 2000); Mustafa Benyaklef, "Socio-economic Disparities in the Mediterranean," in *The Euro-Mediterranean Partnership: Political and Economic Perspectives*, ed. Richard Gillespie (London: Frank Cass, 1997), 93–112.

50. Hafedh Zaafrane and Azzem Mahjoub, "The Euro-Mediterranean Free Trade Zone: Economic Challenges and Social Impacts on the Countries of the South and East Mediterranean," ed. Alvaro Vasconcelos and George Joffe, in *The Barcelona Process: Building a Euro-Mediterranean Regional Community*, special issue of *Mediterranean Politics* 5, no. 1 (2000): 9–32; Gonzalo Escribano and Josep Maria Jordano, "Sub-regional Integration in the MENA Region and the Euro-Mediterranean Free Trade Area," *Mediterranean Politics* 4, no. 2 (1999): 133–48.

51. Maurizio Gianmusso, "The Euro-Mediterranean Decentralized Network," *Mediterranean Politics* 4, no. 1 (1999): 25–52.

52. Annette Jünemann, "Die EU und Barcelona-Prozess-Bewertung und Perspektiven," *Integration* 24, no. 1 (2001): 42–57, particularly pp. 49–53.

9

Conclusions: The Future of Southern European Democracies

SOUTHERN EUROPE AT THE FOREFRONT OF EUROPEAN INTEGRATION

The transformation of southern European politics within the framework of the European integration process has become quite salient since the 1990s. Portugal, Spain, Italy, and Greece are more and more involved in a new political system *sui generis* called the European Union. The dynamics created by the SEM, EMU, and other fields of European public policy led to a growing influence of the European Union in shaping the politics of these member-states. The most impressive changes of behavior could be found in the democracies of Portugal, Spain and Greece, which emerged in the 1970s from former authoritarian dictatorships. The European integration process was a way of consolidating and stabilizing the young democracies. After two and half decades of democracy, these southern European countries were able to improve the living conditions of their citizens and integrate successfully in the club of established democracies. The special case of Italy also had to undergo several changes in the 1990s. In spite of being one of the founding members of the EC/EU, it never was challenged by Brussels until the mid-1980s. The implementation of SEM and the wish to participate in EMU in the first wave led to major transformations of Italian politics.

Although the pattern of weak coalition governnments continued after the collapse of the old party system in 1992, economic, social, and political reforms had to be undertaken to make the Italian political system and the processes of policy making more efficient. At the end of the millennium, we saw all these four southern European countries in the process of overcoming past forms of behavior such as patrimonialism based on clientelism, patronage and extensive corruption. European integration did not only set limits to past practices of behavior but at the same time introduced processes of rational-legal accountability and transparency. For this, statistics and other instruments had to be improved within the European Union framework.

One of the major factors stabilizing the new democracies of southern Europe as well as Italy was the flow of structural funds, which helped link the south and underdeveloped regions of the European Union to the more prosperous ones in the north. Mobility, communication, and infrastructures changed the quality of life of southern European citizens in the past two and a half decades. The inclusion of southern European countries in the decision-making mechanisms of the European Union as equal partners has to be regarded as extremely positive. After centuries of decline, southern European countries are now at the forefront of decision-making in a new political system *sui generis* that certainly will emerge as a new superpower in this millennium. The southern European contribution has been very positive so far. The establishment of the Euro-Mediterranean partnership, the involvement in the creation of the new Balkans, and the proactive role in strengthening a CFSP are some examples of where the southern European contribution could be felt. This enthusiastic support for projects of cooperation and integration within the European Union was the main pillar of European integration in the 1990s, and continues to be so in this millenium, due to the growing Euroskepticism in the northern European countries.

The forthcoming central and eastern European enlargement may strengthen the position of southern European countries in this respect. The original architects of the EC/EU, France and Germany, will have to deal with more and more alliances between southern, central and eastern European countries that may share the same kind of interests in European integration terms.

After the successful alliances of the 1990s in relation to the structural funds, southern European countries may find similar interests in other fields and support each other. Both Italy and Spain are destined to take the lead in shaping the European integration process. Spanish diplomacy has been quite successful since 1986 in pushing forward certain aspects of the agenda such as Social Europe in 1989, the Euro-Mediterranean Partnership in 1995, and the recent stronger cooperation within CFSP. The domestic governmental instability prevented Italy from play ing a more active role in this respect, but the country has been at the forefront of all integrationist projects. The cooperation between Italian and Spanish foreign policy makers has increased substantially in recent years. Cooperation in the field of immigration and in the fight against criminal organizations (Mafia) is becoming more formalized within the Schengen agreement. Greece and Portugal are keen to play a proactive role in the southern European alliance. They share the same security and resource transfer issues with Italy and Spain. The limited possibilities of agenda-setting of the European Union makes it imperative to work closely together with Italy and Spain to enhance their role in the European integration process.

SETTING AN EXAMPLE IN THE MEDITERRANEAN

The difficult roads to democracy in economic, social, and political terms in southern Europe are certainly an example for the southern fringe of the Mediterranean and the emerging new countries of the Balkans. The Euro-Mediterranean partnership and the Stability Pact for Southeastern Europe draw some lessons and inspiration from the southern European countries that were able to improve the living conditions of their citizens by joining the European Union. The main lesson learned is that the European integration process has to be regarded as a successful project for less developed countries. One of the negative aspects of the Euro-Mediterranean partnership is that most of the southern fringe Mediterranean countries are only nominal democracies without substance. This may endanger the whole process of creating a Mediterranean Free Trade Area. The centrality of creating sustainable democracies that are committed to the improvement of living conditions in the long-term perspective will be one of the major challenges to success of the Euro-Mediterranean partnership. If this project succeeds, southern European countries will have a strategic role in strengthening the relationship between the northern and southern fringe of the Mediterranean, which once was a prosperous center of the European economy. Particularly, Spain and Italy may be interested in injecting more ambition into their original projects regarding the Conference on Cooperation and Security in the Mediterranean (CSCM). This naturally also implies a stronger role in creating peace in the Middle East. In the spirit of the principle of "democratic peace" the Mediterranean could become a zone of peace, democracy, and prosperity as it is enshrined in the original purposes of the Euro-Mediterranean partnership.

RESTRUCTURING OF STATE AND CIVIL SOCIETY RELATIONS

This international vision for the future of southern European democracies has to be paralleled by a rebalancing of state and civil society relations. The overdominance of the state in former authoritarian regimes and afterward the creation of patrimonial democratic regimes such as the "First Republic (1948–1992)" under Christian Democracy (DC) in Italy, the period of patrimonial socialism in Spain (1982–1996) and Greece (1981–1989), or Cavaquismo in Portugal (1985–1995) asphyxiated the sound development of civil society in these countries. The growth in complexity in southern European democracies will require a better relationship between state and civil society. Within the European Union project there is a need for retreat of the state in intervening in society as a form of political control. Instead, these democracies will need a very attentive civil society that is able to make people aware of the problems of social inclusion, relative poverty, accountability and transparency. This rebalancing started to happen in the 1990s and will gain more importance in the new millenium. This is crucial to creating a more just society based on genuine equality of opportunities within the SEM.

CREATING A RATIONAL-LEGAL STATE

After decades of patrimonial democratic arrangements, there is a need to reform the state and to reinforce a rational-legal culture in public administration. Accountability and transparency are two crucial elements that gained importance in southern European democracies since the 1990s, but there is much room for improvement and development. The use and abuse of public positions for creating bureaucratic clientelistic linkages between state, party, and civil society have to be replaced by a more transparent process of allocating public positions. This problem is not particular to southern Europe, but can be found in most democracies. Rules of selection have to be backed up by a respective culture. After decades of patrimonial democracy, this takes time to establish.

Another aspect that will become more relevant for Portugal and Greece is that both are highly centralistic states and will have to decentralize their structures in the next decades so that they can offer better public service. This also means that there must be some decentralization of the decision-making process at the regional level. As a consequence regionalization may remain an important issue of public administration reform in the next decades, in spite of the recent backlash in Portugal.

The success of the judiciary in fighting against the old political class in Italy may set an example for the other southern European democracies. Similar events transpired in Spain related to the Socialist governing class during 1982 and 1996. The independence of the judiciary has to be strengthened, all the while preventing either a judicialization of politics or a politicization of the judiciary.

One of the big challenges for public administration will be to strengthen local government, which is the most appropriate level to make democracy work. At the local level, there are more possibilities for direct involvement than at other tiers of the political system.

CONCLUSIONS

Since the mid-1970s, Portugal, Spain, Italy, and Greece have been in a process of democratization and integration into European Union politics. Past forms of patrimonial behavior, which tended to be obstacles to democratization, had to be removed in the 1990s to cope with the demands of the European integration process. Transparency, accountability, the strengthening of the rational-legal state, the independence of the judiciary, SEM, and EMU constrained the possibilities for the political classes to create webs of clientelism and patronage as they existed in the 1980s. The crumbling of patrimonial democratic politics led to a rebalancing of state and civil society relations that in the long-term perspective may make these sustainable democracies examples for other Mediterranean countries and make them more legitimate in taking a proactive role in the European integration process.

Selected Bibliography

Aguiar, Joaquim. "Portugal: The Hidden Fluidity in an Ultra-Stable Party System." In *Conflict and Change in Modern Portugal 1974-1984*, edited by Walter C. Opello and Eduardo de Sousa Ferreira, 101–26. Lisboa, Teorema, 1985.

———. "Eleições, Configurações e Clivagens: Os Resultados Eleitorais de 1995." *Analise Social*, no. 154–55 (2000): 55–84.

Aliboni, Roberto. "Collective Political Cooperation in the Mediterranean." In *Security Challenges in the Mediterranean Region*, edited by Roberto Aliboni and Tim Niblock, 51–64. London: Frank Cass, 1996.

Alivizatos, Nicos. "The Difficulties of Rationalization in a Polarized Political System: The Greek Chamber of Deputies." In *Parliament and Democratic Consolidation in Southern Europe: Greece, Italy, Portugal, Spain, and Turkey,*. edited by Ulrike Liebert and Maurizio Cotta, 131-60. London, New York: Pinter Publishers, 1990.

———. "The Presidency, Parliament and the Courts in the 1980s." In *PASOK 1981-89: The Populist Decade*, edited by Richard Clogg, 65–77. New York: St. Martin's Press, 1993.

Alvarez-Miranda, Berta. *El Sur de Europa y la Adhésion a la Comunidad: Los Debates Politicos*. Madrid: CIS, 1996.

Arango, Ramon. *Spain: From Repression to Renewal*. Boulder: Westview Press, 1995.

Arrighi, Giovanni (ed.). *Semiperipheral Development: The Politics of Southern Europe in the Twentieth Century*. Beverly Hills, CA: Sage, 1985.

Bach, Maurizio, *Die Bürokratisierung Wuropas. Verwaltungseliten, Experten und Politische Legitimation in Europa* (Frankfurt, New York: Campus, 1999).

Bagnasco, Arnaldo. *L'Italia in Tempi di Cambiamento Politico*. Bologna: Il Mulino, 1996.

Baldassare, A., and C. Mezzanotte *Introduzione alla Costituzione*. Roma-Bari: Editori Laterza, 1994.

Bar, Antonio. "Spain." In *Cabinets in Western Europe*, edited by Jean Blondel and Ferdinand Muller-Rommel, 102–119. London: Macmillan, 1988.

Barlucchi, M. Chiara. "Quale Secessione in Italia?" *Rivista Italiana di Scienza Politica* 27, no. 2 (August 1997): 345–71.

Bataglia, Roberto. *Storia della Resistenza Italiana. 8 Settembre 1943–25 Aprile 1945.* Torino: Giulio Einaudi, 1964.

Battegazzorre, Francesco. "L'Instabilitá di Governo in Italia." *Rivista Italiana di Scienza Politica* 17, no. 2 (1987): 285–317.

Belloni, Frank P. *The Single Market and Socio-Economic Cohesion in the EU: Implications for the Southern and Western Peripheries.* Bristol: Center for Mediterranean Studies, University of Bristol, Occasional Paper, no. 8, February 1994.

Ben-Ami, Shlomo. *Fascism from Above: The Dictatorship of Primo de Rivera in Spain 1923–1930.* Oxford: Oxford University Press, 1993.

Bermeo, Nancy. *The Revolution within: Revolution Workers' Control in Rural Portugal.* Princeton, NJ: Princeton University Press, 1986.

———. *A Teoria da Democracia e as Realidades da Europa do Sul.* Lisboa: Difel, 2000.

Boix, Carles. *Partidos Politicos, Crecimiento e Igualdad: Estrategias Economicas Conservadoras y Socialdemocratas en la Economia Mundial.* Madrid: Alianza Editorial, 1996.

Bonime-Blanc, Andrea. *Spain's Transition to Democracy: The Politics of Constitution-Making.* Boulder, CO: Westview Press, 1987.

Braga da Cruz, Manuel. *Instituições Politicas e Processos Sociais.* Lisboa: Bertrand, 1995.

Brassloff, Audrey. *Religion and Politics in Spain: The Spanish Church in Transition, 1962–96.* Basingstoke, U.K.: Macmillan, 1998.

Braudel, Fernand. *La Mediterranée et le Monde Méditerranéen a l'Epoque de Philippe II.* Paris: Armand Collin, 1966.

Bruneau, Thomas C. *Nationhood and Politics: Postrevolutionary Portugal.* New York: Praeger, 1984.

Bruneau, Thomas C. and Alex Macleod, *Politics in Contemporary Portugal: Parties and the Consolidation of Democracy.* Boulder, CO: Lynne Rienner, 1986.

Caciagli, Mario. "La Parabola de la Unión de Centro Democratico." In *La Transición Democrática Española*, edited by José Felix Tezanos, Ramon Cotarelo, and Andres de Blas, 389-413. Madrid: Editorial Sistema, 1993.

Carr, Raymond, and Juan Pablo Fusi. *España: De la Ditadura a la Democracia.* Madrid: Planta Siglo XX, 1979.

Christakis, Michael. "Greece: Competing with Regional Priorities." In *Adapting to European Integration. Small States and the European Union*, edited by Kenneth Hanf and Ben Soetendorp, 84–99. London: Longman, 1998).

Clogg, Richard. *Parties and Elections in Greece: The Search for Legitimacy.* London: Hurst Company, 1987.

——— (ed.). *Greece 1981–89: The Populist Decade.* New York: St. Martin's Press, 1993.

———. *A Concise History of Greece.* Manchester: Manchester University Press, 1994.

Clogg, Richard, and George Yannopoulos (eds.) *Greece under Military Rule.* London: Secker and Warburg, 1972.

Cockfield, Lord F.A. *The European Union: Creating the Single Market*. Chichester: Wiley Chancery Law, 1994.

Commission of the European Communities. *Report on the Implementation of Measures Intended to Promote Observance of Human Rights and Democratic Principles* (for 1994). Brussels, July, 12 1995, COM(95), 1995, 91 final.

———. *Report from the Commission on the Implementation of Measures Intended to Promote Observance of Human Rights and Democratic Principles (for 1995) (1997)*. Brussels, January 17, 1997, COM(96), 672 final.

Conversi, Daniele. *The Basques, the Catalans and Spain: Alternative Routes to Nationalist Mobilisation*. London: Hurst, 1997.

Corkill, David. *The Development of the Portuguese Economy: A Case of Europeanization*. London: Routledge, 1999.

Cotta, Maurizio. "European Integration and the Italian Political System." In *Italy and EC Membership Evaluated*, edited by Francesco Francioni, 204–15. London: Pinter, 1992.

———. "The Rise and Fall of the 'Centrality' of the Italian Parliament: Transformation of the Executive-Legislative Subsystem after the Second World War." In *Parliaments in the Modern World: Changing Institutions*, edited by Gary W. Copeland and Samuel C. Patterson, 59–84. Ann Arbor: The University of Michigan Press, 1994.

Coulombis, Theodore A., Harry Petropoulos, and Harry J. Psomiades. *Foreign Interference in Greek Politics: An Historical Perspective*. New York: Pella Publishing Company, 1976.

Cravinho, João. "The Portuguese Economy: Constraints and Opportunities." In *Portugal in the 1980s: Dilemmas of Democratic Consolidation*, edited by Kenneth Maxwell, 111–65. New York: Greenwood Press, 1986.

Cunha, Carlos. "The Portuguese Communist Party." In *Political Parties and Democracy in Portugal: Organizations, Elections, and Public Opinion*, edited by Thomas C. Bruneau, 23–54. Boulder, CO: Westview Press, 1997.

Dagtoglou, Prodromos. "Verfassung und Verwaltung." In *Südost Europa Handbuch, Bd. III: Griechenland*, edited by Klaus Detlev Grothusen, 13–53. Gottingen: Vandenhoeck and Ruprecht, 1980.

Delgado Sotillos, Irene. *El Comportamiento Electoral Municipal Español, 1979–1995*. Madrid: CIS, 1997.

———. "Comportamiento y Valores: La Cultura Politica de los Europeos." *Revista Mexicana de Sociologia* 59, no. 1 (1997): 139–60.

Della Porta, Donatella. *Lo Scambio Occulto: Casi di Corruzione Politica in Italia*. Bologna: Societá Editrice Il Mulino, 1992.

Della Porta, Donatella, and Alberto Vanucci. *Un Paese Anormale: Come la Classe Politica ha Perso l'Occasione di Mani Pulite*. Roma: Editori Laterza, 1999.

Della Sala, Vincent. "Hollowing Out and Hardening the State: European Integration and the Italian Economy." *West European Politics* 20, no. 1 (1997): 14–33.

———. "The Relationship between the Italian Parliament and Government." In *Parliaments and Governments in Western Europe*, edited by Philip Norton, 73-93. London: Frank Cass, 1998.

Diamandouros, Nikiforos. "Transition to, and Consolidation of, Democratic Politics in Greece 1974–1983: A Tentative Assesment." *West European Politics* 7, no. 2 (1984): 50–71.

——. "Greek Political Culture in Transition: Historical Origins, Evolution, Current Trends." In *Greece in the 1980s*, edited by Richard Clogg, 43-69. Basingstoke, U.K.: Macmillan, 1985.

——. "Politics and Culture in Greece, 1974–91: An Interpretation." In *Greece 1981–89: The Populist Decade*, edited by Richard Clogg, 1–25. New York: St. Martin's Press, 1993.

——. "Southern Europe: A Third Wave Success Story." In *The International Dimension of Democratization: Europe and the Americas*, edited by Lawrence Whitehead, 3–25. Oxford: Oxford University Press, 1996.

Diamond, Larry. *Promoting Democracy in the 1980s: Actors and Instruments, Issues and Imperatives.* New York: Carnegie Corporation of New York, 1995.

Di Palma, Giuseppe. *Political Synkretism in Italy: Historical Coalition Strategies and the Present Crisis.* Policy Papers in International Affairs. Berkeley: Institute of International Studies, 1978.

——. *To Craft Democracies. An Essay on Democratic Transitions.* Berkeley:University of California Press, 1990.

Di Scala, Spencer. *Italy: From Revolution to Republic, 1700 to the Present.* Boulder, CO: Westview Press, 1995.

Downs, Charles. *Revolution at the Grassroots in the Portuguese Revolution.* Albany: State University of New York Press, 1989.

Duggan, Christopher. *A Concise History of Italy.* Manchester: Manchester University Press, 1994.

Durá, Jaime Ferri. "Las Administraciones Públicas," In *Sistema Politico Español*, coordinated by Paloma Roman, 160–81. Madrid: McGraw-Hill, 1995.

Dyson, Kenneth, and Kevin Featherstone. "Italy and EMU as a 'Vincolo Esterno': Empowering the Technocrats, Transforming the State." *South European Society and Politics* 1, no. 2 (Autumn 1996): 272–99.

Eisfeld, Rainer. *Sozialistischer Pluralismus in Europa: Ansätze und Scheitern and Beispiel Portugal.* Köln: Wissenschaft und Politik, 1984.

——. "Portugal and Western Europe." In *Portugal in the 1980s: Dilemmas of Democratic Consolidation,* edited by Kenneth Maxwell. New York: Greenwood, 1986.

——. "Portugal in the European Community 1986–88: The Impact of the First Half of the Transition Period." *Iberian Studies* 18, no. 2 (1989): 156–64.

European Commission, *The New Common Fisheries Policy.* Luxembourg: Office of the Official Publications of the European Community, 1984.

——. *Greece—Common Support Framework 1994–99.* Office of the Official Publications of the European Community, 1994.

——. *Europe 2000+: Cooperation for Territorial Development.* Brussels: Office of the Official Publications of the EC, 1995.

——. *Europe at the Service of Regional Development.* Luxembourg: Office of the Official Publications of the EC, 1996.

——. "Agenda 2000: For a Stronger and Wider Union." *Bulletin of the European Union,* Supplement no. 5, 1997.

——. *Social Protection in Europe 1997.* Luxembourg: Office of the Official Publications of the European Community, 1998.

———. *Managing Change: Final Report of the High Level Group on Economic and Social Implications of Industrial Change*. Luxembourg: Office of the Official Publications of the European Communities, 1998.

———. *The Structural Funds in 1997: Ninth Annual Report*. Brussels: Office of the Official Publications of the EC, 1999.

———. *Sixth Periodic Report on the Social and Economic Situation and Development of the Regions of the European Union*. Luxembourg: Office of the Official Publications of the EC, 1999.

———. *Territorial Employment Pacts: 61 Operational Tools*. Brussels: Office of the Official Publications of the European Commission, 1999.

Fabbrini, Sergio. *Chi Guida L'Esecutivo? Presidenza della Repubblica e Governo in Italia (1996–1998)*. Siena: Centro Interdipartimentale di Ricerca sul Cambiamento Politico. Occasional Papers no. 3, 1998.

———. "Dal Governo Prodi al Governo D'Alema: Continuitá o Discontinuitá?" In *Politica in Italia. I fatti dellanno e le interpretazioni*, edited by David Hine and Salvatore Vassalo, 139–59. Bologna: Il Mulino, 1999.

Featherstone, Kevin. "'Europeanization' and the Centre Periphery: The Case of Greece in the 1990s." *South European Society and Politics* 3, no. 1 (1998): 23–39.

Featherstone, Kevin, and George Kazamias (eds.), *Europeanization and the Southern Periphery*. London: Frank Cass, 2001.

Ferreira, José Medeiros. *Ensaio Histórico sobre a Revolução de 25 de Abril*. Lisboa: Casa da Moeda, 1983.

Ferrera, Maurizio. "The 'Southern Model' of Welfare in Social Europe." *Journal of European Social Policy* 6, no. 1 (1996): 17–37.

Fix, Elisabeth. *Italiens Parteiensystem im Wandel: Von der Ersten zur Zweiten Republik*. Frankfurt: Campus, 1999.

Frain, Maritheresa. *PPD/PSD e a consolidação do regime democrático*. Lisboa: Editorial Noticias, 1998.

Führer, Ilse Marie. *Los Sindicatos en España: De la Lucha de Clases a Estratégias de Cooperación*. Madrid: Consejo Economico y Social, 1996.

Furlong, Paul. *Modern Italy: Representation and Reform*. London: Routledge, 1993.

Gallagher, Tom. "'This Farrago of Anomalies': The European Response to the War in Bosnia-Herzegovina, 1992–95. *Mediterranean Politics* 1, no. 1 (1996): 76–94.

———. "Unconvinced by Europe of the Regions: The 1998 Regionalization Referendum in Portugal." *South European Society and Politics* 4, no. 1 (1999): 132–48.

Garcia Ferrando, Manuel, Eduardo Lopez-Aranguren, and Miguel Beltrán. *La Conciencia nacional y regional en la España de las autonomies*. Madrid: CIS, 1994.

Gilbert, Mark. *The Italian Revolution*. Boulder, CO: Westview Press, 1995.

———. "Le Leggi Bassanini: Una Tappa Intermedia Nella Riforma del Governo Locale." In *Politica in Italia. I fatti dell'anno e le interpretazioni*, edited by David Hine and Salvatore Vassalo, 161–80. Bologna: Il Mulino, 1999.

Gillespie, Richard. *The Spanish Socialist Party: A History of Factionalism*. Oxford: Oxford University Press, 1989.

──. "Spanish Protagonismo and the Euro-Med Partnership Initiative." In *The Euro-Mediterranean Partnership: Political and Economic Perspectives*, edited by Richard Gillespie, 33–48. London: Frank Cass, 1997.

──. *Spain and the Mediterranean: Developing a European Policy towards the South.* Basingstoke, U.K.: Macmillan, 1999.

Giner, Salvador, "Political Economy, Legitimation, and the state in Southern Europe." In *Transitions from Authoritarian Rule*, vol. 2, *Southen Europe*, edited by Guillermo O'Donnell, Philippe C. Schmitter, and Lawrence Whitehead, 11–44. Baltimore, London: Johns Hopkins University Press, 1986.

Ginsbourg, Paul. *The History of Society and Politics in Contemporary Italy.* Harmondsworth, U.K.: Penguin, 1989.

Glenny, Misha. *The Fall of Yugoslavia: The Third Balkan War.* London: Penguin, 1996.

──. *The Balkans, 1804–1999: Nationalism, War and the Great Powers.* London: Granta, 2000.

González Hernandez, Juan Carlos. *Desarollo Político y Consolídacion Democrática en Portugal.* Madrid: CIS, 1999.

Graham, Lawrence. *The Portuguese Military and the State: Rethinking Transitions in Europe and Latin America.* Boulder, CO: Westview Press, 1993.

Graham, Robert. *Spain: Change of a New Nation.* London: Michael Joseph, 1984.

Gualmini, Elisabetta "L'Evoluzione degli Assetti Concertativi in Italia e in Germania." *Rivista Italiana di Scienza Politica* 27, no.1 (April 1997): 101–50.

Guarnieri, Carlo. "The Judiciary in the Italian Political Crisis." *West European Politics* 20, no. 1 (1997): 57–175.

Gundle, Stephen, and Simon Parker (eds.). *The New Italian Republic: From the Fall of the Berlin Wall to Berlusconi.* London: Routledge, 1995.

Gunther, Richard, Nikiforos P. Diamandouros, and Hans-Jurgen Puhle (eds.). *The Politics of Democratic Consolidation: Southern Europe in Comparative Perspective.* Vol. 1 of *The New Southern Europe.* Baltimore: Johns Hopkins University Press, 1995.

Gunther, Richard, Giacomo Sani, and Goldie Shabad. *Spain after Franco: The Making of a Competitive Party System.* Los Angeles: California University Press, 1988.

Guzzini, Stefano. "La Longue Nuit de la Premiére Republique: L'Implosion Clienteliste en Italie." In *Revne Française de Science Politique* 44, no. 6 (December 1994): 979–1013.

Heimer, Franz Whilhelm, Jorge Vala, and José Manuel Leite Viegas. "Padroes de cultura politica em Portugal: Attitudes em relacao á democracia." In *Análise Social*, 25, no. 105–6 (1990): 31–56.

Hentze, Margot. *Pre-fascist Italy: The Rise and Fall of Parliamentary Democracy.* London: Allen and Unwin, 1939.

Heywood, Paul. *Marxism and the Failure of Organized Socialism in Spain 1879–1936.* Cambridge: Cambridge University Press, 1990.

──. *The Government and Politics of Spain.* Basingstoke: Macmillan, 1995.

Higley, John, and Richard Gunther (eds.). *Elites and Democratic Consolidation in Latin America and Southern Europe.* Cambridge: Cambridge University Press, 1992.

Hine, David. *Governing Italy: The Politics of Bargained Pluralism*. Oxford: Oxford University Press, 1993.

Hooghe, Liesbet, and Gary Marks. *European Integration and Multilevel Governance*. Lanham, U.K.: Rowman and Littlefields, 2001.

Hopkin, Jonathan. *La Desintegración de la Union de Centro Democratico: UnaInterpretacion Organizativa*. Madrid: Centro de Estudios Constitucionales, 1993.

——. "Political Parties in a Young Democracy." In *Changing Party Systems in Western Europe*, edited by David Broughton and Mark Donovan, 207–31. London: Pinter, 1999.

Huneeus, Carlos. *La Unión del Centro Democrático y la Transición a la Democracia*. Madrid: Centro de Investigaciones Sociologicas, 1985.

Huntington, Samuel P. *The Third Wave: Democratization in the Late Twentieth Century*. Norman: University of Oklahoma Press, 1991.

Ignazi, Piero. *Il Polo Escluso: Profilo del Movimento Sociale Italiano*, 2nd ed. Bologna: Il Mulino, 1998.

Ioakimidis, P.C. "The Europeanization of Greece: An Overall Assessment." In edited *Europeanization and the Southern Periphery*, edited by Kevin Featherstone and George Kazamias, 73–94. London: Frank Cass, 2001.

Istat. *Rapporto sull'Italia*. Edizione 1999. Bologna: il Mulino, 1999.

Jimenez Sanchez, Fernando. "Posibilidades y Limites del Escandalo Politico como una Forma de Control Social." *Revista Española de Investigaciones Sociologicas* 66 (1994): 7–36.

Kern, Robert W. *Liberals, Reformers and Caciques in Restoration Spain, 1875–1909*. Albuquerque: University of New Mexico Press, 1974.

Koff, Sondra Z., and Stephen P. Koff. *Italy: From the First to the Second Republic*. London: Routledge, 2000.

Kritsantonis, Nicos D. "Greece: Maturing the System." In *Changing Industrial Relations in Europe*, edited by Anthony Ferner and Richard Hyman, 504–528. London: Blackwell, 1998.

Kurth, James, and James Petras, eds. *Mediterranean Paradoxes: The Political and Social Structures of Southern Europe*. Providence, RI: Berg Publishers, 1993.

LaPalombara, Joseph. *Interest Groups in Italian Politics*. Princeton, NJ: Princeton University Press, 1967.

Legg, Keith R., and John M. Roberts. *Modern Greece: A Civilization on the Periphery*. Boulder, CO: Westview Press, 1997.

Leonardi, Robert, and Rafaella Y. Nanetti (eds.). *The Regions and European Integration: The Case of Emilia-Romagna*. London: Pinter, 1990.

Leonardi, Robert, and Douglas A. Wertman. *Italian Christian Democracy: The Politics of Dominance*. Basingstoke, U.K.: Macmillan, 1989.

Letamendia, Francisco, coord. *Nacionalidades Y Regiones En La Unión Europea*. Madrid: Fundamentos, 1999.

Lewis, Norman. *The Honored Society: The Mafia*. New York: Random House, 1972.

Liebert, Ulrike, and Maurizio Cotta (eds.). *Parliament and Democratic Consolidation in Southern Europe: Greece, Italy, Portugal, Spain, and Turkey*. London and New York: Pinter Publishers, 1990.

Lijphardt, Arend, Thomas Bruneau, and Richard Gunther. "A Mediterranean Model of Democracy? The Southern European Democracies in Comparative Perspective." *West European Politics*, no. 2 (1985): 8–25.

Linz, Juan J., and Alfred Stepan (eds.). *The Breakdown of Democratic Regimes*. Vol. 2: *Europe*. Baltimore, London: Johns Hopkins University, 1978.

Lopes, Fernando Farelo. *Clientelismo e Poder Politico na Primeira Republica*. Lisboa: Estampa, 1994.

Machado Pais, José. *Consciencia Histórica e Identidade. Os Jovens Portugueses Num Contexto Europeu*. Lisboa: Celta, 1999.

Magone, José M. *The Changing Architecture of Iberian Politics: An Investigation on the Structuring of Democratic Political Systemic Culture in Semiperipheral Southern European Societies*. Lewiston, NY: Mellen University Press, 1996.

———. "The Assembleia da Republica: Discovering Europe." In *National Parliaments and the European Union*, edited by Philip Norton, 151–65. London: Frank Cass, 1996.

———. *European Portugal: The Difficult Road to Sustainable Democracy*. Basingstoke, U.K., New York: Macmillan, St. Martin's Press, 1997.

———. "The Logics of Party System Change in Southern Europe." In *Comparing Party System Change*, edited by Paul Pennings and Jan-Erik Lane, 217–40. London: Routledge, 1998.

———. "Party System: Installation and Consolidation." In *Changing Party Systems in Western Europe*, edited by David Broughton and Mark Donovan, 232–54. London: Pinter, 1999.

———. "The Portuguese Socialist Party." In *Social Democratic Parties in the European Union*, edited by Robert Ladrech and Philippe Marliére, 166–75. Basingstoke, U.K.: Macmillan, 1999.

———. "Portugal: The Logics of Democratic Regime Building." In *Coalition Government in Western Europe*, edited by Wolfgang C. Müller and Kaare Strom, 529–58. Oxford: Oxford University Press, 2000.

———. "La Costruzione di Una Societá Civile Europea: Legami a Più Livelli Tra Comitati Economici e Sociali." In *Il Comitato Economico e Sociale nella Costruzione Europea*, edited by Antonio Varsori, 222–42. Venice, Marsilio, 2000.

———. "European Regional Policy and Democratization in a Small EU Member-State: The Transformation of the Portuguese Political System" in *Europeanization of Southern European Political Systems*, edited by Kevin Featherstone and Geroge Kazamias, 119–40. London: Frank Cass, 2001.

———. *Iberian Trade Unionism: Democratization under the Impact of the European Union*. New Brunswick, NJ: Transaction Publishers, 2001.

———. The Foreign Policy of Portugal: Reconstructing the Past within European Integration Parameters." In *The Foreign Policies of the Member-States in the European Union*, edited by Ian Manners and Richard Whitman, 162–73. Manchester: Manchester University Press, 2001.

Manuel, Christopher Paul. *Uncertain Outcome: The Politics of the Portuguese Transition to Democracy*. Lanham, MD: University Press of America, 1995.

———. *The Challenges of Democratic Consolidation in Portugal: Political, Economic, and Military Issues, 1976–1991*. London, Westport, CT: Praeger, 1996.

Maravall, José Maria. *Transition to Democracy in Spain*. London: Croom and Helm, 1982.

Mavrogordatos, George T. "From Traditional Clientelism to Machine Politics: The Impact of PASOK Populism in Greece." *South European Politics and Society* 2, no. 3 (1997): 1–26.

Maxwell, Kenneth. *The Making of Portuguese Democracy*. Manchester: Manchester University Press, 1995.

Meier, Viktor. *Yugoslavia: A History of Its Demise*. London: Routledge, 1999.

Merkel, Wolfgang. *Ende der Sozialdemokratie? Machtresourcen und Regierungspolitik im westeuropaeischen Vergleich*. Frankfurt: Campus, 1993.

Montero, José Ramon. "Los fracasos politicos y electorales de la derecha española: Alianza Popular, 1974–87." In *La Transición Democratica Española*, edited by José Felix Tezanos, Ramon Cotarelo, and André Blas, 495–542. Madrid: Editorial Sistema, 1993.

Moran, Maria Luz, and Jorge Benedicto. *La Cultura Politica de los Españoles: Un Ensayo de Reinterpretación*. Madrid: CIS, 1995.

Morata, Francesc. *La Unión Europea:Procesos, actores y politicas*. Barcelona: Ariel, 1998.

Morlino, Leonardo. "Consolidation and Party Government in Southern Europe." *International Political Science Review* 16, no. 2 (1995): 145–67.

———. *Democracy Between Consolidation and Crisis: Parties, Groups and Citizens in Southern Europe*. Oxford: Oxford University Press, 1998.

Morlino, Leonardo, and Mario Tarchi. "The Dissatisfied Society: The Roots of Political Change in Italy." *European Journal for Political Research* 30 (July 1996): 41–63.

Mozzicafreddo, Juan, Isabel Guerra, Margarida Fernandes, and João Quintela. *Gestao e Legitimidade no Sistema Politico Local*. Lisbon: Escher, 1991.

Nanetti, Rafaella Y. *Growth and Territorial Policies: The Italian Model of Social Capitalism*. London: Pinter, 1988.

Nataf, Daniel. *Democratization and Social Settlements: The Politics of Change in Contemporary Portugal*. Albany: State University of New York Press, 1995.

Newton, Michael T., and Peter J. Donaghy. *Institutions of Modern Spain: A Political and Economic Guide*. Cambridge: Cambridge University Press, 1997.

Nugent, Neill. "EU Enlargement and the 'Cyprus Problem.'" *Journal of Common Market Studies* 38, no. 1 (March 2000): 131–50.

O'Donnell, Guillermo, Philippe C. Schmitter, and Lawrence Whitehead (eds.). *Transitions from Authoritarian Rule*. 4 Vols. Baltimore: Johns Hopkins University Press, 1986.

Opello, Walter C. *Portugal's Political Development: A Comparative Approach*. Boulder, CO: Westview Press, 1985.

———. *Portugal: From Monarchy to Pluralist Democracy*. Boulder, CO: Westview Press 1991.

Pappas, Takis S. *Making Party Democracy in Greece*. Basingstoke, U.K.: Macmillan, 1997.

Pasquino, Gianfranco. "Autopsia della Bicamerale." in *Politica in Italia. I Fatti dell'Anno e le Interpretazioni Edizione 99*, edited by David Hine and Salvatore Vassallo, 117–38. Bologna: Il Mulino, 1999.

Pasquino, Gianfranco, and Patrick McCarthy (eds.). *The End of Post-War Politics in Italy*. Boulder, CO: Westview Press, 1993.

Passos, Marcelino. *Der Niedergang des Faschismus in Portugal. Zum Verhältnis von Okonomie, Gesellschaft und Staat. Politik in Einem Europaeischen Schwellenland*. Marburg: Verlag fur Arbeiterbewegung und Gesellschaftswissenschaft, 1987.

Patricio, Maria Theresa and Alan Stoleroff. "Portuguese Communist Party: Perestrojka and Its Aftermath." In *West European Communist Parties and the Revolution of 1989*, edited by Martin J. Bull and Paul Heywood, 90–118. Basingstoke, U.K.: Macmillan, 1994.

Pettifer, James. *The Greeks: The Land and People Since the War*. Harmondsworth, U.K.: Penguin, 1993.

Porch, Douglas. *The Portuguese Armed Forces and the Revolution*. London: Croom Helm, 1977.

Powell, Charles T. *Juan Carlos of Spain: Self-Made Monarch*. Basingstoke, U.K.: Macmillan, 1996.

Pridham, Geoffrey. *Political Parties and Coalitional Behaviour in Italy*. London, New York: Routledge, 1988.

———. "Comparative Perspectives on the New Mediterranean Democracies: A Model of Regime Transition?" *West European Politics*, no. 1 (1984). 1–29.

———. "The Politics of the European Community. Transnational Networks and Democratic Transition in Southern Europe." In *Encouraging Democracy: The International Context of Regime Transition in Southern Europe*, edited by Geoffrey Pridham, 211–54. London: Leicester University Press, 1991.

———. "The International Context of Democratic Consolidation: Southern Europe in Comparative Perspective." In *The Politics of Democratic Consolidation: Southern Europe in Comparative Perspective*, edited by Richard Gunther, Nikiforos P. Diamandouros, and Hans-Jürgen Puhle, 166–203. Baltimore: Johns Hopkins University Press, 1995.

Przeworski, Adam. *Democracy and the Market: Political and Economic Reforms in Eastern Europe and Latin America*. Cambridge: Cambridge University Press, 1991.

Putnam, Robert. *Making Democracy Work: Civic Traditions in Italy*. Cambridge, MA: Harvard University Press, 1993.

Ramirez, Manuel. *Partidos Politicos y Constitución (Un Estudio de las Actitudes Parlamentarias Durante el Proceso de Creación Constitucional)*. Madrid: Centro de Estudios Constitucionales, 1989.

Redmond, John. *The Next Mediterranean Enlargement of the Community: Turkey, Cyprus and Malta*. Aldershot: Datsmouth, 1993.

Regini, Marino. "Still Engaging in Corporatism? Einige Lehren aus Jüngsten Italienischen Erfahrungen mit der Konzertierung." *Politische Vierteljahresschrift* 38, no. 2 (1997): 298–317.

Rhodes, Martin. "Financing Party Politics in Italy: A Case of Systemic Corruption." *West European Politics* 20, no. 1 (1997): 54–80.

Ritaine, Evelyne. *Hypothéses pour le Sud de l'Europe: Territoires et Médiations*. EUI Working Papers, RSC, 1996, 33, no. 96.

Rother, Bernd. *Der verhinderte Übergang zum Sozialismus: Die sozialistische Partei Portugals im Zentrum der Macht (1974–1978)*. Frankfurt: Materialis, 1985.

Rousseas, Stephen. *The Death of a Democracy: Greece and the American Conscience.* New York: Grove Press, 1968.

Rustow, Dankwart W. "Transitions to Democracy: Towards a Dynamic Model." *Comparative Politics* 3 (1970): 337–63.

Ruzza, Carlo, and Oliver Schmidtke. Roots of Success of the Lega Lombarda: Mobilisation, Dynamics and Media." *West European Politics* 14, no. 1 (1993): 1–24.

———. "Towards a Modern Right: Alleanza Nazionale and the 'Italian Revolution.'" In *The New Italian Republic: From the Fall of the Berlin Wall to Berlusconi*, edited by Stephen Gundle and Simon Parker, 147–58. London: Routledge, 1995.

Sablovsky, Juliet Antunes. "The Portuguese Socialist Party." In *Political Parties and Democracy in Portugal: Organizations, Elections, and Public Opinion*, edited by Thomas C. Bruneau, 55–76. Boulder, CO: Westview Press, 1997.

Salmon, Keith. *The Modern Spanish Economy: Transformation and Integration into Europe.* London: Pinter, 1995.

Salomone, William A. *Italy in the Giolittian Era: Italian Democracy in the Making 1900–1914.* Philadelphia: University of Pennsylvania Press, 1960.

Sanchez Cervelló, Josep. *A Revolução Portuguesa e a Sua Influencia na Transição Espanhola (1961–1976).* Lisboa: Assírio e Alvim, 1993.

Sapelli, Giulio. *Southern Europe since 1945: Tradition and Modernity in Portugal, Spain, Italy, Greece and Turkey.* London and New York: Longman, 1995.

Sassoon, Donald. *Contemporary Italy: Politics, Economics and Society Since 1945.* London: Longman, 1986.

Schmitter, Philippe. "Organized Interests and Democratic Consolidation in Southern Europe." In *The Politics of Democratic Consolidation: Southern Europe in Comparative Perspective.* Vol. 1 of *The New Southern Europe*, edited by Richard Gunther, Nikiforos P. Diamandouros, and Hans-Jurgen Puhle, 284–314. Baltimore: Johns Hopkins University Press, 1995.

Schwartzman, Kathleen. *The Social Origins of Democratic Collapse: The First Republic in the Global Economy.* Kansas City: University of Kansas Press, 1989.

Seton-Watson, Christopher. *Italy from Liberalism to Fascism, 1870–1915.* Madison: University of Wisconsin Press, 1968.

Share, Donald. "Transitions to Democracy and Transition through Transaction." *Comparative Political Studies* 19, no. 4 (January 1987): 525–48.

Sotiropoulos, Dimitri A. *Populism and Bureaucracy: The Case of Greece under PASOK, 1981–1989.* Notre Dame, IN: University of Notre Dame. 1996.

Sousa Santos, Boaventura de. "A Crise e a Reconstituição do Estado em Portugal (1974–1984)." *Revista Critica de Ciencias Sociais* 14 (1984): 7–29.

Sousa Santos, Boaventura de, Maria Manuel Leitão Marques, João Pedroso, and Pedro Lopes Ferreira. *Os Tribunais nas Sociedades Contemporaneas: O Caso Portugues.* Porto: Edicoes Afrontamento, 1995.

Spanou, Calliope. "Penelope's Suitors: Administrative Modernisation and Party Competition in Greece." *West European Politics* 19, no. 1 (1996): 97–124.

Spourdalakis, Michalis. *The Rise of the Greek Socialist Party.* London: Routledge, 1988.

Szmolka, Inmaculada. *Opiniones y Actitudes de los Españoles ante el Proceso de Integracion Europea*. Madrid: CIS, 1999.

Tarrow, Sidney. *Democracy and Disorder. Protest and Politics in Italy 1960–1975*. Oxford: Clarendon Press, 1989.

Tezanos, José Felix, José Manuel Montero, and José António Diaz, eds. *Tendencias de Futuro en la Sociedad Española: Primer Foro sobre Tendencias Sociales*. Madrid: Editorial Sistema, 1997.

Thomashausen, André. *Verfassung and Verfassungswirklichkeit in Portugal*. Berlin: Duncker und Humblot, 1981.

Tondl, Gabriele. "EU Regional Policy in the Southern Periphery: Lessons for the Future." *South European Society and Politics* 3, no. 1 (Summer, 1998): 93–129.

Transparency International Reports: http://www.transparency.de

Tuñon de Lara, Manuel. *Poder y Sociedad en España 1900–1931*. Madrid: Coleccion Austral, 1992.

Ullmann, J.C. *The Tragic Week: A Study of Anticlericalism in Spain. 1875–1912*. Cambridge: Cambridge University Press, 1968.

United Nations Development Program (UNDP). *Human Development Report 2000*. New York: United Nations, 2000.

Veneruso, Danilo. *L'Italia Fascista (1922–1945)*. Bologna: Il Mulino, 1981.

Verzichelli, Luca. "The New Members of Parliament." In *Italian Politics: The Year of the Tycoon*, edited by Richard S. Katz and Piero Ignazi, 115–34. Boulder, CO: Westview, 1995.

Verzichelli, Luca, and Maurizio Cotta. "Italy: From 'Constrained' Coalitions to Alternating Governments?" In *Coalition Governments in Western Europe*, edited by Wolfgang C. Müller and Kaare Strom, 433–97. Oxford: Oxford University Press, 2000.

Wallace, William. "The Sharing of Sovereignty: The European Paradox." *Political Studies* 47 (1999): 503–21.

Webster, Richard. *The Cross and the Fascist: Christian Democracy and Fascism inItaly*. Stanford: Stanford University Press, 1960.

Wheeler, Douglas L. *Republican Portugal: A Political History, 1910-1926*. Madison: University of Wisconsin, 1978.

Whitehead, Lawrence. *The International Dimension of Democratization*. Oxford: Oxford University Press, 1998.

Woodhouse, C.M. *Karamanlis: The Restorer of Democracy in Greece*. Oxford: Oxford University Press, 1982.

Index

About the Author

JOSÉ M. MAGONE, M.Phil, D.Phil (Vienna), is Senior Lecturer in Euorpean Politics at the Department of Politics and International Studies, University of Hull, U.K. He was Robert Schuman Scholarship Holder at the European Parliament (1990); Visiting Research Fellow at the Centre for Mediterranean Studies, University of Bristol (1990–91); Assistant Professor at the Instituto Piaget, Lisbon (1992–93); Visiting Researcher at the Instituto Juan March in Madrid (1997); Karl W. Deutsch Guest Professor at the Wissenschaftszentrum Berlin (1999); and Visiting Fellow at the Centre for Political Change, University of Siena, Italy (2002). Among his publications are *The Changing Architecture of Iberian Politics, European Portugal: The Difficult Road to Sustainable Democracy,* and *Iberian Trade Unionism: Democratization Under the Impact of the European Union.*

Lightning Source UK Ltd.
Milton Keynes UK
UKOW06n2159100116

266098UK00008B/85/P

9 780275 977870